Bengali Harlem and the Lost Histories of
South Asian America

Bengali Harlem

and the

Lost Histories

of

South Asian America

Vivek Bald

Harvard University Press

Cambridge, Massachusetts, and London, England

First Harvard University Press paperback edition, 2015

Second Printing

Library of Congress Cataloging-in-Publication Data

Bald, Vivek.

Bengali Harlem and the lost histories of South Asian America / Vivek Bald.

p.   cm.

Includes bibliographical references and index.

ISBN 978-0-674-06666-3 (cloth : alk. paper)

ISBN 978-0-674-50385-4 (pbk.)

1. South Asian Americans—History—20th century.   2. South Asian Americans—
Cultural assimilation.   3. Muslims—United States—History—20th century.
4. Working class—United States—History—20th century.   5. Haidar, Dada Amir.
6. United States—Race relations—History—20th century.   7. Harlem (New York, N.Y.)—
Race relations—History—20th century.   8. United States—Emigration and
immigration—History—20th century.   9. South Asia—Emigration and immigration—
History—20th century.   I. Title.

E184.S69B35 2012

305.891'4073—dc23

2012022231

For my daughter.

Contents

Author's Note

ALTHOUGH MANY OF THE PEOPLE about whom I have written came from regions that are now part of the nations of Bangladesh and Pakistan, most of the period covered here pre-dates the creation of those nations. When I am writing about the pre-1947 period, I have chosen to refer to these individuals as Indian and their place of origin as India in order to maintain historical accuracy. I use the term South Asian when referring either to the post-1947 period or to a stretch of time that includes both the pre- and post-1947 periods. I use the term Bengali to refer to many of the individuals who appear in this book in order to specify their origins in the larger region of Bengal, both West (in present-day India) and East (in present-day Bangladesh). To many of these migrants, regional (Bengali) and sub-regional (e.g.: Sylheti) identity appears to have been more salient on a day-to-day basis than any national identification.

The research for this book entailed piecing together archival documents—ship manifests; census enumerations; birth, death, and marriage certificates—in which British and U.S. officials transliterated South Asian names in multiple ways. The migrants whose lives and travels are recorded in these documents also likely used different English spellings of their names at different times. In the interest of clarity, I have standardized my spelling of specific individuals' names within the text of the book. I have generally chosen the spelling that appears most frequently in the archives or the name that the individual appears to have settled on in his own daily life in New Orleans, Harlem, or elsewhere. These spellings often take forms that might be considered unorthodox by contemporary South Asian readers (e.g., Ally, Fozlay, Surker, Raymond, Box). When I refer to specific archival documents in the footnotes, I use the spellings that appear in those original documents.

I named this project "Bengali Harlem" early on in its development, when it focused primarily on a set of interconnected families of Bengali ex-seamen who had settled and intermarried in Harlem. At that time, the title was literal, referring to a particular set of people in a particular place. Over several years of research, as I followed an expanding trail of archival documents, the history I was piecing together grew far beyond Harlem and it grew to include many other people who were not Bengali—from the Kashmiri seaman and activist Dada Amir Haider Khan to Creole, African American, and Puerto Rican women. Over time, the name has become metaphorical rather than literal, standing for a particular set of encounters and possibilities tied to South Asian life making and place making in U.S. neighborhoods of color.

Each and every identity is extended through a relationship with the Other.

Édouard Glissant, *Poetics of Relation*

Introduction

Lost in Migration

IN MARCH OF 1945, two men from India led testimony before the House Committee on Immigration and Naturalization of the U.S. Congress.[1] One was a Muslim who had settled in Arizona's Salt River Valley in the 1910s, where a handful of farmers from the subcontinent had turned hundreds of acres of land toward the production of rice.[2] The other was a Punjabi Sikh entrepreneur who came to New York City in 1926 and established a business supplying luxury Eastern imports to the city's elites.[3] Both men were lobbying Congress to make East Indians eligible for U.S. citizenship. Their task was not an easy one. In the early years of the twentieth century, Indian immigrants had been vilified. When hundreds of Punjabi workers began to arrive in California and the Pacific Northwest around 1904, they found white citizens' groups and labor unions already lined up against them, emboldened by years of targeting immigrants from China and Japan. The nativists focused their vitriol on the Indian newcomers, whipping up a moral panic over what they called the "tide of turbans" that threatened to swamp white America. At times, the xenophobia boiled over into violence; in September 1907, a mob of white lumber-mill workers rampaged through the northwestern town of Bellingham, Washington, attacking Indian migrants indiscriminately, rounding them up and forcing them from their jobs and homes.[4] By 1917, the federal government had passed legislation barring Indians and virtually all other Asians from entering the United States. The 1917 Immigration Act made East Indians equivalent in the eyes of the law to alcoholics, "professional beggars," and the insane; all were undesirable aliens, to be turned away at the borders. In 1923, the U.S. Supreme Court added a further layer to the exclusion regime by ruling that those East Indians who were already resident in the United States were racially ineligible to become U.S. citizens. Not only had Indians been cast as undesirable, but they had been made permanent outsiders. For the next twenty years, it remained this way: Indians were prevented from immigrating to the United States, from owning land, from voting, and from naturalizing—from becoming an accepted part of the nation.[5]

Mubarek Ali Khan and J. J. Singh sought to change this status quo, and as they stood before the Committee on Immigration and Naturalization, the two Indian lobbyists could not have seemed more different. Khan was a graying middle-aged man who wore spectacles, plain suits, and a cap that marked his Muslim faith. At six feet, J. J. Singh towered over Khan. He was in his late forties, handsome, self-assured, and polished in both demeanor and appearance. He had short hair and was clean shaven, having dispensed with his turban and beard after settling in the United States, and he favored fine suits.[6] The two men had been lobbying Congress over several sessions, each advocating a different approach to redressing Indian exclusion. Khan's proposed legislation was focused and practical; it sought naturalization rights for the roughly three thousand Indians who were estimated to have settled in the United States prior to the Supreme Court decision of 1923. Most of these immigrants were farm and factory laborers—exactly the population of "undesirable aliens" that the 1917 Immigration Act had sought to keep out of the country. However, the three thousand had now been living and working in the United States continuously for more than twenty years, and Khan's bill began from an assertion that they were already Americans in every sense but the law. Singh's bill was more extensive and more ambitious. It would repeal the very logic of exclusion, making Indians racially eligible to become U.S. citizens, and it would create a quota allowing one hundred Indians per year to naturalize. His legislation, however, was focused primarily on the future; it would favor new, and presumably more highly qualified, immigrants over pre-1923 settlers, reserving seventy-five of each year's naturalizations for such applicants.[7]

As different as the two bills were, Khan and Singh and their respective supporters had come to lean on similar arguments when they went before Congress. Both men's camps bolstered their cases for repeal of the naturalization laws by stressing the accomplishments of "leading" Indian Americans of the day, and each presented lists and biographies of these scientists, engineers, and scholars. Such individuals, they argued, were wronged by the current laws; they were prevented from becoming American citizens even though they had contributed their considerable knowledge and expertise to the United States. Khan also stressed the injustice suffered by large-scale Indian farmers, like those in Arizona, who could not own the land they had made productive. Singh spoke of the Indian businessmen who could not do meaningful business in the United States because they were restricted to short-term tourist visas. Both sides stressed the participation of Indian forces and Indian men in the war effort and touted the benefits of expanded U.S. trade with an India that would likely gain its independence at the war's end.[8]

The majority of Indians who were living in the United States in 1945 and who were being prevented from becoming U.S. citizens were, in fact, not scientists, not businessmen, not engineers, scholars, or even large-scale agriculturalists. They were farm laborers and industrial and service workers. But in the 1945 hearing, this was mentioned only sporadically and often obliquely. Even Mubarek Ali Khan, who represented this group, was cautious in how he described "the three thousand." J. J. Singh made a few references to the farm and factory workers, but always in the negative: that is, he assured the committee that because his bill required that most of the one hundred naturalizations per year be filled by Indians *from* India (rather than by those already living in the United States) his legislation would not result in a flood of Indian workers becoming U.S. citizens. Acknowledging that some congressional committee members were still "worried about the so-called laboring classes," Singh went so far as to assure them that "with the industrialization schemes that are afoot in India, I do not anticipate that [any workers] would care to leave India" to come to the United States.[9] As the hearings

progressed, no one seemed willing to speak boldly for the silent majority
of Indians in the United States, for a shadow population of migrants,
spread across the country, who had dropped "out of status" as the immigration laws changed around them. No one, that is, except a Bengali
from New York City named Ibrahim Choudry.

Choudry was a seaman turned community activist: former director of
an Indian merchant sailors' club in Manhattan and secretary of the India
Association for American Citizenship. Although allied with Mubarek
Ali Khan, he was willing—and likely felt bound—to be more forceful
than Khan in his advocacy. In the midst of the March 1945 hearings
before the Committee on Immigration and Naturalization, a letter that
Choudry had written was introduced into testimony. There is no indication that it was read aloud, which likely means that it was simply handed
by Khan to the appropriate clerk to be added to the typed record after
the conclusion of the hearing. Shuffled into archival obscurity, Choudry's
letter spoke up unequivocally for a population that other witnesses
were less forthright in acknowledging. "I do not speak . . . here for the
few," Choudry wrote:

> I speak for the many. I am not speaking for the transient element—
> the student the business man, the lecturer, the interpreter of India's
> past and present, whose interests and ties in this country are tempo-
> rary, the man or the woman whose roots are in India and who even-
> tually returns home. I talk for those of us who, by our work and by
> our sweat and by our blood, have helped build fighting industrial
> America today. I talk for those of our men who, in factory and field,
> in all sections of American industry, work side by side with their fel-
> low American workers to strengthen the industrial framework of
> this country. . . . We have married here; our children have been
> born here. . . . I speak for such as myself, for those of my brothers
> who work in the factories of the East and in Detroit. . . . I speak for
> the workers and the farmers of our community whose lives have
> been bound to this country's destiny for 23 years or longer. I speak
> for these men who while they themselves have no rights under orien-
> tal exclusion have seen their sons go off to war these last years to
> fight for a democracy which they—their fathers—could not them-

selves enjoy. I speak for men who . . . expect to die in the country to which they have given their best years. . . . [W]e simply ask you for justice—American justice.[10]

Despite his eloquence, Choudry was on the losing side of U.S. immigration history. Although the naturalization bill that President Harry S. Truman signed into law in July 1946 did make all Indians already resident in the country eligible for citizenship, the law was grounded in the ideas that J. J. Singh and his allies had championed and to which Mubarek Ali Khan had largely assented. These ideas—that U.S. immigration policies toward India should favor scientists, engineers, and businesspeople and be driven by national considerations of trade and foreign policy—not only won out in 1946 but were eventually enshrined in the Hart-Celler Act,[11] which opened the door to tens of thousands of skilled professionals from the subcontinent in 1965. These are the South Asian immigrants whom Americans would come to know in the 1970s, 1980s, and 1990s—the doctors, the engineers, the entrepreneurs. While it seemingly put an end to the exclusion era, the 1965 act essentially maintained the exclusion of working-class immigrants. Choudry's letter is like a flash in the midst of this history. For a brief moment, it revealed a hidden population of Indian laborers who had no legal status but who by the mid-1940s had already long become part of the fabric of U.S. society, living, working, and bringing up families in the shadows of its restrictive anti-Asian immigration laws. The ex-seaman from New York had attempted to bring these men out into the open, to lay claim, on their behalf, to official belonging in the U.S. nation.

In the years since, the migrants for whom Choudry spoke have passed away, and as their stories have disappeared from public memory, we have been left with a history that is fragmentary and partial. The fullest narrative we have of an early South Asian presence in the United States is that of Punjabi migrants to the Canadian and U.S. West Coast. Between 1904 and 1924, these predominantly Sikh workers entered Vancouver, were driven southward into the Pacific Northwest by Canadians' "whites only" policy, encountered outbreaks of racial violence after entering the lumber mills of Washington and Oregon in the early 1900s, and then made their way into the rich agricultural areas stretching along inland

California to the Mexican border and the U.S. Southwest. For more than three decades, scholars have explored Punjabi migrants' experiences, building a rich understanding of their encounters with local populations; their involvement in the expatriate anticolonial Ghadar movement; and their attempts to fight the imposition of anti-Asian immigration, naturalization, and landownership laws.[12] But we have come to understand this West Coast history as if it were the full story of early South Asian America and we have too often assumed that the story came to a definitive end when the 1917 Immigration Act criminalized Asian immigration and the 1923 Supreme Court decision in *United States v. Bhagat Singh Thind* closed off the pathway to citizenship. As a result, thousands of South Asian migrants who settled across other parts of the country—the East Coast, the South, the Midwest—and who either arrived or stayed in the United States under the radar of racist immigration laws, have been lost to history. Their lives have remained hidden in disparate archives and fading family memories.

Ibrahim Choudry was one of these migrants. He was part of a phenomenon that has gone unaccounted for in both popular and scholarly accounts of Asian immigration to the United States. Beginning around the time of the First World War, hundreds of Indian maritime workers, men who labored in the engine rooms and kitchens of British steamships, escaped into the crowded waterfronts of New York, Philadelphia, and Baltimore in search of less brutal and captive work and better wages onshore. These men were predominantly Muslims from rural backgrounds. The largest number were from villages in East Bengal—a region that would later become the nation of Bangladesh. Others hailed from regions that are part of present-day Pakistan—Punjab, Kashmir, and the Northwest Frontier. After signing on to ships in Calcutta and Bombay, they worked under indenture-like conditions at the mercy of British ships' masters for months and years at a stretch. During the war, however, these men found that their labor was in demand in U.S. steel, shipbuilding, and munitions industries, and they formed clandestine networks to help one another jump ship and make their way inland to factory towns. Their networks helped sustain an Indian presence onshore even after the passage of the 1917 Immigration Act, so that by the 1920s, Indian workers could be found across the whole of the U.S. industrial belt. In New York City, the largest port of entry for this population, ex-seamen also entered the service economy. They lived in shared apartments near the west-side waterfront and on the Lower East Side, and worked as line cooks, dishwashers, doormen, and elevator operators in Manhattan restaurants and hotels.

This was by and large a transient population. Over time, hundreds of Indian seamen cycled through the networks that their co-workers and kin had first set up in the 1910s, and most eventually returned to the maritime trade and the subcontinent. But some stayed in the United States for good. By the time Ibrahim Choudry made his petition to Congress, he and other ex-seamen were part of a population of Indian workers that had put down roots throughout the U.S. Northeast and Midwest. Denied official belonging, they became part of another nation, a nation beneath the nation, in working-class neighborhoods of color from New York to Baltimore to Detroit. The greatest number appear to have settled in Harlem. Many married local women here, had children, and even as they maintained ties to one another, developed Puerto Rican, African American, and West Indian extended families and friends. Some opened restaurants or started small businesses, and as they settled, they became a quiet but integral part of the daily life of their adopted neighborhood.[13]

Astonishingly, this community had an even earlier precedent. In the 1880s, groups of Bengali Muslim peddlers from the present-day Indian state of West Bengal had begun making their way to and through the United States. These men brought embroidered silks and other "exotic" goods to sell to an American public that was in the grips of a fashion for all things "Indian" and "Oriental." As hundreds of these peddlers followed the pathways of U.S. leisure travelers and consumers, their trajectory took them to the beach boardwalks of New Jersey, the streets of southern cities, and the emerging Euro-American tourist destinations of the Caribbean and Central America. At the U.S. border, they faced a restrictive immigration regime, focused most pointedly on the exclusion of Chinese labor migrants but increasingly suspicious of and hostile toward "Asiatics" in general. Once inside, they found a United States—north and south—that was riven by racial segregation; the subordinate social status of African Americans was delineated in the geography of the cities and towns to which they came, and was enforced by law, custom, and violence. As dark-skinned men from "the East," the peddlers occupied a slightly different position, but one that was inconsistent and unpredictable; while their place within the country's black-white racial imagination was not quite fixed, and to a degree was even manipulable, their place on the streets and within the residential neighborhoods of segregated cities was much clearer. So, as they accessed white consumers with fantasies of India, their pathway into and across the United States was a pathway through working-class black neighborhoods; they established outposts in these places and then moved outward to sell their goods.

The most important neighborhood to their operation was New Orleans' Tremé. Here, some of the Bengalis married and started families with African American women, who were part of recent black migrations into the city, or with Creole of Color women who had deep generational roots in Tremé. These local women of color became as important to the operations of the network as the women who remained in West Bengal villages; while Bengali women produced the embroidered goods that would be sold in the United States and tended to the homes, land, and families that the peddlers left behind for months or years at a time, women in New Orleans helped Indian men settle and establish themselves locally; they gave the peddler network stability and longevity.[14] Between the 1890s and 1920s, hundreds of Bengali peddlers were thus able to cycle through to sell their wares. After the network ceased to operate, a small number of the men stayed behind, and in the ensuing years, they, their wives, their children, and their descendants became part of the history of black New Orleans.

The stories of these Muslim peddlers and seamen from colonial India are as remarkable as they are unknown. They are remarkable for what the men had to navigate, for the places they ended up, and for the kinds of communities and families they formed once they reached the United States. They defy most assumptions and expectations about South Asian migration to the United States— about who South Asian migrants are, where they come from, what trajectories they follow, how they navigate the U.S. landscape of race and class, and how they assimilate. In fact, these stories force us to reconsider some deep-held beliefs about U.S. immigration. The Indian Muslim migrants of the late nineteenth and early twentieth centuries did not experience the welcome that was promised to the world's "tired . . . poor . . . huddled masses." Most came with no expectation that they would stay; they did not come, in historian Sucheta Mazumdar's words, as "part of incipient settler families clutching a one-way ticket in their hands and the American Dream in their hearts." These men were sojourning laborers, or what we now would understand more broadly as global labor migrants. They were among the many populations of peasants and workers whose traditional means of livelihood had been disrupted by colonization, industrialization, and the mechanization of agriculture, and who traveled across oceans to access the jobs and markets available in the United States. As such, the peddlers and seamen illuminate the larger displacements and mass migrations that characterized their era.[15] At the same time, they point to one of the United States' most enduring contradictions: in the very years that the United States became what its leaders would later call a "nation of immigrants" it also became a nation of immigrant exclusion.[16]

These Indian migrants provide us with a different picture of "assimilation." The peddlers and seamen did not form ethnic enclaves, as did Italians, Greeks, Germans, or, for that matter, South Asian immigrants of later generations. Nor did they follow the iconic path of immigrant upward mobility that would lead so many members of these other groups out of their ethnic enclaves into predominantly white suburbs. The networks that Indian Muslims formed—networks that were embedded in working-class Creole, African American, and Puerto Rican neighborhoods and entwined with the lives of their residents—represent a different pathway into the United States. All of the places where the peddlers and seamen put down roots—and Harlem more than any other—were receiving-stations for migrants and immigrants of color, particularly those displaced by white-supremacy in the U.S. South, and the military and economic pursuits of Britain and the United States in the Caribbean. These were as much spaces of the global black diaspora as they were neighborhoods of the United States.

It was here that South Asian Muslims were able to forge complex and syncretic new lives and build multi-ethnic families and communities at a time when the U.S. nation saw them only as aliens and criminals. And they were not alone in this; South Asians were just one of several smaller groups—many living under the radar of the immigration laws—who found homes and built lives in these places. They included Chinese, Filipinos, and Arabs in Tremé; Filipinos, Chinese, and Roma in West Baltimore; Arabs, Afghans, and Greeks in Black Bottom; Mexicans, Argentines, and Peruvians in Harlem, among others.[17] The stories of the men who were described in Mubarek Ali Khan's legislation simply as "three-thousand Eastern Hemisphere Indians," thus tell us a great deal about U.S. neighborhoods and communities of color in the first half of the twentieth century—about their heterogeneity, their openness, and the unacknowledged role they played in U.S. immigration history.

CHAPTER 1

Out of the East and into the South

There are some thirty Indians, fresh from East India who landed in Atlanta about two weeks ago and every one of them has been peddling notions in and around the city.

—*Atlanta Constitution,* November 21, 1912

ELLIS ISLAND WAS ON FIRE. The grand, three-story immigration station had cost more than $75,000 and had taken almost two years to build. It had been in operation for no more than five and a half years, and now, in the middle of the night of June 15, 1897, a fire had broken out. More than two hundred immigrant detainees were rushed out of the building as the flames spread. Across the water, on the southern tip of Manhattan, fire crews scrambled into action, but before their boats could reach the island, the entire pine structure was engulfed in smoke and fire; the ceiling quickly caved in and the federal government's flagship immigrant-processing station collapsed to the ground.

Three days later, the SS *St. Louis* sailed into New York Harbor from Southampton, England. It was a beautiful early summer evening; the sky was clear and the weather was warm. The *St. Louis* approached the Statue of Liberty, still a relatively new addition to the waters below Manhattan, and turned gently to the left toward the mouth of the North River. Twelve Muslim men from Calcutta and Hooghly, West Bengal, were on board the steamship, preparing to disembark after their six-day journey across the Atlantic. Ahead and to the ship's right, they would have seen southern Manhattan's impressive outcrop of skyscrapers—the tallest reaching more than twenty stories above the ground—aglow in the evening sun. On their left, where their ship was supposed to dock, lay a pile of rubble.

Since the conflagration, the Bureau of Immigration had been scrambling to deal with incoming passenger ships. Each day, two or three more ships arrived, bearing thousands of immigrants from Europe and points farther east. In the absence of a processing facility, the Bureau had ordered arriving steamships to proceed to their respective piers along the Manhattan waterfront. A team of medical and immigration inspectors would meet each ship as it docked, examine its passengers, and admit or detain them as warranted. So, after passing the embers of Ellis Island, the *St. Louis* made its way up the North River to Pier 14, the terminal for its parent company, the American Line. This was one of the largest and most modern structures on the waterfront, extending into the river from West Street between Fulton and Vesey, exactly where, a century later, the north tower of the World Trade Center would stand.[1]

The Bengali men on board the *St. Louis* were peddlers, on their way to the beach resorts of New Jersey—Atlantic City, Asbury Park, and Long Branch. In their home villages, their wives, mothers, sisters, and daughters produced finely embroidered silk and cotton fabrics—handkerchiefs, bedspreads, pillow covers, and tablecloths—in a style known as *chikan*; no doubt, the luggage that each man carried was filled with such goods. At some point earlier in the year, perhaps as recently as May, the twelve men had made their way by ship from Calcutta to Southampton, England. They had then crossed the Atlantic in the SS *St. Louis,* with more than two hundred other migrants, immigrants, and travelers. They shared the cramped quarters of third class with a German butcher, an Armenian student, a Japanese cook, two Russian Jewish tailors, and a number of returning Americans: a dressmaker, a cigar worker, a cattleman, an upholsterer. More than half the passengers were Scandinavian immigrants on their way to New York, Pennsylvania, Illinois, Minnesota, and North Dakota. The majority of these men and women were farmers, laborers, and domestic workers.[2]

What were the Bengali peddlers anticipating as their ship docked on West Street? The older members of the group, Mintoz Mondul, Moksad Ali, and Moosha Mondul, had been making voyages to the United States since the 1880s. In those early years, they had been through immigration procedures at Manhattan's Castle Garden depot, and they may have seen the Ellis Island station under construction, sailing past it on their way in and out of port. In more recent years, a few of the peddlers had passed through Ellis Island's imposing new processing facility and made their way through its maze of metal pens, going from one type of inspection to the next.[3] It is hard to know whether these previous experiences would have eased the Bengalis' anxiety as they approached Pier 14 or increased it. The men likely knew what to expect as they faced the indignity of the medical exam, in which they were poked and prodded like cattle, their hair combed through for lice, their eyelids pulled back with a metal hook to check for trachoma. However, the number of questions that the immigration examiners asked them had been increasing and the speed at which they were asked these questions had grown more rapid. And in the days following the Ellis Island fire, the examiners were, no doubt, under pressure to be extravigilant, to prove that the adverse conditions would not hamper their ability to prevent "undesirable aliens" from entering the country.[4]

When Mintoz and Musa Mondul, Moksad Ali, their colleagues Abdul Aziz, Abdul Ahmed, Basiruddin, Obidullah, and Fazleh Rahman, and the rest of their group went up before the examiner, they gave a single set of answers to a quick succession of questions: Occupation? Merchant. Nationality? East Indian. Last residence? Southampton. Final destination? New Jersey. Who paid for your ticket? Myself. How much money do you have with you? £6. Been in the United States before? Yes. Joining a relative? No. Been in prison? No. Polygamist? No. Under contract to work in the United States? To this last question, they all answered "no"—or at least this is what was recorded on the incoming ships' manifest. But something must have happened when the men were face-to-face with the immigration examiner. Something was said; something was misunderstood; someone hesitated; or the examiner simply decided that the dozen Indians were suspicious, that they looked like contract workers, entering the country in violation of the law. He ordered them detained. As the Scandinavian farmers and workers disembarked onto West Street to start new lives, meet eagerly waiting relatives, or make their way to points farther west, the twelve Muslim peddlers from Bengal were taken away to the southern tip of Manhattan, to a makeshift detention center on the top floor of the Barge Office—a facility that one contemporary reporter described as "grimy, gloomy, [and] more suggestive of an enclosure for animals than a receiving station for prospective citizens." Across the water, a few miles down the New Jersey coast, the beach boardwalks were filling up with thousands of summer vacationers, thousands of potential customers for the "fancy goods" that sat packed away in the peddlers' trunks. But this summer's trip was not to be. After holding them in detention for eight days, the Bureau of Immigration's Board of Special Inquiry ordered the twelve men deported, declaring that "inasmuch as they peddle goods not their own, they are held to come under provisions of the Contract Labor law." On the ship that took them back to London, the men were now listed as "laborers" rather than "merchants."[5]

What is remarkable about this story is not the harshness of the treatment to which the twelve Bengali peddlers were subjected—or the cursory nature of the Board of Inquiry hearing that turned them back from U.S. shores. In the closing years of the nineteenth century, as the numbers of immigrants arriving at U.S. ports swelled, the federal government had taken over the processing and evaluation of arriving passengers—a role previously played by individual states. The government's Immigration Bureau began rationalizing, regularizing, and tightening the criteria according to which "alien passengers" would be admitted. The Chinese Exclusion Act of 1882 and the Alien Contract Labor Law of 1885 were two of the first elements of the new border regime. Both were suffused with racist assumptions about the nature of Asian laborers, and both complicated the Bengali peddlers' ability to cross into the United States, making their treatment in 1897, at the very least, unsurprising.[6] What was remarkable was the peddlers' ability to adapt to their deportation and operate within a much larger field of possibilities. Within a month of their arrival in London, five of the deported men—Musa Mondul, Basiruddin, Abdul Aziz, Abdul Ahmed, and Obidullah—signed on with a group of fifty miners from England, Scotland, Ireland, and Northern and Eastern Europe and set off by steamer for South Africa, which, along with Australia, was another market for their goods.[7] Within a year or two, almost all twelve men would return to the United States, traveling in smaller groups, trying different ports, finding a way to get back in, reunite with kin and co-villagers, and carry on their work.

These men were part of what may be the first significant settlement of South Asians in the United States. Beginning sometime in the 1880s, Muslim peddlers from a cluster of villages just north of Calcutta began traveling to the United States to sell "Oriental goods"—embroidered cotton and silk, small rugs, perfumes, and a range of other items. Indian demand for their handicrafts had declined under colonial rule, as the British imported cheap factory-made textiles and established greater control over the subcontinent's internal markets.[8] But overseas, middle-class consumers in Britain, Australia, South Africa, and the United States were in the midst of a fin de siècle fashion for the exotic ideas, entertainments, and goods of India and "the East." Other Indian traders had made their way outward from the subcontinent to sell handicrafts to European travelers in the Mediterranean and North Africa.[9] The Bengalis ventured into new territories, establishing an extensive network that stretched through the East Coast of the United States, into and across the southern states, and as far south as Panama. Even as U.S. laws and attitudes turned against Asian immigrants, these men worked the India craze to their advantage. Between the 1890s and the 1920s, as the policing of immigration shifted from the regime of the Alien Contract Labor Law to that of the explicitly exclusionary Immigration Act of 1917 (also known as the Asiatic Barred Zone Act), these men built upon existing ties of kinship and newly established connections within U.S. communities of color to build, maintain, and expand their operations. In their own day, they became a regular fixture at North American tourist sites and on the streets of major U.S. cities. Yet they have vanished from historical memory.

Buried in hundreds of fragmentary archival documents—ships' logs, census records, marriage certificates, local news items—the stories of these men illuminate a very different trajectory of migration to the United States from those celebrated in the national mythology. The peddlers did not leave their homeland behind in order to start new and better lives in the United States. Like other sojourning laborers of their day, they moved often, following the temporary openings and shifting demands of the U.S. and other economies. In their case, the "opening" was an expanding

American culture of travel, tourism, and consumption and a broad demand for Oriental goods. Rather than reconstituting their Indian families in the United States, they forged different, sometimes temporary, forms of affiliation in the places they peddled goods, while continuing to function—through remittances and return visits—as part of economic circuits that stretched back to their families and home villages on the sub-continent.[10] Rather than forming their own enclaves in U.S. cities—ethnic neighborhoods where they sought to replicate in miniature the places they left behind—these peddlers built a global network that was multiethnic and rooted in segregated black neighborhoods. The men who moved through this network had to navigate the economic circuits, national borders, social spaces, racial ideologies, and consumer desires of both Great Britain and the United States. They were living, working, and moving in the shadows of two empires.

Peddlers of Notions

Today, when we think of U.S. fads and fashions for India, we tend to focus on the recent mass popularity of yoga and Bollywood films or on narratives of self-discovery in the East such as Elizabeth Gilbert's best-selling *Eat, Pray, Love.* The hippie counterculture of the late 1960s, with its obsessions for Indian music, fabrics, and spiritualities, also remains strong in the public memory. It is largely forgotten that at the turn of the twentieth century the United States was in the grips of a craze over India and "the Orient" that was, in some ways, larger and more pervasive than anything that has occurred since. Between the 1880s and 1920s, Americans from all classes and walks of life were drawn to an "India" that was, in essence, a collective fantasy. Elites of cities such as New York, Chicago, Boston, and Philadelphia explored Vedantist philosophy and attempted the contortions of "tantrik" yoga. A young Isadora Duncan performed her interpretations of Eastern dance, in bare feet and flowing robes, on the lawns of Newport, Rhode Island's finest mansions, while Ruth St. Denis performed in Indian-style on Broadway, bedecked with jewels and wrapped in a colorful silk sari. The New Thought writer and publisher William Walker Atkinson built a national audience for his mail-order books on clairvoyance, mind control, and the "Hindu-yogi science of breath," published under pseudonyms such as Swami Panchadasi, Yogi Ramacharaka, and Swami Bhakta Vishita.[11]

Meanwhile, the sexualized figure of the Indian "nautch" dancer became a staple of American burlesque theaters. Southern growers marketed tobacco under brand names such as Hindoo, Mecca, Mogul, and Bengal, with labels that depicted Ameers and maharajahs, palaces, hookahs, and dancing girls. Tin Pan Alley songwriters churned out show tunes such as "My Hindoo Man" and "Down in Bom-Bombay," which middle-class Americans sang to amuse themselves in the piano parlors of their homes. Circuses and exhibitions competed to present ever-larger menageries of Indian elephants and camels and ever-more spectacular re-creations of Indian, Sinhalese, and other "native" villages. Such exotic public spectacles reached new heights in 1904, when the owners of Coney Island's Luna Park turned fifteen acres of the Brooklyn amusement park into a replica of the city of Delhi and "imported" three hundred Indian men, women, and children, forty camels and seventy elephants to live there for the summer season. Several times a day the "natives" and their animals marched through Luna Park, performing a re-creation of the Delhi Durbar—the grand procession that had occurred in India the year before to mark the ascendance of King Edward VII of England to the imperial throne. By 1909, even the Wild West showmen Buffalo Bill Cody and Gordon "Pawnee Bill" Lillie joined in the craze, touring a "Far East Show" across the U.S. Midwest and South that featured Arabian horsemen, a troupe of Sinhalese dancers, a "Hindu fakir," and a "nautch dance ballet."[12]

For Americans of the era, "India" was presented as part of a mysterious and exotic "Orient" that took in the entire swath of North Africa, the Middle East, India, and Ceylon. This "Orient," in turn, was a blur of images, stories, references, and fantasies, derived from the contexts of the British, French, and other European empires. In their original context, Orientalist narratives and imagery had performed a particular kind of work. The British portrayal of India as the seat of a once great but now decaying civilization provided moral and political justification for the imposition and maintenance of colonial rule.[13] In the American context, Orientalist notions were more free-floating. Unmoored from the daily exercise of colonial power, they entered the realm of the United States' growing cultures of self-improvement, mass entertainment, and mass consumption. Ideas about India took on new life and meaning in a society in which people's identities and social standing were increasingly defined by what they consumed and displayed.[14]

This was nowhere more apparent than in the turn-of-the-century fashion for "Oriental goods." As "Indian" and "Oriental" ideas, images, and amusements proliferated, Americans developed a seemingly insatiable desire for items that connected them to the East of their imaginings: silk scarves and shawls, cushion covers, wall hangings, rugs, brassware, carved and enameled boxes, jewelry, incense, perfume. This was a trend that had, over a very short span of time, traveled across both geographic and class lines. Earlier in the 1800s, the fashion for fine silks, rugs, and porcelain from India, China, Japan, and the Middle East had begun among the upper classes of London and Paris, for whom the display of luxury goods from the far reaches of empire was a sign of both power and sophistication. Elites in U.S. cities quickly followed the lead of their class counterparts in Europe, using "Oriental" and other foreign commodities to assert their own worldliness—at precisely the moment that the United States itself was growing as an imperial power. Men in New York, Chicago, and elsewhere outfitted their smoking rooms with plush Oriental rugs, hookahs, tiger skins, elephant tusks, daggers, scimitars, and images of "eroticized Eastern women"—goods that simultaneously conveyed the conquest of far-off lands and conjured the fantasy world of the Eastern harem.[15]

Upper-class women used Oriental goods to create lavish schemes for the interiors of their homes. Chicago's society matron Bertha Honoré Palmer, for example, decorated her Lake Shore Drive mansion in a series of regionally themed rooms. According to historian Kristin Hoganson, the home "had a Spanish music room, English dining room, Moorish ballroom, Flemish library, and French and Chinese drawing rooms. Upstairs, Bertha Palmer slept in a bedroom copied from a Cairo palace."[16] Such women, Hoganson argues, used themed interiors to push beyond domestic constraints—to assert their connection to a wider world. At the same time, American women drew upon the cache of meanings that surrounded Oriental goods to challenge the propriety of the Victorian era; as the century came to a close, the American "New Woman" marked her independence and liberation by owning, wearing, and displaying goods that conjured Western ideas of a sensual and exotic East.[17] By this time, a wave of popular writing about interior design promoted a scaled-down version of upper-class decorative styles to middle-class American women. Unable to furnish multiple themed rooms, women of lesser means were encouraged to combine several themes in a single room. They could "stuff the entire world into their parlors, confident that this was au courant."[18] Oriental goods thus became a marker of class status, and a vehicle of class striving, at multiple levels of society. While upper-class American women displayed high-end items from "the East" to assert their equivalence to European elites, the possession of items at the lower end of the scale—embroidered fabrics, cushions, throws, and other small goods—allowed middle- and lower-middle-class women, in turn, to emulate the American upper classes and lay claim to their own "sense of European sophistication."[19]

As Oriental goods entered the realm of mass consumption, the spaces in which they were bought and sold also expanded. Earlier, the sale of Oriental goods had largely been limited to high-end department stores and suppliers such as Liberty in London, Samuel Bing in Paris, and Tiffany in New York.[20] By the 1880s and 1890s, a broader array of importers, retailers, and department stores were providing such goods to the middle-class market.[21] In New York City, these included Erich Brothers, W. & J. Sloane, Macy's, Lord and Taylor's, Cowperthwaits, and the specialty retailer A. A. Vantine, which boasted of being the "largest Japanese, Chinese, and India house in the world." Under the banner of its unique logo—the flags of Japan and China, crossed, beneath the crescent moon and star of Islam—Vantine's sold an astonishing variety of goods, from rugs and silks to teas, coffees, dinner gongs, teak furniture, "Kutch" sandalwood talc, and perfumes with names like "Java Lily" and "Delhi Heliotrope."[22] Oriental goods also found a ready market within the growing spaces of middle- and working-class leisure: resorts, amusement parks, exhibitions, and beach boardwalks. Here, Oriental gift shops and pack and pushcart peddlers sold exotic souvenirs, curios, and handicrafts to Americans on weekend day trips and holiday travels.[23]

It was in this context that a handful of small-scale traders from West Bengal set out for the United States. The men were from a Muslim community in the district of Hooghly. Here, in a cluster of villages thirty miles northwest of the city of Calcutta, members of the local peasantry had engaged in the production of cotton and silk handicrafts for generations, supplementing what they produced and earned through farming with the sale of clothing and domestic goods embroidered in the intricate decorative style known as *chikan*. Accounts suggest that most of the needlework was done in the home during times of the year "when work on the farm is slack" and that it was predominantly women who produced the embroideries, while "their men" traveled out to "sell these products in home-markets."[24]

It is difficult to pinpoint the exact origins of the operation that brought Hooghly's handicrafts halfway around the world to the United States. In what is perhaps the only detailed narrative account of the network's activities in the United States, the expatriate Indian nationalist newspaper the *Hindusthanee Student* suggested in 1917 that the peddlers had first been forced beyond their regional orbit under the rule of the British East India Company. In the early nineteenth century, the British had flooded Indian markets with their own machine-made textiles and imposed high tariffs on Indian goods, undermining the indigenous textile industry and weakening internal demand for cotton and silk handicrafts like those of Hooghly's villages.[25] The British also pushed aggressively to regulate and dominate the arenas in which goods were bought and sold on the subcontinent, the bazaars in which Hooghly's *chikondars* would have operated.[26] During this period, to which the *Hindusthanee Student* simply referred as "the decline," men from Hooghly were forced to find new markets for *chikan* goods and began to travel overseas. These small traders, or *chikondars*, first made their way outward from Calcutta to South Africa and Australia, and by the 1880s, after prospering in these locations, "the first batch, consisting of ten or twelve men, dared the perils of the unknown" and set out for the United States. Having been displaced by colonial pursuits on the subcontinent, these men used the very infrastructure of the British Empire to go beyond the empire's reach. They traveled thousands of miles through the circuits of colonial seaborne trade to a place where the scarves, handkerchiefs, tablecloths, and wall hangings embroidered in Hooghly villages had become the stuff of fashions, fancies, and fantasies.[27]

Hooghly's *chikondars* were not the first Indian traders to make such a shift, and the story of one group that preceded them sheds some light on the dynamics that may have led Hooghly's peddlers overseas. In the 1860s, Sindhi Hindu merchants from the city of Hyderabad, west of Karachi, began making trips outward from the subcontinent to sell a range of regionally produced handicrafts. At the height of their operations, the Sindhi networks stretched eastward from Bombay through Singapore, Shanghai, and Manila to Kobe, Japan, and westward through Port Sudan, Port Said, Valetta, and Gibraltar—or via Cape Town and Freetown—to Panama. According to historian Claude Markovits, the Hyderabad network grew out of a confluence of events tied to the expansion of the British Empire. In the 1800s, the British created an infrastructure for the extraction of goods and raw materials from northwest India: a deepwater port in Karachi; rail lines between rural Punjab and Karachi's port; steamships traveling outward, both to the east and to the west; and the canal at Suez, which drastically reduced the time and expense required to transport goods from India to Europe. In shifting the commercial center of Sindh from Hyderabad to Karachi, the British disrupted previous economic relations and means of livelihood in the Hyderabad region, among other things weakening the traditional markets for local handicrafts such as textiles, lacquerwork, and embroidery. A small number of Hyderabadi handicraft dealers began making sales trips to Bombay and discovered that there was a strong demand for their goods among Europeans in the expanding colonial port city. This information was brought back to Hyderabad, and regional merchants decided not just to sell their goods in Bombay, but also to move out to other sites with large numbers of traveling Europeans. They began, in the early 1860s, by making their way to Egypt, which had become a destination of choice for British and other European tourists. As colonial conquests, steam navigation, and the construction of major shipping canals opened the world up to European leisure travelers and the modern-day phenomenon of tourism began to take shape, these Sindhi merchants established outposts everywhere that Europeans sailed, selling "silk and curio items from the Far East and India" at sites throughout the world.[28]

Hooghly's peddlers of cotton and silk went through a similar process, establishing a base of operations in Calcutta and then moving outward.

Like the Sindhi traders, they began by selling their goods along British imperial circuits—in South Africa and Australia—but then branched into a vast territory that the Sindhi peddlers had left untouched: the United States. Here they carved their own pathway for the sale of embroideries and curios, moving through a series of U.S., Caribbean, and Central American sites of travel and tourism. They began with New Jersey, whose beach boardwalk towns were some of the era's premier sites of popular recreation on the Eastern Seaboard. During the summer season, the hotels, beaches, and amusement parks of Long Branch, Atlantic City, and Asbury Park drew hundreds of thousands of working people from Philadelphia and New York City. It was a crowd that was newly able to partake of regular leisure activities, what New Jersey historian Charles E. Funnell has described as the "lower middle classes . . . lesser white collar workers of all varieties including the many different kinds of clerks staffing the commerce and retail trade of Philadelphia . . . [and, increasingly] women, employed [in the cities] in growing numbers as salesgirls."[29] The resorts made their money by encouraging and catering to this group's desire to regard itself as class ascendant; as Funnell puts it in his description of Atlantic City, "the values expressed in the resort's entertainment were those of citizens vigorously striving for the good life which . . . they imagined the upper middle-class and rich to enjoy."[30] "Oriental" items such as silks, embroidered cloth, and small trinkets and curios were accessible and affordable markers of this good life; the demand for them among New Jersey's holiday makers was significant enough that "Oriental gift shops" became a prominent feature of the resort towns' boardwalks, and Long Branch, Atlantic City, and Asbury Park became fertile ground for individual fancy goods peddlers from "the East."[31]

The earliest fragments of evidence that place Hooghly's *chikondars* in the region of New Jersey date back to the mid-1880s. Ships' manifests show that small groups of Indian Muslim "traders," "hawkers," and "merchants" were entering the United States through the port of New York roughly once a year during fall and winter months. In September 1884, for example, two Indian "merchants," Sheik and Gorhan Ally, arrived in New York on the SS *Edam* from Boulogne-sur-Mer, France; in January 1885, the merchants Waheed Bux and "Moostakim" arrived on the SS *California* from Calcutta; and in February 1888, four Indian "hawkers," Sultah Ahmed, Saidh Bhoole, and Mohammad and Shaikh Hossain, arrived on the SS *Waesland* from Antwerp, Belgium.[32] These appear to be the Hooghly peddlers' first forays into the United States— trips that laid the foundations for their network. Two of the men on these early voyages, Waheed Bux and Mohammad Hossain, would continue to make journeys into, out of, and across the United States for the next twenty years. By the end of the 1880s, they and others from their region had established a distinct pattern of sojourning migration centered on the summer season of New Jersey's beachside resorts.[33]

It was around this time that U.S. commentators began to take notice. On May 29, 1889, Mohammad Hossain accompanied nine other men from India to New York, traveling the final leg from London on the SS *Egyptian Monarch*. Although the ships' manifest listed the men as "laborers," the *Brooklyn Eagle* reported the true nature of their business, noting the day after their arrival that the *Egyptian Monarch* had "brought about a dozen Hindoo peddlers who will do business at Long Branch in shawls and tablecloths."[34] In the racial vernacular of the turn of the century, these Muslim men, along with Hindus, Sikhs, and all others from the subcontinent, would be marked with the term "Hindoo." Two years later, on July 19, 1891, Hooghly's *chikondars* again came to the notice of the press. This time, they warranted a full paragraph in the *Chicago Tribune*. Under the headline "Hindoos in America," a reporter wrote: "The dark-skinned Hindoo peddlers who infest the seaside resorts of the Jersey coast in summer are very interesting people. They are invariably courteous and their general shrewdness when trying to affect a sale is most engaging. As a rule, they are handsome men with clean-cut features and intellectual faces. They speak Hindustanee and occasionally Bengali, while their English is excellent."[35] While steeped in condescension, this news item publicly marked the beginnings of what would be a decades-long presence of Bengali peddlers within the cultural and commercial arena of New Jersey's seaside resorts.

From 1889 onward, the peddlers' voyages became more regular and their population in the United States increased. In the 1890s, groups of *chikondars* arrived at Ellis Island like clockwork during the first half of each summer season, on their way to the New Jersey boardwalks to sell their wares. As the earlier traders gained their footing in the United States and remittances began to flow back to their villages, the number of Bengali peddlers arriving each year grew.[36] Seven *chikondars* arrived from Calcutta in June 1894; the following June it was twenty, then eleven in June 1896 and twelve in June 1897. By this time, the Bengali peddlers' operations had taken the shape of a full-fledged and well-organized network. At the end of each season, between two and seven men typically left the United States to return to Calcutta, and then another group of peddlers sailed from Calcutta to New York at the beginning of the following summer, presumably with a fresh stock of embroidered silks, cottons, and other small saleable items. Each of these groups included a core of five or six men who had traveled to the United States in previous years. They included Abdul Subham, Sofur Ally, Jainal Abdeen, Roston Ally, and Solomon Mondul in 1895 and Abdul Rahman, Mohammad Hossain, Eshrak Ali, Mubarak Ali Mondul, Abdul Wahab, and Abdul Latif—as well as Abdul Subham and Solomon Mondul again—in 1896.[37] Only a few of these peddlers returned to the subcontinent at the end of each summer season; the others continued to expand the network's reach within the United States. From the late 1880s onward, New Orleans became the center of their operations during the fall, winter, and spring. According to one account, "In September, when the summer resorts . . . closed, [they came] down to the South along with the climate-changers and pleasure-seekers and continued their business as in the north, to move back to the north the next summer."[38]

In the late nineteenth century, New Orleans was one of the United States' most important hubs of travel and transport and was becoming a tourist attraction in its own right. New Orleans was connected by rail to every major city in the South as well as to the cities of the north. Trains ran, either directly or through connecting lines, northeast to Atlanta, Charlotte, Baltimore, Philadelphia, and New York; northward to Birmingham, Chattanooga, St. Louis, Louisville, Cincinnati, and Chicago; and westward to Houston, Dallas, and beyond.[39] The port of New Orleans was the second busiest in the country; it connected the United States to the Caribbean and Central and South America.[40] New Orleans' political and business elites were also in the process of remaking the city, transforming it from a port town tied to slave trading and the dwindling economies of cotton and sugar into a progressive metropolis on par with the great cities of the North. Under their stewardship, the Crescent City was to become a showcase of the modern South—one that would attract a year-round flow of tourists and travelers from all over the world.[41]

In the 1880s, New Orleans developers turned Canal Street, which ran from the river up through the center of the city, into a glittering commercial thoroughfare, with shops, department stores, and offices on either side and a streetcar running through the middle.[42] The nearby French Market, in the meantime, was promoted as a kind of portal to a romanticized version of New Orleans' Creole past. A travel feature that circulated in U.S. newspapers in December 1903 described the French Market as "an eighteenth century market in a twentieth century city," hailing its "quaint customs," its "kaleidoscope of sights and . . . Babel of sounds."[43] Boosters promoted and advertised the yearly celebrations of Mardi Gras with the aim of drawing ever-greater crowds from outside the city, while simultaneously, if less explicitly, they built an international reputation for the city's sex district, Storyville. In these years, New Orleans became a city associated with pleasure, fantasy, and consumption. By the turn of the century, tens of thousands of tourists were flocking to Mardi Gras each winter, and hundreds of thousands were visiting the city each year.[44]

New Orleans' growing tourist trade and its evolving identity as a site of pleasure and fancy made the city fertile ground for the men from Bengal, for these "peddlers of notions" from far-off India. Fantasies of and goods from "the East" already circulated widely in the city. Over the years that Mardi Gras grew as a national attraction, the city's elite Anglo-American parading krewes—Comus, Proteus, Momus, and Rex—frequently presented lavish Indian- and Eastern-themed processions. When New Orleans held its International Cotton Exhibition in 1884–1885, the items displayed in the Asian pavilions were so popular that an Oriental Exhibition Store was opened on Canal Street in the heart of the city's commercial district. Across the avenue, Canal Street's fanciest department store, Maison Blanche, sold items at the high end of the Orientalist economy—plush carpets, fine silks, and porcelain—to local elites and wealthy travelers. A few blocks away, Storyville's madams thickly decorated the interiors of their brothels with Eastern rugs and wall hangings, drawing in customers through the era's fantasies of the harem and hiring "Oriental danseuses" to work alongside the Districts' more famous "mulattas," "quadroons," and "octaroons."[45]

Turn-of-the-century New Orleans was also a city full of peddlers and neighborhood markets. For years, women of African descent had worked independently as peddlers and market-stall vendors selling various perishable and dry goods.[46] This was also the case among members of new immigrant groups, who, between the 1870s and 1890s, became a presence all over the city. "The Poydras and Dryades street markets," writes historian Richard Campanella, "attracted Orthodox Jewish vendors from Russia and Poland; the French Market drew Sicilians; the Irish dominated the Suraparu and St. Mary's markets, and the Chinese created a series of shops on Tulane Avenue, which became known as Chinatown."[47] By the turn of the twentieth century, the tourists and locals who visited the French Market could find stalls and vendors representing every one of New Orleans' many communities, from the oldest to the most recently arrived. "Nowhere else within such a small compass can one discover so great a variety of nationalities, languages and quaint customs," wrote the author of the 1903 travel feature. "Within a few steps of where one stands are stalls presided over by Germans, Frenchmen, Chinamen, Hindoos, Jews, Englishmen, Irishmen, Malays, Spaniards, American Indians, Moors, Italians, Mexicans, Cubans, Creoles, as well as Africans of all shades and blends."[48] It was in this arena that the Bengali sellers of embroidered silks appear to have found their niche. They sold their "Oriental" wares amid the purveyors of every possible kind of produce and small good, in the French Market and on the city's streets.

In 1900, the federal census recorded twelve men from "Hindoostan" living in New Orleans. All were members of the peddler network—men who had begun making trips through Ellis Island in the 1880s and 1890s to peddle goods on the New Jersey seaside. Ten of these men lived together in two shared apartments on the outskirts of the Storyville sex district. Alef Ally, Aynuddin Mondul, and Ibrahim Musa lived at 1428 St. Louis Street; Jainal Abdeen, Solomon Mondul, Abdul Subham, Sofur Ally, and Eshrack, Bahadoor, and Majan Ali all lived at 1420 St. Louis Street. The men were mostly in their midthirties to late forties and already had years of experience behind them selling Oriental goods to

U.S. consumers. They had moved to St. Louis Street around 1895, two years before the creation of Storyville, when the block was part of an area consisting of boardinghouses, bars, clubs, brothels, and low-rent residences. Here, the peddlers were within walking distance of three areas of the city that would have been crucial to their work: the French Market, where some of them sold from stalls; the commercial district along Canal Street, which offered crowds of tourists and middle-class window-shoppers; and the railway terminal on Rampart Street, which connected the Bengalis to points north, east, and west.[49]

The chikondars had been living on St. Louis Street for about five years when they next garnered the attention of the press. On May 25, 1900, the *Daily Herald* of Biloxi, Mississippi, published a detailed dispatch from one of its correspondents in New Orleans, describing a group of "Hindoo peddlers" who were working on the streets there. Published under the heading "Not Very Dignified–Amusing Story of an Oriental Who Took a Bicycle Ride," the article opened with its author's musings about a growing population of new immigrants in New Orleans: "You know we have quite a colony of East Indians here who wear black skullcaps and long-tailed frock coats and prowl about town peddling rugs and such like. I must confess there [has] always been something strangely fascinating to me in the appearance of these fellows. They look so preternaturally solemn, and have such an air of oriental mysticism . . . that I can't help believing they are as wise as Solomon and are laughing in their sleeves at us poor barbarians while incidentally they are loading us up with their ridiculous rugs." The writer then relayed a longer anecdote about his encounter with one of the peddlers. While walking down an unspecified side street in the city, the author had looked up to see an Indian man heading toward him on a wobbling bicycle. He described the rider as "a lean bronzed gentleman with a scraggy, coal-black beard and piercing eyes" and noted with evident pleasure that the man was "humped over like a camel and making desperate efforts to keep his balance." While he granted that the peddler "preserved a certain indescribable dignity," the author immediately went on to undermine it. "There was something monstrously incongruous in the idea of a Hindoo on a bike," he wrote: "I would as soon think of seeing a bishop on a trapeze, and I stood transfixed with amazement, while he very nearly ran me down. But instead of saying, 'Make way, oh! Sahib, for thy servant to pass,' as he should have done, he called me an old fool in very good English, and asked me whether I wanted to be killed." Claiming that he was "too surprised to get mad," the *Daily Herald*'s correspondent provided another self-satisfied description of the rider losing control of his bicycle, flying through the air "with his arms spread out like a frog," and slamming onto the pavement. To bring home his central point, the writer concluded with the claim that "according to the books [the peddler] should have accepted the misadventure with oriental stoicism. On the contrary, he scrambled up and proceeded to kick the stuffing out of both tires."[50]

If we can look beyond its tone of racial superiority and its obvious satisfaction with an Indian immigrant's misfortune, the *Daily Herald*'s article is revealing in many ways. First, the article acknowledged the presence of Indian Oriental goods peddlers as part of the social and economic landscape of New Orleans at the turn of the twentieth century. Second, it implied, in musing that the peddlers were "laughing in their sleeves . . . as they are loading us up with their ridiculous rugs," that they were selling such goods on the basis of what the author saw as a ruse of Eastern authenticity. Third, it demonstrated a clearly developed set of fantasies and expectations about who the men were and how they *should* be behaving—as "mystic" and "stoic" Orientals—ideas that the author clearly assumed his readership would recognize and share. Finally, the article inadvertently recorded these Indian peddlers' capacity both to use (as salesmen) and to defy such Orientalist ideas and expectations. What the *Daily Herald*'s reporter likely did not know was that the men he was describing—and ridiculing—were in fact part of a complex global trade network that would soon stretch from the villages of West Bengal to the Canal Zone of Panama.

From the Hooghly to the Mississippi to the Panama Canal

By the first decade of the twentieth century, the Bengali peddlers' operation worked like a well-oiled machine. If its origins lay with small-scale peasant-traders, as early reports suggest, the *chikondars*' network eventually came to resemble the operations of much larger Indian merchant and banking groups. It involved a group of "merchants" or "dealers" based in Calcutta and another group of distributors in U.S. cities, while it continued to draw in less-experienced and -traveled young men from rural Hooghly to peddle goods overseas. A 1908 report by the U.S. Department of Commerce and Labor described an operation that was small but complex and highly coordinated. Over the course of each six to twelve months, a few merchants based in Calcutta purchased batches of *chikan* goods from producers in Hooghly's villages. When they had collected enough to fill "a medium-size dry goods box" on an outgoing steamer, they shipped these goods to the customhouses in New Orleans, Charleston, Savannah, and Philadelphia, where other members of the network, usually their kin, distributed the embroidery to individual *chikondars*, who then fanned out to sell the goods to American tourists and leisure travelers.[51] New peddlers were drawn into the network through family and kinship ties and largely hailed from the cluster of villages where the *chikan* goods were being produced.[52] These included Babnan, Sinhet, Alipur, Chandanpur, Mandra, Bandipur, Bora, Dadpur, and Gopinathpur.[53] Archival records indicate that, once a year, these new recruits made their way over land or down the Hooghly River to a predominantly Muslim neighborhood in the southern part of Calcutta known as Collinga Bazar.[54] Here, a number of more senior traders with ties to the Hooghly District—likely the men described as "merchants" in the 1908 report— occupied a series of addresses on Kerr Lane and Collin Lane, two small side streets off Collinga Bazar Street. Novice members of the network came from their villages to these addresses before setting off for New Jersey and New Orleans. It is probable that, like the first members of the network, who had voyaged to the United States in the 1880s, they brought additional goods in their luggage, to demonstrate to customs officials that they were independent traders and to supplement the items shipped in advance to the U.S. nodes of the network.[55]

Two descriptions of Collinga Bazar in the late nineteenth and early twentieth century—one quoted in P. Thankappan Nair's *A History of Calcutta's Streets* and the other written by Rudyard Kipling—both identify it as an area of inexpensive accommodations and drinking establishments that was home to a semi-permanent population of female European sex workers and the many sailors of different nationalities who passed through the port of Calcutta. Although British colonial officials did not officially "legalize" the activities of these women, Nair states that officials did actively attempt to contain what they called "white prostitution" within a closely circumscribed area in and around Collinga Bazar Street.[56] Kipling's melodramatic account of this neighborhood, from his essay "City of Dreadful Night," gives a sense of the heterogeneous population that frequented the area, even as it reveals an attitude of racial and class superiority that Kipling shared with his white contemporaries in the U.S. South: "There are Seedee Boys, Bombay *serangs* and Madras fishermen . . . Malays who insist upon marrying native women, grow jealous and run amok: Malay-Hindus, Hindu-Malay-whites, Burmese, Burma whites, Burma-native-whites, Italians with gold earrings and a thirst for gambling, Yankees of all the States, with Mulattoes and pure buck-n[——]ers, red and rough Danes, Cingalese, Cornish boys . . . tun-bellied Germans, Cockney mates . . . unmistakable 'Tommies' who have tumbled into seafaring life by some mistake, cockatoo-tufted Welshmen spitting and swearing like cats, broken-down loafers, grey-headed, penniless, and pitiful, swaggering boys, and very quiet men with gashes and cuts on their faces."[57] The similarities between Collinga Bazar in Calcutta and Storyville in New Orleans would have been numerous, but perhaps most significantly for the men who were moving from the former location to the latter was these neighborhoods' particular kind of cosmopolitanism—stemming from the intermixture of local working-class residents with a mobile, international population of sailors, peddlers, sex workers, and participants in various underground economies.[58] So, while members of the peddler network that stretched from Bengal to Louisiana had their origins in the villages of rural Hooghly, their entry into global circuits of trade and their travels to cities such as London, New York, and New Orleans were preceded, mediated, and no doubt conditioned by time already spent in this complex urban space within Calcutta.

Although occasionally, early on in their network's formation, Hooghly's peddlers managed to sail directly from Calcutta to New York, their voyages were rarely so straightforward. More often, the peddlers traveled by one British steamship westward from Calcutta to London and then after a few days caught another from either Southampton or Liverpool to the United States. On a number of occasions, the men traveled on one ship from Calcutta to Colombo, another from Colombo to London, and a third from Southampton or Liverpool to New York. The journey that eleven of Hooghly's peddlers took in 1896 was typical. These men spent close to a month on two steamships before arriving in New York and moving onward to the beach boardwalks of the New Jersey coast. They left Calcutta in early May on board the SS *Goorkha*, operated by the British India Steam Navigation Company (BISNC).[59] Although it was a private company, the BISNC was deeply entwined with the operations of the British Empire. Its steamers transported mail, cargo, passengers, troops, military supplies, and indentured laborers between British colonial ports in South, Southeast, and East Asia and East Africa, as well as running long-distance services between Britain and Australian and Indian ports. Hooghly's peddlers may have known of or favored the line because it had a share in the traffic of Indian Muslim pilgrims to Mecca each year, or simply because it was one of the few lines that readily took "native passengers" between Calcutta and London. Although they were listed as "cabin" passengers on the *Goorkha,* one source states that British India Steam Navigation kept Indian passengers on deck for the duration of the journey.[60]

The *Goorkha* first traveled down the eastern coast of India, picking up passengers in Madras and Colombo, then rounded the tip of India and sailed westward across the Arabian Sea. It stopped again to pick up passengers at Aden in Yemen, traveled northwest across the full length of the Red Sea, passed through the Suez Canal into the Mediterranean, and docked at Port Said, Egypt. In May, this journey would have been extremely hot, especially for those who had to remain on deck. From Port Said, the *Goorkha* sailed onward to London. It first took on more passengers in Naples, Italy, then crossed through the Strait of Gibraltar into the Atlantic Ocean, steamed northward to the mouth of the Thames River at Southend-on-Sea and made its way upriver, completing its journey in London's East End docklands.[61] Soon after the eleven peddlers disembarked on May 28, they traveled overland eighty miles southwest to the port of Southampton, where they boarded an outbound steamship for New York, the SS *St. Paul.* They then spent the next eight days crossing the Atlantic Ocean in the steerage section of the *St. Paul.* Here, their accommodations would not have been much better than on the first leg of their trip. "Steerage" compartments in this era typically consisted of a series of large spaces below deck with low ceilings, dim light, and minimal air circulation that shipping companies filled with rows of three-tiered metal-frame bunks. In the case of the *St. Paul*, the eleven traders from Bengal shared steerage with 350 other travelers, 325 of whom were migrants, immigrants, or sojourners like themselves.[62]

From the 1890s through the 1910s, the Bengali peddlers' annual journey to the United States followed a similar pattern.[63] The activities of the peddlers on the U.S. side of the network, however, became more coordinated and complex. After passing through Ellis Island, each group of peddlers split up to cover the different New Jersey seaside towns. One or two members each would head to Atlantic City, Asbury Park, and Long Branch, suggesting that they may have been acting not only as peddlers, but also as couriers, transporting a fresh stock of goods for other members of the network to sell over the course of the summer. These other men were already in the United States, having come on previous years' journeys and moved on to New Orleans and elsewhere to sell goods in the nonsummer months. In order to join the newly arrived peddlers in each New Jersey resort town, they would have traveled north on the Southern Railway's Fast Mail or Southwestern Vestibuled Limited—lines that were segregated until they reached Washington D.C.—or on one of the coastwise ships that were, in these years, bringing the first waves of black southerners to North Atlantic cities as part of the Great Migration. At the end of the summer season, a few members of the Hooghly network returned to Calcutta, while the majority headed to the southern states once again.

Each year, more of the peddlers appear to have remained in the United States and the network ventured farther afield across the South. The population of Bengali Muslim peddlers operating in the United States steadily grew. In New Orleans, the U.S. Census captured a fivefold increase in the Indian peddler population between 1900 and 1910. There were now more than fifty Indian Muslim peddlers living in eight households around the perimeter of Storyville (Table 1). Of these, five were residences in which several peddlers lived together in groups, and each of these five group households included both older, more experienced traders in their thirties, forties, and fifties and younger, more recently arrived peddlers in their teens and twenties. Four of the *chikon-*

dars, including thirty-eight-year-old Haji Haq and sixty-year-old Abdul Aziz, lived on North Johnson Street. Eleven, including at least two who were part of the group deported from Ellis Island in 1897—Solomon Mondul and Fazleh Rahman—lived on North Roman Street. Five more peddlers lived on Conti Street, and six, including fifty-one-year-old Abdul Goffer and forty-six-year-old Abdul Majid, lived on North Claiborne Avenue. Both Goffer and Majid appear to have been part of a group that entered the United States through Castle Garden twenty-two years earlier, in 1888. Perhaps the most significant New Orleans address was 1428 St. Louis Street. Here, Alef Ally, an embroiderer and merchant who settled in New Orleans in the mid-1880s, had turned the building into a boardinghouse for twenty other peddlers from the network. These included a number of younger men who had arrived in the United States in the years since 1903, as well as a handful of more experienced and senior men, including what appears to be two members of the group turned away from Ellis Island in 1897: Musa and Mintoz Mondul. The presence in New Orleans in 1910 of at least half the men deported from Ellis Island in 1897 is a testament to the persistence of these traders, to the continuing demand for the goods they were selling in the United States, and, as will become apparent in the next chapter, to the labor of local women who helped ground the network in the city.[64]

The reporter who penned the *Biloxi Daily Herald*'s dispatch about a "Hindoo on a Bicycle" was clearly prone to embellishment, but his comment that "East Indian peddlers" were "prowling all about town" suggests that even as early as 1900, the men were numerous enough and spread out enough to be a noticeable presence on the streets of New Orleans. Given that the main tourist and commercial areas of New Orleans comprised an area of only about one and a half square miles, this is hardly a surprise, and by 1910, as their numbers grew, and as they likely split up the city into territories, their presence would have been even more striking. At the same time, there is evidence that from early on, groups of Hooghly's peddlers were making extended forays from New Orleans into other southern cities. As early as 1897, a Texas newspaper made note of two men, "Mohammed and Hamid Hassain," identified as "vendors of Oriental goods," returning to New Orleans after a period of time peddling in Fort Worth. In 1912, the *Atlanta Constitution* described

Table 1.   Indian Peddler Households in New Orleans, 1910

Address	Name	Age	Arrived	Status	Occupation
1428 St. Louis St.	Alef Ally	50	1885	Na	Merchant—Merchandise
	Mahoma Moassa	40	1903	Al	Merchant—Merchandise
	Abdul Jabbar	39	1896	Pa	Merchant—Retail
	Tarafat Ally	38	1903	Al	Merchant—Retail
	Tazer Ally	32	1907	Al	Merchant—Retail
	Manzur Ally	24	1907	Al	Merchant—Retail
	Devan Husan	32	1909	Al	Merchant—Retail
	Rohamat Ally	28	1909	Al	Merchant—Retail
	Mazed Ally	28	1907	Al	Merchant—Retail
	Bakshee Rohaman	22	1907	Al	Merchant—Retail
	Mintez Mandal	60	1904	Al	Merchant—Retail
	Joynal Abdin	45	1905	Al	Merchant—Retail
	Abdul Jalil	23	1907	Al	Merchant—Retail
	Imraz Zaman	23	1909	Al	Merchant—Retail
	Abdul Rohim	26	1908	Al	Merchant—Retail
	Abdul Sircar	28	1907	Al	Merchant—Retail
	Nawazes Ally	38	1906	Al	Merchant—Retail
	Sher Ally	24	1906	Al	Merchant—Retail
	Sari Raddin	24	1908	Al	Merchant—Retail
	Tawakul Hussain	29	1909	Al	Merchant—Retail
	Fazla Sayed	25	1909	Al	Merchant—Retail
	Jagatbandhu Dev	25	1908	Al	Student
	Viola Ally	12			none
	Celestine Gardner	65			none
415 N. Claiborne St.	Bundy Ally	48	1904	Al	Peddler—Dry Goods
	Abdul Mozid	46	1904	Al	Peddler—Dry Goods
	Abdul Goffer	51	1905	Al	Peddler—Dry Goods
	Ilias Mondol	25	1905	Al	Peddler—Dry Goods
	Monibur Rohman	29	1906	Al	Peddler—Dry Goods
	Nozoff Ally	27	1907	Al	Peddler—Dry Goods
1711 Conti St.	Motiaz R. Mondol	22	1909	Al	Peddler—Fancy Goods
	Boolie Mohla	35	1909	Al	Peddler—Fancy Goods
	Sooleman Mohla	28	1909	Al	Peddler—Fancy Goods
	Itias Rohman	23	1909	Al	Peddler—Fancy Goods
	Sokas Sukiluddin	36	1909	Al	Peddler—Fancy Goods
320 N. Roman St.	Abdul Mondol	33	1904	Al	Peddler—Fancy Goods
	Fazla Rohman	31	1904	Al	Peddler—Fancy Goods
	Solmon Mondol	40	1904	Al	Peddler—Fancy Goods
	Roudal Huck	39	1907	Al	Peddler—Fancy Goods
	Abdul Osama	45	1909	Al	Peddler—Fancy Goods
	Golam Rub	26	1909	Al	Peddler—Fancy Goods
	Abdul Malick	24	1909	Al	Peddler—Fancy Goods

Table 1. (*continued*)

Address	Name	Age	Arrived	Status	Occupation
	Wajed Ally	30	1908	Al	Peddler—Fancy Goods
	Abdul Rub	19	1909	Al	Peddler—Fancy Goods
	Abdul Rouf	24	1908	Al	Peddler—Fancy Goods
	Tazli Moddin	55	1908	Al	Peddler—Fancy Goods
323 N. Johnson St.	Hadgi Hojik	38			Peddler—Dry Goods
	Atowbbor Sny	30			Peddler—Dry Goods
	Abdul Kholock	25			Peddler—Dry Goods
	Abdul Aziz	60			Peddler—Dry Goods

Names are spelled as they appear in the original census documents. Reported arrival dates often appear to reflect most-recent rather than first arrival. Immigration status: Al=Alien; Pa=First Papers (ie: the individual has filed an Intention to Naturalize); Na=Naturalized.

Source: USDC/BC, *Population Schedules* for New Orleans, LA (various).

a group of thirty Indian peddlers who had traveled to Atlanta and had been selling goods there, "in and around the city," for two weeks.[65]

Such trips depended on a smaller number of Bengali men who settled, or stayed for extended periods, in cities throughout the South. Most of these men were members of the network who had worked the New Jersey seaside resorts or lived in New Orleans for some time and had then branched out to other southern cities, where they usually lived in and often married into local black communities.[66] Once they were settled in these places, their function in the network was likely twofold: they both sold goods themselves, expanding the reach of the network's market, and provided an infrastructure for larger groups of peddlers to pass through from town to town, selling the network's silks and other goods. In port cities like Charleston, Savannah, and New Orleans, these men could also now act as middlemen, receiving goods shipped by kin in Calcutta through the local customhouses that could then be distributed to other peddlers. In the opening decades of the twentieth century, members of the network established outposts in several southern cities.[67] Draft registration records give us a snapshot of the network's reach by the time the United States entered the First World War. In 1917–1918, thirty-five Indian peddlers filed their mandatory registration cards in New Orleans, seven registered in Charleston, South Carolina; six in Jacksonville, Florida; four in Memphis, Tennessee; and between one and three in Chattanooga, Tennessee; Galveston, Texas; Dallas, Texas; Birmingham, Alabama; and Atlanta, Georgia (Table 2).[68]

As the Hooghly network gained its footing in New Orleans and expanded through the southern United States, some of its senior members also moved farther south, bringing their wares to a series of ports in the Caribbean and Central America. Here, the colonial engagements of Britain and the United States had opened up multiple sites to Western tourism and leisure travel: Jamaica, Cuba, Puerto Rico, Panama, Trinidad.

Table 2. Draft Registrations of Indian Peddlers in Southern Cities, 1917–1918

New Orleans, LA	Abdul Jobber Mondul, Abdul Ganie, Abdul Ganie Mondul, Abdul Jalil Mallick, Abdul Kholick Mollah, Abdul M. Mollah, Abdul Rohim Sarker, Abdul Surker, Abdul Ganie Mondul, Abdul Hamed Mondul, Abdul Wahed, Aminoola Rohimoody, Babur Alli, Dawood Rohman, Elias Mondul, Fozlay Rohman, Hafez Mosihor Rohman, Hassan Abdul, Jonean Sarker, Kiramuth Ali Mondul, Kolimudden Mondul, Monebor Rohman Mollah, Mocklajar Rohman, Mohammed A. Isscas, Monsur Ally Mondul, Mortoza Hassain, S. Atear Rohaman, S. F. Mowla, Shaik Rohim Boksh, Syed Abdul Fara, Syed Monsur Ally, Toffozul Hossain, Towakal Hossain Halder, Volu Mollah
Charleston, SC	Sadeck Ali Mollah, Abdul Gaffer Mondul, Jogadish Chandra Goswami, Keramoth Ally, Mosud Ally, Rajab Ali, Syed Abdul Ganny
Memphis, TN	Abdul Khalick, Abdul Robe Mondul, Azad Bauksh, Rashidul Hock
Chattanooga, TN	Abdul Wade Mondul
Galveston, TX	Abdul Ganie Mondul, Abdur Rohim Mondul
Dallas, TX	Abdul Karim Mondol, Golam Robbaney
Birmingham, AL	Ayub Mondul, Noserul Hawk Mondul
Atlanta, GA	Abdul Rubby, Mohammed Yeakub, N. H. Mondul
Jacksonville, FL	Abdul Gany Mondul, Abdul Rohim Meer, Abraham Mondal, Roohul Amin Sircur, Sheik Abdul Rohman Mondul, Syed Awlad Ali

Names are spelled as they appear in the original draft registration documents. Jogadish Goswami (Charleston) appears to have originally come to the United States, via San Francisco, as a student in 1907, and later joined the network. USDCL/BINi *Declaration of Intention*, J. C. Goswami, U.S. District Court of Charleston, SC, January 29, 1910.

Source: USSS/DRC, *WWI Draft Registration Cards*, Local Registration Boards of New Orleans, LA; Charleston, SC; Memphis, TN; Chattanooga, TN; Galveston, TX; Dallas, TX; Birmingham, AL; Atlanta, GA; and Jacksonville, FL.

American periodicals of the day described such places to an increasingly mobile middle-class readership, while shipping lines promoted them as destinations for winter escapes, emphasizing their "delightful" climate and their easy accessibility via "luxuriously equipped ocean liners" sailing regularly from U.S. ports. Over the winter of 1907–1908, the New York–based *Travel Magazine* presented the Caribbean as if it were merely an extension of the United States; its monthly feature articles on seasonal destinations spoke in virtually the same breath of New Orleans, Savannah, Puerto Rico, and Trinidad, of Florida, Barbados, and Havana, while shipping companies advertised "Tours to the Tropics" that included Jamaica, Colombia, Costa Rica, and Panama. The Royal Mail Steam Packet Company's ad juxtaposed the January weather forecasts for New York ("Min. 10/Max. 15") and Kingston ("Min. 68/Max. 68") and offered "all inclusive" tours of Jamaica and the Isthmus of Panama. Hooghly's *chikondars* were one of several groups of peddlers who followed the winter "climate-changers and pleasure-seekers" from the United States and Europe into this circuit of warm-weather sites.[69]

The port to which they sailed most frequently was Colón, on the Caribbean coast of Panama. Between 1905 and 1909, several of the men who had begun peddling Hooghly's embroidery to vacationers along New Jersey's boardwalks in the 1890s—Panch Courie Mondul, Abdul Barrick, Abdul Aziz, and Solomon Mondul—all made trips to Colón, listing their occupations variously as "merchants," "traders," and "silk-sellers." Colón was a key city for the era's travelers—it was at one end of the fifty-mile Trans-Isthmian Railway, which had been used for decades to cross between the Caribbean and the Pacific Ocean. The route was now newly in the hands of the United States after more than a century of attempts—by the Spanish, the French, and even the Scottish—to control the crucial passage of people and goods between the Atlantic and Pacific worlds. In 1903, Panama had been a province of Colombia. The United States put its military might behind a group of local elites who sought to secede and in exchange gained sovereign control over the strip of land along which the railway ran, including its termini, Colón and Panama City. In 1904 the U.S. government's Isthmian Canal Commission and Army Corps of Engineers began construction of the canal along that route. It was to be, for the time, the jewel in the United States' imperial crown.[70]

By the time Panch Courie Mondul and three other members of the Hooghly network arrived on an initial visit in 1905, the number of tourists, travelers, and workers making their way to and through Colón was growing exponentially. Thousands of laborers made their way to Panama from the Caribbean, Europe, Asia, and the United States to work on the construction of the monumental canal and to make improvements to the railway, which was now transporting not only travelers and goods but workers, equipment, and the tons of earth and stone dynamited and dug up from the canal's route. The Bengalis were not the only Indians in the Canal Zone. Punjabi Sikh men were among the laborers working on the railroad, sent by labor recruiters on the subcontinent.[71] Sindhi traders also set up their first shop in Colón in 1905 to sell Oriental goods to the other group of outsiders that began to visit Colón in increasing numbers: the "ships passengers who disembarked there and had time to engage in purchases while their ship was in harbour." Although by the late 1920s, Markovits writes, the Sindhis had gained a "complete monopoly" on this lucrative trade, Hooghly's peddlers appear to have had part of it in these early years.[72]

From 1905 through the 1910s, the Bengali *chikondars'* trips to Colón formed a secondary circuit of their network's yearly migrations. Groups of peddlers traveled from Calcutta to London and then split up; some sailed on to New York, while others took the Royal Mail's ships from Southampton, England to Panama and eventually sailed back to New Orleans, New Jersey, or Southampton. Initially, smaller groups of *chikondars* made their way through this circuit: after Panch Courie Mondul's initial foray in 1905, three peddlers made the trip to Colón in 1906, and six did so in 1907. By 1908, other points in the Caribbean had been incorporated into the larger framework of the Hooghly traders' movements. That year, ten members of the network set out together from Calcutta to London and then split up to proceed to different territories: three continued onward to 1428 St. Louis Street in New Orleans, two sailed to Trinidad, and five sailed to Colón, Panama. Over the coming years, they would circulate in small numbers between New Orleans and New Jersey in the United States; Panama, Honduras, and Belize in Central America; and Trinidad, Jamaica, and Cuba in the Caribbean.[73]

The presence of Indian peddlers in these regions did not go unremarked upon. A 1909 article titled "School Teaching in Panama," published in the U.S.-based weekly *The Independent*, placed both work-ers and traders from India within the larger context of international travel and migration to "The Zone" during the construction of the canal. "On the street, our children meet men from all parts of the world," the author, a missionary schoolteacher, wrote: "The East Indian wearing his bright yel-low or blue turban drives a dirt cart for the railroad or serves in the office of a watchman. Every other store is a Chinese shop filled with the ivories, carved woods, and silks from the Orient . . . Assyrian peddlers and Hin-doo merchants in their queer costumes go from house to house selling their wares. And on every hand, the child meets Spaniards, Frenchmen, and Italians."[74] In August 1901, the *Atlanta Constitution* had provided a similar description of Indian traders in Havana, Cuba, where the number of American tourists and military personnel had quickly grown since the United States occupied the island in the wake of the Spanish-American War. In a travel article focusing on the Cuban city's "quaint" and "color-ful" populations of peddlers, a *Constitution* correspondent described the "colony of Hindoos" that had taken root in Havana—made up, it would seem, of both Muslims and Sikhs, in that they were described as wearing "turbans or embroidered fezes." She claimed these men were "the most attractive and prosperous class of street vendors here," and walked from place to place carrying "a pack on the back weighing many hundred pounds, consisting of gorgeous East Indian and Oriental stuffs." The men were said to have "a large store down on Paula Street, and a dozen or more [men who] travel about the city and suburban towns within a radius of thirty miles, disposing of their things." As for the goods themselves, the author wrote, admiringly: "They have curious eastern embroideries in silk and cottons. . . . They make a specialty of draperies, and find ready sale for these, particularly among the Americans and in Columbia [mili-tary] barracks . . . where the bare rough walls cry aloud for some artistic covering."[75]

In the Shadows of Empires

The travels of Bengali Muslim peddlers within and beyond the borders of the United States are all the more remarkable for the fact that they oc-curred at a time of increasing anti-immigrant and anti-Asian sentiment in the United States. The period between the 1880s and the 1910s—the

years in which Hooghly's traders established and expanded their operations in the United States—saw a rapid rise in immigration to the
United States. Immigrants from all over the world were coming through
New York, San Francisco, and other U.S. ports in numbers the country
had never before experienced. It was also a period of rising xenophobia,
directed largely at the poorest and least skilled of the workers who were
coming to U.S. shores—from Chinese railroad workers to Sicilian peasants. Over these years, the U.S. government developed an ever-more selective regime of immigration laws that explicitly used criteria of class
and race to turn immigrants away from the United States. This process
began with the Chinese Exclusion Act of 1882 and the Alien Contract
Labor Law of 1885 and continued with the 1917 Immigration Act, which,
among other things, instituted the Asiatic Barred Zone, the provision
that brought virtually all legal migration from Asia to a halt.[76]

From the 1890s to the 1910s, the most significant obstacle that
Hooghly's peddlers faced at U.S. borders was the Alien Contract Labor
Law. The Contract Labor Law was ostensibly enacted to stop U.S. employers from "importing" foreign laborers who might undermine the
wages and conditions of U.S. workers. The law was also, however, an
extension of the Chinese Exclusion Act and was suffused with anti-
Asian sentiments and assumptions. The 1885 law relied on a distinction
between "free" and "unfree" migrants; it sought to limit labor immigration to people who were entering the country on their own initiative as
"free migrants"—that is, to block the entry of indentured or contract
laborers, who had been recruited, assisted, and bonded by their employers.[77] The enforcement of this law was difficult and uneven, but the Bengali peddlers would have been more likely than many others to be accused of being bonded laborers. According to historian Adam McKeown,
immigration inspectors were guided by Western notions of Asian societies as backward and despotic; Asian migrants were marked by the image
of the "coolie," seen as inherently subservient and "unfree." At the same
time, the Contract Labor Law made no distinction between large-scale
employers, agents, and recruiters, and smaller kinship and family-based
networks.[78] The Bengalis' operation was a variant of the latter, but the
more organized and coordinated it became, the more easily immigration
officials could claim that arriving peddlers were "assisted" migrants,

"bonded laborers," entering the United States in violation of the law, and were therefore to be detained and turned back.

The Bengali peddlers who were deported in 1897 came up against the Immigration Bureau's broad enforcement of the Contract Labor Law, and they were not the first. In 1890, a group of thirty-two Arab peddlers were detained when it was claimed that they worked for a "dealer in rugs and Oriental goods" with offices in Paris and New York. Hooghly's peddlers could be treated in the same way. The structure of their operation—in which new peddlers were brought into the United States by more established traders whose business extended from Calcutta through New Jersey, New Orleans, and Charleston—was such that U.S. authorities could construe the new members as men bonded to a larger concern, whose peddling was therefore a form of "unfree labor" and whose entry should be prohibited. This appears to have been the argument put forward by the Immigration Bureau's Board of Special Inquiry in 1897; although Moksad Ali, Obidullah, Fazleh Rahman, and the others were coming to the United States to sell handicrafts that had been made in their home villages—perhaps even by their relations—for generations, the twelve detainees were accused of being part of a scheme in which they were contract workers "peddling goods not their own." Each time they stood before Ellis Island's immigration inspectors, the Bengali peddlers faced the possibility of being accused again, pulled aside, put in detention, and deported. This risk would have only increased as anti-Asian politicians and citizens' groups became more active and vocal in the years leading up to the creation of the Asiatic Barred Zone.[79]

How, then, did the Bengali *chikondars* establish such a wide-ranging presence in the United States and continue to move in and out of the country, year after year, for more than three decades? The peddlers succeeded in large part because they operated as a network; they shaped, structured, and coordinated their activities to ensure that people, information, money, and goods continued to flow across borders, even as conditions on the ground changed.[80] Their response to the 1897 deportations is a prime example of this agility. The peddlers who were already in the United States at this time appear to have used the years immediately following the deportations to shore up their presence and activities in cities such as New Orleans and Charleston. A number of these men began naturalization procedures—an option that was yet still open to them.[81] But something else happened. The peddlers found other, more surreptitious routes in and out of the country. Ships' manifests for the period between 1897 and 1902 show almost none of the Bengali peddlers entering the United States officially through New York, Philadelphia, Baltimore, or New Orleans. Yet a number of these men did make their way out of and back into the United States over the course of these years. Solomon Mondul, for example, left New York for Liverpool with four other members of the network in September 1898 and had returned to New Orleans by 1900. Moksad Ali, one of the men detained and deported in 1897, also successfully made his way back to New Orleans by 1900, then left the country once again around 1901, presumably on his way to India, and then crossed back into the United States via Quebec, Canada, with one other member of the network in September 1902.[82] When Hooghly's peddlers began to travel openly through Ellis Island again in 1903, they had changed tactics. They now entered the country in small groups in an effort, no doubt, to avoid arousing the suspicion of immigration authorities that they were under the employ of large-scale Oriental goods dealers.

They also began, around this time, to make use of the Contract Labor Law's loopholes and exceptions. The law contained a provision that allowed existing residents of the United States to assist family members and personal friends to come to the United States "for the purpose of settlement."[83] So in 1903, when Hooghly's peddlers resumed their yearly journeys through Ellis Island, each now claimed to be entering the United States to join a relative or friend. Of the four men who arrived on the SS *Teutonic* on June 2, 1904, for example, Abdul Rajack stated that he was joining his "uncle, S. Serajuddin," Abdul Lotiff was joining his "father, S. Serajuddin," and Abdul Mojidda was joining his "friend, S. Serajuddin," in Atlantic City, while Joynal Abdin was meeting his "cousin, Majan Ali," in Asbury Park, before moving on to 1428 St. Louis Street in New Orleans.[84] On board the SS *Oceanic* in July 1912, Kalimodden Sirkar was traveling from his brother, Hajee Abdul Bux, at 10 Kerr Lane, Calcutta, to his son, Abdul Rohim Surker, in Asbury Park; Abdul Khalik was traveling from his father, Nastik Ally, at 13 Kerr Lane, to his uncle, Rahim Bux, in Atlantic City; and Ebadur Rahman was traveling from his father, M. Mohram, at 13 Kerr Lane, to his brother,

Fazla Mohla, in Asbury Park.[85] It is quite possible that these claims of family connection were true, as there are indications that the network grew organically along lines of kinship as members recruited other family members and co-villagers to come to the United States.[86] Indian familial relations were also broader in their interpretation than those in the United States, so that the traders may have referred to male cousins as "brothers" and their fathers' friends or elder co-villagers as "uncles." But familial claims were also a canny means of navigating the Contract Labor Law. Whether they were marking or exaggerating their connections to one another, ships documents clearly show that these peddlers constituted a group that was broadly related by village and region, if not by direct and extended family ties, and, at the borders, they used these ties to stake a claim for entry into the United States.

The *chikondars'* network survived, in other words, because it was dynamic. Between 1897 and 1902, peddlers bypassed Ellis Island and made their way into the United States through either Canada or smaller U.S. ports; after 1903, they entered Ellis Island in groups of four or five rather than ten, twelve, or twenty; and they came equipped with the names and addresses of relatives or friends who were residents in Atlantic City, Asbury Park, New Orleans, or Charleston. All these changes in the wake of the 1897 deportation suggest that members of the network brought information back to the subcontinent about the changing conditions in the United States and at its borders, and that the network adapted its strategies to these conditions. Information and coordination also played key roles at the local level. When younger and newer members of the network traveled with older traders or joined them in group households in New Jersey, New Orleans, and elsewhere, they would have been directed by the more experienced men, provided with information about each individual city or town, perhaps assigned neighborhoods or territories, and taught about how to approach customers to make sales. In this sense, the men who lived for extended periods in the network's regional hubs and outlying cities would have built a store of information crucial to the work of those members who were newer and more transient.

The wide-ranging circulations of some of the Bengali *chikondars*—and of the goods they were selling and the earnings they were generating—are a testament to just how strong and effective their network became over time. Evidence of the movements of individual peddlers is scattered across a range of archives from the 1910s and 1920s—passport applications, draft registration cards, census records, and the manifests of ships coming through Ellis Island and the port of New Orleans. Pieced together, they trace out a remarkable set of movements, as the cases of Fazleh Rahman, Abdul Gannie, and Noorul Huck demonstrate. In October 1913, Fazleh Rahman applied for a U.S. passport at the offices of the American Legation in Panama City, on the Pacific Ocean side of the soon-to-be-completed canal. This appears to have been the same "Fauslay Roman" who was living at 15 Wesley Place in Asbury Park, New Jersey, at the time of the 1900 U.S. Census. In applying at the American Legation, Rahman listed his place of birth as Calcutta and his occupation as "merchant." He stated that he had come to the United States from Southampton, England, in 1898, lived in Asbury Park for twelve years, until 1910, and then moved to Atlantic City. He had naturalized at May's Landing, New Jersey, on April 14, 1905. In 1912, Rahman had left New Jersey, returned to Calcutta, and after a brief stay there, traveled onward to Panama, where he had now been living for several years. In his passport application, Rahman claimed that he soon intended to return to Atlantic City but, prior to doing this, required the passport "for the purpose of engaging in business in Costa Rica."[87]

Five years later, in 1918, Abdul Gannie, another Indian "merchant" who had naturalized with Fazleh Rahman at May's Landing in 1905, applied for a passport to travel to India via Japan and China "on business and for health." Originally from the village of "Batta, near Calcutta," Gannie had come to the United States via Southampton in 1896, and since then, his movements had been almost as far-reaching as Rahman's. In addition to having lived in "New Orleans, Long Branch, [and] Atlantic City," Gannie had been back to India twice, spending a total of eighteen months there in 1907 and 1909. His 1918 passport application was his third attempt to get U.S. traveling papers, and to support his application, he pointed to the case of a cousin, Noorul Huck, who had recently been granted a U.S. passport to travel to Calcutta for similar reasons. According to ships' manifests, census records, and his own passport application, Huck was another trader who had been headed for Fazleh

Rahman's address in Asbury Park when he originally came to the United States on a ship from Liverpool in 1909. He had subsequently lived in Atlantic City for a year, stayed briefly in New Orleans, and then traveled to Galveston, Texas, before ultimately settling in Houston.[88]

One of the earliest indications of the volume of the trade these men were doing comes in the form of a short news item that ran in the *Philadelphia Inquirer* at the end of July 1902. The *Inquirer* reported the theft of a bag of items from the Atlantic City residence of an "East Indian peddler named Fahi Uddin"—an apparent mis-transliteration of Mohi Uddin Mondal. Mohi Uddin was a member of the Hooghly network who, at the time of the U.S. Census two years earlier, was living with six other Bengali peddlers in a cluster of households halfway between Atlantic City's train station and its boardwalk. The burglar had "put a ladder against [Uddin's] house and climbed in a second story window," making off with "a rich haul of fine fabrics valued at $500 and . . . $113 in cash." This was a rich haul, indeed, and would have represented a significant loss to the peddlers; it was equivalent to approximately $13,000 in today's dollars. It likely represented the earnings that Uddin and his associates had generated during the first part of the summer season, and the remaining complement of goods that they were drawing on for their peddling each day.[89]

The stories of Mohammed Issa and Shaikh G. R. Mondul suggest the structure and size of the trade that the network was doing fifteen years later. In July 1917, Issa, a peddler born in "District Hooghly," traveled from Belize to New Orleans. On ships' documents, he listed Belize as his "last permanent residence" but stated that he had lived in New Orleans in 1916 and was now intending a three-week stay in the city, at one of the key addresses associated with the Hooghly network, 1825 St. Ann Street. Issa listed the "friend or relative" he was joining in New Orleans as "S. Karamat Ali"—who would show up three years later on the 1920 U.S. Census as a "Bengalese"-speaking peddler of silks. Issa was, in other words, connecting with other members of the network, and the fact that he intended only a three-week stay in the United States before returning to Belize suggests a trip made for the purpose of delivering earnings, renewing supplies of goods, or both.[90] More telling is a trip made in November 1919 by Shaikh G. R. Mondul, a thirty-year-old merchant who, on ships' documents, listed his last residence as Tela, Honduras, and his languages as "Bengalese" and Spanish. On this trip, Mondul had made his way by land from Tela to the port of La Ceiba, Honduras, where he caught a steamship and sailed northward through the Caribbean and the Gulf of Mexico to New Orleans, carrying an astounding $3,250—an amount roughly equivalent to $40,000 in today's dollars. From New Orleans, Mondul was to sail back down through the Gulf and Caribbean to Panama, and ultimately from Panama to "Bengal, India." This strongly suggests that Mondul's purpose was either to deliver cash to his compatriots in New Orleans or to collect their earnings to add to his own, to courier back to Calcutta.[91]

Why has this group of South Asian migrants remained hidden to U.S. history? By the 1910s, Hooghly's peddlers were traveling extensively through the United States, the Caribbean, and Central America. Their presence was significant enough in places like New Jersey, New Orleans, and Atlanta to attract the attention of turn-of-the-century reporters and correspondents. "Hindoo peddlers" in general were numerous enough in sites of U.S. tourism such as Havana and the Canal Zone to attract such notice as well. These men have been "lost" to history in large part because popular understandings, expectations, and myths about immigration to the United States render them invisible or illegible. Hooghly's peddlers of Oriental goods did not do what we have been told immigrants have done since the eighteenth century: namely, give up their lives and homes in a distant land to seek a better life and a promising new future in an America that welcomed them with open arms. These men came to the United States on a thin edge between Indophilia and xenophobia—they arrived at a time in which fantasies of and goods from India were valued, even as immigrants from the subcontinent and other parts of Asia were being vilified, attacked, and excluded. For most Bengali peddlers, cities like Atlantic City, New Orleans, and Charleston were not final destinations, but places of opportunity for the sale of their villages' handicrafts, and were only a few among many nodes in a network that originated in South Asia and stretched beyond U.S. borders. Most remained sojourning itinerant peddlers, moving in and out of the country and from place to place.

To this extent, Hooghly's peddlers had much in common with participants in other overseas commercial networks emanating from India in the late nineteenth century. Claude Markovits has provided the most extensive and detailed account of these Indian networks and estimates that the number of Indian merchants and financiers operating outside the subcontinent rose from a few thousand to a quarter of a million in the century between 1830 and 1930. Most of the growth occurred between 1880 and 1910, precisely the period that traders from Hooghly began journeying outward from Bengal to find Western markets for their goods.[92] What sets Hooghly's *chikondars* apart from their contemporaries is the extent to which they moved beyond British imperial circuits to engage the consumer desires of a nation that was just beginning to challenge Britain as a world power. While Sindhi merchants did eventually establish outposts in places like Kobe and Panama, their network largely followed the global expansion of the British; they sold their goods primarily within a circuit of British and European sites of travel and tourism. The Bengali peddlers, on the other hand, crossed deep into U.S. spaces—establishing markets for their "fancy goods" and "notions" both within U.S. borders and in areas such as Cuba and Panama, which had been recently occupied or colonized by the United States.

Although men from Hooghly were also moving through British colonial circuits—selling *chikan* goods in Australia and South Africa—theirs appears to have been the only overseas Indian trader network of their era to have established an extensive presence across U.S. sites of consumption and commerce. Hooghly's peddlers were thus involved in a curious imperial balancing act: they traveled in British steamships, along the supply routes of the British Empire, only to face American immigration officials as they crossed U.S. borders to sell Indian goods to U.S. consumers, who were eager to demonstrate their worldliness and class credentials as their nation became a power on par with Britain. Nothing in these movements was guaranteed. In India, the men were colonial British subjects, rather than citizens; their travels were allowed but subject to the oversight and restrictions of a ruling power. Their status in the United States was equally unsteady: as they entered the country each year, they did so through a narrow opening in an increasingly unfriendly immigration regime. As they discovered early on, they always ran the risk of detention and deportation. The trips they took were simultaneously made possible and made precarious by the power of Britain and the United States.

Ultimately, the transience of the Hooghly network's peddlers, the global nature of their movements, and the fact that their relationship to the United States was based largely on the vagaries of consumer demand all place these men at the margins of U.S. immigration history. They should, however, be no less important to our understanding of immigrant America. In their own day, these men were part of a much larger phenomenon in which tens of thousands of migrants from many regions of the world entered the United States as sojourning laborers.[93] The fact that these workers came without an intention to settle, and most returned to their home villages, does not make their stories any less significant. Most of the Bengali Muslim peddlers, for example, spent extended periods of time in the United States, and, as a group, they constituted a continuous and visible presence in New Jersey, New Orleans, and other parts of the U.S. South over the course of more than three decades. As globally extensive as it was, their network was also embedded within U.S. communities of color, and members of the network married into these communities; some started families and spent the rest of their lives in the United States. This group's inclusion in the American story requires us to reimagine the structure of the early-twentieth-century migrant experience to recognize the kinds of transnational lives, connections, and dynamics we normally only associate with the present day.[94] In the case of Hooghly's peddlers, this means not just tracing the global movements of these men, but also understanding the rootedness of their network in black neighborhoods in cities such as New Orleans and accounting for the women—both in these neighborhoods and on the subcontinent—whose lives and labor made the peddlers' work possible.

CHAPTER 2

Between Hindoo and Negro

Mose stood looking at his visitor. He was an old man . . . dressed in tuxedo, tucked shirt and black tie. His small head and face seemed smaller under a turban of pale blue silk. *Daddy Splane, Doctor of Spiritual Science.* Mose knew at a glance the reason for the bizarre costume . . .

"You ever lived Jim Crow?"

"Plenty. But I have ways of getting around it. I just put on my turban and pass as a Hindu. No trouble at all."

—William A. Owens, *Walking on Borrowed Land*

IN HER 1940 AUTOBIOGRAPHY, *A Colored Woman in a White World,* suffragist and civil rights activist Mary Church Terrell told the story of a friend who had had a curious experience on a visit to the South. The friend, whom she described as an African American "real estate man who lives in Washington [DC]," had traveled to Charleston, South Carolina, to visit his sister. When he arrived, an exposition was being held and his sister "was very enthusiastic about an East Indian with an unpronounceable name who had astounded the [locals] with his wonderful feats of legerdemain." The man's sister brought him to see the East Indian magician and the two men immediately recognized each other. As it turned out, the two had been boyhood friends in Charleston; the "East Indian," Terrell wrote, had been "born and brought up as a colored boy in that very southern city" and was now posing, working, and traveling as a Hindu fakir. Now that the exposition was in Charleston, Terrell continued, the magician had taken to removing his garb at the end of each night to visit some of his local relatives, "until he grew so bold about it" that an African American friend "warned him to exercise more caution."[1]

Terrell relayed this story to illustrate the strategies that African Americans developed over the course of many decades to "pass" in the segregated South—to cross the color line and temporarily, contingently, outwit the racial apartheid of Jim Crow. By the midtwentieth century, stories of passing circulated widely in African American communities; many of these stories focused on individuals who had successfully passed as white in order to access better jobs and accommodations, but for those who were darker skinned, posing as a "Hindu" or "East Indian" was a recurring and prominent theme. One national black magazine wrote that "some of the race's best folk tales are tied up in turbans and a half dozen other ways dark negroes 'pass' down south." The writers went on to cite the cases of Joseph Downing, who in the early 1900s became the spiritualist "Joveddah de Rajah," and the Reverend Jesse Routte, "who traveled unmolested through the deep south . . . lived in a white [Mobile,] Alabama Hotel and ate in downtown restaurants simply because he wore a velveteen robe and a [turban] on his head."[2]

We will probably never know which black southerner first employed this ruse, first discovered that it was possible to move across the line between "Negro" and "Hindoo," from a denigrated to an exotic otherness, from an unacceptable to a nominally acceptable blackness, by simply donning a different costume, speaking in a different way, performing a different identity. It may have been that this individual witnessed men from India doing just this and saw that whites treated them differently, afforded them greater privileges of movement, or even sought them out for the goods they sold, the "wisdom" they bore, or the "magic" they performed. If such witness occurred, it could very likely have involved one of the Bengali peddlers. There were other Indians passing through the U.S. South in the late nineteenth century—performers with traveling circuses, merchant seamen moving on and off the waterfronts of New Orleans, Charleston, and Galveston. But the peddlers constituted the first long-term Indian presence on the streets of southern cities, and descriptions of these men in the act of selling their silks, rugs, and curios make clear that they had learned to perform a well-calculated Indianness. They approached potential customers with a particular bearing, style of dress, mode of speech, and, it appears, even some replication of the servility of the imagined colonial subject. In this daily act, they validated and accentuated the ideas that Americans associated with "India" and "the East" and in so doing gave authenticity and value to the goods they sold. The men, in their "fezes," "frock coats," and "interesting blouses," were "courteous," "shrewd," "graceful," and "handsome"; they "enter[ed] stores and offices and cafes, with gentle persistency begging to show the contents of their packs"; they had "fathomless eyes," "brilliant smiles," and an "air of oriental mysticism" and were "so attractive . . . that we will buy in spite of resolutions to the contrary."[3]

When the Bengali peddlers began to set up their operations in New Orleans, Charleston, Savannah, and elsewhere in the 1890s, these cities were, in some ways, perfect locations for the men to enact their performances of authentic "Hindoo"-ness and to sell their exotic goods. As the phenomenon of middle-class tourism took hold in the United States, southern cities became popular winter destinations for white northerners, each locale offering its own "quaint" charms, customs, and cuisine, and each boasting bustling local markets, where travelers could buy gifts and mementos. New Orleans was a particularly suitable place for the *chikondars* to do business. By the final decade of the twentieth century, New Orleans was emerging as the South's preeminent tourist destination—as a place of unbridled pleasure and consumption.[4] "India" and "the East," moreover, were already woven into the fabric of tourist New Orleans. Fantastical images of "the Orient" saturated the Mardi Gras parades of this period, while "Eastern" fantasies thrived within the walls of the city's brothels. When they plied their trade as "Hindoo peddlers" in New Orleans' markets and on its streets, Hooghly's *chikondars* could capitalize on a well-established set of notions about "the East."

However, the Bengali peddlers also arrived in the U.S. South at one of the most violent and perilous moments for its "colored" populations, as state and local governments were imposing legally—and whites were enforcing extrajudicially—a broad regime of racial apartheid. The 1890s were marked by the passage of laws segregating transportation, schools, hospitals, and virtually every other arena of public life—and by a dramatic upsurge in lynchings of black men. The peddlers' trade required mobility, but for most men of their color, the stakes of move-ment across the South's dividing lines were high. "Travel and move-ment," writes historian Leon Litwack, "no matter what the distance, exposed blacks to a variety of risks and humiliations. Whether on the streetcars or railroads, at the ticket offices or in the . . . waiting rooms, they faced Jim Crow restrictions and the insults and violence that often accompanied them."[5] African Americans could move from "Negro" to "White" spaces only to perform a specific, circumscribed, and subor-dinate role—as a servant, a maid, a driver, a washerwoman. In this context, the Indian peddlers' politeness, servility, and self-exoticizing airs did a particular kind of work. This performance not only helped them to sell their goods, but also allowed them to move; their "Hindoo" dress and mannerisms gave the peddlers greater safety and mobility as they traveled by train from New Jersey through Virginia, North Caro-lina, Georgia, Alabama, and Mississippi to New Orleans; as they moved by foot from one neighborhood to another in New Orleans; or as they fanned out to sell their goods in other segregated cities: Atlanta, Mem-phis, Chattanooga, Charleston, Dallas. In an uncommonly direct refer-ence to the peddlers' strategies of comportment and dress, *The Hindust-hanee Student* noted in 1917 that the men had taken to donning fezes, a choice the writer saw as unusual for Muslims from the subcontinent, "principally as protection against prejudice."[6]

However, the peddlers' exotic appearance could only shield them up to a point. As figures who could conjure popular fantasies of the East, they may have gained temporary passage through areas that were other-wise off-limits to men of color. But the dark hue of their skin ultimately determined where they would return at the end of each day, the type and quality of the houses in which they would live, the health conditions they would face, the public facilities they could and could not access, and the risks that attended their daily movements. They built their operation within the constraints of Jim Crow, shuttling back and forth between an Indianness they performed for their customers and a blackness they shared with New Orleans' and other cities' populations of African de-scent. Black neighborhoods thus came to play a central role in the Hooghly traders' operations; it was here that that their efforts were rooted and here that they gained neighbors, acquaintances, lovers, and wives. As much as their peddling depended on the movement of people, goods, and money through global circuits, these circuits needed to be anchored in particular cities. None of these cities was more important than New Orleans, the hub that gave Hooghly's peddlers access to consumers throughout the South, the Caribbean, and Central America, and within New Orleans they became anchored in the neighborhood of Tremé.

Over the course of almost four decades, the Hooghly network operated out of a series of households in this historic downtown neighborhood. The network gained a footing here as a core group of Bengali Muslim peddlers married local women of color. Some of these women were members of Tremé's longstanding Creole of Color community while others had roots in the rural South and were of the first generation born outside slavery. While perhaps not acknowledged as such, these New Orleans women were also part of the Hooghly network, grounding it in the city through their local knowledge and connections and their daily labor to maintain boardinghouses, businesses, and families. By the 1920s, when the number of new peddlers moving through the network began to wane, Bengali traders had become integrated into the life of Tremé. Most lived just off the neighborhood's main commercial thoroughfare of North Claiborne Avenue, and many gave up the tourist trade entirely to sell clothing and other goods to black customers in their adopted neighborhood. In the ensuing years, their descendants and the memories of their presence would disappear into the history of black New Orleans.

Hindoo Heavens and Jim Crow Streets

The first records of the Bengali peddlers in New Orleans are scattered across the 1880s and 1890s. Census enumerations suggest that Alef Ally, the first of the Bengali traders to settle in the city, arrived around 1885. Ships' manifests record small groups of Bengali peddlers passing through New York on their way to New Orleans in 1890, 1893, and 1896. About eight members of the Hooghly network turn up in New Orleans marriage records between 1890 and 1903, and the first dozen children of these unions appear in the city's birth records stretching from 1892 to 1904. In these years, New Orleans was fertile ground for the peddlers' business. The fashion for "Oriental goods" had spread across the entire country, but in New Orleans the Bengalis found a manifestation of the Oriental "craze" in the local idiom of Mardi Gras that was grand in scale. In the final years of the nineteenth century, Mardi Gras was not only the centerpiece of local boosters' efforts to turn New Orleans into an international tourist destination, but also became the stage for some of the era's wildest spectacles of India and "the East."

Before the United States took control of Louisiana in 1803, Mardi Gras had been an event that the city's racially heterogeneous but predominantly Catholic population celebrated on the day before the beginning of Lent. In the latter half of the century, however, the city's new American political and business leadership—white Protestants with roots in the U.S. Northeast—moved to co-opt the yearly celebration. They began to use Mardi Gras to attract outside visitors and assert their own cultural heritage over that of the city's Catholic French, Spanish, and Creole inhabitants.[7] Between 1857 and 1882 members of New Orleans' Anglo-American elite formed a series of white male secret societies—the city's first krewes—to stage masked parades and balls on Mardi Gras. Each year, the Krewes of Comus, Proteus, Momus, and Rex designed costumes and built floats and, on Fat Tuesday, took over the main streets and thoroughfares of New Orleans with elaborate themed processions that referenced English and Greco-Roman history, literature, and myth. This meant that Mardi Gras parades were often multifloat illustrations of scenes from well-known English masterworks: Milton's *Paradise Lost*, Spenser's *Faerie Queene*, Dickens' *Pickwick Papers*.[8]

In the years that the Bengali peddlers established their operations in the city, the krewes partook in the larger fin de siècle fashion for "the East" by drawing liberally from Britain's large store of Orientalist literature. The Krewe of Comus had made the first gesture in this direction in 1868 by staging a Mardi Gras procession and ball enacting scenes from Thomas Moore's epic poem *Lalla Rookh*, about a Mughal princess who falls in love with a poet on the eve of her wedding. It featured, among other sights, the exotically costumed "princess" riding atop a life-size papier-mâché elephant. In 1882, not long before Alef Ally arrived in New Orleans, Proteus paraded a series of floats illustrating "Ancient Egyptian Theology," while the Krewe of Momus rode New Orleans'

streets on floats depicting scenes from the Hindu epic *The Ramayana*.
On average, at least one of the four major New Orleans krewes staged a
procession and ball based on an "Oriental" theme every other year from
1880 to 1910. These included "Tales of the Genii," "Aladdin, or The
Wonderful Lamp," "The Moors of Spain," "The Semitic Races," "Myths
and Worships of the Chinese," "Shah Nameh," two versions of "The Ma-
habharata," and "Mahomet: Incidents in the Life of the Great Prophet."[9]

Two of the most elaborate of this era's Mardi Gras parades were staged
by the Krewe of Proteus: 1889's "Hindoo Heavens," which presented a
series of floats based on the work "The Curse of Kehama" by the British
Orientalist poet Robert Southey, and 1908's "Light of Asia," based on the
epic poem by Sir Edwin Arnold telling the story of Buddha.[10] Both were
spectacular renditions of the most exotic ideas about India, its people,
and its religions. "When darkness arrived," the *Montgomery Advertiser*
reported of the 1908 procession, "twenty big floats of the Krewe of Proteus were wheeled out of their hiding places and began a night parade.
These floats and the masked and costumed men riding on them illustrated the subject 'The Light of Asia.' Hindu beliefs and Buddhistic and
Brahminical customs were portrayed, including allegories of Yasodhara
the Fair, the dancers of Indra's temple; The Lords of Light; Parihga and
Mano; Kama the King of Passions, Mara and the Tempter; and The
Abode of the Rishis. A *bhodi* tree, some huge dragons and monsters without names were portrayed on the floats."[11] Year after year, thousands of
locals and visitors came out to line the Mardi Gras parade routes, and in
procession after procession, New Orleans' Anglo-American krewes filled
the imaginations of these eager spectators with fantastical ideas about
"the East." The lines between India, China, the Middle East, and North
Africa blurred, as did those between Islam, Hinduism, and Buddhism.
All were part of a single Oriental imaginary—a store of exotic notions
upon which the Bengali peddlers could draw each day they stepped out
to sell their goods.

The remaking of Mardi Gras into an Anglocentric tourist spectacle
was just one part of a larger transformation that New Orleans' white
leadership was imposing on the city during the years Bengali peddlers
put down their roots. Over the same two decades in which Mardi Gras
was saturated with "Oriental" imagery—the same period in which the

men from Hooghly and Calcutta established households in the city and found sites, routes, and customers for their goods—the daily life and racial geography of New Orleans were being remade by Jim Crow. From the time that the Anglo-Americans arrived from the North to take control of New Orleans in 1803, they began what would be a decades-long, uneven, but unrelenting process of "Americanizing" the city. They first pushed to marginalize and displace New Orleans' existing "white Creole" elite—a group who were of French, Spanish, and mixed French-Spanish ancestry. New Orleans' free persons of color, or Creoles of Color, were also a threat, particularly after the end of the Civil War. Although less powerful than the white Creoles, the city's *gens de couleur libre* had carved out a considerable cultural and political presence in Tremé and other neighborhoods on the downtown side of New Orleans and included a segment of relatively prosperous tradespeople and craftsmen.

After men of color swept into Louisiana's state legislature over the period 1868–1872, the Anglo-Americans mounted an often violent campaign to reassert themselves and prevent the leadership of the free person of color community from establishing lasting political power.[12] By the 1880s, white Americans had regained control of the state government, and in 1890, around the time that the first Bengalis settled in New Orleans, Louisiana's legislature began to construct the legal edifice of Jim Crow. Their first step was a law that required railroad and streetcar companies to provide "separate accommodations for the white and colored races" and prohibited "colored" passengers from riding on cars or in sections designated for whites. Although members of New Orleans' free person of color community challenged the Separate Car Act, the U.S. Supreme Court, in its *Plessy v. Ferguson* decision, upheld the law's constitutionality. This cleared the way for Louisiana to enact a series of other segregation laws as well as a new state constitution that effectively disfranchised the state's citizens of African descent.[13]

Over the next several decades, Jim Crow changed the social and physical geography of New Orleans, and Tremé—the seat of Creole of Color power—was particularly affected. At the end of the nineteenth century, Tremé, was still a heterogeneous neighborhood. The neighborhood's Creole of Color community was broadly varied across lines of class and skin color; it included *gens de couleur libre* who were dark skinned and others who, like Homer Plessy, were light enough to pass as white. Some engaged in manual work, while others owned businesses, practiced professions, or edited newspapers. Tremé was also home to some of the thousands of Americans of African descent who had migrated to New Orleans from other parts of the South in the years following Emancipation, and to a smaller number of working-class European and other immigrants— Irish, Italian, German, Syrian, and Chinese.

Anglo-American rule had already begun a process of flattening New Orleans' heterogeneity into "a rigid, two-tiered structure that drew a single, unyielding line between white and nonwhite." This process accelerated from the post-Reconstruction era into the 1920s and 1930s as segregation and disfranchisement politically weakened and isolated Tremé's inhabitants. Tremé was made into a "negro district" in the image of others across the segregated South and the rest of the United States—its population excluded from power, its housing and infrastructure neglected, and its residents and borders policed. By the turn of the century, Tremé was one of two such areas near the center of New Orleans. The other was not far away; across Canal Street on the uptown side of the city, many of New Orleans' recent black American migrants were concentrated in a small area of low-grade housing referred to as "back of town" or "the Battlefield." The lines dividing both these neighborhoods from "white" parts of New Orleans became more pronounced as the city passed residential segregation ordinances and as the expansion of streetcar lines and the drainage of swampland opened up new neighborhoods and spurred white flight out of the city's core.[14]

The stakes of the post-Reconstruction racial order were made clear by an event that occurred soon after the first group of Bengali peddlers established their footing in New Orleans. On July 23, 1900, a young African American man was questioned by New Orleans police. The man, Robert Charles, had recently made his way to New Orleans from rural Mississippi. He ended up working a range of odd jobs while becoming active in an association advocating African American migration to Liberia. Charles had, according to later accounts, been enraged by the recent killing of Sam Hose, a young black man roughly the same age and generation as Charles, who had been brutally lynched by a white mob in

Georgia. New Orleans police officers questioned Charles because he was seen sitting on the porch of a white family's house on a racially mixed block on the uptown side of the city. As the confrontation quickly escalated, Charles pulled out a pistol and fired, then ran to his apartment, and as the police and a crowd of thousands of white New Orleanians closed in on him, he opened fire with a rifle, killing seven men before being killed himself. New Orleans was now engulfed in antiblack violence: "For four days, mobs surged through New Orleans, seizing control of downtown sections, killing at least a dozen black people and injuring many more, and destroying black property," including the city's leading school for children of color, the Lafon School, which was burned to the ground.[15]

Six weeks before this incident, U.S. Census takers had recorded ten members of the Bengali peddler network residing on St. Louis Street, in downtown New Orleans. July was high season for the New Jersey seaside resorts, and it is possible that many of these men—Solomon Mondul, Abdul Subham, Bahadoor Ali, and others—had left to work the boardwalks of Atlantic City and Asbury Park not long before New Orleans erupted in racial violence. A smaller number, however, were almost certainly present to witness the rampage. Sofur Ally, for one, had just got married to a local Creole woman days before the riots broke out. And those who traveled to New Jersey for the season returned in the fall to a New Orleans still reverberating from the events of July.

It is difficult to say exactly what the peddlers experienced in the ensuing years, how they were regarded and treated as men of color operating within a volatile racial order. Even the most exoticizing descriptions of Bengali peddlers in turn-of-the-century U.S. newspapers—and of the Bengali, Punjabi, and other Indian seamen who were now beginning to appear with frequency in U.S. ports—focused in on the men's complexion and tried to place them according to the United States' binary racial logic. One 1900 story about Indians in the sailors' quarter of New York City stated that these men were "all so dark as to be taken easily for Negroes, but their features are Caucasian and their hair is straight, stiff, and wiry." It described their character in terms that drew on notions of both Asian "inscrutability" and African American "criminality," saying that they "are peaceable and orderly up to a certain point and then they lose all self-control and generally resort to the knife." Another story, focusing on a group of Bengali peddlers who were working on the streets of Atlanta, Georgia, declared that these Indian men were "not like American Indians, of course, but look like Mexicans, only three shades darker." In this case, the peddlers were represented, as African Americans often were in the white press, simultaneously as wily and dim-witted.[16] Government documents from the same period reflect a certain confusion about the "color" and "race" of the Bengali peddlers. In 1900 and 1910, federal census takers marked most of the men "Black," others "Mulatto," and a few "White," before a supervisor often scratched "Hin" for Hindu over the top of the original classification. During the First World War, draft registrars described the peddlers' "race" variously as "Black," "White," "Oriental," "Turkish," and "Malaysian." The officials who processed a handful of the Bengalis' passport applications in the 1910s mostly described their "complexion" as "dark" but in one case wrote "copper," in another "ruddy," and in another "light."[17]

There was clearly a difference between these official classifications and the lived experiences of segregation the peddlers faced. While the Bengalis may have benefited from the kind of ambiguity that is apparent in official attempts to classify them, their position within the racial order ultimately appears to have been provisional and uncertain. Like the distinctions between "Creole," "free person of color," and "negro," the various ways of describing, categorizing, and distinguishing these Indian peddlers meant little when it came to the most basic aspects of Jim Crow. The Bengalis' darkness, no matter what shade or category, made them vulnerable to individual acts of violence and was a deciding factor when they sought out family homes, boardinghouses, neighborhoods, and communities in which to live.

Two of the only records we have of the Bengalis' direct confrontation with Jim Crow make clear the contingency of their position in the segregated South. In the opening years of the twentieth century, a small number of Bengali traders began naturalization proceedings in various southern cities. These included Alef Ally, Sofur Ally, Abdul Hamid, and Abdul Jobber Mondul in New Orleans and Mohamed Kauser, Abdul Aziz, Elahi Baksh Mondul, Abdul Rohim Mondul, Abdul Haq Mondul, Mohammed Idris, and Syed Abdul Ganny in Charleston.[18] The most well-known naturalization case from this group is that of "Abba Dolla," a trader of Afghan descent who became a member of the Hooghly network in Calcutta, worked the New Jersey summer resorts in the 1890s, and then settled in Savannah around the turn of the century. There, Dolla became a local supplier, receiving shipments of embroidered silks and cottons through the Savannah customhouse, and then distributing these goods to other members of the peddler network to sell throughout the city and its vicinity. It is difficult to locate Abba Dolla in shipping, census, and other records because his name was either changed or mis-transliterated in the process of applying for citizenship, but it appears that Dolla was the same member of the network who traveled through New York to New Jersey several times in the 1890s under names recorded as "Obidullah" and "Abad Ally." Dolla filed a Petition of Intention to Naturalize in Savannah in 1907, and then in 1910 submitted his application to naturalize, along with supporting statements from two witnesses. At the time he went up before a judge in the Federal District Court in Savannah in 1910, people of only two "races" were allowed to become U.S. citizens—"white persons" and "persons of African ancestry"—and like a handful of other East Indians in the years immediately before and after him, Dolla applied for and was granted citizenship as a "white person."[19]

Immigration historians have described Abba Dolla's case in this context; it is understood as one of a number of instances in the early twentieth century in which immigrants from India successfully "claimed whiteness." The details of both his case and his daily life in segregated Georgia, however, present a less clear picture. Having determined that Abba Dolla had followed the correct procedures in his application for citizenship, the judge examining Dolla held that the only issue to determine at his hearing was "whether or not he was a white person within the meaning of [the] naturalization laws." To this end, Dolla presented an argument in several parts: he described his ancestry—he stated that he was born and raised in Calcutta and was of Afghan descent; he cited the case of Abdul Hamid, another Calcutta silk peddler with whom he had entered the country in 1894, and who had been naturalized as a "white person" in 1908; he testified that he was the owner of a plot in Savannah's white-only cemetery; he offered to produce a series of (presumably white) leading citizens to attest to his good character—"the deputy collector of the Port at Savannah, certain merchants of the city, one of the attaches of the United States court"; and he offered to produce "a leading white physician" who had once operated on him for appendicitis and who would confirm that he was "of pure Caucasian blood." The judge heard all this and first seemed concerned to determine that Dolla had not developed any social affiliations with the black community. Ultimately, however, the judge called no witnesses; instead he relied on a close examination of Dolla's skin, asking the silk trader to roll up his sleeve and noting that while his face and hands had been darkened by the sun, his unexposed skin was "several shades lighter . . . and was sufficiently transparent for the blue color of the veins to show very clearly."[20]

Although Dolla was granted citizenship, this was not a larger indication that "East Indians" were widely considered or treated as "white." The U.S. government in fact vigorously opposed Dolla's naturalization, as it had in other similar cases, sending an assistant U.S. attorney, Alexander Ackerman, to challenge its own federal district court judge at Dolla's hearing. Ackerman presented an argument that failed to sway the judge, that Dolla, as an Asian, was not a "white person" and was therefore racially ineligible to become a U.S. citizen. The method that the regional district court judge used to determine that Dolla *was* "a white person" was unorthodox even for 1910—more in line with the daily practices of southern segregation than with any legal precedent. His judgment also belied the subjectivities and inconsistencies of an early-twentieth-century naturalization system that put decision-making powers in the hands of a range of lower federal court judges. There were opportunities but no guarantees for members of the Bengali network seeking citizenship in southern courts. While a few of Abba Dolla's fellow peddlers may have also had skin "sufficiently transparent for the blue color of the veins to show," any number of them could have failed the visual inspection to which he, a presumably lighter-skinned man of Afghan descent, had been subjected by this particular district court judge. Many would have also failed to convince this judge that they had not developed affiliations with the local "colored" population.[21]

In truth, Dolla's own relationship to Savannah's black community was less clear-cut than he presented and than the judge chose to see. For

all the white citizens he offered to present at his hearing, Dolla's two official witnesses, who had, in sworn written affidavits submitted with his
application, confirmed his presence in Savannah over the previous three
years and attested to his good character, were both African American
men. This suggests that Abba Dolla had been in closer proximity and
developed greater familiarity—if not also closer ties—with members of
Savannah's black community than with its white citizens. And although
the judge at Dolla's hearing determined to his own satisfaction that
Dolla pursued his trade "among whites and blacks indifferently" and
that he lived together with "several of his countrymen" and only maintained "relations of a social nature" with "those of his own nationality,"
federal census records show that the Bengali peddlers operating in Savannah all lived within black neighborhoods or on predominantly black
city blocks. In 1900, the single member of the Hooghly network who
appeared in the census in Savannah was Abdul Barrick, who was renting a room from a widowed African American laundress and living with
her three children and niece. The 1910 census recorded one Bengali
group household in Savannah, and it was located in the same working-
class African American area on the east side of the city.[22]

Abdul Hamid, whose successful naturalization Dolla cited as a precedent, also appears to have lived a more complex relation to blackness
and to the black community than his naturalization as a "white person"
would suggest. By the time he applied for naturalization in New Orleans in 1908, Hamid had already been married to a local Creole of
Color woman for eight years, and in the years that followed he lived and
worked within the "negro" community in the heart of Tremé.[23] It is of
course impossible to know how individual members of the Hooghly
peddler network saw themselves in relation to color, "race," and the
racial order that surrounded them in the South, but there is enough
evidence to suggest that for many, naturalization was a strategic move
to give greater stability to their business pursuits rather than an identification with white supremacy and a disavowal of African American
and Creole neighbors, acquaintances, and extended families. And
they would have clearly understood after even a short time in the Jim
Crow South that legal citizenship was not equivalent to full citizenship, that racial determinations were made not only in the courts where

they sought to naturalize but also on the streets where they plied their trade.

If, in the courts, the subjectivity of racial judgments could work in the peddlers' favor, in this other arena of their daily lives, the subjective execution of segregation could just as easily turn against them. This is brought home in another incident involving a Bengali on the streets of New Orleans in 1922. The case of Abdul Fara is recorded in *The Negro in Louisiana*, an unpublished manuscript authored by the African American poet and historian Marcus Christian, based on research he directed as head of the Works Progress Administration's Louisiana Negro Writers Project in the 1930s.[24] In a chapter describing the evolution of Jim Crow laws in post-Reconstruction Louisiana, Christian wrote that by the 1920s, a variety of New Orleans residents, including "persons of colored races such as Japanese, Chinese, American Indian, Puerto Rican, Philipinos [*sic*]," as well as persons whom he described as "dark whites . . . Turks, Indians, and Spaniards," and some number of "light-skinned Negroes," were all regularly seating themselves in the "white" section of the city's segregated streetcars. The conductors of these streetcars, he continued, normally let these riders be, "having been warned of the costly consequences of mistaken racial identity." In Abdul Fara's case, however, the conductor was not the problem.

Fara boarded a streetcar on Canal Street and took a seat in the last row of the "white" section, next to a white World War I veteran named Fitzhugh Davis. After two blocks, Christian writes, the conductor left the back of the streetcar and came to investigate. He approached Abdul Fara and asked him "whether he was a white man or Negro." Fara claimed neither identity; he "replied that he was a native of Calcutta, India, whereupon the [conductor], apparently satisfied, returned to his place on the platform." Soon afterward, however, the white passenger sitting next to Fara took matters into his own hands. After an exchange of words, he grabbed the "screen" that marked the dividing line between the "white" and "colored" sections of the streetcar—a heavy wooden sign with two thick metal prongs that was slotted into the back of his seat—pulled it out, and attacked Abdul Fara with it, striking him twice over the head. When Fara later brought suit against Davis, the white judge hearing the case declared that it was reasonable that Davis might have thought Abdul Fara was a "negro" and that he was thus justified in having become incensed at Fara's riding in the "white" section of the car and in striking him. The judge held in favor of Fara's attacker and ordered Fara to pay the costs of the court. In an arena in which individuals were empowered to enforce white supremacy in its multiple daily manifestations, the Bengali peddlers' access to white spaces and privileges was always going to be provisional and subject to revocation at a moment's notice. These spaces may have provided them with customers who would buy their goods, but black neighborhoods were where the Bengalis became rooted and built their lives.

Into Tremé

The first federal census of the twentieth century, conducted in June 1900, gives us a snapshot of the Bengali peddlers at work across several states. Heroo Shaikh, who traveled from Calcutta to New York with ten other members of the network in 1896, was now living in a lodging house for southern black migrants in Pittsburgh. Abdul Latif was renting a room from an African American family in Cleveland, Ohio, and Rahim Bux lived in an all-black neighborhood in the seaside town of St. Augustine, Florida. Abdul Surcar was peddling goods in Houston, Texas, where he had married a young African American woman named Sadie, and Bell Ali was living as a dry-goods peddler in a predominantly African American neighborhood in Galveston, Texas. In Charleston, seven members of the network were living in black family homes or neighborhoods, and three had married local black women. In Atlantic City, where segregation was enforced by practice rather than by law, the Bengalis' place was clear by contrast to that of their Syrian competitors: while Syrian Oriental goods peddlers had settled in white lower-middle-class areas among members of Atlantic City's permanent population, the Bengali men were living with other seasonal workers of color—stewards, cooks, chambermaids, bartenders, laundresses, and musicians—in a segregated black section of town.[25] At the turn of the century, everywhere the Bengalis peddled their goods, they lived in working-class African American homes, apartment buildings, or neighborhoods.[26]

New Orleans was no different. From the moment the Bengali peddlers arrived in the city, they lived among its residents of African
descent—both southern black migrants and Creoles of Color. Over the
course of decades, they appear to have experienced alongside these
groups the encroachments and effects of the city's implementation of Jim
Crow. Between 1895 and 1930, the Bengalis made their homes almost entirely in Tremé. Some of the men established group households and
boardinghouses in a handful of neighborhood buildings that subsequently provided shelter for dozens of fellow members of the Hooghly
network—cousins, uncles, nephews, sons, and co-villagers. Others married into local New Orleans communities, starting families with Creole
of Color women and women connected to the more recent African American in-migration. Still others moved from one residence to another over
decades spent cycling in and out of New Orleans but always within the
bounds of Tremé.

In these years, the Bengalis' lives became entangled in the neighborhood's transformations. As New Orleans' leadership implemented Jim
Crow and opened up other parts of the city, as many of Tremé's European immigrant residents moved out, the Bengalis became more integrated into the neighborhood.[27] Tremé experienced two major shifts in
its geography and make-up. First, just one year after the *Plessy* decision,
New Orleans' aldermen carved thirteen poor, largely black residential
blocks out of the southwest corner of Tremé in order to create the city's
new sex district. Then, in the 1910s and 1920s, as Canal Street and
other commercial areas across New Orleans came to be restricted to
whites, a new black cultural and commercial core formed along the
wide tree-lined boulevard of Tremé's North Claiborne Avenue. New
Orleans' Bengali peddlers moved with both these shifts. In the 1890s, the
first group of men from Hooghly and Calcutta established their operations
in the section of Tremé that was to become, before their eyes, the Storyville sex district. Some of the peddlers remained here as local residents
were pushed out, and others followed displaced residents of color to the
blocks just outside the District. The Bengalis were here at Storyville's
edges as the neighborhood's brothels, bars, and barrelhouses rose and
fell. By the 1920s and 1930s, the handful of Indian peddlers who remained in New Orleans moved again—this time into the new heart of

black Tremé along North Claiborne Avenue, where they sold textiles, embroidery, and ready-made clothing not to tourists, but to the local residents of the neighborhood.

Bengali peddlers of silks started making trips from New Jersey to New Orleans between the mid-1880s and the early 1890s. The first members of the network to do so—Alef Ally, Moksad Ali, Jainal Abdeen, and Aynuddin Mondul—all arrived in New Orleans during this period. By 1895, another group had joined them—Solomon Mondul, Abdul Subham, Sofur Ally, and Majan, Eshrack, and Bahadoor Ali. Most of the men found accommodations on a block of St. Louis Street between Marais and Tremé Streets, near Congo Square and a stone's throw from St. Louis Cemetery No. 1. The two residences they rented, 1420 and 1428 St. Louis Street, were on a block of two- and three-story wooden structures built in the simple "shotgun" style common in much of this section of New Orleans. Some of the streets in the surrounding area were dirt, others were gravel, some were paved with cobblestones, and still others with wood planks. This was a vibrant corner of Tremé. The Bengalis' neighbors were working-class and primarily of color, a mix of families and unmarried adults. The families were often extended and multigenerational, with parents, grandparents, adult siblings, in-laws, and children living under the same roof. There were also a few white households interspersed through the area tied to various waves of European immigration: German, French, and Irish. The neighborhood included the Union Chapel—an African Methodist Episcopal church—as well as a "Negro public school" and a handful of black lodges and meeting halls. Many of the neighborhood's women and men, like the Bengalis, would have fanned outward each day to go to their jobs in other parts of the city—as construction workers and day laborers, as dockworkers, porters, and cooks, and as laundresses, maids, and house servants.[28]

In 1897, this part of New Orleans became the first in the city to experience the post-*Plessy* regime of residential segregation. That year, the city passed ordinances that made prostitution illegal everywhere in New Orleans except two specified areas; the larger of these two, which would come to be known as "Storyville," or simply "the District," encompassed the thirteen blocks bounded by St. Louis, Basin, Customhouse, and Robertson Streets, including at its edge the block where the Bengali peddlers were living. As Alecia P. Long has argued, the legal delineation of these blocks was not an act of racial segregation per se. Yet in carving "the District" out of this poor, predominantly black locality, she writes, "city leaders implied a rough equality between its population of 'lewd and abandoned women,' . . . and the African Americans who lived, went to school, and worshipped in the neighborhood." The disruption of the latter group's existing community was of little importance to those who penned the ordinances, if the features of this community were even legible to them. Both populations—the city's sex workers and the more than two thousand existing residents of this section of the city—were to be spatially separated from "respectable" New Orleans; both were to be controlled and contained.[29] In the years that followed, the logic and rhetoric that had supported the creation of Storyville would be extended: "Segregationists would argue that, like prostitutes, African Americans should be separated from respectable whites because of their [supposed] propensity toward disorder, sensuality, immorality, filth, and disease."[30]

Soon after Alef Ally, Solomon Mondul, and the other Bengali *chikondars* settled into this area, they would have seen their street and the surrounding neighborhood go through a transformation. In 1900, three years after the legal delineation of the sex district, the U.S. Census recorded a number of people in the immediate vicinity of 1420 and 1428 St. Louis Street who were clearly connected to Storyville's dance halls, saloons, and brothels. But, at this stage, a significant portion of the area's population still consisted of Creole of Color and black American residents who had little or nothing to do with the District's businesses. They included teamsters, dockworkers, railroad workers, slaters, sailors, day laborers, and likely some number of the women listed as cooks, washerwomen, and maids.[31] This changed quickly after 1900. Between 1900 and 1910, the owners of buildings in the area—who were usually whites who lived in other parts of the city—took to subdividing their residential properties into multiple single-room "cribs"—spaces that they could rent out in two shifts a day, at a high premium, to the neighborhood's sex workers. Although it was on the outer edge of Storyville, St. Louis Street was not immune to this trend. By 1908, seven of the buildings on the 1400 block had been converted into sex workers' cribs.

This included 1420, the building where seven members of the Hooghly network had lived just a few years earlier, and 1426, the building next door to Alef Ally and his two daughters. By 1914, in addition to the seven cribs, the 1400 block featured a saloon on each corner, and Alef Ally's building was one of only two residential dwellings left on the block.[32]

This trend appears to have displaced much of the area's remaining working-class population, pushing them to the undesirable blocks just outside the borders of the sex district or to other parts of the city.[33] Unlike many of his former neighbors, however, Alef Ally did not move from the area, and his was the block to which increasing numbers of Bengali peddlers came to live in the 1910s. When the census was conducted in April 1910, Ally was fifty years old and a naturalized citizen, and had been a resident of New Orleans for more than half his life. He had now turned the building at 1428 St. Louis Street into a boardinghouse for other members of the Hooghly network. While Ally's occupation was listed as "merchant," he was also recorded as head of a household that included his younger daughter, Viola, a sixty-five-year-old "mulatto" woman named Celestine Gardner, and twenty-one Indian peddlers. The peddlers included a small number of older men who were veterans of the Hooghly network, but most were recent arrivals to the United States.[34] The building at 1428 St. Louis Street appears to have become a key part of the New Orleans operation, where older members of the network introduced younger members to the city and the trade. In the decade between 1904 and 1914, a series of younger peddlers from Hooghly villages declared at their Ellis Island inspections that the St. Louis Street residence was their final destination and named a group of senior Bengali peddlers—Fazleh Rahman, Abdul Barrick, Monsur Ali, and Moksad Ali—as the "relations" whom they were joining there.[35]

What did these men from Babnan, Chandanpur, Sinhet, and Alipur make of the world around them? What did they make of the changes that were occurring on their block and in the neighborhood beyond St. Louis Street in the months and years after the creation of the sex district? In Calcutta, they were connected to a neighborhood not unlike the one Storyville was becoming. The "vice" in the area around St. Louis Street also was not new. There were a significant number of brothels, saloons, and dance halls in the area even when the first group of Bengalis moved to this part of New Orleans in the 1890s.[36] This is likely the reason they were able to find affordable accommodations on St. Louis Street in the first place. One nearby property owner testified in an 1897 court case that "she had tried on several occasions" to rent three of her houses on St. Louis and Franklin Streets " 'to respectable people, but they wouldn't live in the neighborhood,' so she rented them to prostitutes or question-able characters instead."[37]

In the years after 1897, the Bengalis would have seen the sex trade take over their area. The cribs and brothels on the blocks around them became an integral part of New Orleans' growing tourist economy— these establishments were the illicit side of the same phenomenon of warm-weather "pleasure seeking" that had drawn the first members of the Hooghly network to the city.[38] Each night this area was inundated with hundreds of men—both locals and visitors—on their way into and out of sex and drinking establishments in search of pleasure, power, and fantasy. And the growth of the sex industry was not the only change oc-curring in the area. The brothels and saloons were full of music: particu-larly ragtime and the evolving style that would become jazz. So were the large halls that were all a stone's throw from St. Louis Street—Globe Hall, Economy Hall, Equity Hall, Friends of Hope Hall. From the time they arrived, the peddlers would have regularly heard the sounds of brass bands playing funeral marches as they passed Alef Ally's boardinghouse en route to St. Louis Cemetery No. 1 half a block in one direction or St. Louis Cemetery No. 2, two and a half blocks in the other. Now they would have also heard the sounds of the new music pouring out of neigh-borhood establishments each night.[39]

Their black and Creole neighbors did not all respond to these changes in the same way. A group of neighborhood residents—the lead-ership of Union Chapel Methodist Episcopal Church and some of the six hundred members of its congregation—fought to prevent the cre-ation of the sex district in 1897. Black women and men who had attended the church all their lives were now being priced out of their neighbor-hood homes as landlords doubled and tripled rents in anticipation of the area's conversion to sex work. The chapel's minister argued that the creation of the vice district would "destroy the value of the [church] property for the purpose for which it was intended . . . as a place of worship."[40] The courts' rejection of this legal challenge demonstrated how little power local residents of color had in the face of the city's expanding regime of residential segregation.[41] After these local residents' claim was denied, however, other New Orleanians of color engaged with the District as a source of work. Besides many of the sex workers and a small number of Storyville's madams, the neighborhood's businesses employed hundreds of entertainers and service workers, who were predominantly African American and Creole: "two hundred musicians, about five hundred domestic workers, and a hundred fifty saloon employees," according to one account.[42]

It is impossible to know where the Bengali peddlers were on the spectrum between those who objected to and fought Storyville and those who accepted and partook in its daily business. It is possible that some of the men from Hooghly, like the members of Union Chapel's African Methodist Episcopal congregation, objected to the trade that was flourishing on their doorstep and on the streets all around them. However, for the veterans of the peddler network—even those from Hooghly's villages—their experiences in Calcutta, and later London, Liverpool, New York, and elsewhere, would have made them accustomed to areas like the one springing up around them. They were also businessmen who may have recognized the District as a site for their own trade. It is beyond the scope of archives and popular memory to know for certain if the Bengalis sold within Storyville. What we do know is that the kinds of goods these men purveyed were prominent throughout the sex district. The fantasies of India and "the East" that New Orleans' elite white krewes paraded through the streets during Mardi Gras each year were also manifest in Storyville brothels where "Oriental dancing girls" regularly performed. These performances involved women who were likely Creole, African American, Jewish, or Southern European who dressed in scant "Oriental" fabrics and were surrounded by rugs and wall hangings meant to evoke the imagined harems of Arab, Persian, or Mughal emperors.[43] Later advertisements for the goods that Bengali peddlers sold in New Orleans list precisely the kinds of items that would have been used to construct such sexualized fantasies of the "East"—"real lace [and] hand embroidered shawls from faraway India" along with "negligee waists, silk lingerie, undergarments, hosiery, [and], camisoles."[44]

Oriental goods also appear to have played the same function within the interiors of Storyville brothels as they played within the mansions of the United States' elites—as markers of worldliness and class distinction. The madams who ran the District's large upscale brothels along Basin Street emulated the lavish interior designs that were in fashion among European and American upper-class women of the late nineteenth century. The Arlington, run by Josie Arlington, rivaled Bertha Palmer's home in its opulence; it boasted "a Turkish Parlor, a Hall of Mirrors, a Japanese Parlor, a Vienna Parlor, an American Parlor," but also added rooms that were specific to the building's primary use: "seemingly countless luxury 'dens' and 'boudoirs,' . . . with quantities of wall hangings, chandeliers, drapes, rococo furniture, afghan spreads, [and] oriental, deep-pile rugs."[45] Houses like The Arlington appear to have set a standard that less exclusive brothels were quick to follow. Photographs from the period, including those by E. J. Bellocq, show brothels thickly decorated with "Oriental" rugs, scarves, cushions, tablecloths, and tapestries.[46] The Bengali peddlers on the edge of Storyville had access to such goods and would have found lucrative business among the District's madams, who were known to local traders for their tendency to make a show of wealth and luxury. "[M]erchants 'sold high' to owners of *maisons de joie* and madams prided themselves on their willingness to 'pay the price.'"[47]

Whether they were selling within Storyville or confining themselves to New Orleans' tourist trade, by 1910 the number of Bengali peddlers operating in the city had grown significantly. The federal census recorded more than fifty *chikondars* residing in the city in April of that year, but an Indian account suggests that the number of Bengalis moving through New Orleans may have actually been in the low hundreds by this time.[48] While a number of the earliest peddlers had married in New Orleans by 1910, and others appear to have returned to their villages in India, another group had chosen to live a different kind of life; they settled on neither end of the network, but instead remained mobile, living and working in the company of other men. These older *chikondars* traveled and plied their trade together in the same pairs and small groups over many years and across the full breadth of the network. They also appear to have been the members of the network who shepherded younger peddlers through its circuits, initiated them into its workings, and maintained a shifting set of households for the network in key cities.

Between 1900 and 1910, a group of these network veterans—Solomon Mondul, Abdul Aziz, Tazlim Uddin, Abdul Goffer Mondul, Abdul Majid—followed Storyville's displaced working-class population into the blocks of houses just outside the borders of the sex district.[49] The peddlers crowded into the homes here; between four and a dozen men lived together at each address, in simple spaces that were rarely larger than eight hundred square feet.[50] Although they spread out across the city to sell their goods each day, here in these houses they shared the domestic and intimate aspects of their lives, cooking and eating together, washing and cleaning, likely sharing beds, caring for those who fell ill, helping each other navigate the challenges of their daily lives, and spending leisure time with one another. In one of the few accounts that exists from this era of the Bengali peddlers at rest, a visiting Indian student wrote that "here in the South, they live in groups [and] you often notice them in their pajamas, sitting at ease, playing cards and gossiping, mostly about old-fashioned things."[51]

It is not clear how much these men interacted with the others around them, but there was a tenor of daily experience that they would have all shared with one another. The character and landscape of the neighborhood were similar to those of St. Louis Street before the creation of Storyville. The Bengalis' neighbors were predominantly of color—classified on census enumerations as "Black" and "Mulatto"—and the buildings around them included many multigenerational, extended-family households that were often female led. These neighbors included washerwomen, porters, riverboat and ocean-bound sailors, railroad and levee workers, a "wine rectifier," and a barber. The streets were still unpaved and the houses were packed closely together—long, one-story shotgun homes made of wood and tin, a door every ten feet. When it rained hard, the streets here would have run with mud and sewage. When New Orleans experienced its frequent outbreaks of diseases such as tuberculosis, smallpox, and yellow fever, they spread fastest in overcrowded areas like this, and the results are evident in the death certificates of those who died here in the opening years of the century, including the handful of Bengalis who passed during these years: Jainal

Abdeen, dead at thirty-three in 1900, Bahadoor Ali, dead at forty-two in 1906, Moksad Ali, dead at forty-six in 1918, all from tuberculosis.[52] In addition to these conditions, most of the men from Bengal shared with their neighbors a set of social constraints—varying levels of literacy and education, marginal economic status, and dark skin—which relegated them to some of the most neglected housing in the city.[53]

Of the group of Bengali residences that appeared on the federal census in 1910, two stood out from the rest, as they were farther from the edge of the sex district and several blocks deeper into the center of Tremé. Significantly, these were the homes of two of the Bengali men who had married local women of color. Joseph Abdin was living with his wife, Viola, an African American woman from Mississippi, four blocks east of the District, on Orleans Avenue. They had a household of ten that included Joseph and Viola's two children and Viola's mother, sister, three nephews, and niece. Sofur Ally was living with his wife, America, a New Orleanian of Creole and Cuban descent, and their three children a few blocks farther up Orleans Avenue, near the corner of North Derbigny. Both of these men were near commercial areas that catered not to white tourists but to the predominantly black working-class residents of the neighborhood. Abdin's residence faced the covered Tremé Market, and Ally's was one block away from the emerging "Negro" shopping and entertainment district on North Claiborne Avenue. In 1910, Abdin and Ally were at the front edge of a shift that New Orleans' Bengali peddlers would make over the next decade and into the 1920s, as anti-Asian immigration laws made the crossing of U.S. borders more difficult for the peddlers and as New Orleans' commercial segregation became more stark.[54]

The group households that Alef Ally, Solomon Mondul, and others had established on the outskirts of Storyville continued to function as hubs for a transient population of scores of Bengali peddlers at least into the late 1910s. The network's global activities appear to have been at their height, however, around 1914. The same Indian student who described the lives of Hooghly peddlers in the South in late 1917 noted that a series of circumstances, including "competition with machine-made goods" and "the stringency of the recent [U.S.] immigration laws," meant that the peddlers were "dwindling in number year after year."[55] By this time, some of the men had already begun to shift their business activities, following Joseph Abdin and Sofur Ally's lead, to sell clothing and other "East India Fancy Goods" to members of downtown New Orleans' black working-class population. The peddlers who made this transition were largely members of the Hooghly network who had married local women, put down roots in the city, and established supply lines of cloth goods from their associates and kin in India. In the 1920s and 1930s, these men took part in another shift in the city's racial landscape, moving into the area around Tremé's North Claiborne Avenue as it became the new heart of black New Orleans.

From the time the earliest members of the Hooghly network arrived in New Orleans, a small number had married or cohabited with local women of color. Alef Ally, for example, was already living with a young Creole woman of color, Emily "Minnie" Lecompte, by about 1891.[56] A number of other peddlers followed suit: Jainal Abdeen married Florence Perez in 1893; Moksad Ali married Ella Blackman in 1895; Abdul Hamid married Adele Fortineau, and Sofur Ally married America Santa Cruz in 1900; Joseph Abdin married Viola Lewis in 1906; Hassan Abdul married Viola Wilson in 1914.[57] The overall number of these marriages was small—fewer than two dozen were recorded between the 1890s and the 1910s—but they were clearly crucial to the Hooghly operation. While the boardinghouses and group households provided spaces of mentorship, companionship, and coordination for the large numbers of transient men who were moving through the network, the marriages—or more specifically, the women whom Bengali peddlers married—appear to have facilitated the network's integration into local neighborhoods, communities, and economies. A few of these women, such as Ella Blackman and Viola Lewis, were from the areas of African American in-migration that had developed on the uptown side of New Orleans in the decades following Emancipation. Others—such as Emily Lecompte, Florence Perez, and Adele Fortineau—were from Creole of Color families on the downtown side of New Orleans. None of these women were well-off, and most were in their teens when they married the Bengalis. All but one, however, were born and grew up in New Orleans. In some cases, the women had deep generational roots in the city, and in Tremé in particular. They had local knowledge, local networks, and a local cultural fluency far beyond those of their immigrant husbands.[58]

As they brought this knowledge and fluency to their partnerships, New Orleans women of African descent came to be connected across oceans to women in West Bengal.[59] The peddlers' impressive mobility—their capacity to move goods and money back and forth across thousands of miles—depended upon the presence and the work of women at every node in their network, from Hooghly villages to southern U.S. cities. The division of labor between "male migration and female domestic labor," was a defining feature of sojourning networks of this era.[60] While men traveled to find work overseas, the women who remained in their villages performed the crucial role of keeping up homes, land, and livestock. In Southern Italy, for example, women "took over all household responsibilities," while growing food and engaging in small handicraft production and wage work. When Italian women began emigrating to the United States in greater numbers, they took on similar roles in New York, New Jersey, Philadelphia, and elsewhere. Their domestic and reproductive labor, homework, and garment factory work provided their households with stability while men engaged in manual labor that was inconsistent and poorly paid. Women's work, in the household and in factories, was also the precondition for Italian immigrant men to open and operate small businesses.[61]

The network of Bengali Muslim peddlers that took hold in New Orleans and other parts of the South was similar; most of the *chikondars* were sojourners who maintained their ties to families and villages on the subcontinent and eventually returned, relying on others to maintain their land holdings in the interim.[62] But as much as the Hooghly peddler network relied upon the work of Indian women in home villages, it functioned in North America because of the labor of U.S. women of color. Women in Babnan and Chandanpur produced embroidered goods and maintained the Indian side of split families and households. African American women anchored the network's operations in New Orleans and elsewhere in the South. They worked in the boardinghouses that Indian men established, in at least one case living as the only woman among large groups of sojourning men, apparently cleaning, cooking, and laundering. Widowed women of color took in peddlers as boarders in the spare rooms of their apartments where they likely also looked after their domestic needs. The women who married Bengali peddlers kept up their households in the United States even as the men continued to travel through the network, raised their children, and would have connected the peddlers to their own circles of family, friends, and acquaintances; they provided their partners with the intellectual and domestic labor that enabled them to establish and run businesses and allowed hundreds of other, more transient, members of the network to work in New Orleans and to pass through on their way to other locations further east, west and south.

Were these simply marriages of convenience? Archival records suggest no clear answer. The relationships between Bengali men and local

Table 3.   Indian Mixed Marriages, New Orleans, 1890–1920

Year	Groom	Age		Bride	Age
c1891	Alef Ally		m.	Emily Lecompte (CR)	
1892	Moksad Ali	27	m.	Ada Wallace (AA)	17
1893	Jainal Abdeen	26	m.	Florence Perez (CR)	20
1895	Moksad Ali	29	m.	Ella Elizabeth Blackman (AA)	24
1896	Shaik Aynnaddeen Mondol		m.	Rita Albrier (CR)	
1897	Asa Alli	40	m.	Aurelia Urbain (CR)	18
1900	Abdul Hamed	25	m.	Adele Fortineau (CR)	19
1900	Sofur Ally	28	m.	America Santa Cruz (CUB/CR)	16
1901	Shaik M. Alley		m.	Corinne Villar (CR)	
1905	Bahador Ali Molar	38	m.	Florence Gertrude Wilbert (AA)	22
1906	Joseph Abdin	45	m.	Viola Ida Lewis (AA)	22
1909	John A. Martin (AA)	22	m.	Nofossu Abdeen*	18
1909	Victor Dupart (CR)	21	m.	Sadie Ally*	18
1910	Ensan Ally	35	m.	Camille Basset (CR)	18
1911	Abdul Rub	21	m.	Olga Santa Cruz (CUB/CR)	18
1911	Maxest Ally	31	m.	Ananise Sylvester (CR)	16
1911	Denis Schaff	22	m.	Viola Alley*	20
1914	Hassin Abdul	28	m.	Viola Wilson (AA)	21
1914	Frank Carey Osborn (AA)	32	m.	Nofossu Ella Abdeen*	20
1916	Nazaf Alli	31	m.	Juanita Marita Lambert (AA)	24
1917	Abdul Hamid	21	m.	Emma Fortineau (CR)	19
1918	Hassan Abdul	32	m.	Leonora Pavageau (AA)	24
1919	Joseph Anthony Jensen (AA)	23	m.	Hazel Adele Alley*	18
1920	Abdul Jalil	25	m.	Jeanne	18
1928	Monibur Rohfman	38	m.	Lillian	23

Abbreviations in parentheses indicate the best determination of each spouse's racial/ethnic ancestry. (CR) refers to Creoles of Color; (AA) refers to African Americans with roots outside of New Orleans; (CUB/CR) is used for the Santa Cruz sisters, who were of Cuban and Creole descent.

Source: City of New Orleans, Bureau of Health, *Certificates of Marriage,* Louisiana State Archives, Baton Rouge.
*Child of earlier interracial family.

women of color appear to have been varied in their nature, dynamics, and longevity. Alef Ally and Emily Lecompte never married but had two children together whom Alef continued to care for after Emily died. The evidence also suggests that Alef brought Emily and their first daughter, Mary Sadie, with him to visit India in 1896, a gesture that indicates a level of intimacy beyond mere convenience. Some marriages, however, were very short-lived. Moksad Ali's first marriage, to Ada Wallace, lasted less than three years; Aynuddin Mondul's marriage to Rita Albrier lasted less than four. In 1920, ten years after her marriage to Ensan Ally, Camille Bassett Ally was living with her mother, and Ensan was nowhere to be found. Ensan Ally's case was probably closer to the norm than Alef Ally's; that is, when members of the Hooghly network returned to India for extended periods of time—or for good—they left their American wives and mixed-race children behind in the United States. Nevertheless, there were other New Orleans marriages, like those of Sofur Ally and America Santa Cruz, Moksad Ali and Ella Blackman, and Abdul Hamid and Adele Fortineau, that lasted many years, until one or the other spouse passed away.[63]

The evidence does suggest a pattern: between 1900 and 1920, an increasing number of the Bengali peddlers' marriages were to women from Tremé, and by 1920, the majority of the Bengalis in the city had moved into the neighborhood's center (see Map 1). This shift may have occurred in a couple of different ways. The men may have begun selling their goods in the emerging commercial area along North Claiborne Avenue in the 1910s and as a result come in contact with more women from the neighborhood. Or those men who first married and partnered with local women from Tremé may have gained greater footing in the neighborhood over time, become more rooted there, and facilitated other Bengalis' shift to selling goods there. It is likely that the two phenomena were simultaneous—that each fed into the other. There were, however, other factors leading the Bengali peddlers further into black New Orleans. In addition to the events that were making the Hooghly network's continued global operation more complicated—the world war, the new U.S. immigration regime, continued competition from machine-made textile goods—New Orleans' residential and commercial segregation was becoming more pronounced. In the same years that the Bengalis were moving further into

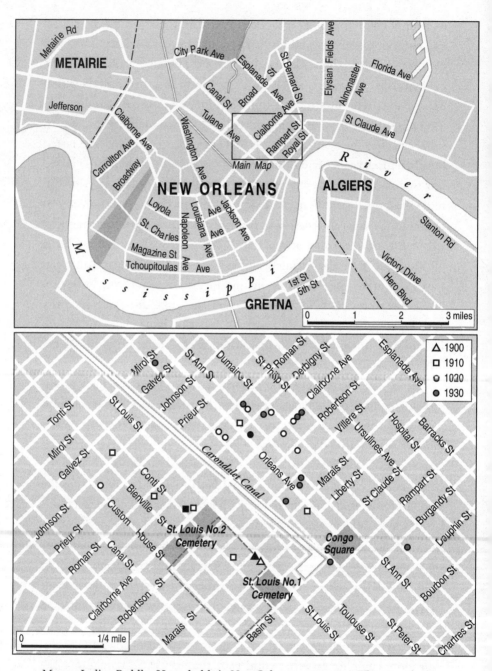

Map 1. Indian Peddler Households in New Orleans, 1900–1930. Those marked in black indicate addresses that were listed on two or more consecutive decennial censuses as homes of Indian peddlers: 1428 St. Louis Street (1900, 1910, 1920), 1711 Conti Steet (1910, 1920), and 1719 Orleans Avenue (1920, 1930). Source: USDC/BC, *Population Schedules* for New Orleans, LA (various, 1900–1930).

Tremé, the European immigrants who had been part of the neighbor-hood for at least two generations were moving farther out, relocating to new, predominantly white areas beyond the city's core.[64]

Just as significantly, New Orleans' shopping districts became racially segregated. Canal Street, the centerpiece of the city's modern new im-age, was increasingly off-limits to black New Orleanians as customers, workers, merchants, or businesspeople. As early as 1913, writes geogra-pher Michael Crutcher, "[an] advertisement for the Success Restaurant and Confections, located at 1428 Canal, boasted that the establishment was 'The Only Restaurant on Canal Street for the Accommodation of Colored People' . . . [and] African Americans were prohibited from working in visible positions alongside whites." The result was the growth of commercial and business districts elsewhere that catered specifically to African Americans; one such district formed in uptown, along South Rampart and Dryades Streets, and another, much larger one formed in Tremé along North Claiborne Avenue.[65]

Crutcher's description of the North Claiborne district sheds light on the role that members of the Hooghly network came to play in the Tremé community. The area, he argues, first formed around three key forms of black independent business: "insurance companies, funeral homes, and pharmacies." All of these were rooted in the nineteenth-century medi-cal, benevolent, and burial societies that downtown's poor and working-class communities of color developed for pooling resources to cover the costs of illnesses and deaths. In the early twentieth century, black fu-neral homes, pharmacies, and insurance companies came to play the roles that neighborhood associations had once done, offering services in which members of the community could pay small amounts over time to ensure that they could afford future medical and burial expenses. The growth of these businesses was also tied to New Orleans' segregation; according to Crutcher, white undertakers found it too expensive to maintain separate facilities for black customers and were willing to give up their black business, while white insurance companies were simply so arrogant and abusive toward their black customers that local black-owned companies successfully competed for and took over their busi-ness. Collectively, these three types of black enterprise became the an-chor for the new commercial district on North Claiborne Avenue. New Orleans' Bengali peddlers found their own niche on North Claiborne setting up businesses that followed the same logic as that of these enter-prises.[66] As their tourist-based trade in *chikan* embroidery began to wane and kin and co-villagers returned to India, a group of Bengali peddlers remained in Tremé, opened shops, and sold a mix of Indian embroidered and "fancy" goods and American ready-made clothes—suits, dresses, and women's silk undergarments—on installment to lo-cal black customers.[67]

These men were at the very heart of the Claiborne Avenue district in the 1920s and 1930s, where, in Crutcher's words, businesses "catered to the community's specific needs for food, clothing, and entertainment." Sofur Ally's "dry goods shop" was located just off the main strip of North Claiborne on St. Peter Street. Abdul Rahman ran a "ladies dress store" at 826 North Claiborne Avenue in the center of the district, where he em-ployed three other former members of the Hooghly network as salesmen. On the 900 block of North Claiborne, Towakkal Haldar and Abdul Jalil, both former itinerant peddlers, operated a "ready-to-wear store," at num-ber 914, and Abdul Rohim Surker, a younger member of the Hooghly network who had been living as one of Alef Ally's boarders in 1910, opened another shop selling women's dresses and "East India fancy needlework," at 928 North Claiborne. Abdul Hamid had a silk store nearby and later operated a soft-drink stand. These businesses were in the liveliest part of Claiborne Avenue's black commercial district. Abdul Rahman's shop was two doors down from one of Tremé's most important black-owned businesses, the Lebranche Pharmacy. Rahman's, Haldar's, and Hamid's shops were also all just half a block on either side of the corner of North Claiborne and Dumaine, a location that jazz musician Danny Barker described as "one of the most famous corners in New Orleans" in this period. The corner, which was home to "the Chattard Brothers' barber shop and Big Al Dennis' shoe shine stand," was a site where local men would gather to gossip and talk about boxing. "Around the corner on Dumaine," Barker remembered, "was Joe Sheep's . . . [which] had the best hot sausage sandwiches in town," and down the middle of North Claiborne was the shady "neutral ground," a strip of green space where neighborhood kids played and black "Mardi Gras clubs paraded." Sid-ney Bechet also remembered this stretch of North Claiborne Avenue as the main "meeting place" when local bands and clubs were parading:

"the people they'd be up by Claiborne Avenue and St. Philip. They knew you'd be coming there. You *had* to pass some time." The Bengalis were not the only Asian immigrants here. Next to the Chattards' barber shop, on Dumaine, was a Chinese laundry, and the Chattards employed a young man who was "half-Chinese, half-black," possibly the son of the laundry's proprietor.[68]

Because of their location and the business they conducted, the Bengalis would have become a well-known part of Tremé in this era. The nature of their layaway business would have meant that they developed long-term relationships with their customers, which would have likely required a sense of mutual trust. Unlike many other immigrant businesspeople operating in African American areas in this era, the men lived in the neighborhood where they sold their goods. As the U.S. operations of the Hooghly network eventually came to an end, these men remained anchored in Tremé, became woven into the fabric of the neighborhood: through their marriages to local women and relations with their families, through a web of relationships with customers, and ultimately through their children. Alef Ally had his two daughters; Moksad and Ella Ali had one daughter and six sons; Joseph and Viola Abdin had two children; Jainal and Florence Abdeen had four; Abdul and Adele Hamid had one; and Sofur and America Santa Cruz Ally had nine. While the fathers had been part of a network that stretched back to Calcutta and Hooghly, Bengal, their children were of black New Orleans.[69]

Traces of Lives

The stories of Sofur Ally, Jainal Abdeen, and Moksad Ali—three of the first Bengali peddlers to settle in New Orleans—provide a glimpse of the different trajectories that mixed families took over the early years of the twentieth century. Sofur Ally arrived in New Orleans in 1895. He had traveled from Calcutta to New York with twenty other peddlers that year, heading for the New Jersey beach resorts at the beginning of the summer. By the time of the 1900 U.S. Census, he was living in the joint household at 1420 St. Louis Street with Solomon Mondul, Eshrack Ali, Abdul Subham, and others on the edge of Storyville. Later that year, Sofur married America Santa Cruz, a Louisiana-born woman whose father was Afro-Cuban and mother was of local Creole and Cuban descent. By 1910, the couple had had three children, Abraham, Isaac, and Mohammed, and moved to a house at 1806 Orleans Avenue on a residential block not far from North Claiborne Avenue. Here, Sofur was listed as a "street peddler." Ten years later, the 1920 census found Sofur and America living on St. Peter Street on the northern edge of Tremé. They now had six children, including the youngest three, Abdul, Belle, and Fatima. Sofur Ally had naturalized and was listed as the proprietor of a dry-goods store. The Ally's eldest son, Abraham, now eighteen, was working as a delivery boy for his father.

By 1930, at the height of the Depression, Sofur and America Ally were living on St. Ann Street, back around the corner from where they had lived in 1910, just off Tremé's commercial thoroughfare. They had three more children, Hassan, Corinna, and Alema. In what is perhaps a sign of the family's financial struggles, the U.S. Census no longer listed Sofur as the proprietor of a shop; he had gone back to street peddling, and now three of Sofur and America's New Orleans–born, Bengali-Creole sons had joined their father and other remaining members of the Hooghly network in the trade: Abraham, twenty-eight, and Abdul, eighteen, were listed as peddlers of "retail perfumes," and Mohammed, twenty, as a peddler of "retail merchandise." Apparently pooling their resources with the family, these three adult sons lived with their parents and most of their siblings in a household of nine.[70]

Sofur Ally had at this point lived in New Orleans for thirty-five years and had been married to America for thirty. Over that time, he became increasingly rooted in his wife's native city and began to play a middleman role for other Indians. While Sofur Ally was one of the first Bengali peddlers to move into the commercial and cultural heart of Tremé, members of America's family had lived there for at least two generations. Sofur and America's home at 1806 Orleans Avenue became a destination for other peddlers from the Hooghly network making their way to New Orleans, including Fortik Sheik and Taslimuddin Mondul, who traveled from Calcutta in October 1908. According to his descendants, Sofur worked with local city officials and leaders in Tremé's predominantly black Catholic Church parish to build bridges between the men from Bengal and the local community and founded a "welcome center" for men arriving from the subcontinent, helping them adapt to New Orleans and likely taking them in for extended periods of time. After going through the process of opening a business, he helped other Bengalis with official paperwork, signing as a witness, for example, on the passport application of another Indian peddler, Roston Ally, in 1918. As for America, over the course of three federal censuses, she was consistently listed with the word "none" written in the "occupation" column—a notation that obscures the role that she played in easing Sofur Ally's own transition to New Orleans and providing a bridge between Sofur and other members of her family and community. It also belies the decades of domestic and reproductive labor she provided to sustain the Ally household as a family, as a functioning economic unit, and as place of residence and space of welcome for other men from the subcontinent. One descendant of Sofur and America Ally understatedly describes the couples' sons—Abraham, Isaac, Mohammed, and Abdul—as men who "expected a lot from their women," a trait they clearly learned from their father.[71]

The trajectory of Jainal Abdeen and his family demonstrates how uncertain life was for the working-class communities of color within which Indian Muslim migrants settled in turn-of-the-century New Orleans. Jainal came to the city around 1888. In the early years, he appears to have played some of the roles that Sofur Ally later came to play within what was then a quite small population of Bengalis in New Orleans. In the absence of an imam, Jainal performed the wedding rites when his friend Moksad Ali married Ada Wallace in 1892, being forever recorded on their wedding certificate as "Reverend" Jainal Abdeen. The next year, five years after his own arrival in New Orleans, Abdeen married Florence Perez, a local Creole woman. The 1900 U.S. Census, compiled in June, showed that Jainal and Florence Abdeen were living about two and a half miles northwest of Storyville, in a racially mixed working-class residential area of New Orleans' Third Ward. They had four children, Arthur, nine, Nofossur, six, Kahdidje, three, and Jainal Jr., seven months. Despite this listing in the census, however, records show that Jainal Abdeen Sr. had in fact died from tuberculosis six months earlier, in January of that year. His appearance in the census record suggests that Florence

Abdeen may have hidden his death from the census enumerator and from her landlord, a likely scenario if she feared being evicted and put out on the street with her four children. The Abdeens were absent from the next census, in 1910, when they were perhaps without a fixed address, and then in 1912, Jainal and Florence's daughter, Kahdidje, died at the age of fifteen from smallpox. Marriage records show that Kahdidje's sister, Nofossur, had married a man named John Martin in June 1909, when she would have just turned sixteen years old. This marriage did not last; in 1914, at the age of twenty, she was married a second time, to thirty-two-year-old Frank Osborn, an African American man who had come to New Orleans from Alabama.[72]

Frank and Nofossur were the only members of the extended Abdeen family to appear in the 1920 U.S. Census. At this time, their household seemed to have regained some footing: the young couple were living in a mixed working-class area of the Third Ward with their four children, whose ages ranged from eight months to seven years, as well as with a sister-in-law, an uncle, and a cousin from Frank's side of the family. There were three wage earners in the household, all part of the large black workforce on New Orleans' waterfront: Frank was working as a longshoreman, his uncle as a cotton "weigher," and his cousin as a dock laborer.[73] Four months after the census was enumerated, however, whatever stability this extended family had achieved began to unravel. In April of 1920, Nofossur died at the age of twenty-six, and four years later, her husband, Frank, died at the age of forty-three, leaving their four young children orphaned. By 1930, the only traceable members of this family line, begun by Jainal Abdeen and Florence Perez in 1893, were two of their orphaned grandchildren: Florence Osborn, now a fourteen-year-old girl and the adopted daughter of a sixty-eight-year-old Creole of Color woman, Wicker Aguerila, and Raymond Osborn, listed as an eleven-year-old boarder in a household consisting of a seventy-six-year-old street peddler, a fifty-two-year-old laundress, and a fifty-one-year-old ship's carpenter, on the edge of the former Storyville district.[74]

Moksad Ali settled in New Orleans around the same time as Jainal Abdeen and married a local African American woman, Ella Blackman. Ella's family had come to New Orleans from other parts of the South in the years before and after the Civil War. Her father's side came from

Tennessee, her mother's from Virginia. Moksad and Ella married in May 1895, when Ella was seven months pregnant with their first child, Monzure. On Monzure's July 12 birth certificate, Moksad Ali listed his occupation as "silk merchant" and penned a clear but labored signature in Roman/English cursive letters. Five years later, the 1900 U.S. Census recorded that Ella could read and write English but Moksad could only speak the language. At this time, Moksad and Ella were living in New Orleans' Third Ward as heads of a large, mixed, extended family. Their household included their first three children, Monzure, Kara-mouth, and Roheamon, Ella's younger sister Fanny, Fanny's husband, John Brooks—who was from Georgia, and was of Haitian and Jamaican descent—and Fannie and Ella's eighty-year-old grandmother, Hannah Judah. Judah was a freed slave from Virginia who had come to New Orleans in the 1840s and had supported Ella, Fanny, and their mother in earlier years, working as a housekeeper. It was a diverse family, spanning four generations with roots in multiple southern states, the Caribbean, and the Indian subcontinent, as well as in at least two religious traditions, and in experiences of both colonialism and slavery. Blurring these multiple histories, the census taker recorded everyone in the household as "Black" and did the same for the majority of residents on the same block, with the exception of Moksad and Ella's next-door neighbors, an Italian immigrant family with five Louisiana-born children. The adults in the immediate surroundings of the Ali-Judah-Brooks household worked different jobs on the lower rungs of the city's economy: Moksad Ali was a peddler of silks, his neighbor Antonio Borasso was also a peddler, of vegetables, his brother-in-law John was a day laborer, and among their African American neighbors were three cooks, two seamstresses, a midwife, a butcher, and four other day laborers.[75]

Moksad and Ella Ali's was one of several East Indian-African American families from New Orleans that took part in the Great Migration. These included Nazaf and Juanita Lambert Ali, who married in New Orleans in 1916 and migrated to Chicago around 1918, where Nazaf worked alongside the thousands of African American men from southern states in the city's stockyards. It also included John and Jennie Abdullah and Charles and Albertine Barber, married in New Orleans in 1911 and 1912, respectively, who were all living together in Los Angeles in 1920. Here, the two men—Indians who had changed their names after settling in the United States—found work that would have been familiar to Indian seamen of this era, firing the furnaces of "stationery engines," probably in a factory or railroad setting.[76]

In the case of Moksad Ali, he, his wife Ella, and their three children moved from New Orleans across the Mississippi River delta to nearby Hancock County, Mississippi, sometime around 1903. Here, Moksad and Ella had four more sons, Rostom, Abdeen, Bahadour, and Arfin. The 1910 U.S. Census recorded the Alis as a family of seven living in a predominantly black area of rural Mississippi, near the town of Waveland, and listed Moksad, a "merchant," as the only wage earner. Although Moksad and Ella had eight children over the course of fifteen years, there are indications that Moksad kept circulating through the peddler network over this period, leaving Ella on her own with their children for extended periods of time. In 1918, when Moksad Ali was afflicted with tuberculosis, he died not in Mississippi with Ella and his children, but at the boardinghouse at 1428 St. Louis Street in New Orleans. Sometime either just before or soon after Moksad Ali's death, Ella joined the northward flow of the Great Migration, bringing six of her children to New York City to move in with her sister Fannie in the Bronx.[77]

By the time they had reached their teens and early twenties, Moksad and Ella Ali's children Roheamon, Rostom, Abdeen, and Bahadour were all living at the edge of Harlem, and it was not long before all three moved the short distance across the Harlem River into a neighborhood beginning to crackle with possibility for people of color from all over the country and all over the world. Bahadour moved right into the center of Harlem's growing black community, to an apartment on West 133rd Street between Seventh and Lenox Avenues, and married a young woman who had also come from the South, twenty-four-year-old Margaret Carree, from Savannah, Georgia. On their marriage certificate, Bahadour gave his age as twenty-three and his occupation as "actor," and both Margaret and Bahadour were officially classified as "colored." Rostom moved just two blocks away to an apartment on 135th Street and married seventeen–year–old New York–born Pearl Pierce. Their 1924 marriage certificate also records husband and wife as "colored" and shows that Rostom had found a far less glamorous occupation than his younger brother; Rostom was working as a "fireman," which in this case most likely referred to the job of shoveling coal and stoking furnaces in the basement boiler rooms of hotels and other large buildings. Around this same time, sister Roheamon married Arthur Straker, a former boarder in their family's Bronx apartment. In 1930, the two were living on St. Nicholas Avenue between 151st and 152nd Streets. Their occupations were recorded as "housewife" and "laborer," respectively, and both were racially classified as "negro." Younger brother Bahadour was now living with them, along with a second wife, Thelma, a twenty-six-year-old African American actress from Texas.[78]

Bahadour's classification as an "actor" turned out to be an understatement; Moksad and Ella's fourth son would go on to have a long career in black show business. Sometime in the 1920s, Bahadour changed his name to Bardu. He began performing as a dancer on the era's black vaudeville circuit, partnering with a young woman, possibly his wife, Thelma, as the team "Baby and Bardu Ali" and with his younger brother, Abdeen, as "The Ali Brothers." In 1926, young Bardu came to the notice of the Baltimore *Afro-American*, which profiled him on their theatrical page, describing him as the son of a "Turkish" father and "Creole" mother—neither of which was quite true: "Ali is the son of Makrad [*sic*] Ali, a Turkish silk importer who came to America many years ago and engaged in the silk importing trade in New Orleans. The father married the now Elizabeth Ali, a Creole girl of that city and from the union have been born nine children, Abdeen, Bahadour, Mohammed, Aklemia, Roheanon [*sic*], Monseur [*sic*], and others with names just as unusual among the colored populace." Although the *Afro-American* set the Ali siblings apart in this way from "the colored populace," it simultaneously claimed them, reporting that Bardu was "proud of his Negro ancestry" and that his brothers "seem quite capable of taking care of themselves, they were raised in New York City and 'know their stuff' as the current parlance of the day expresses it."[79]

Bardu quickly made a name for himself in black theatrical and music circles as a suave and crowd-pleasing emcee and in the 1930s was recruited by one of Harlem's leading swing jazz bandleaders, Chick Webb. In this role, Bardu Ali is often credited with introducing Webb to a young Ella Fitzgerald and insisting he hire her as a singer for the Chick

Webb Orchestra, an event that launched her own long career. After Webb's death, Bardu Ali moved to Los Angeles, where he became an instrumental part of the city's Central Avenue music scene in the 1940s. Here he teamed up with the drummer Johnny Otis to open the Barrelhouse, the country's first nightclub devoted to the emerging style of rhythm and blues. Ali closed out his career in the 1970s as the business manager for the comedian Redd Foxx, at the time that Foxx was acting in his own situation comedy, *Sanford and Son*. By the time he died in 1982, Bardu Ali, one of the first children born of the migration of Bengali peddlers to New Orleans, had been involved in multiple phases in the development of twentieth-century black entertainment, from 1920s vaudeville to swing-era jazz, to rhythm and blues, to one of the first African American sitcoms on prime-time U.S. television.[80]

Embedded, Enmeshed

The lives of Bengali Muslim peddlers and their descendants became embedded within black communities and entwined with their histories. Over the decades that men from West Bengal lived, worked, and established roots in New Orleans, migrants from the subcontinent were barred from entering the United States as immigrants, from owning property, and from becoming citizens.[81] Over the same period, a broadly heterogeneous New Orleans was divided by both the laws and practices of Jim Crow into unequal "White" and "Negro" worlds. Although their livelihood still likely depended on crossing back and forth between these two worlds, "Negro" New Orleans provided a home for the handful of Bengali traders who chose to settle permanently in the United States and an anchor for the scores of others who continued to travel through the global and regional circuits of the Hooghly network to ply their trade. As a result, these Muslim migrants from colonized India made their lives with and among black southerners who had survived slavery or were the children of slaves, with members and descendants of a Creole community that was engaged in mounting legal and political challenges to Jim Crow, and with immigrants and children of immigrants who had escaped political upheavals in the Caribbean.

African American women were also deeply embedded in the structure of what might, at first glance, seem to be simply a Bengali peddler network. Because neither they nor the women who labored in Hooghly villages moved through its circuits, however, these women had a different experience of the *chikondar* network. The men were globally mobile. They encountered and interacted with multiple different people in varied spaces. They traveled together and built new connections to people in the places they worked. The lives of the women on either end of the network depended much more on their local circumstances; in the absence or loss of their own local support systems, the women's experience of this dynamic global network could be one of hardship and isolation. The women likely never met their counterparts on the other sides of the ocean; the two groups likely knew little of one another. But they shared the experience of being alone in the absence of their peddler husbands, just as they shared some of the network's greatest risks. These risks are brought home in the stories of two women—Jennat Bibi and Minnie Wade Mollah—captured in fragments of archival evidence from the 1910s and 1920s.

Jennat Bibi made her way into the archives in 1918 when she sent a letter to her husband, Roston Ally, urging him to return from New Jersey to his home village in Bengal. Roston Ally was one of the earliest members of the Hooghly network to come to the United States. By the time of Jennat Bibi's letter, he had naturalized and had been moving back and forth between Atlantic City and New Orleans, peddling goods, for twenty-three years. Roston submitted Jennat Bibi's letter to U.S. authorities as part of an application for a passport to return to India, stating that his wife had asked him to return to "settle his affairs." Roston Ally may have included Jennat Bibi's letter simply as part of a strategy to strengthen his case for traveling papers—conveying to U.S. authorities that he had a wife on the subcontinent who needed him to "come home" to address pressing family matters. In fact, other records indicate that Roston Ally had married and had a child with another woman in New Orleans after coming to the United States.

When Roston Ally arrived in the United States in June 1895 as part of a group of twenty Bengali peddlers on their way to Long Branch, New Jersey, it is likely that he had only recently been married to Jennat Bibi.

Records indicate that he had made only one trip back to India since that time, in 1905, after successfully gaining U.S. citizenship. Now, more than a decade after this visit, Jennat Bibi spoke of the growing difficulties she was experiencing, trying to fulfill her role looking after property that belonged to a husband she had barely known. For his part, Roston Ally had clearly abdicated his own role in maintaining a family economic unit across oceans and national borders. "It is two years since my health is broken," Jennat Bibi wrote. "My mother and father have both died. I have no relatives with whom to live. Unless you come, all of your lands and property will be taken away. . . . [Y]our cousin never gives me anything of the produce of your lands. . . . [Y]ou must come home immediately. And after you come home, we both could go to America to live, after selling all the lands and property."[82]

Jennat Bibi's letter suggests the tenuousness of the Hooghly network in terms of its ability to provide a secure life for the women on the Indian end of the circuit. At the same time, it points to the importance of the role these women played, maintaining a place for their husbands in their home villages while they were away for extended periods of time. There are different ways of reading her letter. It is possible that all of Jennat Bibi's support networks had indeed broken down in Roston Ally's absence, leaving her vulnerable to the machinations of his other male relatives. It is also possible that Jennat Bibi had come to fear that Roston Ally would never return (perhaps hearing from others in the extended kinship network that he had married another woman in the United States) and was using the potential loss of his property as an oppurtunity to get him to come back to his village. In either case, it was Jennat Bibi's inability to hold on to the land that was central to her plea for Roston Ally's return. She appears to have known that the land would most likely motivate him to travel back to India even after living in the United States for more than two decades. Tellingly, Roston Ally did travel to India soon after being granted a passport and, after presumably seeing to his land, returned to the United States in 1923 on his own, again leaving Jennat Bibi behind.[83]

Minnie Mollah, the wife of Bengali peddler Abdul Rub Mollah, was in French Lick, Indiana, far at the other end of the network. Minnie was the daughter of former slaves. Her father, recorded in the 1880 U.S.

Census as "Capt. Wade," was born in Tennessee in 1847. Her mother, Alice Wade, had been born into slavery in Mississippi in 1855 and had gained her freedom along with her mother and a younger sister at the end of the Civil War. By the time Minnie was born, in 1879, her parents were living in St. Louis, Missouri, where her father was working on one of the regional railroads. Minnie did not marry early, like many young women of her era did, but instead became a public school-teacher in St. Louis and continued to live with her mother and a stepfather into her early thirties. Around 1915, when she was thirty-six years old, Minnie married Abdul Rub Mollah, a peddler ten years younger than she who had come to the United States in 1909. Mollah had first worked in New Orleans, where he lived in a group household at 320 North Roman Street with Fazleh Rahman, Taslimuddin Mondul, and other senior members of the Hooghly network, and then made his way to St. Louis, where two other members of the network had begun peddling goods around 1910.[84]

It is unclear where and how they met, but soon after Minnie and Abdul Rub Mollah were married, the couple moved to French Lick, a predominantly white rural town two hundred miles due east of St. Louis. French Lick was a regional tourist destination; it was home to one of the Midwest's premiere health resorts, centered around the town's natural springs and springwater. Here, on Maple Street, the small town's main commercial thoroughfare, Abdul Rub Mollah opened an "Oriental Gift Shop" next to a clothing store and the offices of the local electric company. He also filed a Declaration of Intention to naturalize soon after his marriage to Minnie, and in 1918 he was granted U.S. citizenship in the Circuit Court of Orange County, Indiana. Almost immediately afterward, Mollah applied for a U.S. passport, and in 1919, he left Minnie in French Lick to tend the shop while he went back to India for two years. Although he returned to Indiana in 1921, Abdul Rub took at least two more two-year trips to India over the next fifteen years, presumably to send and bring back stock to sell in Mollah's Oriental Gift Shop, which Minnie was left to run in his absence.[85]

This arrangement would have been quite different from leaving Minnie to run a business in her hometown of St. Louis, where she had family and where there was a large African American community. Although

French Lick had a historical connection to the Underground Railroad, by the time Minnie and Abdul moved to the town, its black community consisted of a small number of service workers employed at the French Lick Springs resort hotel. This was not friendly territory for Minnie. Not only had the nineteenth-century founder of French Lick Springs been a Confederate sympathizer who had organized a white secret society to stop abolitionists' activities in his town, but by the 1920s and 1930s, the state of Indiana itself was home to the largest branch of the Ku Klux Klan outside the South. In this era, up to 30 percent of Indiana's adult white male population were in the Klan, and the organization's members were deeply integrated in local and state government.

Even in such a context, Minnie successfully ran Mollah's Oriental Gift Shop for more than twenty years, both with and without Abdul's help. It is now impossible to know what kind of community she built for herself in French Lick, and how she coped in potentially hostile surroundings. The 1920 U.S. Census, conducted when Abdul Rub Mollah was in India, provides one curious piece of information. Minnie Mollah appears to have been written into French Lick's enumeration by a local census taker, without being directly interviewed. The census taker recorded her place of birth as "India," her mother tongue as "Unknown," and her race as "White," presumably because she was assumed to be Indian. As the proprietor of the town's Oriental Gift Shop, Minnie Mollah appears to have been either unintentionally or intentionally passing as Indian.[86]

The lives of these women—Jennat Bibi in West Bengal and Minnie Wade Mollah in French Lick—were deeply entwined with the trade in Oriental goods that had been established when men from Hooghly and Calcutta began making trips to Atlantic City and New Orleans in the 1880s. Their labor contributed to one of the earliest manifestations on U.S. soil of what we would now refer to as the South Asian diaspora. The same can be said for numerous other women in Louisiana, South Carolina, New Jersey, and elsewhere: America Ally, Ella Ali, Celestine Gardner, Florence Abdeen, Adele Hamid, Aurelia Mondul, Olga Abdul, Anaise Ally, Juanita Alli, Leonora Hassan. In some cases these women were involved with Bengali peddlers for short periods of time, and in some cases for most of their adult lives. The work in which they engaged, however, provided rootedness to a trade network that stretched from villages in Hooghly through Calcutta, New Jersey, and the neighborhood of Tremé in New Orleans to multiple points in Central America and the U.S. South. The hundreds of Bengali Muslim peddlers who moved through the United States between 1885 and 1935 have remained lost to South Asian American history because these men did not immigrate and settle, did not "become American." Those few who did stay, and the descendants who remain in New Orleans and elsewhere, have been lost to South Asian American history because they integrated into black neighborhoods and communities. And the U.S. women of color who helped the Bengali peddlers put down roots, both temporary and permanent, the women with whom so many of the peddlers shared their lives, have remained doubly lost because they confound the set of ideas we employ when we construe this history simply as "South Asian."

CHAPTER 3

From Ships' Holds to Factory Floors

Recently, thirty-nine Indian workers of the Bethlehem Steel Company were arrested without warrants at the gates of the factories in Bethlehem, Pa. . . . and were taken to Ellis Island. . . . At this gate of America, they were lodged in filthy cells full of vermin. . . . [T]he British Captain of the *Lucerus* appeared on the scene and the Hindusthanees were summarily ordered to follow him to the boat, and there [return to] work as seamen. But when they came to know it was a British ship . . . they flatly refused to obey the order. Asked the reason, they said that to work on board a British ship was worse than working in "hell."

—Basanta Kumar Roy, *The Independent Hindusthan,* October 1920

O N A SUNDAY MORNING at the end of December 1907—a time of year when Hooghly's peddlers were selling their wares far from the cold Northeast—a different set of Indian Muslim men appeared on the waters of New York Harbor. Several small groups set out in rowboats from piers all over the area—from the east-side and west-side docks of Manhattan and from the waterfronts of Brooklyn, Staten Island, and New Jersey. In the brisk winter morning air, the men rowed south and eastward across New York's crowded, choppy waterways, weaving past freighters, tramps, schooners, and ferries toward Bush Docks in South Brooklyn. There, at the edge of the neighborhood now known as Sunset Park, they climbed onto the upper deck of a German steamship, the *Stolzenfels,* where they prepared to mark 23 Dhul Qi'dah, the martyrdom of Ali Raza, the eighth Imam of Shi'a Islam.[1] These men were sailors, or more precisely, maritime laborers; they were stokers, firemen, coal trimmers, and stewards from various steamships that were then in port. Over the course of the day, groups of these seamen—"lascars," as the British called them—kept turning up, in one small boat after another.[2] By the time of the ceremony and feast, fifty Indian Muslim men had arrived from every part of the New York waterfront and were gathered on the deck of the *Stolzenfels*. A crowd that included the ship's European officers, a press photographer, and a *New York Times* reporter stood at a distance to watch. The reporter's story appeared prominently on page 3 of the *Times* the next morning. His narration of the sailors' activities was a mixture of fantasy, news-speak, and condescension. "For hours before the beginning of the feast," the *Times'* reporter wrote:

> little Lascar sailors came. . . . The South Brooklyn pier at the foot of Forty-second Street was the Mecca toward which all the Lascars headed. . . . [The] little brown sailors squatted on the forward deck of the German freighter, and the sheep's head was pointed to the sun. It was then massaged by one of the Lascars until those who viewed the ceremony from the bridge felt sure that the sheep was hypnotized. Quick as a wink the animal was dispatched, and before any of the flesh was touched, every drop of blood in the animal had been allowed to trickle into a pan on the deck . . . Nor was a knife used in skinning the animal. The Lascar butcher did that with his thumb so skillfully and in such a short time that a stockyard butcher could not have beaten him. While this was going on, the "band" played the sacred music incidental to the Feast of the Malah [*sic*]. The "music" sounded, to American ears, much like that heard at Coney Island side-shows.[3]

This was just one of a number of stories that appeared in U.S. newspapers at the turn of the twentieth century describing the arrival of "strange" and "curious" "Hindoo" sailors in port cities along the Atlantic and Gulf coasts. Writing from the marginal spaces of the United States' docklands and waterfronts in New York, Philadelphia, Baltimore, and Galveston, reporters ushered lascars onto the terrain of the U.S. popular imagination.

Most of these writers fell back on familiar tropes, describing the Indian seamen in much the same way they wrote about the "Oriental" magicians and performers who had become a staple of the era's circuses and exhibitions. Some reporters chose to focus on high-seas adventures: the *New York Daily Tribune* reported on a live Punjab goat that ran amok on a transatlantic voyage and butted a lascar seaman overboard. The *New York Times* described a steamship that arrived in Philadelphia with a "choice cargo of tales from the Far East"; the ship's captain had wrestled a cobra for two hours after it slipped on deck in Calcutta, and a lascar seaman "died of fright" after meteors fell alongside the ship while it sailed through the Mediterranean Sea. Most American reporters, however, chose to focus on the incongruity of Indian Muslim seamen in local waterfront areas and attempted to describe the "queer customs" these men brought with them: daily prayer observances, dietary strictures, religious celebrations, burial practices. When two British ships carrying 125 Indian crew members docked in the port of Galveston, Texas, the *Dallas Morning News* launched a sensational exploration of the lascars' diet, eating habits, and religious beliefs. "One thing the Lascars will not tolerate is pork," the paper declared. "They are more afraid of pork than a woman is of a mouse. It is believed not only to contaminate the body, but also the soul, as the swine is thought to be an agent of their devil."[4]

To American readers at the turn of the century, Indian seamen might as well have been fictional characters; judging by the press reports of the day, they were equal parts exotic and peculiar, inscrutable and fanatical, ridiculous and treacherous. At the same time, these articles offer us a glimpse into the lives that this population of workers from the subcontinent were fashioning for themselves as they spent days, weeks, and months in U.S. ports, waiting for their ships to unload, reload, and set back out to sea. Most poignant are the accounts of Indian seamen who were faced with burying comrades who had died during their ships' voyages. Even the most voyeuristic descriptions of these moments hint at the care the seamen took to prepare their coworkers' bodies in accordance with Muslim practice and to maintain the privacy and dignity of burial rites in unfamiliar and unsympathetic surroundings. When a Galveston newsman reported on a funeral that visiting Indian seamen held for a member of their crew, he recounted a set of deliberate steps these men took to guard and prepare their friend's body and ensure his proper placement in a grave facing Mecca. Another account focusing on the death of an Indian steamship cook described a "weird ceremony" at New York's Bellevue Hospital in which "each of the friends of the deceased removed his shoes and stockings and taking a pail of water, sat down on the curb outside the Morgue door and bathed his feet." Even the *New York Times'* 1907 account of the "Feast of the Malah," with its demeaning descriptions of "little brown men" performing like a "Coney Island side-show," revealed that Indian seamen were organized and determined enough to secure the use of the upper deck of the *Stolzenfels* for their observances and then to communicate and coordinate among Muslim crew members on multiple ships spread across several miles of New York waterfront.

In the years that the U.S. operations of the Hooghly peddler network were slowing down, Indian seamen were arriving in Atlantic ports in increasing numbers. New York, Baltimore, and Philadelphia were at the edge of a maritime world that stretched far beyond the comprehension of local American newsmen. The events that had compelled and enabled Hooghly's peddlers of silks to cross oceans—the expansion of the British Empire, the opening of the Suez Canal, the arrival of steam power, and the growth and acceleration of world travel and trade—had also given rise to a new industrial workforce on the subcontinent, one that was semicaptive and hyperexploited but globally mobile. In the early decades of the twentieth century, Indians comprised almost one-quarter of the laborers on British merchant vessels. They moved through the circuits of British seaborne trade and became a regular presence in and around port cities from Asia to the Middle East to Britain and beyond. The majority of these men came from rural areas, many from small-holding farming families that were under pressure due to colonial taxation policies. In their villages and on the waterfronts of Calcutta and Bombay, there were thousands of other men like them, waiting for months or even years to find work on outgoing ships. They had to take out loans to pay middlemen in order to get hired and then, at sea, they faced indenture-like contracts and brutal conditions at the hands of British masters.[5] Even in this setting, however, Indian seamen developed strategies to challenge the industry's inequities and improve their lives, from mutiny to black marketeering to jumping ship in ports overseas.

By the 1910s, tens of thousands of these Indian seamen were working globally on British ships, thousands were moving into and out of the Port of New York each year, and hundreds were successfully jumping ship and disappearing into the crowded waterfronts of Manhattan, Brooklyn, and Staten Island.[6] Some deserted in order to find better work and wages on other outgoing ships; others did so to find jobs in factories and restaurants onshore. They stayed in the United States for months or years at a time, maintaining clandestine networks in neighborhoods that stretched from the Tenderloin and the Lower East Side in Manhattan to Black Bottom and Paradise Valley in Detroit to the Pennsylvania Avenue district in West Baltimore. Their journey to the United States was remarkable because of the arduousness of the labor they had to perform—many shoveling coal and firing furnaces in the bellies of steamships on and off shift continuously for more than eighty hours a week—and the policing and ill treatment they faced from their British captains and officers on board.[7] After 1917, those who reached the United States also faced a harsh new immigration regime, one that barred their entry into the country on explicitly racial grounds. Nevertheless, hundreds of seamen from the subcontinent were left in port or escaped British ships in search of higher wages and better lives onshore in the United States.[8] As was the case with Hooghly's peddlers, they did so through a combination of ingenuity, cooperation, and coordination, building networks of their kin and countrymen onshore and at sea. Indian seamen, ex-seamen, and sympathizers passed information to one another, helped one another jump ship, and found one another work, often far from their ports of desertion across the industrial belt of the U.S. Midwest.[9] They first deserted in large numbers during World War I, when there was a demand for their labor in U.S. munitions, shipbuilding, and steel factories. But once they had established their networks, Indian seamen branched out to a wide range of onshore labor, working as cooks, dishwashers, doormen, and elevator operators in New York City, silk dyers in Patterson, New Jersey, and assembly-line workers in the auto industry in Detroit.

Thirty Feet below the Sea

The most common images of merchant seamen tend to be drawn from the seventeenth and eighteenth centuries, from the days in which ships were crafted out of wood and canvas and the crews that sailed them were a breed apart, drawn from all over the world, but more connected to the sea than to any particular place on land. In novels, comic books, and films, this world of whalers, adventurers, pirates, maroons, and mutineers has defined the popular understanding of maritime labor. In the era of sailing ships, crews were indeed often mixed; they drew members as they moved from port to port, from Liverpool to Buenos Aires to Shanghai. The division of power between a ship's officers and its crew was stark, but the crew members themselves were on a relatively even plane; while they played different roles, each sailor had to have a core set of skills, and all the members of a crew—whether European, Asian, or African in origin—had to work together to navigate difficult stretches of ocean and get through stormy seas. These crew members also shared similarly harsh conditions of labor. As historians Peter Linebaugh and Marcus Rediker have put it, the sailing ship, "provided a setting in which large numbers of workers cooperated on complex and synchronized tasks, under slavish, hierarchical discipline." Out of this context grew a seafaring underclass made up of sailors and pirates who had been brought together across differences of color, ethnicity, and language by common experiences of labor and subjection. The sailing ship "became . . . a meeting place where various traditions were jammed together in a forcing house of internationalism." Some of the most powerful images of Asian and African seamen—from Herman Melville's *Moby Dick* to Amitav Ghosh's *Sea of Poppies*—derive from this period, in which sailors of color were part of a large, broadly heterogeneous, international workforce.[10]

With the coming of steam power in the latter half of the nineteenth century, however, the nature and structure of maritime labor changed dramatically. If the wind-powered sailing ship could be described as a "prototype of the factory," the steamship was a factory fully formed.[11] The move to steam power created, in one historian's words, "totally new categories of labor."[12] Below deck, coal passers wheeled masses of coal from dark, cavernous storage bunkers to the ship's engine rooms; coal trimmers hammered away at these pieces to prepare them for the fire and then wheeled them to the mouths of the furnaces; firemen shoveled the coal into the fiery furnaces; stokers stood at the furnace doors, working the fires to keep them burning at optimum heat; and oilers and greasers moved from one part of the engine to another to keep the machinery functioning at maximum efficiency.[13] This was industrial labor afloat, and some of the worst industrial labor of the era, with workers toiling in the depths of each steamship, as one Indian seaman described it, "thirty feet below the surface of the sea with no fresh air or daylight."[14] By the turn of the twentieth century, these grueling engine-room jobs accounted for nearly half the positions on merchant ships, but in Britain, white seamen shunned engine-room labor and the "coolies" brought in to perform it; this was not the work of true sailors, they claimed, of skilled men of the sea.[15]

The transition from sail to steam threatened British shipping companies' dominance of seaborne trade. Other European nations now competed with Britain to build bigger and faster steamships, and British seamen successfully organized unions, developed allies in Parliament, and gained concessions on wages and working conditions. The British shipping industry responded by turning to the colonies as a source of cheaper and more controllable labor.[16] Huge pools of workers were available to them in India, Egypt, Yemen, Malaysia, Somalia, and elsewhere, and it was here that they came to hire crews to work the engine rooms of their vessels and, ultimately, to cook in the ships' kitchens, serve in the cabins and mess halls, and clean the rooms and decks.[17] By the turn of the century, Indians came to comprise the single largest group of colonial laborers working on British steamships; tens of thousands were hired out of the subcontinent's ports. The largest number of these men were Bengalis engaged from their home port of Calcutta. They were predominantly Muslims who hailed from villages in a few key regions, especially Sylhet, Noakhali, and Chittagong. Thousands of other steamship workers were engaged out of the port of Bombay where the seafaring population included men from Punjab, Kashmir, the Northwest Frontier, and Goa, while smaller numbers of men were hired in other ports, such as Karachi and Colombo.[18] Although British shipping companies hired from all these groups and many others across the colonies, they divided their crews by language and region to minimize the likelihood of workers banding together against their white officers: on a large steamship, the engine crew might all be from one part of the world or the subcontinent, the saloon crew from another, and the deck crew from another.[19] As seafaring became industrialized, British ships were transformed from sites of heterogeneity and intermingling into factorylike workplaces, with groups of laborers sharply divided along lines of race, ethnicity, language, and colonial subjecthood.

While the subcontinent had long traditions of seafaring, most Indian seamen of this era were from areas newly incorporated as supply centers for maritime labor. They came from villages that were often far inland from the main colonial ports of Calcutta and Bombay, where farming had been the main means of livelihood for generations.[20] Their entry into the maritime trade was tied to a larger restructuring of the Indian economy under British colonial rule. Over the course of the nineteenth century, the British imposed private property and a new regime of taxation, which, coupled with recurring instances of drought and famine, threw members of the peasantry off their lands and spurred large-scale internal and external migrations.[21] Hundreds of thousands of the poor, landless, indebted, and displaced migrated to the major colonial cities of Calcutta, Bombay, and Madras. In 1911, almost two thirds of Calcutta's population of 900,000 were in-migrants. Others—more than three-quarters of a million—migrated across Northern India to work on Assam's tea plantations or in mines in West Bengal, while some of the poorest were recruited into indentured labor on plantations in the Caribbean, Fiji, Ceylon, Malaya, and Mauritius.[22]

The men who made their way to the docks of Calcutta and Bombay and eventually traveled across oceans to the waterfronts of London, Liverpool, New York, and Baltimore were, by and large, not the worst off of the uprooted, even if they became one of the most exploited groups of laborers on British steamships. Those who came from smallholding farming families were still working the land but struggling under the colonial regime to hold onto the property they owned.[23] Land taxes under the British were not only high, but also inflexible to yearly fluctuations in crop yield. Smallholders had to pay their taxes annually in full, even in the years that floods or droughts wiped out their crops. In these bad years, farmers borrowed from or mortgaged portions of their land to local moneylenders in order to pay their taxes. In good years, they often borrowed as well, to expand or improve their holdings. Over time, more and more smallholders defaulted on loans and had to give up their property, piece by piece, to cover their debt. Farming families saw their holdings dwindle as money lenders, larger property owners, and the British colonial state came to control more and more of the land that once supported them.[24] According to historian Ravi Ahuja, it was "often the younger sons" of such families who were drawn into the maritime trade via networks of recruitment that stretched from Calcutta inland to rural districts like Sylhet, and from Bombay all the way into Punjab, Kashmir, and the Northwest Frontier.[25] They entered the trade hoping to make enough money as coal-passers, firemen, cooks, and stewards to bring back to their home villages, repay their families' debts, and keep what remaining farmland they had from slipping into the hands of the money-lenders. In this sense, Ahuja and others have argued, the changes the British introduced on the sea were inseparable from those they wrought on land; the imposition of a colonial economy both unmoored these young men and redirected their labor. They moved from farms and villages to the industrial furnace rooms, coal bunkers, kitchens, and pantries of steamships that hauled away cotton, jute, tea, and other goods from the colony to the mother country and beyond.[26]

By the early twentieth century, the waterfronts of Calcutta and Bombay had swelled with such men, and the future that awaited them in the maritime trade was not an easy one. Faced with the combined power of shipping companies and the British colonial state, they entered the industry at a huge structural disadvantage. In the 1890s, British maritime unions won a set of victories that required their employers to use a standard contract (British, or European, articles of engagement) that specified wages; guaranteed standards for hours, working conditions, food, and sleeping quarters; and provided compensation for work-related injuries. But the shipping industry exacted a key concession: workers hired out of Indian ports were not given the same protections and guarantees as their European counterparts. Indian workers were engaged on lascar, or Asiatic, articles—a form of agreement which was closer to indenture than to a contract between free parties. Under this two-tiered system of seamen's articles, British companies could hire Indian steamship workers at wages four to six times lower than those commanded by British seamen. They could provide lascars with food of lesser quality and quantity and cram them into bunks that were barely larger than coffins. There was no guaranteed compensation for Indian seamen if they were injured or for their families if they were killed on the job. When they signed on to a ship under Asiatic articles, these men were bound to work for the shipping company not just for the duration of one journey, but for a contracted period of one or two years. During that time, the shipping company could pass them from ship to ship; the Indian men had no right to leave their employment, no matter what the circumstances or conditions, until their contract was over. And when the contract *was* over, shipping companies were required to return lascars to the subcontinent, ensuring that they could not access the rights and wages available to seamen who were hired out of British and other European ports.[27]

When a prospective seaman traveled from his home village to the port of Calcutta or Bombay, he thus found a system that was structured against him in multiple ways. But the contracts that would define his working life were only part of this system. There were up to three times as many workers as there were jobs on outgoing ships—a situation that helped shipowners keep Indian workers "docile" and wages low.[28] The British colonial government banned the formation of labor unions on the subcontinent, hampering Indian maritime workers' efforts to address their lot collectively well into the 1920s.[29] Prospective seamen not only faced months of waiting, searching, and competing to get signed on to ships, but also had to navigate an arena of middlemen that the authorities did little to regulate. There were the *ghat serangs,* men who ran dockside boardinghouses and acted as employment brokers for British shipping companies, and the *serangs,* men who assembled outgoing crews, signed these crews on to a ship, and then managed them on board for the duration of each contract.[30] Individual seamen had to make payments to *serangs* in order get onto their crews, and when they returned to their home port at the end of a journey, they also had to pay off their debts to the *ghat serangs* who had provided them room and board during the long periods they were unemployed.[31]

Accounting for a year's pay in the 1910s, one Indian seaman wrote: "In addition to the two months' wages that would go towards the Sarong's bribe and various other collections, at least one month's pay would be needed for working clothes . . . and other necessities. Two months' earnings were required for the [boardinghouse keeper] at whose home one lived on credit while searching for a job, and it took almost one month's pay to cover train fare and other traveling expenses in returning to one's village. . . . Thus, toiling under degrading and unhealthy conditions for an entire year, the best that one could hope for would be to have sixty or seventy rupees left over." Given what was at stake, however, most seamen had little choice but to work within the system's constraints. The sixty or seventy rupees, "would be most welcome as it helped pay back the user-er's loan. . . . This saved a few acres of land from being expropriated by moneylenders or the state."[32]

For the thousands of Indian seamen who successfully secured work on outgoing ships, things were hardly better at sea. Engine-room labor was particularly brutal. Recalling his experiences on a series of voyages outward from his home port of Bombay, Dada Amir Haider Khan writes: "Working in the coal bunkers through the Red Sea was [s]uch hell that the firemen had to pour buckets of sea water over their bodies before opening the furnace door to throw coal inside, or rake the fire. By the time they finished a round, their overalls would already be dry. Immediately they would douse themselves again with sea water. . . . Still, some firemen, scorched and asphyxiated, had to be carried to the decks by their workmates with others taking their places."[33] Such work took a harsh toll, both mentally and physically, on colonial laborers. At the turn of the century, British and American newspapers were littered with stories of "lascar" sailors "going mad" after hours in the stokehold. In one instance, the *New York Times* recorded the effects of a heat wave on two workers of the SS *Haleric* as it passed between Calcutta and Colombo. The heat had driven one man "crazy" and sent the other overboard. "The crazed man," wrote the *Times*, "was at work in the boiler room at a time when the deck temperature was 108, [and] complained of feeling dizzy. He came up on deck and began to circle crazily. Just as he started to . . . lunge at one of the [white] engineers who had followed him, he was seized" and "pinned to the deck by British officers." The second man "staggered to the ship's side and was in the water before his absence was noted. . . . Though the ship circled for two hours, he was never found."[34] Tragically, this seaman was not alone in his death; as Ahuja has noted, British colonial records show "a remarkable recurrence of the theme of lascar suicides, especially among firemen," from the turn of the century through the 1930s.[35]

British shipping companies justified their exploitation of Indian workers with a racial mythology that portrayed men from the colonies as inferior to Europeans. Indian men were "weaker," "less capable" sailors; the companies thus claimed they had to hire several Indians, at lower wages, to do the work of a single European. Indian men were also more "suited" to the heat of the boiler room (because they were accustomed to a "tropical" climate) or to servile and domestic tasks above deck. These ideas were reinforced by the attitudes of white British seamen. Although firing and stoking a ship's furnaces and monitoring, regulating, and maintaining the steam in its boilers required a combination of strength, stamina, and skill, this work was derided by British sailors as "not seafaring . . . it is arduous, dirty and hot . . . with no seagoing traditions to support it"—and thus fit only for lesser workers. The labor of those in the saloon and catering crews was simply "dismissed as 'women's work.'"[36] The prevalence of illnesses such as tuberculosis, pneumonia, ulcers, and fevers among Indian sailors was also explained in racialized and gendered terms, "attributed to their [natural] lack of stamina not to their inferior rations or their appalling conditions of service."[37] "In the shipboard mythology," writes historian Rozina Visram, "lascars became inferior, lacking in masculinity, self-reliance and initiative . . . [and] could [only] make excellent seamen . . . when led by European officers."[38] In fact the one-sidedness of Asiatic articles left British officers free to work their Indian crews relentlessly. Ships' masters wielded "practically unlimited control over the person of the lascar, who risked being charged with breach of contract if he refused to be at the disposal of the shipmaster at any time, either when the ship was at sea or when it lay in port."[39]

Still, Indian seamen consistently pushed at the boundaries of the maritime system. As they moved through the circuits of imperial trade, a significant number of these men succeeded in outwitting the shipping companies and their officers and used the industry to expand their opportunities beyond the subcontinent. They moved from port to port, shifted back and forth between maritime and onshore work, and pursued better wages and working conditions in countries far from their homes.[40] There were many ways they could make use of their mobility once at sea. In order to supplement their meager wages, seamen commonly engaged in small-scale trade—or in the words of one sailor, "buying cheap" in one location and "selling dear" in another. This kind of activity did not always require seamen to travel great distances. One group of Indian seamen who were docked near the port of Basra in the midst of the First World War made money catering to the basic needs of soldiers passing by on their way to the battlefront. The seamen

> would obtain leave from the[ir *serang*] in exchange for a share in the profits, engage small row boats, and . . . purchase a variety of fruits such as grapes, oranges . . . raisins, dates, and pomegranates [from fruit sellers onshore]. After loading the local fare into small boats, they would station themselves in the middle of the river and greet [the] incoming troop ships that would arrive daily in Basra loaded with soldiers from India and other theatres of the war. These men could often not stomach the tasteless food provided aboard their ships or would be suffering from sea sickness. They were happy to pay whatever they had for these fresh fruits.[41]

In the 1920s, British authorities were alarmed by another trade that Indian seamen had developed that was global in its scope and threatening in its implications. In a letter to the Intelligence Bureau of the British colonial government, Bombay's commissioner of police claimed that Indian seamen "import cocaine from Kobe, Japan, and sell at a profit in Bombay. With the proceeds, drugs, mostly *charas* [hashish], are bought in Bombay and taken to Port Said [in] Egypt where they are sold at a profit; with the proceeds of these sales, arms are bought in Marseilles and taken to China, where their disposal is not so difficult and likewise profitable."[42] A little more than a decade later, during the Second World War, Indian seamen in British ports took advantage of the local system of ration coupons; they "used to go to the ships—[in] Tilbury, Liverpool,

Cardiff—and buy coupons from [departing] sailors—they didn't need them [anymore]—and then get sweets, chocolates, clothes, and sell them around the factories [on the] black market."[43]

On board ship, Indian seamen engaged in everything from petty theft to mutiny. Dada Khan describes instances in which he and his coworkers stole goods from their ships' storeroom either to trade for fish and meat in different ports or simply to eat when their officers were depriving them of sufficient food.[44] On one voyage, a sixteen-year-old Khan crawled through an air shaft in his ship's storage area to steal onions and potatoes. A shipmate then cooked them up with ghee and spices to feed the Indian crew.[45] Seamen were not always so nonconfrontational, however. In 1890, the *New York Times* described the case of a British ship, manned by a "mixed" crew, whose Indian cook unilaterally stopped working two days after the ship left Dundee, Scotland. "The Captain sent for him," the ship's first mate told the *Times*, and two hours later, the captain was found stabbed to death, slumped in a pool of his own blood, with the cook reportedly sitting nearby with a knife in his hand, "crouched like some wild animal . . . upon a large flower pot of geraniums which he had ruthlessly crushed beneath him."[46] An article from 1913 tells a similar story, of "four Hindu seamen . . . of the Mohammedan faith . . . [who were] charged with killing . . . an assistant engineer on the British steamship SS *Kundia*,"[47] and a story from 1930 describes a "riot" on board the SS *Irisbank,* in which "Lascar stokers and oilers of the vessel's crew attacked their superiors with crowbars, shovels and belaying pins . . . shortly before the ship was to have sailed."[48] While American newspapers described the sailors' actions as "murders" and "riots" and the men involved were described as "irrational" and "deranged," such events were clearly rational, if desperate, responses to the severe conditions and daily indignities these men faced on board.

Desertion was another step that Indian steamship workers took in the face of such conditions; it was at once an assertion of agency, a reassertion of humanity, and a denial of labor to those who would relentlessly exploit it. In her *Asians in Britain: 400 Years of History,* Rozina Visram tells the story of a crew of Indian Muslim seamen who found themselves at the mercy of a violently sadistic ship's officer. "They had been 'hung up with weights tied to their feet', flogged with a rope and forced to eat pork.

The[n] . . . the tail of the pig had been 'rammed' into their mouths and the entrails twisted around their necks." Upon arrival in London, the entire ship's crew deserted en masse. "Desertion," writes Visram, "was . . . akin to an act of resistance."[49] At the same time, Visram and other historians of the era have made clear that "jumping ship" was not an easy matter, nor was it simply a spontaneous act that seamen undertook to escape the harrowing conditions on specific vessels. It was one of a larger set of strategies that Indian and other colonial maritime workers developed in order to gain greater control of their lives and labor, particularly once their ships had reached British ports, where they could assert a set of rights as subjects of the Empire. In some instances, men jumped ship in order to work at higher-paying factory or service jobs in British cities and then returned to the maritime trade after a stretch of months or years. For other colonial seamen, desertion was a means of gaining higher-paid maritime work; after deserting in port cities like London, Cardiff, Liverpool, and Glasgow, they used their status as British subjects to establish residency in the United Kingdom and then reentered the industry on British rather than lascar articles. This allowed them to access the higher wages and greater protections that European articles guaranteed.[50] Still other men from the colonies went a step further, successfully mobilizing their status as subjects of the Crown to remain in Britain—to live and work there for good.[51] As G. Balachandran has put it, deserting seamen were able to turn the British steamship to their own ends, to give "an instrument of control . . . the sharp edge of dissent."[52]

Shipping companies watched their workers closely and policed their movements while in port, but over time, hundreds of Indian, Arab, African, and Chinese seamen successfully jumped ship, and distinct multi-ethnic enclaves began to develop in many of Britain's major port cities. Some of the earliest men to desert successfully in the 1890s and early 1900s married local working-class British women and, with their help, opened boardinghouses, restaurants, and cafés.[53] This meant that by the time of the First World War, when tens of thousands of Indian seamen were sailing into and out of British ports on merchant and supply ships, these men could access established networks of local men and women who would help them jump ship and find work onshore.[54] During the war, jobs were also plentiful. Indian men found more opportunities to sign on to ships in British ports at British wages, and Indian and other colonial workers were in great demand onshore in steel and munitions factories, sugar refineries, and shipbuilding firms. Shipping companies and onshore industries now openly competed for Indian workers, with the former accusing the latter of "entic[ing] sailors away by offering higher wages than under ships' articles."[55]

At the end of the First World War, dockside settlements of working-class Indian, African, Arab, and other Asian men numbered in the hundreds and, in larger ports like Cardiff and London, in the thousands.[56] Indian seamen sailing into Britain, however, found a less welcoming and hospitable environment. When thousands of white British seamen returned from their war service and sought to reenter the maritime trade, British port cities experienced a wave of riots aimed at driving out "coloured seamen." Afterward, the British government launched a series of its own efforts, as historian Laura Tabili puts it, "to uproot Black residents from Britain by persuasion or compulsion."[57] African, Arab, and Asian residents of dockside settlements were now required to "produce documentary proof of British nationality" and to register as aliens and faced heightened policing and harassment.[58] In this context, local networks became the key to the survival of Indian seamen and ex-seamen in Britain. Networks of boardinghouses, private homes, restaurants, and work sites not only provided escaped seamen with places to live and work under the radar of local authorities, but also enabled the circulation of people, knowledge, and information from one locality to another and back out into maritime circuits that stretched all the way to the subcontinent.[59]

At the Nation's Edge

In recent years, British historians, ethnographers, and genealogists have built an increasingly detailed picture of the Indian men who jumped ship in Britain and the communities they formed onshore in places like East London, South Shield, Cardiff, and Liverpool—some of the first South Asian communities in all of Europe. It is clear that many Indian seamen chose to jump ship in British ports because of the colonial relationship between Britain and India—because Indians could make claims to

live and work in the United Kingdom that they could not make elsewhere. But by the early twentieth century, Indian seamen were traveling
to ports all over the world, including the United States. In the years that
newsmen in Galveston, Baltimore, Philadelphia, and New York were
providing American readers with descriptions of the "queer customs" of
"Hindoo seamen," these seafarers were bringing descriptions of Galveston, Baltimore, Philadelphia, and New York back to their families and
fellow workers on the subcontinent. This information appears to have
included news of the opportunities that were available in U.S. port and
factory towns for those seamen who could successfully jump ship. It also
likely included details about the laws pertaining to Asian immigrants
and seamen, the practices of shipping companies and U.S. authorities to
prevent desertion, the strategies that seamen had developed to outwit
the shipping companies and the authorities, and the names and locations
of people onshore who could help deserting seamen find lodging and
work.

Over time, a seaman departing from Calcutta or Bombay with hopes
of finding work elsewhere engaged in a complex calculus about where,
when, and how to jump ship, and U.S. ports were part of the equation.
This was the case, for example, with Shah Abdul Majid Qureshi, a seaman from Sylhet, East Bengal, who settled in London only after trying
and failing to jump ship in New York in 1935.[60] In an interview with
ethnographer Caroline Adams in the 1980s, Qureshi described both
Britain and the United States as destinations that his contemporaries
sought to reach through the maritime trade; these were places that
many of them had in mind for desertion, even before they left the subcontinent. In Qureshi's case, it was the success of co-villagers who had
jumped ship in the United States that drew him into maritime work in
the first place: "My aim was to get a job in the sea and either go to
America or to England. England was not much attraction to me—
America, at that time America was the attraction, because . . . [t]hose
who managed to escape and somehow settle in America, they always
used to send [home] big money orders. Some of them came back [to the
village] and that gave me the idea that we were poor, down and out . . .
if I could manage to go to America, somehow or other I could earn
enough money—that was my ambition."[61] Qureshi did sign on to a ship

that was bound for the United States, but because he was literate and had more education than his shipmates, his British officers considered him a risk, denied him shore leave in New York, and closely watched him for the days they were in port. But hundreds of men succeeded where Qureshi failed, both before and after him.

The barriers these men faced were considerable. Both British and U.S. maritime unions wanted to keep low-wage Indian seamen out of their members' home ports and off their primary sea routes, and both fought hard to pass laws and influence public opinion to achieve their goals. British seamen's organizations won an early victory when they secured the inclusion of the "lascar line" provision in the 1894 Merchant Shipping Act. This provision forbade British steamship companies from employing Indian workers on voyages to Atlantic ports above 38 degrees north latitude—Baltimore, Philadelphia, New York, and Boston—between October and March of every year. The unions drew on the racial mythology surrounding Indian seamen to justify this clause, arguing that the warm-blooded Indians could not withstand the work on these routes during the "winter months" and asserting that the provision would protect them from illness. In fact, the British unions sought to discourage the hiring of Indian workers on U.S.-bound ships entirely and to make the North Atlantic routes the exclusive province of white seamen—at least for six months of each year.[62] To comply with the provision, British shipping companies with Indian crew members would have to drop these men off in the southern port of Newport News, Virginia, put them up in boardinghouses at the shipping companies' own expense, temporarily hire other seamen to work in their place, proceed up the coast with this alternate crew, and then return to pick up the Indian crew from Newport News before making their return trip. Although some shipping companies did go through this routine, the unions' goal seems to have been to make the process so cumbersome and costly that British shipping lines would be compelled to employ white British seamen instead of Indians on U.S.-bound journeys to avoid the extra time and expense.[63]

U.S. maritime unions were also doing their best to keep Indian seamen out of the United States. Among U.S. labor leaders, one of the most vociferous opponents of Asian immigrant workers was Andrew Furuseth, the head of the San Francisco–based International Seamen's Union.

While remembered as the heroic architect of the 1915 Seamen's Act, which regulated wages and working hours and set health and safety standards for American maritime workers, Furuseth was also one of the founding members of the violently xenophobic Asiatic Exclusion League in 1905.[64] For decades, until his death in 1938, this Norwegian American agitated for the exclusion of Asian immigrants from the United States and of Asian seamen from ships entering U.S. ports. At Furuseth's insistence, the Seamen's Act included a language requirement for crews moving in and out of U.S. ports that was aimed specifically at keeping Chinese and Indian seamen from either working on American merchant ships or entering the United States on foreign ships. Furuseth also made dramatic and repeated claims in public and in congressional hearings that Chinese and "Hindu" seamen were sneaking into U.S. ports by the thousands and engaging in the large-scale smuggling of people and drugs. His testimony helped fan the flames of the growing moral panic about an America "flooded," "swamped," and "infiltrated" by Asian immigrants, sentiments that ultimately led to the passage of the Asiatic Barred Zone provisions of the 1917 Immigration Act.[65]

The 1917 act raised the stakes even further for Indian seamen who attempted or hoped to jump ship in the United States. While best known for its anti-Asian provisions, the 1917 act also included a series of clauses intended to tighten U.S. borders by policing the movements of foreign seamen while they were in U.S. ports. These clauses created a system for tracking all noncitizen seamen arriving in and departing from U.S. ports, defined classes of seamen whom foreign shipping companies were not permitted to land or discharge in the United States, and set steep fines for shipping companies who brought barred immigrants into the country in the guise of seamen or failed to prevent the desertion of their workers while in port. Although these provisions pertained to seamen from Britain, Norway, Greece, and other European countries, the combination of the anti-Asian and the alien seamen's clauses of the 1917 act established a particularly strong set of regulations for seamen from India, China, and other parts of the "barred zone."[66]

The 1917 legislation placed the burden of surveilling and controlling Asian seamen on the shoulders of their employers. It specified that the "negligent failure" of a shipowner to "detain on board any . . . alien excluded from admission into the United States," would make the owner liable for a penalty of $1,000 per deserting seaman and could result in his ship being seized by immigration authorities until the fine was paid.[67] As a result, Indian seamen faced even greater policing by their ships' officers than they had before 1917 while in port in the United States. For those who might elude their employers, the threat of imprisonment in and deportation from Ellis Island was also a clear disincentive to desertion. As the new legal regime went into effect after 1917, news traveled through maritime networks of the conditions and treatment that captured Indian deserters experienced at Ellis Island. Ahuja describes the case of a group of Indian seamen who jumped ship in New York in 1921 in order to bring suit against their employers for denial of sufficient clothing and food rations. The *New York Globe* reported that the "lascars" were "panic stricken" at the idea of being sent to the Bureau of Immigration and Naturalization's holding cells at Ellis Island: "Through an interpreter, they said they knew all about this terrible place, and would not go there."[68]

Together, these varied laws, mechanisms, and practices added up to a formidable set of barriers; on their face, they should have ensured that few Indian seamen were even sailing into the major ports of the U.S. Atlantic coast and that, at least after 1917, those who came were held on board their ships and not given the opportunity to desert. But this was not the case. Indian seamen did make their way to ports along the Eastern Seaboard, they did step onshore, and many found ways to leave their ships and stay. There were other forces at work in the 1910s that made desertion in the United States not only possible for Indian maritime workers, but also worth the risk. In 1902, British shipping companies successfully lobbied their government to partially repeal the "lascar line" provision of the Merchant Shipping Acts, so that they could use Indian engine and saloon crews below deck on winter voyages to U.S. Atlantic ports. They then convinced the British Government to drop the ban entirely for the duration of the First World War, which allowed them to use Indian crews above deck as well. There is evidence that major British shipping lines continued this practice on voyages to New York for more than a year after the war's end.[69] Thus, as a result of British companies' efforts, the number of Indian seamen sailing into U.S. Atlantic ports rose after 1902, and for an extended period in the late 1910s and into 1920, these companies employed Indian engine and deck crews on voyages to U.S. Atlantic ports all year round. Manifests show that, throughout this latter period, ships operated by the Ellerman Line, the Clan Line, and the Cunard Line regularly made runs into New York during the winter months using low-wage "lascar" crews, sixty, seventy, eighty men at a time.[70] In January 1919, for example, eight British steamships brought more than 450 Indian engine-room and saloon workers into the port of New York in a single month. The vast majority of these workers were Bengali Muslims—from Sylhet, Noakhali, Myensing, Tipperah, and Calcutta.[71] This month was on the high side, but the shipping companies in question appear to have been consistent in their use of Indian workers; through the winters of 1917 to 1924, between 50 and 300 Indian seamen arrived at the New York waterfront on British ships every month. Because Indian crews were sailing into New York with even greater frequency during the spring and summer, these numbers added up. In the decade between 1914 and 1924 alone, 20,000–25,000 Indian steamship workers moved in and out of New York's docklands.[72]

These men were arriving at the United States' maritime borders during a large-scale expansion of U.S. industry. In the years before the United States' entry into the First World War, between 1914 and 1917, U.S. industries were supplying their European allies with millions of dollars worth of munitions, fuel, ships, and other goods and materials vital to the war. When the United States officially joined the conflict in 1917, the country's factories, shipyards, and steel mills were operating at full steam. The entry of thousands of young American men into the military created a labor shortage that U.S. industries addressed by hiring women, African American migrants from the U.S. South, and immigrants.[73] While the flow of immigrant workers was significantly curtailed by the 1917 Immigration Act, Indian and other seamen had a unique advantage. Most arrived in U.S. ports as experienced industrial laborers; they had a well-honed set of skills working with furnaces, engines, and machinery. This appears to have made them especially desirable to U.S. factory owners, who, just like in Britain, began to recruit members of the Indian and Chinese crews of ships passing in and out of New York, Philadelphia, and Baltimore. In the years immediately following the war, as U.S. labor unions mounted a series of regional and nationwide strikes, factory owners continued this practice, hiring Indian and Chinese seamen off the docks and using them alongside African American workers as strikebreakers.[74]

Both British shipping companies and U.S. industries were bending and breaking their countries' laws in pursuit of Indian seamen's labor. The steamship lines were pushing back against Britain's Merchant Shipping Acts in order to use Indian workers without restriction on ships bound for North Atlantic ports, and U.S. munitions, steel, and auto companies were violating immigration and labor laws by enticing Indian workers off the waterfronts to work in their factories. For these men from Bengal, Punjab, and the Northwest Frontier, U.S. immigration law was a wall that was supposed to separate the maritime and onshore industries, to prevent workers moving from one to the other. But the pursuit of profit by powerful interests on both sides ensured that the wall would not be impermeable. These industries' efforts and violations created opportunities for workers from the subcontinent both to reach U.S. ports and to escape their ships for higher-paying factory work onshore.

To be sure, those who successfully took this route often found themselves in situations that were only nominally better than what they had experienced in the maritime trade. Dada Amir Haider Khan's experience after jumping ship in New York in February 1918 is a case in point. In the weeks following their desertion, Khan and one of his shipmates failed to find work, and with dwindling resources, limited skills in English, and barely enough clothing to keep them warm, the two fell prey to one of the city's unscrupulous labor recruiters. This middleman and his team of "employment agents" were rounding up unemployed immigrants from throughout the city to supply to New York–area factory owners. "He told us to sit down in a hall where there were some benches," writes Khan, "while a few more groups were brought in from elsewhere by some of his agents. . . . We were [then] herded together and put on a train for some unknown location." This, it turned out, was one of DuPont's wartime munitions plants in New Jersey—most likely their sprawling complex of factories at Carney's Point. Here, according to Khan, immigrant workers were housed in row after row of wooden barracks with "cots resembling ships bunks." They worked long shifts "sorting and separating some peculiar brownish coloured ingredient, like Italian spaghetti," were paid 30 cents an hour in a combination of cash and company scrip, and were policed by the compound's "own militia, secret service, [and] officials responsible for discipline and enforcement of rules." Like many of the spaces through which Indian men moved after deserting, the factory was wildly heterogeneous; Khan worked alongside Italian, Spanish, Polish, Russian, and Eastern European workers but was domiciled with the Puerto Rican "camp" since "there were not enough Indians for an Indian camp." "We [were] just like all the other ignorant, illiterate, poverty-stricken men employed at the plant," Khan wrote.[75]

A group of Indian and Chinese seamen found themselves in an equally dire situation after the war, emerging as targets of violence during a 1922 railroad shop-workers' strike in Jersey City, New Jersey. These workers stepped off the waterfront directly into the racial politics that would define U.S. interwar labor struggles. As soon as the strike had started, the Erie and Lackawanna Railroads sought out low-wage, nonunionized Indian, Chinese, and African American workers to sidestep white workers' organizing efforts. A series of local employment agents quickly emerged, who supplied the railroad owners' needs by canvassing the docks and facilitating the desertion of Indian and Chinese seamen to take up strikers' jobs in the railroad's steam-power shops. As a result, at the end of the first week of the strike, most of the violence that had arisen was not between workers and employers but between the striking white workers and their Asian and black nonunion replacements.[76] It is unclear whether these seamen knew when they took the rail-yard jobs that they were being thrown into the middle of a labor dispute. According to a Jersey City police captain, "a Bowery employment agency had promised [Indian and Chinese seamen] $3 a day and lodging and meals." After they were brought across the water from Manhattan, these men were housed in buildings within the rail-yard compound, where "close guard was being maintained over the imported men" by an armed security force that the Erie Railroad had hired. The seamen, however, were put upon by all sides. The Indian workers, according to the police captain's report, had to be "rescue[d] . . . from a mob which was threatening them with clubs and stones." Significantly, the Jersey City police neither arrested the

Asian seamen nor did much to prevent them from coming back. Nor did federal immigration officials cite the Erie Railroad for hiring "alien" workers in violation of the labor and immigration laws or go after the "Bowery employment agents" for their role in this violation.[77] When an industrial concern as large as the Erie Railroad needed to use Asian seamen to ensure the continuation of rail services in the face of a strike, local and federal officials were apparently willing to look the other way, letting the railroad's agents and hired guns circumvent the laws as they saw fit and concentrating their own energies on simply keeping things from boiling over into violence. Asian seamen, for their part, were largely left to fend for themselves.

Clandestine Networks, Onshore Worlds

While Indian maritime workers found an unwelcoming, even hostile, environment awaiting them in the United States—one in which they faced the controls of their ships' officers, the punishments of immigration officials, the ire of white labor unions, and the exploitation of industrial employers—they were able to navigate this environment and benefit from the options for working onshore by building networks of kin, fellow workers, and local residents that stretched from the waterfronts of Atlantic port cities far into the industrial heartland of the United States. The networks took root between 1914 and 1917, in the brief window of time after U.S. factories had shifted into wartime production and before the restrictions of the 1917 Immigration Act tightened the reins on Asian immigrants and "alien seamen." As in Britain, these networks were rooted in a population of ex-seamen whose presence onshore grew steadily in the final years of the nineteenth century. As early as 1900, the *New York Post* noted a small "colony" of Indian seamen living in the sailors' boardinghouse district at the southern tip of Manhattan, where the "lascars" shared quarters with other maritime workers from the Middle East, Singapore, and the Malay peninsula.[78] While this was likely a transient population of men who were moving on and off the ships, in the 1910s some of the seamen began to make their way inland to work factory jobs in New Jersey, Pennsylvania, upstate New York, and beyond. The first of these men may have been recruited by agents working for specific factories, but by the time wartime production reached full stride, Indian seamen had built up their own circuit that stretched through multiple factory towns across hundreds of miles and several state lines. When immigration laws subsequently tightened, the Indian presence throughout this circuit was already well entrenched; in New York, Philadelphia, and Baltimore and in at least a dozen major factory towns, there were groups of ex-lascars, some of whom had married local women; in each location there were shared apartments and boardinghouses; and in the factory towns, there were avenues for newcomers to secure work—in steel, in shipbuilding, and on automotive assembly lines. Twenty years earlier, Hooghly's peddlers had created a network that tied together multiple sites of tourism, commerce, and consumption; now these seamen created a network that connected multiple sites of industrial production. The infrastructure they laid down enabled a steady stream of escaped Indian seamen to work in U.S. factories for the duration of World War I and for many years afterward and allowed these men to live and work under the radar of the new anti-Asian immigration regime.[79]

While the Bengali peddlers had moved southward into Louisiana, South Carolina, Georgia, and Texas, the seamen moved in an arc north and westward from the Atlantic coast. Many of the factories and mills to which they traveled were close at hand. In Patterson, New Jersey, just across the Hudson River from Manhattan's West Side waterfront, Indian ex-seamen found a niche stoking the fires that heated vats of dye in the town's silk-manufacturing plants. In Hamilton, New Jersey, thirty-five miles up the Delaware River from Philadelphia's waterfront, they worked in the Zonolite asbestos factory. In Chester, Pennsylvania, just fifteen miles downriver from Philadelphia and eighty miles from Baltimore, Indian ex-seamen worked in the Sun Shipbuilding Company's shipyard and on the assembly line of a Ford auto factory. In Bethlehem, Pennsylvania, not more than a day's journey for a seaman who had jumped ship in Philadelphia, New York, or Baltimore, Indians worked in Bethlehem Steel's massive steel-production compound. Other opportunities took these men farther afield: dozens of Indian seamen made the 400-mile journey into the colds of upstate New York to work in the Lackawanna (later Bethlehem) Steel plant near Buffalo; others traveled deep into the

Midwest to work in U.S. Steel's mills in Youngstown, Ohio, and Gary, Indiana, and the Ford, General Motors, and Packard auto factories in Detroit and Dearborn, Michigan.[80]

During the 1920s and 30s, some of the largest populations of Indian factory workers were in these more distant locations: particularly Buffalo and Detroit. The former was the site of what was then the largest steel plant in the world, operated until 1922 by the Lackawanna Steel Company. This plant came to occupy more than 1,000 acres of land; it had, according to one description, "its own ship canal, locks, bridges," and railway lines and produced steel "bars, sheets, rail, tie plates" and fabricated parts for construction and other industries.[81] By 1920, there was already a well-established infrastructure for escaped Indian seamen to live and work in Lackawanna. Two men who had arrived in the United States in the early 1910s—one an Indian named Meah and the other listed as "East Indian" but whose name, Abdul Djebara, suggests he may have been Arab—ran boardinghouses for Indian workers on Fifth Avenue and Ridge Road, just outside the steel plant's doors. On the day federal census takers came around to these addresses in January 1920, Meah was lodging two dozen men and Djebara another dozen; they were all young, between eighteen and thirty-five, all had entered the country over the course of the war, between 1914 and 1919, and all now worked as firemen, likely stoking the flames that turned iron ore to molten steel in the Lackawanna plant.[82] At the peak of the war, draft registrars recorded close to fifty Indian men who were engaged in this work at Lackawanna. They had come from the precise demographic of the Indian maritime population: all were Muslim, they were predominantly from Bengal, and one member of the group was even known by the surname "Serang"—indicating his former occupation as the headman of an Indian steamship crew. Few of these workers appear to have had formal education; eight signed their draft cards in rough Bengali, one signed in clearly drawn English script, and the rest were unable to sign their names in either Bengali or English, instead marking the bottom of their draft cards with an *X* or a check mark. The men had, however, turned the skills they had developed in the boiler rooms of British steamships to equivalent and probably better-paid work in steel production.[83]

In Detroit, the number of Indian ex-seamen working in Ford auto factories grew in the immediate postwar period and continued through the 1920s.[84] As in Lackawanna, this Indian presence was built on a network of ex-maritime workers, boardinghouse keepers, and others who guided escaped seamen from New York and other port cities to Detroit and set them up with lodging and factory jobs. Here, they joined multiple streams of labor migration. By 1930, Detroit's Ford plants and the city's working-class neighborhoods and rooming houses were full of workers from all over the country and all over the world: African Americans who had come north as part of the Great Migration, as well as Afghans, Arabs, Syrians, Turks, Greeks, Maltese, Poles, and other immigrants from Europe, the Middle East, and the Americas. Although Indian men usually roomed together, they lived in buildings and areas that they shared with all these other groups.[85]

Over time, most came to live in a series of Indian boardinghouses and group households in a corner of the working-class African American neighborhood of Black Bottom on the east side of downtown Detroit. On their immediate blocks, their neighbors were predominantly Greek and Muslim immigrants; three or four blocks to the north was one of Black Bottom's main entertainment and commercial districts, around St. Antoine Street and Gratiot Avenue, which was home to a variety of African American small businesses, nightclubs, restaurants, and vaudeville and movie theaters. On the blocks beyond, to the north, east, and south were the residential areas of Black Bottom and Paradise Valley, where, as a result of the city's segregation, up to three hundred thousand southern black migrants came to share some of Detroit's poorest housing.[86] In the 1920s, one of the ex-seamen opened a small Indian restaurant here, possibly Detroit's first, which became a place of congregation for the city's workers from the subcontinent.[87] Whereas in Lackawanna, most of the Indian men were able to translate their existing furnace and engine-room skills directly from maritime to factory labor, the Indians in Detroit became part of a new industrial paradigm; they were deskilled and spread out across countless individualized tasks. On 1930 census sheets, their jobs read like an enumeration of every position on the Fordist assembly line: "Abdul Wahid—tool maker," "Mohammed Khan—molder," "Noor Alli—drill press," "Asod Ali—punch press," "Ishak Ali—motor assembly," "Abdul Karim—ignition assembly," "Sefit Ali—body builder," "Jamshed Ali—oiler," "Ali Ullah—sander," "Idris Ali—polisher."[88]

The population of Indian ex-seamen laboring in places like Lackawanna, Detroit, Chester, and Youngstown seems to have been in constant flux; men came and went from each city, and some worked in multiple industrial locations over the course of the months or years they spent in the United States. Onshore networks not only created conduits for men to travel from port cities to individual factory towns but also connected factory towns to one another; the communication and coordination among former seamen in these places was such that deserters could keep moving from one factory town to another, sometimes with stints at sea in between. The story of Mustafa "John" Ali, a Bengali seaman who spent several decades in the United States, illustrates just how mobile these men could be. Ali jumped ship in Baltimore in the early to mid-1920s, worked onshore for a time, then reentered the maritime trade, worked his way back to India, and returned to his village in Sylhet. In the late 1920s, Ali set out again for Calcutta, secured work on an outgoing steamship, and when his ship got to Maryland, he deserted a second time and settled in Baltimore, where he married an African American woman and had three children. In the 1930s, he left his family in Baltimore to work in the Ford auto plant in Chester, then traveled north to Buffalo to work in the Bethlehem Steel works, then returned to Baltimore to move his family back with him to Chester, where he worked either for Ford or for Sun Shipbuilding during World WII. After the war, Ali moved his family back to Baltimore, while he went to work first at the U.S. Steel plant in Gary, Indiana, and then in a General Motors auto factory in Detroit. When he retired from General Motors in the 1950s, Ali went back to his village in Sylhet.[89]

In order to achieve such mobility, Indian seamen needed to know or learn certain things—how to elude ships' officers, how to time a desertion, how and where to lay low until their ships left port, where to go for work—and they needed the help of others who were already living onshore, people who would put them up in the short term, feed them and hide them from authorities, and direct them to other people and locations that were often many miles away from the places they jumped ship. Some men may have planned to desert and had a specific destination in mind—Buffalo, Bethlehem, Youngstown, Detroit—before they even reached U.S. shores. These men might have communicated with friends or family who were already in the United States or might have learned about these American industrial towns from shipmates once they were at sea.[90] Other deserters may have heard of such places only after they jumped ship and were directed to the factories and steel mills by recruiters or by the Indians who were living onshore in New York, Philadelphia, or Baltimore. Whatever the case, most first-time deserters would have arrived in the United States with hardly anything in hand. Their British employers gave them work clothes that were thin, ragged, and largely inadequate to the northeastern weather. Lascar crews were not paid off fully until they had reached the end of their contracts and returned to their home ports, so these men would have had little to no money on hand when they jumped ship.[91] Most had minimal English-language skills and very little knowledge of where to go once they were onshore. So, after deserting, they first needed a place to hide, food to eat, and a new set of clothes. Then, when they set out for one of the factory towns, they needed directions for travel and an address and person to go to on the other end.

Physically, onshore networks began with the ships and docks and extended inland through various spaces: lodging houses and residences, factories and other job sites, and places of gathering and leisure. They were also chains of people—countrymen, kinsmen, and allies who provided deserters with assistance and information as they passed through these spaces in a series of steps, from the moment of desertion at the waterfront to a period of hiding in the port city to the subsequent journey to a factory town to the navigation of daily life in the context of that town. For those workers who did not use the mails and wire transfers, earnings often moved back through these same circuits: the men who were working at factories handed off money to trusted kin and co-villagers who were still working in the maritime trade, and these earnings would be carried on the ships back to their families on the subcontinent. At the same time, men on incoming ships communicated news of family, friends, and ongoing events on the subcontinent to those who were living and working onshore in the United States. The waterfront, in other words, was the hinge between the onshore and maritime worlds. Indian men who were living onshore would visit the ships during the days they were lying in port, pass news, information, money, and other items to individual seamen whom they knew onboard, or in some cases helped these men to desert. The seamen onboard would pass information to their friends onshore and in some cases help these men find work on outgoing ships.[92]

For all the controls on their movement, for all the legal restrictions they faced, and for all the public outcry against their presence in the United States, Indian seamen used their networks to render the waterfront more permeable and the United States more navigable. The record of these men's lives is fragmentary; it exists in a scattering of archival documents and news reports and a handful of firsthand accounts. But, together, these sources make clear the varied makeup of Indian maritime work-ers' onshore worlds. These men clearly relied on one another; as In-dian seamen deserted and found work in the United States, they fueled a chain migration in which they helped others from their families, villages, regions, and former ships desert and find work as well. However, this was only one part of the story. Indian seamen drew on the knowledge, assis-tance, and labor of many other people, from the American women of color a number of them married to waterfront shopkeepers, anticolonial exiles, and other sailors—Arab, Irish, and British. The spaces they in-habited and moved through were comprised of and animated by all these other people.[93]

The accounts of individual seamen make this clear. Dada Amir Haider Khan's desertion in January 1918 was striking for the variety of non-Indians who came to his aid. He and one of his shipmates were first en-couraged to desert by the Jewish proprietor of a waterfront provisions store on Manhattan's West Side. While exploring the docks on a two-hour shore leave, Khan and his friend wandered into the shop, where "Mr. S. Doctor" put the idea into their heads of jumping ship, described the higher wages they could get working on U.S. ships, and coached them on what to do. One evening a few days later, Khan and his friend took shore leave again, "telling our shipmates we were going for a stroll," but they did not return. When they found themselves wandering the streets of Manhattan in the middle of a severe winter night, "wrapping our-selves in whatever we had—an old pair of pants, a cotton shirt and a coat, a cheap cap and a coloured piece of cloth for our heads," it was an African American boardinghouse keeper in the Tenderloin district along Seventh Avenue who ultimately took them in and helped them hide. "[M]y companion had a talk with the Negro landlady," Khan writes, "and explained to her that we had deserted a ship and did not want to return [and] it was necessary for us to remain indoors while the vessel was still in port, so that we would not be apprehended and taken back. [So s]he arranged for a young Negro girl who was living in a room on the same floor to [go] purchase our food [for us]—bread, butter, eggs etc. which she cooked for us in the house." After a few days in hiding, under the boardinghouse keeper's care, Khan and his shipmate returned to the shop on West Fourteenth Street, where Mr. Doctor exchanged their few remaining British pounds for dollars, advised that they remain near the waterfront in order to find work, and directed them to the Seamen's Institute, a sailors' boardinghouse nearby where they could stay cheaply for a longer stretch of time. Here, Khan and his friend told the man in charge that they had deserted their ship, and he took them in with no questions asked.[94]

At the Seamen's Institute, Khan and his friend met "a young British-er" who helped them through the next step in their journey. The British sailor had also just jumped ship and explained to the Indians how "alien seamen," as a class distinct from "immigrants," could attempt to sidestep the bulk of U.S. immigration laws. After filing a petition of intention to naturalize, he told them, seamen could obtain the right to work on U.S. merchant ships, join U.S. maritime unions, and then apply for full U.S. citizenship after three years of work. While it ran counter to the recent laws of 1917, this provision provided a loophole through which Indian and Chinese seamen could enter the American merchant marine. Khan followed the steps as they were explained to him and succeeded in taking this path; within months of deserting his British steamship, he was working on U.S. ships at higher wages, with New York City as his home port. After Khan had spent almost a year sailing in and out of New York, it was finally an Arab sailor who connected him to the city's network of Indian ex-seaman. On the waterfront, Khan bumped into an "Arab coal-passer" with whom he had worked on a previous ship. This friend "had come into contact with some Indians and took me to meet them." Khan now found a community of "like-minded countrymen" in New York City but had arrived at this point through the assistance of a Jewish shopkeeper, an African American boardinghouse keeper, a white British sailor, and an Arab coal passer.[95]

The motivations of these men and women likely varied. While all four showed some sympathy for Khan, the shopkeeper, Mr. Doctor, was part of a complex dockside economy that depended on long-term relationships with seamen. In addition to supplying seafarers with provisions and clothing and helping them find work on the ships going in and out of port, Mr. Doctor operated an informal banking system in which seamen could save money between voyages. Khan and other sailors left considerable sums of money with him as deposits during the months they were away at sea and then drew on these sums when they were in port. This was a mutually beneficial structure; seamen were afforded the security of keeping their savings safe during their voyages, and, as Khan explains, "since everyone did not return or demand all their money at once, [Mr. Doctor] could make use of the deposits to finance his business operations."[96] The African American boardinghouse keeper also derived some business from Khan and his friend in the first days they were onshore—like many single and widowed working-class women in the city, she took lodgers in order to support herself financially. Khan makes clear, however, that she took in the two bedraggled Indian men even when several other boardinghouse keepers would not, and took very little in exchange; he implies that her actions were motivated by something more—by an empathy or racial affinity that others he encountered did not have.[97]

As heterogeneous as his initial allies were, Dada Khan's subsequent experiences illuminate the ways that Indian ex-seamen in U.S. port cities were helping other men from the subcontinent gain greater power over their mobility, labor, and lives. After his chance meeting with the Arab coal passer, Khan became part of a predominantly Indian circle of "seafaring men" who moved through and congregated in a series of spaces in the blocks that extended inland from New York City's West Side waterfront. As one moved from the docks toward the center of Manhattan, the bustle and commerce of the waterfront—ships, barges, people, goods, trucks, trolleys, crates, and horses—gave way first to the

poor and working-class Irish American neighborhood known as Hell's
Kitchen and then to the crowded tenements and licit and illicit entertainments of the Tenderloin. At the turn of the century, the Tenderloin
stretched from Twenty-Third to Fifty-Second Streets and Eighth to
Fifth Avenues. Clubs, cafés, saloons, theaters, and burlesques were concentrated along and near the north-south–running avenues, while blocks
of four- and five-story working-class residences ran in between, along the
east-west–running streets. Working- and middle-class African Americans lived in concentrated pockets throughout the area, particularly in
the corner of the neighborhood farther downtown and toward the river,
where Indian seamen began to settle in the 1910s. Though by this time,
the violence of white immigrants and New York City police had pushed
much of the black population farther uptown to San Juan Hill and Harlem, and sections of the neighborhood's entertainments were evolving
into a professionalized theater district, the lower Tenderloin was still a
racially mixed part of the city with crowded tenements and a sizable
transient population.[98]

It was here that a small population of Indian maritime deserters began
to find rooms and open small-scale businesses. One of these was a laundry on West Twenty-Third Street run by two Punjabi ex-seamen, and
another was a hole-in-the-wall Indian restaurant on West Thirty-Seventh
Street, run by a Goanese man who was likely a former steamship cook. A
little farther up the West Side at Forty-Third Street and Eighth Avenue
was the Ceylon India Restaurant, run by K. Y. Kira, a Sinhalese former
circus performer who appears to have taken in escaped seamen from
Ceylon and elsewhere, providing them with short-term lodging above
his establishment. In the restaurant itself, Indian seamen shared space
with political exiles and students from the subcontinent, who had made
the Ceylon India into a hub of expatriate nationalist activity. At Eighth
Avenue and Forty-Seventh Street was a large single-room-occupancy
hotel that, at least for a short time, became a kind of halfway house between the Indian maritime and onshore worlds. At the time of the 1930
census, the hotel was home to a population of more than fifty Indian
men; a handful held jobs on steamships—as cooks, waiters, stewards,
and seamen—while the others worked in similar capacities in restaurants in the city or supported themselves doing "odd jobs." Amir Haider

Khan also helped open two businesses on the West Side. In late 1920 or early 1921, he invested much of his savings to help a Punjabi student open a restaurant around Seventh Avenue and Thirty-Eighth Street, which, though short-lived, became another space of gathering for the city's Indian seamen and students. Later, Khan partnered with another ex-sailor to open a laundry and dry-cleaner's shop in the basement of a residential tenement building on West Forty-Third Street.[99]

These small businesses played dual roles. They were commercial ventures, but they were also dynamic community spaces where Indian workers gathered daily to socialize and exchange news and information. The men who operated the laundry on Twenty-Third Street received an Urdu newspaper in the mail and so provided their countrymen in New York with access to detailed information about ongoing political events in India. The laundry and restaurants were also places where members of the seafarers' community could meet up and keep track of each other and they were hubs for finding either onshore or maritime work. One of Khan's extended voyages out of New York in 1919 came about after he met a Punjabi seaman "while dining at one of the Indian restaurants," who engaged Khan in conversation, asked if he was employed, and told him of a ship about to leave for Italy that was in need of a crew member with his skills.[100]

On at least one occasion, Dada Khan used his dry-cleaning shop to move seamen in the opposite direction, off the ships and into the city. In 1922, an acquaintance of Khan's, Abdul Rehman, was canvassing the waterfront, moving on and off various ships that were then in port, looking for work, when he met an older seaman who was asking after his nephew "Amir Haider." Rehman conveyed the news to Khan, who then visited his uncle's ship in port in Brooklyn. He wrote later that although "I was not well off financially at the time . . . [I] asked him whether he wished to leave the ship at New York." At their request, Khan helped both his uncle and another shipmate desert, hiding them in a sleeping area at the back of the laundry, where "we served them their food until we could provide suitable clothes so that they could appear more presentable in the New York surroundings." Khan and his friends then found jobs for the men, who eventually moved on to live with a group of other ex-seamen elsewhere in the city.[101]

When an escaped seaman left the port city in which he had deserted and traveled farther away to one of the factory towns that were part of the Indian circuit, he depended on another set of contacts and relationships. On arrival at one of these destinations, he found a constellation of people and spaces similar to those he had encountered in the port city: boardinghouses, shared apartments, and private residences; boardinghouse keepers, middlemen, and other escaped seamen. By the 1920s, there were Indian ex-seamen who had settled in each of the major factory towns who could help the newly arrived. They fell roughly into two categories. One group had opened restaurants or were running boardinghouses and other small businesses. They could set up new arrivals with a place to stay, perhaps on credit to begin with, and direct them toward work. Their businesses were places where other ex-seamen congregated and where new arrivals may have met men whom they knew from maritime work or through family and kinship connections. This was especially the case in larger cities like Detroit. Another group who could assist newcomers consisted of those Indian ex-seafarers who had lived and worked in specific factory towns for extended periods of time—men who had gained a footing in these places and developed local knowledge and connections. Just as in New Orleans, a small number of these men had married local women of color. They and their wives could provide invaluable guidance and assistance for Indian deserters who were newly arrived.

In Detroit, a small number of Indians were among the groups of predominantly Muslim men—Afghans, Arabs, Turks—who turned a section of Black Bottom apartment buildings into makeshift rooming houses. During and immediately after the First World War, an increasing number of buildings along Monroe, Fort, Congress and Lafayette Streets were turned over to such use, becoming temporary homes for various transient populations of immigrants workers. By 1920, two Indian men who had entered the United States in the early 1910s, Idris Ali and Anoar Mohammed, were operating boardinghouses for other Indians in this area. On the day of the 1920 federal census, Ali was boarding twelve Indian men and Mohammed was boarding thirteen, all of whom worked on the auto assembly lines. In 1930, Wozid Ali was running a rooming house in the same area with fourteen Indian autoworkers as boarders, and a second Mr. Allie had a smaller apartment nearby where he was lodging five more men. By now, entire blocks in this part of Black Bottom were dominated by boardinghouses full of Muslim immigrant workers. Among them were dozens of Afghans—men who may have had a similar background to the Bengalis and Punjabis, as seamen who escaped British ships after sailing out of ports on the subcontinent. Two doors down from Wozid Ali was an Afghan named Chanan Din, who had entered the United States during World War I and was now boarding a dozen Afghan and Arab autoworkers. A block farther away, Jacob Khan, another Afghan, was boarding twenty-one. The Indian restaurant in this neighborhood could also act as a conduit for men who were new to the city; Indian seamen could come here in order to track down friends or acquaintances and be directed toward nearby rooming houses. An Indian seaman, newly arrived in Detroit from New York, Baltimore, or Philadelphia, had only to find his way to this part of Black Bottom and he would have been able to draw upon the local network here for food, lodging, and work.[102]

The Indian rooming houses here bore some resemblance to the boardinghouse that Alef Ally ran in New Orleans for members of the Hooghly peddler network, but they also differed from Alef Ally's in important respects. One of these was the relationship between boardinghouse keeper and boarders—and among the different men living together in a single boardinghouse at any given time. Most of the Bengali peddlers who were operating in New Orleans from the 1890s to the 1910s came from a small cluster of villages in the same district of West Bengal, and many appear to have been related to one another as uncles and nephews, fathers and sons, brothers and cousins. They also were working in a coordinated manner when they peddled their goods. The connections between seamen were less familial and the work they were doing onshore was more individuated. These men did share bonds of language, region, religion, and occupation, and individual crews were often recruited from a single village or locality. These bonds remained important within the onshore networks of maritime deserters, but the industry drew workers from multiple regions of the subcontinent, and onshore populations were varied and marked by much individual transience. Friends, co-villagers and shipmates spent intensive periods of time together at sea and onshore but often were separated from one another for months or even years at a time as the demands of maritime and factory work pulled them in different directions.[103] So, while the Indian boardinghouse keepers in Detroit and elsewhere may have had sympathy for their boarders as countrymen and former seamen, the assistance they offered many of these men would no doubt have been of a different tenor than the assistance offered by senior to junior members of the Hooghly peddler network.

The structure of the boardinghouses was also such that even the most generous and helpful boardinghouse keeper had a relationship to his boarders that was, at the end of the day, financial. The men who ran these establishments were not property owners, but rather ex-seamen who had gathered enough resources to rent a large apartment building, convert it to use as a rooming house, and then sublet it to their boarders. The boardinghouse keepers were responsible at the end of each week or month to pay rent on the entire building—anywhere from $25 to $125, depending on its size—which they had to collect from their boarders. The proprietor of such a rooming house, then, would have been motivated at least in part by self-interest to help recently arrived ex-seamen find employment in the local factories.

Where such establishments resembled Alef Ally's was their dependence on the labor of local women—often women of color. Wherever they were, these boardinghouses required a considerable amount of daily upkeep. Someone needed to clean rooms, launder bed linens, and in some cases, prepare breakfasts and other meals for between ten and twenty men. Alef Ally engaged Celestine Gardner, an older African American woman, to do this work at 1428 St. Louis Street in New Orleans, and many of the boardinghouses in Black Bottom, Detroit—whether Indian, Afghan, Syrian, Turkish, or Greek—were structured in the same way. One woman often lived among all the male boarders and did the work of keeping up the house. In some cases, this was the wife of one of the autoworkers residing at a given rooming house; Wozid Ali's boardinghouse at 584 Fort Street, for example, was maintained by Marguerite Alli, the Mexican wife of one of the Indian lodgers at the address, and Jean Shah, the wife of one of Chanan Din's lodgers, may have played the same role at Din's rooming house. In other cases, Black Bottom's boardinghouse keepers hired single and widowed older women to live and work in their buildings; Sadie Abdou, a Syrian boardinghouse keeper at 556–560 East Lafayette Street, like Alef Ally, employed a widowed African American woman, Mary Stokes, to perform the daily labor of cooking, washing, and laundering.[104]

In addition to those men who ran businesses catering to Indian maritime workers in U.S. factory towns, there were certain members of the Indian population who simply took on the role of helping other seamen transition to life onshore. These were typically men who had been in the country for a longer stretch of time, had married and settled in U.S. port cities or industrial towns, had built up knowledge and language skills, and were more acculturated and integrated into local communities. These men were particularly important in towns with smaller numbers of Indian factory workers, where, instead of a structure of established Indian boardinghouses, the newly arrived seamen found informal networks of shared apartments and private homes. Mustafa "John" Ali came to play such a role in Chester, Pennsylvania, where, throughout the 1920s and 1930s, the town's auto factory and shipbuilding yards drew small groups of Indian men who had jumped ship in Baltimore and Philadelphia. Ali's story parallels Haider Khan's in some respects: both men shifted in and out of maritime work and moved through multiple factory jobs; both became part of Indian communities in the gray areas of the immigration regime; and both aided other seamen to jump ship and work in the United States. While Haider Khan left the United States after seven years, eventually returning to the subcontinent, Ali married a local African American woman after jumping ship in Baltimore in the early 1920s, and he spent more than thirty years in the country before retiring and returning to his village in Sylhet. The majority of Indian men who deserted their ships to work in the United States in the 1910s, 1920s, and 1930s appear to have taken a path closer to Haider Khan's, but Ali was part of a smaller group who, after jumping ship, stayed in the United States for most or all of the rest of their lives. Like the Bengali peddlers who settled in New Orleans, these men helped anchor the broader network of escaped seamen in a series of key locations.

When John Ali moved to Chester, Pennsylvania, in the late 1930s, he had already been living in the United States for close to a decade, moving from one job to the next. He had learned English, in part by listening to the radio, and had worked in Baltimore, Buffalo, and, for a brief time once before, in Chester itself. Chester was a city dominated by industry. Its Sun Shipbuilding plant, which took up almost sixty acres along the banks of the Delaware River, was the largest of its kind in the United States, employing tens of thousands of workers—white, black, immigrant and U.S.-born—while a series of other factories were interspersed through other parts of the town. Indian ex-seamen had been working in Chester since the First World War, so when John Ali returned there, he joined a well-entrenched community that included one of his cousins, Nickar Ali.[105] Because of his language skills, local knowledge, and acculturation, and presumably because of the experience and connections he had built in several other industrial towns in the Midwest, John Ali became a leader among Chester's group of Indian workers. He was in constant contact with the members of this community; the men regularly came to his house after work and on weekends to meet, talk, play cards, and listen to the radio together. According to John Ali Jr., his father always had a big pot of rice and curry on the back burner of their stove in order to feed the visitors who inevitably dropped by. He had learned to season his fish, shrimp, and beef with curry powder, paprika, and whatever other spices were available in the local stores. Ali translated news broadcasts for his visitors, from English into Bengali, as they sat in his home. "India was in the news a lot those days," says John Ali Jr., and his father's friends would gather to hear about the latest developments in the independence struggle, which he would translate as the broadcasts ran, and which they would all then discuss afterward.[106]

Ali also became one of the people whom newly arrived deserters sought out for help. Local officials eventually learned that he was playing this role—feeding and guiding the Indian seamen who came to see him—so when a ship in port in Baltimore or Philadelphia reported that members of their Indian crew had jumped, immigration officers often turned up at Ali's door. According to John Jr., two of the officers used to occupy the Alis' house on such days. They would invite themselves in and wait for half the day for the escaped seamen to arrive. "They would come around," remembers Ali, "and I'll never forget they would sit down and they would eat sardines out of cans—with a suit and tie on, they would sit at our dining room table and eat sardines while they waited for these fellows who jumped ship to contact my father." It was perhaps a sign of how effective the local network was that none of the Indian deserters ever showed up at John Ali's house when the immigration officers were in. "The word must have got out," remembers his son.[107]

John Ali Sr. and other ex-seamen like him managed to stay in the United States because of a three-year statute of limitations on their desertions. If these men jumped ship in the United States and managed to evade capture for three years, the immigration authorities could no longer arrest and deport them; they could stay in the United States.[108] But these men were not welcomed as other immigrants might have been; they had no legal footing in the country and lived for years in this marginal status. Yet they did find homes and build communities—largely because they joined and were accepted by others on the nation's margins. John Ali and other Indian Muslim men simultaneously integrated into working-class families and neighborhoods of color in U.S. cities and built pockets of Indian community within those spaces. In fact, the latter phenomenon depended on the former. While localized Indian networks in places like Chester supported and sustained an ongoing flow of deserters from British ships, these networks were themselves made possible by Indian intermarriage within African American and other communities of color, and, more broadly, by these communities' acceptance of Indian and other immigrant men of color into their fold.

John Ali's trajectory illustrates these intertwined dynamics. Soon after Ali jumped ship for the second time in Baltimore, he met a young African American woman from the city, Mamie Chase, at a class he was taking at a local school. The two courted, married, and over the next few years had three children together. Although John Ali moved in and out of his family's life over the next several years as he went off in search of industrial work, his son, John Ali Jr., recalls that both his mother's family and the larger West Baltimore neighborhood in which they lived provided a home for his father. Ali developed a close relationship to his mother-in-law, Mamie's mother—who John Jr. remembers loved to dance with the young Bengali whenever he was visiting the family—and with Mamie's older brother, with whom he used to share drinks at the local Elk's Lodge. The neighborhood along Pennsylvania Avenue in which Mamie's family lived and where John Sr. and other escaped Indian seamen settled was the cultural heart of Baltimore's African American community, but at the same time, a wide variety of immigrants had settled among the black population: Filipinos, Portuguese, Chinese, and Roma, among others. Sometime in the 1930s, another Bengali ex-seaman named Ali opened an Indian restaurant here along the same stretch of Pennsylvania Avenue that included the Royal Theater, Baltimore's equivalent of Harlem's Apollo, and the other black nightclubs and movie houses that were the life of the district. It was in this part of Baltimore that John Ali Sr. first gained his footing in the United States, learned English, and built local relationships, all of which eventually enabled him to help others in the Indian worker community when he moved with Mamie and his children to Chester.[109]

In both Baltimore and Chester, John Ali and his Indian contemporaries stepped into a United States that was defined by the color line, and it appears to have become clear to them and to those around them which side of the line they were on. Although Chester, Pennsylvania, was technically in the North, in the 1930s, its neighborhoods full of industrial workers as well as its theaters, primary schools, and public facilities were all racially segregated. As in Baltimore, Indian and other immigrant men of color lived in black neighborhoods, and the lines that separated these neighborhoods from white ones, remembers John Ali Jr., were clearly enforced, particularly by members of Chester's Italian and Italian American population. In Chester's main movie theater, African Americans were seated on the left side of the house, while whites were seated in the middle and on the right. "When the center and the right became full," says John Ali Jr., the manager "would move the minorities from the left-hand side into the back and let the whites come over and sit in front of them." When the Indian men went to see a movie, "they would sit on the same side as the black people sat, because as far as the white people were concerned, they were doing it based on color." The same division held for those Indian ex-seamen who managed to save enough to open small businesses. As was the case in New Orleans, these men set up in black neighborhoods and became part of these areas' commercial and cultural landscapes. This was true for one of John Ali's circle in Chester, who left industrial work to run the main grocery and bar in a small, semirural, and predominantly black neighborhood in Chestertown, Maryland, seventy miles away.[110]

"Indian Sailors Strike for Grub"

In 1925, around the time Amir Haider Khan was leaving the United States and Mustafa "John" Ali was arriving, the Baltimore *Afro-American,* one of the county's national black weeklies, ran a banner headline across the top of page 9 about a group of Indian seamen who had arrived in port in Baltimore. In some ways, the article resembled those stories about "curious lascars" that had run in more mainstream U.S. newspapers at the turn of the century, and continued to appear in those papers even in the 1920s. The *Afro-American*'s article, for example, spoke of a "mutiny" on the high seas; it focused in on one of the Indian men's "peculiar red whiskers" (presumably his beard, died with henna) and mentioned that the men would not eat food "prepared by unbelievers." But the similarities ended there. The main point of the article was in fact to explain how a group of Indian seamen now under arrest in Baltimore had come to the verge of attacking their employer. It described the men's poor working conditions on their ship and detailed their mistreatment at the hands of the ship's officers. It explained that the captain had refused to provide them with food prepared according to the tenets of their "Mohammedan faith" and highlighted the stand they took midvoyage by refusing to work. The *Afro-American* dispatched a reporter to speak not to the ship's captain, but to the arrested men, to hear their story in their own words. The paper also sent a photographer, so they could show their readership the six sailors who stood up for their rights on board. The headline that ran in bold letters across the full length of one page of the newspaper spoke of the "alleged" mutiny of these men, and the subheads fleshed out the details: "India Seamen Arrested; Tell Harrowing Tale—Five Dollars Monthly Wage and Meatless Diet Caused Near Mutiny on Ship— Brutality and Hard Life of Jack London Stories Are Recalled at Police Station." Above the photograph of the six men, displayed prominently at the top of the page, was the heading: "East Indian Sailors Strike for Grub." Just below, the photo caption indicated one man among the

Indians who was more likely of Somali or North African descent and pointed out that he was "undoubtedly of African parentage."[111]

In its important respects, the *Afro-American*'s article could not have been more different from those of the era's white-owned papers. The six seamen were presented here as human beings and, specifically, as workers of color, whose stories were important and whose actions were logical, reasonable, and even commendable. Their dietary observances were not the focus of ridicule or voyeurism but were rather aspects of their faith that their captain was wrong to deny them. Just as Mamie Chase's family and others on Baltimore's African American Westside welcomed Indian men into their families and communities—men who had otherwise been rendered "illegal" by the nation's racialized immigration regime—this black newspaper embraced a group of Indian seamen who had struck against an injustice and ended up in a Baltimore jail. Their story would have resonated with the others that filled the *Afro-American*'s pages every week, of African American women and men subjected to the violence and injustice of white supremacy and criminalized for fighting back. The affinity that the *Afro-American* showed for these Indian "mutineers" was not isolated; this was a historical moment in which African American and Indian nationalist leaders were coming to recognize and articulate the connections between their struggles.[112] Maritime desertion, however, led to its own arena of contact between the two groups, and as the story of Dada Amir Haider Khan makes clear, that arena could produce its own understandings and transformations.

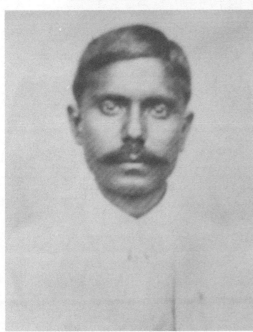

Figure 1. Photographs of two of the Bengali peddlers operating in the United States in the 1890s–1920s: Roston Ally (Atlantic City, NJ, and New Orleans, LA) (top) and Abdul Rub Mollah (New Orleans, LA, St. Louis, MO, and French Lick, IN) (bottom). (Source: U.S. National Archives)

LIST OR MANIFEST OF ALIEN IMMIGRANTS

Required by the regulations of the Secretary of the Treasury of the United States, under Act of Congress appro...

vessel having such passengers on board

S.S. *St Louis*   sailing from *Southampton*

No. on List.	NAME IN FULL.	Age Yrs. Mos.	Sex.	Married or Single.	Calling or Occupation.	Able to Read Write	Nationality.	Last Residence.	Seaport for Landing in the United States.	Final destination in the United States. (State, City or Town.)
1	Joseph Hekimian	18	m	S	Student	y/s	Armenian	London	New York	Boston Mass
2	Noah Lemon	25	m	S	Shoe Maker	y/s	American	"	"	" Mass
3	Jacob Miller	36	m	m	Buckler	y/s	German	Southampton	"	Philadelphia Pa St Louis
4	Lipot Lepecler	18	m	S	Book keeper	y/s	Hungarian	London	"	New York
5	Thomas George	29	m	S	Cook	no	Japanese	"	"	"
6	Carl J. B. Anderson	23	m	S	Clerk	y/s	Swede	"	"	Hartford Ct
7	Henry Smith	17	6	m	S	Sailor	y/s	English	"	"	New York
8	Isaac Levin	21	m	S	Buckler	no	Russian	"	"	"
9	Lazarus Silverstein	14	m	S	Tailor	o/s	"	"	"	Detroit
10	Israel Goodman	27	m	S	Sailor	"	"	"	"	"
11	Abel Goodman	15	m	S	—	—	do	do	do	do
12	Niatoy Mondel	40	m	m	Merchant	y/s	East India	Southampton	NY	"
13	Moocha	30	m	m	"	"	"	"	"	"
14	Abdul Aziny	25	"	"	"	"	"	"	"	Deported
15	Busuudaen	30	"	"	"	"	"	"	"	Deported
16	Obiaulll	19	"	"	"	"	"	"	"	Deported
17	Ali Almia	20	"	"	"	"	"	"	"	Deported
18	Mx Aid Ali	32	"	"	"	"	"	"	"	Deported
19	Glolm Rubbani	30	"	"	"	"	"	"	"	Deported
20	Golan Box	28	"	"	"	"	"	"	"	Deported
21	Danray Alm	28	"	"	"	"	"	"	"	Deported
22	Iholmuleddia	18	"	"	"	"	"	"	"	Deported
23	Faylai Alma	16	"	"	"	"	"	"	"	Deported
24	Richard Carne	22	M	m	Laborer	y	English	Penzance	"	Wyoming
25	Elizabeth do.	23	F	"	wife	y	do.	"	"	"

Figure 2. Detail of ship manifest for the American Line's SS *St. Louis*, which arrived in New York on June 18, 1897, carrying twelve members of the Hooghly peddler network who were on their way to sell goods on the boardwalks of New Jersey. The twelve were detained and then deported for violation of the Alien Contract Labor Law. (Source: U.S. National Archives)

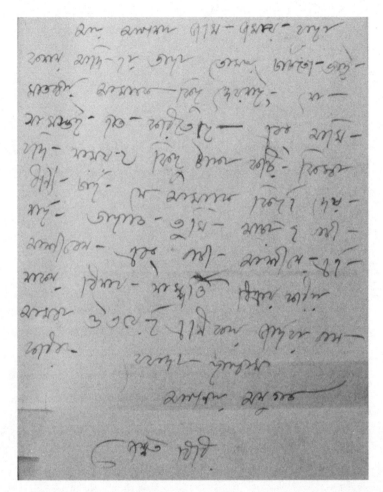

Figure 3. Detail of a letter sent from Jennat Bibi in West Bengal to her husband, Roston Ally, in New Orleans, asking that he return. (Source: U.S. National Archives).

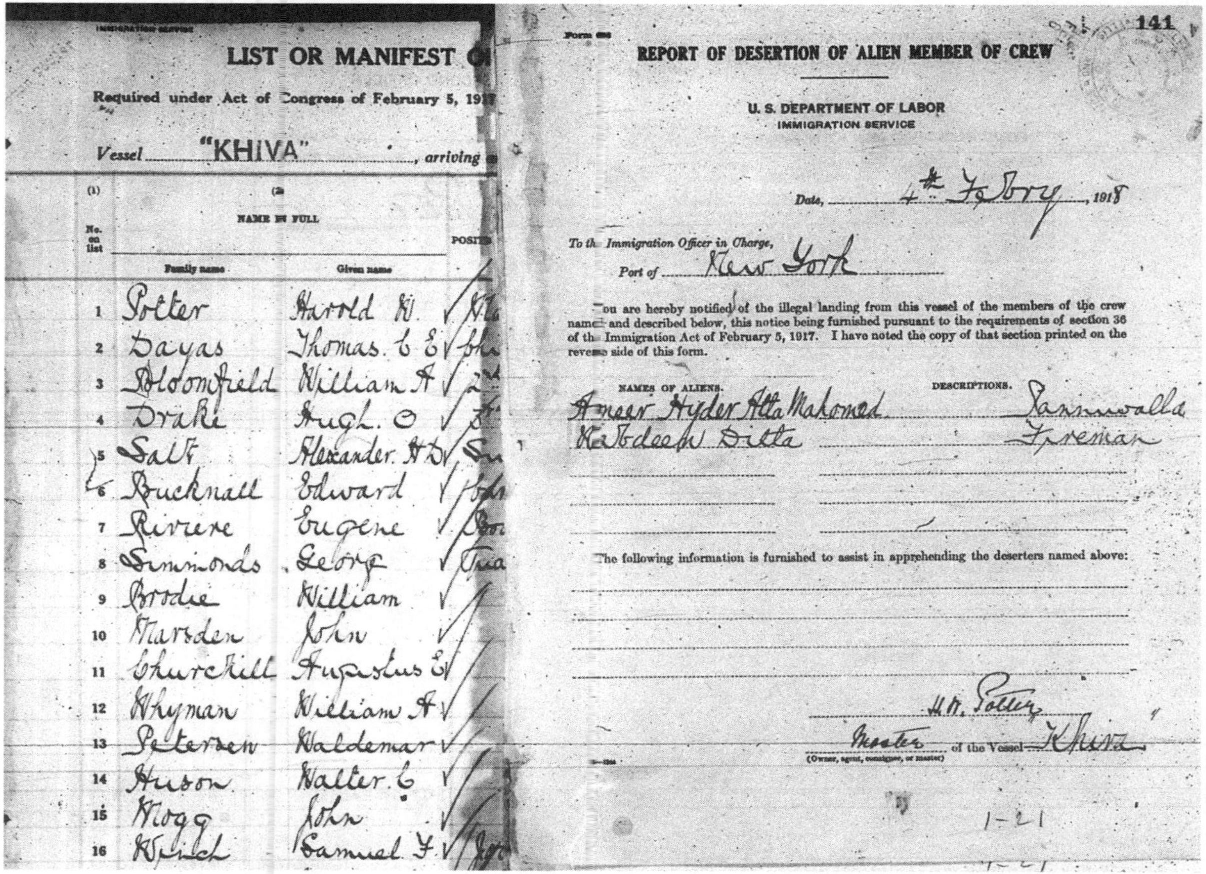

LIST OR MANIFEST O[F]

Required under Act of Congress of February 5, 1917

Vessel "KHIVA", arriving

(1) No. on list	(2) NAME IN FULL Family name	Given name	POSITION
1	Potter	Harold W.	
2	Dayas	Thomas C. E.	
3	Bloomfield	William A.	
4	Drake	Hugh. O	
5	Salt	Alexander H. D.	
6	Bucknall	Edward	
7	Riviere	Eugene	
8	Simmonds	George	
9	Brodie	William	
10	Marsden	John	
11	Churchill	Augustus E.	
12	Whyman	William A.	
13	Petersen	Waldemar	
14	Huson	Walter C.	
15	Hogg	John	
16	Welch	Samuel F.	

141

REPORT OF DESERTION OF ALIEN MEMBER OF CREW

U. S. DEPARTMENT OF LABOR
IMMIGRATION SERVICE

Date, 4th Febry, 1918

To the Immigration Officer in Charge,
Port of New York

You are hereby notified of the illegal landing from this vessel of the members of the crew named and described below, this notice being furnished pursuant to the requirements of section 36 of the Immigration Act of February 5, 1917. I have noted the copy of that section printed on the reverse side of this form.

NAMES OF ALIENS.	DESCRIPTIONS.
Ameer Hyder Atta Mahomed	Pannewalla
Kabdeen Ditta	Fireman

The following information is furnished to assist in apprehending the deserters named above:

H. W. Potter
Master of the Vessel Khiva
(Owner, agent, consignee, or master)

1-21

Figure 4. Record of the 1918 desertion of Dada Amir Haider Khan, sailing here under the name Ameer Hyder Atta Mahomed. (Source: U.S. National Archives)

SLOGAN OF ISLAM TO MINGLE
WITH CHRISTMAS CAROLINGS

"SERANG" AND GROUP OF LASCARS

Figures 5 and 6. Images of Indian seamen from U.S. newspapers.
Top: *Philadelphia Inquirer*, December 25, 1903. Bottom: *Baltimore
Afro-American*, August 1, 1925. (Source: *Philadelphia Inquirer*; Afro-American
Newspapers Archives and Research Center, Johns Hopkins University)

Figure 7. Bardu Ali, one of the first children of Bengali–African American intermixture in New Orleans, who went on to work as a dancer on the black vaudeville circuit in the 1920s; became emcee for Harlem's famed Chick Webb Orchestra in the 1930s, and then teamed up with Johnny Otis to open the Barrelhouse Club in Los Angeles in the 1940s. (Source: Afro-American Newspapers Archives and Research Center, Johns Hopkins University)

NANOO MEAH

Thin and malarial, he has spent 27 years at sea, is a boatswain. He has been in one ship sunk by bombing, another in a convoy collision. He comes from Purangao near Calcutta in Bengal, where famine has been stalking the fields. Like all others here, he has one wife, though Moslem law allows him more. He is afraid of Hindu interference with Moslem worship.

ABDUL KARIM

Weighing 90 pounds and only 19 years old, he is one of the best-educated men shown here. He went to high school and speaks English carefully and well. He comes from Ballygunge near Calcutta and is a steward. One Lascar as frail as Karim was one of two survivors of 16 men on a raft 52 days. Karim has been at sea for two years and he wants to fly an airplane.

NOJIBUL HAQUE

Tense, excitable and 21, Nojibul Haque has also received some education, in Calcutta. He has been at sea two years as a messboy. He shows the glistening blue-black hair and fine features of a typical Bengali. Some Indians see no great difference between British and other imperialisms, but others say this view is not typical of young, intellectual Moslems.

Figures 8 and 9. Images from the British Merchant Sailors Club for Indian Seamen, run by Ibrahim Choudry during World War II on Thirty-Eighth Street in midtown Manhattan. In 1944, *Life* magazine ran a feature about the club that included profiles of Indian seamen then in port. Top: the club's prayer room (Choudry is second from left, front row, facing camera); bottom: three of the men featured in *Life*. (Photo: Nelson Morris, illustrations: Martha Sawyers, source: *Life* Magazine)

Figure 10. Habib and Victoria Ullah (back row, left and middle) with their children, Habib Jr. and Zubeida, and friends, Doña Juana (standing, right), Fina, and Feyo (kneeling, left and right), at Orchard Beach in the Bronx, New York, circa 1950. (Source: Habib Ullah Jr.)

Figure 11. Saad "Victor" Ullah and his son, Victor Jr., late 1950s. (Source: Helen Ullah)

Figure 12. Saad (back left) and Helen Ullah (back right) with friends, circa 1964. (Source: Helen Ullah)

Figure 13. Habib Ullah Jr. (foreground) with two of his cousins, Ralph (top) and Martin (bottom) Caballero, on the lake at the northeastern corner of Central Park in Manhattan, late 1950s. (Source: Rafael Caballero Jr.)

Figure 14. Moheama Ullah (Habib Ullah Sr.'s second wife) with her sons Alaudin (front) and Karim (rear) in the playground at the George Washington Carver Housing Project, East Harlem, circa 1973. (Source: Alaudin Ullah)

CHAPTER 4

The Travels and Transformations
of Amir Haider Khan

When the appeal was made for contributions for Dr. Sweet's defence fund, everyone contributed whatever [they] could. By me
were sitting some Negro working women of different ages. When
the collection basket came, those who had no cash with them took
off their earrings, finger rings, or whatever else they had to contribute towards the defence funds. . . . That day I saw how in face
of a common danger, the Negro [community] stood united in defence of [a] man of their race.

—Dada Amir Haider Khan, *Chains to Lose:*
Life and Struggles of a Revolutionary

B Y THE TIME AN INDIAN SEAMAN reached the waterfront of New
York, Philadelphia, or Baltimore, he had already gone through a
kind of transformation. Most had spent their early lives in rural areas far
from the ocean before making their way to Calcutta and Bombay. They
had often spent months in these cities' crowded docklands and then
weeks, months, or years working at sea in the company of men from their
own and other villages and regions, as well as moving in and out of large,
bustling, cosmopolitan port cities across the globe—Alexandria, Naples,
Tunis, London, Liverpool, Glasgow, Antwerp, Kobe, Shanghai, Singapore. The decision to jump ship in a Northeastern port—to escape the
inequities of the British maritime trade and break the immigration laws
of the United States—was itself the sign of a confidence that for many

would have grown over their time spent in the maritime trade. Many would have witnessed and been encouraged by other seamen who had developed knowledge about moving on and off ships as they docked in different places, or who had told of the opportunities and networks that awaited deserters onshore. But what happened to these seamen once they jumped ship in the United States? What happened to their sense of self, their sense of possibility, and their sense of the world once they entered into the spaces of U.S. port cities and factory towns as workers, as migrants, and as men of color in a society deeply divided by race and class? This is a question that cannot be answered for most of the Indian seamen who deserted in U.S. ports in the 1910s and 1920s. There are likely as many answers to the question as there were men who jumped ship, and now, years after this generation has passed away, there is little record of their experiences, let alone of the changes they underwent. The vast majority of these men were nonliterate, and those who were literate appear to have had little opportunity or inclination to record their stories in writing.

There is, however, one remarkable exception: the memoir of Dada Amir Haider Khan.[1] The first volume of his *Chains to Lose* was written from a British Indian jail cell between 1939 and 1942, after Khan had been imprisoned for his activities in the independence movement and his organizing work for the Communist Party of India. More than four hundred pages long, it details the early part of Khan's life, from his birth in a small village in northwestern Kashmir to his years as a teenage coal trimmer on British steamships, through the period of his life, from 1918 to 1926, that Khan spent moving into, out of, and across the United States. In this relatively short period, he worked as a member of the American merchant marine, with New York as his home port, as a boiler-maker in a railway workshop near Buffalo, New York, and as an auto-worker in Detroit, Michigan. He rode the rails in the segregated South, earned certification as a steam engineer, via a correspondence course, and became a licensed pilot, after attending an aviation school in rural Southern Illinois. Khan's memoir is perhaps the only existing firsthand account of the life and movements of an Indian maritime worker in the United States before the 1930s.

Dada Khan was exceptional in many ways. He possessed a boldness and intolerance for injustice that led him to challenge superiors and organize fellow workers on British ships from the time he was just sixteen years old and then to plunge himself into the political landscape of cities such as New York and Detroit in his twenties. By the time he was twenty-six, he had been recruited by representatives of the Communist International in the United States and sent to Moscow to train and study. As exceptional as he was and as singular as some of his experiences were, Dada Khan's story is important because it illuminates so many different aspects of the history of Indian seamen in the United States, and it moves through so many of the spaces these men inhabited. As Khan recounts his movements and observations, we gain a first-hand account of the lives that Indian seamen forged for themselves throughout the networks they set up in U.S. port cities and industrial towns. Khan describes his time on and near the New York City waterfront; encountering recruiters and middlemen; working on ships with Indian crews, mixed crews, and white crews; laboring in factories in New Jersey, upstate New York, and Michigan; living with other Indian "seafaring men;" congregating in restaurants, laundries, and rooming houses; attending political meetings in ships' quarters, hotels, and Baptist churches. Khan's story gives us a sense of just how different were the pathways through which Indian ex-seamen moved after jumping ship in the United States, compared to the smaller number of Indian elites—students, intellectuals, and professionals—who lived in the United States during the Asian exclusion era and the much larger numbers who arrived after 1965. As racialized and criminalized workers, Indian maritime deserters inhabited different spaces onshore, they encountered different people, ideas, difficulties, and challenges.

As a result, they were presented with different possibilities for reimagining themselves as social, cultural, and political actors, and this is what Dada Khan's memoir illuminates so clearly. From his jail cell in India, Khan described the "political awakening" he experienced as he moved through three spaces where Indian seamen became a presence in the United States during the 1910s and 1920s: the American merchant marine, the waterfronts and expatriate nationalist circles of New York City, and the social and political worlds of Black Bottom and Paradise

Valley in Detroit. His was a long and circuitous journey. After his desertion in New York City in 1918, and his short stint working at the DuPont munitions factory in Carney's Point, New Jersey, Khan spent four years working in the engine rooms of American steamships, returning to live in New York at the end of each journey and shipping back out whenever he found work on another ship.[2] Khan's trips took him to French and Italian ports within the war zone in the final year of World War I, and then on a series of shorter voyages to Mexico, Brazil, Argentina, and Trinidad after the end of the war. While in port in New York City, Khan was drawn deeply into anticolonial politics, joining other seamen who were working in coalition with the expatriate organization Friends of Freedom for India (FFI). Ultimately, Khan found work on a voyage that took him around the world: southward through the Caribbean and the Panama Canal, then to Yokohama, Shanghai, and Hong Kong, then across the Indian Ocean, through the Suez Canal, across the Mediterranean, and northward to England before returning to New York again. As U.S. shipping began to slump in the early 1920s, Khan increasingly experienced racial discrimination within the American merchant marine. In disgust and frustration, he left New York City and the maritime industry and ventured into the industrial belt of the U.S. Midwest. Here he spent three years repairing boilers on railway engines in Olean, New York, south of Buffalo, then several months pursuing his aviation license in rural Ohio before traveling to Detroit in 1925, to join the other Indian ex-seamen who were living in Black Bottom and working in the city's booming auto factories.[3]

Amir Haider Khan was transformed through his travels and encounters in the varied working-class spaces of ships and factories, port cities and industrial towns. Every step of the way, the escaped seaman from rural Kashmir forged friendships and alliances across differences of ethnicity, class, gender, and nationality that expanded his conceptions of justice and injustice, broadened his racial consciousness, and sharpened his convictions as a political actor. The ships' crews that Khan joined in New York differed from those on British steamers. In the absence of a strong American merchant marine, U.S. shipping companies drew in a much more diverse work force.[4] As a result, Khan's shipmates included white and "Negro" Americans, Scots, Irish, and Irish Americans, Mexicans, South Americans, Italian Americans, Hawaiians, as well as other seamen from India.[5]

New York City itself was not only full of immigrants from all over the world, but was, by the early 1920s, a meeting place for expatriates, exiles, and seamen from India, Ireland, and Egypt, who found common cause and forged working alliances in their struggles against British colonialism.[6] In these contexts, Khan saw his political focus expand from the struggles he had experienced on British steamships to the struggles of all peoples living under the domination of British imperialism. Ultimately, Khan's witness, experiences, and negotiation of U.S. racism—and his engagement with the African American community in Detroit—expanded his political vision even further. Beyond detailing his varied travels, Khan's memoir is striking for the way it records these changes in consciousness. Over the course of the memoir's first volume, Khan describes his journey as he is transformed from an "ignorant and impoverished" teenage coal passer to a committed young internationalist and anti-imperialist.

From Coal Passer to Revolutionary

Dada Amir Haider Khan came of age at a moment when Indian expatriates were organizing against British rule from outposts across the world—in North America, Europe, South Africa, and East and Southeast Asia. In the opening decades of the twentieth century, and particularly after the start of the World War, British authorities attempted to police the wide range of these anti-colonial activities. In the United States, they worked with U.S. authorities to disrupt the work of the nationalist Ghadar party on the West Coast, and of a variety of allied radical students and intellectuals, predominantly from Bengal, who were active in New York City. One of many British concerns at this time was the fact that Indian radicals were disguising themselves as seamen and using the maritime trade to move into and out of India undetected. This was the method, for example, by which Sailendranath Ghose, one of the expatriate leaders in New York, had used to elude capture on the subcontinent and reprise his nationalist activities in North America. By the 1920s, British authorities had also begun to worry about another threat—of Indian nationalist elites like Ghose "using" Indian seamen to transport guns and propaganda from the United States and Europe back to the subcontinent.[7] The British assumption was that the seamen themselves were simply conduits—that they were dangerous not because they had developed an ideological opposition to British rule, but because their movements in and out of the world's port cities were so extensive and difficult to police. Lascars, in other words, were a threat not because they were thinking people but because they were mobile. Khan's story makes clear, however, that maritime workers were thinking independently and incisively about the injustices of British rule, and that in his case, it was precisely his mobility—and the varied conflicts, encounters, alliances, and friendships that he experienced as he moved through and eventually out of the maritime world—that led to the radicalization of his thought.

Before deserting in New York, the young Khan already had a bent for organizing his Indian shipmates on British ships whenever he perceived an injustice had taken place. At the beginning of one voyage from England to Southeast Asia a sixteen-year-old Khan strategized with and represented his crew to force the firing of a particularly cruel and unfair *serang* and have him replaced by the crew's own elected representative.[8] Despite such ship-based activism, Khan described himself as politically unaware at this stage in his life, his activities confined to a world of localized disputes over conditions on specific steamships. In the first volume of his memoir, as he narrates the twists and turns of his early "wandering life" Khan accounts for how he developed from these early attempts at righting wrongs on steamships to the point of having a broader political vision. In this sense, the memoir is a unique chronicle of how the events a seaman witnessed, the people he met, and the things he experienced within and beyond the networks of Indian maritime deserters in the United States ultimately led to the expansion and maturing of his political consciousness.

What stands out in Khan's account is the variety of both Indian and non-Indian spaces, encounters, and friendships that drove this process of transformation. Khan locates the beginnings of his "political awareness" in his friendship with an Irish American shipmate during one of his first voyages out of New York as an American merchant marine. On this trip, which took Khan to Saint-Nazaire, France, at the end of the First World War, the impending Versailles peace treaty "created a vague interest in the political minded members of the crew, particularly the engine-room staff," and it was the Irish American Joe Mulkane who became Khan's source of political information and analysis. "He and I worked together as extra firemen in the engine room," writes Khan, "[we] slept in adjacent bunks, and while the majority of those in our quarters spoke Spanish, he was the only one with whom I could chat in my broken English. Though he was sixteen years my elder, he treated me as an equal in every respect." When news reached them that Joe's father, also a sailor and an active Irish nationalist, had been murdered under suspicious circumstances in Egypt, Khan was not only witness to his friend's grief and anger, but now learned from him, over the course of several months of conversations, about the Irish struggle against British rule. "Being the son of an Irish revolutionary," Khan recounts, "Joe knew all about the sins and misdeeds which the British had perpetrated on Ireland, including the way they pitted one portion of the Irish people against the other. . . . He would frequently relate to me the various tactics by which a small country like England was able to dominate so many races and nationalities in different parts of the world."[9]

Through his friendship with Joe Mulkane, Khan's previous understanding of the dynamics of British power in the context of steamships and maritime labor began to develop into an understanding of British imperial power across the globe, and Khan began to see the United States not merely as a place where he could find better pay for his work as a seaman, but also as a nation that offered him a haven from the injustices of British rule. Khan thus describes his relationship with Mulkane, set against the human devastation they both saw at the end of the war, as a key moment of transition in his early life: "Through my constant association with a man like Joe, my interest and knowledge about the United States increased and I began to love and respect Americans while my dislike for the British grew. The seeds planted by the vicissitudes and ever-changing surroundings of my wandering boyhood and the more recent events connected with the World War began to germinate into a political consciousness, sown by a pro-U.S., anti-British, American-born son of an Irish revolutionary. It was through Joe that my first anti-British, pro-Indian sentiment began to grow." An Irish nationalist sailor had turned Khan into a nascent Indian revolutionary through a friendship that began in the engine room and sleeping quarters of an American steamship.[10]

Khan's political development took its next step after he returned to New York, met other Indian seamen who had gone through a similar process of "awakening," and became involved with the expatriate organization the Friends of Freedom for India (FFI). Interestingly, although Khan now came in contact with the FFI's founder, Sailendranath Ghose, and the other elite male leaders of the Indian nationalist community in New York, including Taraknath Das and Basant Kumar Roy, these were not the figures who most affected him and stoked his own revolutionary sentiments. Rather it was Ghose's American partner, Agnes Smedley, an older Sikh representative of the Ghadar Party, and Khan's own cohort of "seafaring men" who collectively fostered his nationalism and helped draw him further into radical politics. In this period, around 1920–1921, it was the Twenty-Third Street laundry and dry-cleaning shop run by his friend Azim, an ex-seaman from Punjab, that became Khan's primary space of political community. Azim's shop was the place Khan would "rush" back to whenever he returned from a job at sea. "This," writes Khan, "was one of the places where Indian [ex-seamen] would frequently meet and one could get information regarding political developments in India." After returning from a short trip to Trinidad in 1920, Khan writes, he went straight to Azim's shop and "met some of the members of this social group who gave me the most glowing and optimistic account of the progress of the National Anti-British Movement in India." While Khan's description of this group of Indian workers may reflect his own political vision in the 1940s, it is clear that he and these men had not only begun to come together in New York City around ties of kinship, language, and work, but also now encouraged among one another a shared sense of possibility for an independent India. "Under normal circumstances, they would have no interest in politics," says Khan, "yet now these humble sons of India were living in anticipation and hope of momentous changes—changes that would shake off all the old fetters, the religious and caste prejudices . . . which had split our people into innumerable divisions."[11]

At Azim's laundry on Twenty-Third Street, among this group of "politically minded seafaring men," Khan also met the man whom he describes simply as the "Ghadr Sikh"—a forty-year-old veteran member of the Ghadar Party, whose background, like that of the ex-seamen, appears to have been rural or working-class, and who had come to New York City to work among the Indian community there.[12] Through his friendship with this Ghadr Sikh, Khan continued the political tutelage he had begun with Joe Mulkane on board the SS *Applease.* According to Khan, he "had devoted himself wholly to the cause of freedom for our people and could detail the litany of British misdeeds and episodes of brutality towards members of various revolutionary organizations. . . . He would often narrate stories of the struggles that were going on in various British colonies, particularly Ireland and Egypt. When he was not speaking to us, he used to sing or recite selected pieces from 'the Gadar Ki Goonj.'" What is significant here is that the Ghadr Sikh's appeal to Khan and his group of ex-seamen relied on a specifically working-class publication of the Ghadar Movement—*Ghadar di Gunj*—as well as modes of address rooted in working-class political traditions on the subcontinent: storytelling, singing, recitation. It was, in other words, from within their own radicalized community of steamship workers, and through this representative of the Ghadar Party, that Khan and his cohort of ex-seamen came into the larger fold of Indian and other anti-British nationalist groups in New York City. Khan himself writes that he "became very attached to the 'Ghadr Sikh' and would spend all [his] free time in his company," and it was as a result of this relationship that the Sikh "acquainted [Khan] with a variety of anti-British radical organizations and institutions and a number of personalities associated with these movements who were staying in New York at this time." This included the young American radical Agnes Smedley.

Although it is unclear from Khan's account how much direct interaction he had with Smedley, he was deeply affected by the example of her work for the Indian cause, devoting several pages to her in his memoir. By the time he met her, Smedley had already been involved in Indian politics in the United States for several years, having been tried, along with Sailendranath Ghose and a group of West Coast Ghadarites, in the so-called Hindu-German Conspiracy Case of 1917, in which she and the others were accused of working with the German government to smuggle weapons and ammunition from the United States to revolutionaries in India. Three years later, Khan describes her as the driving force behind the Friends of Freedom for India, revealing in his observations the gendered dynamic of expatriate nationalist politics at that moment. While figures like Ghose, Das, and Roy were the recognized founders and spokesmen of the organization, who garnered the attention of New York's political circles, Smedley was, according to Khan, the person whose organizational work, alliance building, and strategic decisions made the organization run. This was particularly apparent to Khan in the months leading up to the FFI's first annual conference in December 1920, when Smedley organized a small army of young women to put everything together. "[I]t was Agnes Smedley alone," writes Khan,

> whose dynamic energy and magnetic personality had enlisted and brought together support . . . for the cause of Indian freedom from various American liberal politicians, Irish Americans and other anti-British elements. Many young women helped in the office as secretarial staff, preparing for the first congress of the organization by collecting an enormous store of facts and literature on India. Then they typed innumerable letters of invitation, circulars, notices and press reports . . . collected money, made arrangements for propaganda meetings, etc. Finally, they had to manage the tremendous workload connected with the open congress of the "Friends of Freedom for India."[13]

Khan was equally impressed by a campaign that Smedley headed up in which the FFI sought to intervene in the raids that the U.S. government was pursuing against the hundreds of Indian seamen working in U.S. factories at this time. On learning about the thirty-nine Indian seamen who were rounded up from western Pennsylvania factories in July and August of 1920 and imprisoned at Ellis Island in preparation for deportation, Smedley secured a lawyer for the men under the banner of the FFI, then wrote to elected representatives and rallied others to their cause. Khan, who was present in New York, between voyages, as this case unfolded, writes that Smedley "moved every quarter to get these poor, illiterate workers released from the clutches of the U.S. Immigration Department. First they were released on bail, then she continued the fight until they were permitted to live in the United States unconditionally."[14] As a maritime worker, Khan was clearly moved by the fact that Smedley could shift her political energies from pursuing the lofty goal of Indian independence to addressing the everyday difficulties and concerns of Indian ex-seamen in the United States—and that she could see, as he no doubt felt, that both efforts were part of the same struggle. Agnes Smedley further advanced Khan's understanding of the necessity for and possibilities of political organizing, as well as his own sense of himself as a political actor. "The manner in which she struggled unceasingly, day after day, without proper rest, working passionately in the great American metropolis for a country she had never seen . . . intensified my vaguely awakened patriotic feelings. She was the first political woman [to win] my spontaneous admiration and respect, and even subconsciously inspired me, though she never knew it and I did not let her know."

After detailing a gradual process of politicization, which grew from his relationships with Smedley, Joe Mulkane, the Ghadr Sikh, and his own cohort of politically minded "seafaring men," Khan describes the 1920 FFI convention, at the Hotel McAlpin in midtown Manhattan, as a moment of personal catharsis. Khan attended the two-day congress alongside other Indian seamen and workers, as well as representatives of the Ghadar Party, the FFI leadership, delegates from Irish and Egyptian nationalist organizations, a wide range of American liberals, radicals, and sympathizers with the Indian cause, and "[m]ost of the [other] Indians who were in New York at that time," including students, businessmen, and tourists. He was enthralled both by the passionate speeches and calls for India's freedom that ran over the course of both days and by the sheer spectacle that Smedley had orchestrated. Strategically mobilizing Orientalist fantasies to the cause at hand, Smedley had passed out colored turbans to the Indian students and workers and had dressed all her young female volunteers in colorful saris. This not only "enchanted and thrilled the sophisticated American visitors . . . [and] attract[ed] the attention of the . . . public towards the gathering," but aided Smedley's fund-raising efforts; as "the volunteers went through the rows and galleries with their collection boxes," Khan writes, "the attractive and novel appearance of the young girls, with their pleading eyes, helped evoke a generous response." Khan's own bright red turban, which he thought people might associate with communist Russia, became a sign of his newfound political confidence. After leaving the FFI convention with a group of Ghadar revolutionaries, he recounts: "Passers by would gape at our strange head gear as we walked along 8th Avenue toward the [Ceylon India] restaurant, particularly at my red turban which was jolting [to] some American sensibilities. . . . [But] I was now bold enough to act according to my own opinions, and did not worry if other people liked it. . . . I had begun to fancy anything radical, proudly and demonstratively walking through the crowded streets in the company of representatives of the Gadar Party."[15]

For Khan, the 1920 conference of the FFI thus marked the consolidation of a radical anti-imperialist politics that had begun with his earliest experiences of British power and injustice on board steamships. His political ideas had gained greater focus and clearer articulation as a result of his encounters, interactions, and conversations with Joe Mulkane, Agnes Smedley, and other Indian ex-seamen in New York. His decision to carry a trunk full of copies of *Ghadar di Gunj* on his next steamship out of New York City—along with a pistol provided to him by the Ghadr Sikh[16]—was the culmination of these years of developing "awareness." It is at this stage that he joined the ranks of an unknown number of other Indian seamen who took a similar route into nationalist politics and who, because of their global reach and the porousness of the ports they visited, became one of the more vexatious problems with which British authorities were dealing in this era as they sought to contain the growing independence movement. In Khan's case, he approached his role in the movement with evangelical zeal, not merely transporting Ghadar literature but using every stop along his ship's journey—which took him from New York to Boston and then through the Caribbean and the Panama Canal to East and Southeast Asia—as an opportunity to find local communities of expatriate Indians and bring them into the nationalist fold.

Khan spent his spare moments on board ship memorizing revolutionary poems and songs, so like his mentor in New York, he could most effectively engage his audiences, who were mostly farmers, work-ers, or sailors like him.[17] Before his ship left the United States, as it loaded on goods in Boston, Khan spent "most of my free time . . . deliv-ering political discourses on board a British ship from Calcutta that was lying nearby." He describes these efforts at "political speaking" as a progression from his earlier experiences addressing ships officers as an advocate for the crews he worked with as a teenager; his effectiveness and insight as a speaker, in other words, came from his own day-to-day experiences in the maritime trade. "Every evening," he writes:

> I would go onboard the British ship to speak to the Indian crew. Among them were many middle-aged men who had served on Brit-ish ships for many years and might have traveled much more than I did. Yet they would sit attentively late into the evening listening to my pleas of support [for] the struggle to liberate the land of their birth. My arguments were based on my practical experiences as a toiler . . . I put to them the question of why we should be treated so badly and given such meager wages by the British. "Because we do not belong to an independent nation which can enact legislation to protect us," I said to them. Then I asked, "Why is it that we are looked down upon by the people of other countries . . ." respond-ing, "Because we are slaves under foreign domination at home" . . . Before leaving, I gave them copies of Gadar ki Goonj to take back to India.[18]

This was a routine that Khan now repeated among groups of Indians at port after port, in the Panama Canal Zone, in Yokohama, Japan, and in Singapore, until finally British authorities caught up with him in Hong Kong and a bunkmate had to throw Khan's pistol and remaining Ghadar literature overboard to protect him from arrest. Although his activities were aborted for the rest of the voyage, this trip brought a further matur-ing of Khan as a political actor—it was the moment he made the transi-tion from learning about, discussing, and protesting British imperialism to actually working as part of an expatriate movement for the over-throw of British colonial rule. At the same time, Khan's account of this voyage is important for what it reveals about the larger community of maritime workers around him: namely, that there was an independent realm of nationalist activity among Indian seamen in New York and other ports in the 1910s and 1920s—a realm that was connected to that of the "educated" radicals like Sailendranath Ghose, Taraknath Das, and others, but which had its own distinct spaces, circulations, interactions, and vernacular, to which these elite men had little access.

Race, Racism, and Internationalism

Amir Haider Khan and the other Indian seamen who jumped ship in the United States during this period also occupied a realm of work and everyday life that set them apart from elite radicals and introduced them in a more immediate way to the realities, and often the violence, of American racism. While Khan's entry into Indian nationalist politics is central to his narrative, his account of his developing consciousness around race and racism is equally significant. Although this parallel "awakening" had a longer arc, it was a crucial part of his experience in the United States, in the U.S. merchant marine, and in his transformation from coal passer to revolutionary. Khan's writing about race is striking in its honesty, particularly as he assesses, after the fact, his own blind spots in his regard for African Americans and in his understanding of antiblack racism. Over time, Khan came to recognize that his nationalism was at the root of this blindness—that because his rejection of British subjecthood was predicated upon an embrace of the United States as a land of freedom and opportunity, he was unable to see the negative aspects of American society that were right in front of him. This changed over time, as Khan witnessed racial injustices and experienced them himself, and as he and other Indian ex-seamen lived near and among working-class African American migrants in Detroit at a time of major political mobilization in the black community.

Khan's account of his shifting consciousness around race is largely written in a reflective past tense in which he simultaneously records the instances of racial injustice, large and small, that he witnessed after jumping ship in the United States in 1918, and notes his often inadequate responses to or understanding of these events at the time they occurred. A striking example came early on in his career as an engine-room worker on American vessels. In the fall of 1918, the ship on which he was working, which was en route from New York to Saint-Nazaire, France, to deliver supplies to U.S. troops, struck a rock in the shallows outside Saint-Nazaire and began taking on water. The barges that arrived to save the ship, Khan writes, brought pumps to keep the ship from sinking, along with "groups of Negro Army workmen," who were sent into the icy water deep inside the hold of the sinking ship to salvage its cargo. Khan watched as these black men, "at the instruction of their white overseers, would fish out pieces of cargo night and day." This process continued for two months, even after the end of hostilities. "Though Christmas is the biggest [holiday] in the United States," Khan remarks, "there was no relief from the ceaseless toil of the Negro workers, whose bodies had become numbed by continuously working in cold weather and using the same wet overalls without any change. While standing nearby, I heard a Negro sergeant complain on behalf of his men that they were ready to collapse from exhaustion. His white overseer threatened that . . . the slightest hesitation would result in punishment. Although the war had ended, the harsh treatment of the Negroes who were among the U.S. expeditionary forces in France did not improve."[19] Khan was equally struck by the way U.S. military officials imposed American racial hierarchies upon the French port cities where American forces were concentrated, noting that while, in French cities like Paris, "one could often see Negroes, Chinese, or men of other colonial nationalities accompanied by French ladies in the most fashionable shops and cafes," in Brest and Saint-Nazaire, "the Americans . . . compelled the . . . French to segregate the American Negroes, and all the local businesses including restaurants, catered only to Whites. . . . [T]he Negroes were allowed only into some of the ugliest backstreet dumps."[20]

At this stage, however, Khan did not appear to have been moved beyond the act of observing and remembering, and in fact admits to having been "infected" by American racism himself. Having caught cold while his ship was docked in Brest, Khan was sent to an army hospital onshore. Here, because of his dark skin, he was put in the black medical ward that U.S. authorities had set up, but instead of protesting the segregation in principle, Khan sought to be reassigned. "Seeing that they had put me in a Negro ward, I did not want to stay and told the nurse I was really not that sick. . . . She reported this to the admitting doctor who probably sensed the real reason for my refusal to stay. . . . [H]e asked me where I was born and I replied, 'I was born in India.' He instructed that I be put in a ward with whites and told me that I should remain in the hospital for treatment. . . . This I was [now] quite content to do and I received very good care."[21] Writing more than twenty years later, Khan used this episode to illustrate that "American racism often takes the form of a contagious disease," accounting for his own actions and attitudes in these naturalized terms: "Even I, whose skin was not much fairer than the average Negro, had subconsciously been infected by a superiority complex within a few months of my arrival in the United States, though I knew absolutely nothing of the country and could not even speak its language."[22] Over the next few years, Khan's response to repeated personal experiences of racism in the American merchant marine would continue to take this form—he attempted to disassociate himself from African Americans and "prove" his worth as a seaman to his white American shipmates while explaining away these shipmates' racism through the metaphor of disease, or being "infested with the germ of this peculiar psychological illness."

However, Khan's attempts to explain away racism as an anomoly rather than a central feature of American society eventually began to break down. Amid a postwar slump in shipping, Khan writes, the American Legion and Ku Klux Klan gained increasing influence among white American seamen. Now he experienced one incident after another in which white crew members shunned him the minute he stepped on board a new ship. Although his response was to work even harder once on board, to gain the respect of these racist shipmates—to help them overcome their "illness"—he reached a breaking point in 1922, when, assigned by the Shipping Board in New York to an outgoing steamer, he experienced, once again, a "complete social boycott." When, on his second day on board, with the ship still in port, the "sneering" first engineer accused him of arriving late to his shift and "pick[ed] a quarrel," Khan quit on the spot, leaving the ship, and maritime work, for good. Khan's narration makes clear that this moment was the culmination of many years of growing self-confidence and racial consciousness and the beginning of the end for Khan's belief in the promise of American equality and opportunity. Interestingly, this loss of faith in the national myth was grounded in an equally strong faith in the "cosmopolitanism" of New York City:

> I was not surprised or offended [by the racism on my previous ship] because the crew was from the southern part of the United States and I had joined the ship at Norfolk, Virginia where racial and co-lour prejudice was rampant. But I did not expect . . . such prejudice around the port of New York . . . Indeed, I was proud of New York and its cosmopolitan life of which I always spoke very highly. I felt more confident in New York than in India . . . I had innumerable friends and acquaintances in the city from various walks of life. Thus I was not willing to tolerate any racism or be looked down upon on account of my foreign birth or the colour of my skin. I had suffered through nasty personal experiences in the past . . . and the additional treatment on this ship added insult to injury.[23]

Ironically, it was this incident that sent Khan running from New York City, its waterfront, his friends, and his political work to take the first job he could find in the industrial interior of the country—in this case a job in rail yard in Olean, in far upstate New York.[24]

The move upstate initiated a series of events that gave Khan a view of American racism that was less clouded by his faith in the abstract prom-ises of his adopted country. In Olean, he almost immediately found himself in an altercation and fistfight with a white coworker, who re-ferred to him as a "little Hindu" and threatened, "I shall kill you and send you back . . . where you came from."[25] When he took leave from his job for two months to pursue a course in small plane aviation in rural southern Illinois, Khan was confronted by a local man "with the handle of a gun protruding from his hip pocket" who told him to "leave this place on the next available train." He discovered that "not a single Negro was allowed to work, live, or enter the vicinity of the town." Khan still felt compelled, when he met his aviation instructor, to insist that "I am not a coloured man, but . . . come from India." At the same time, when he describes the lengths that his instructor now had to take in order to convince the owner of the town's hotel that he is "not a Negro," Khan relates this act of racial distinction in a sarcastic rather than matter-of-fact tone: "I presumed he was giving the owner a discourse in anthropology, and probably sociology . . . to convince the man that I was not a Negro [and h]ence no outrage would be committed against the white race in renting me a room. . . . After completing all the arrangements, he came back and, smiling triumphantly, announced his formidable achievement."[26] By the time that Khan, resting in an Indiana hospital room after crashing his plane on a test flight, looked out his window to see a white-hooded phalanx of the Ku Klux Klan marching through the town's main street, he had already come to a clearer understanding of his position in the United States' racial hierarchies—closer to "Negroes" than to the white shipmates he had once tried to "cure" of their "illness"—and his belief in "America" had been deeply shaken.

It was in this state that Khan came to rejoin his network of Indian ex-sailors in the Detroit neighborhood of Black Bottom, where he went through a final transition in his understanding of race and racism in the United States. Khan and the other Indian Muslim seafaring men living in Detroit in 1925 had come to the city at a significant moment for its African American residents. Marcus Garvey's influence in Detroit and in black communities across the United States was at its height, and this year, after appeals against manufactured charges of mail fraud failed, Garvey was sent to jail. Also in 1925, Duse Mohammed Ali, a Sudanese Egyptian Pan-Africanist and adviser to Garvey, began holding Muslim meetings and prayer services in Detroit that brought African American and immigrant Muslims together within the same organization, the Universal Islamic Society. These meetings, which were attended by some of the city's Indian ex-seamen, may have influenced the development of two of the most important African American Muslim groups, the Moorish Science Temple and the Nation of Islam.[27] Finally, 1925 was the year in which an African American doctor, Ossian Sweet, went on trial for murder after he and his friends took up arms to defend his new home in a previously white Detroit neighborhood from a violent mob. While Dr. Sweet's case garnered widespread national attention, it was a particularly strong rallying point for Detroit's own African American community, which included thousands of residents of Black Bottom and Paradise Valley who were recent migrants from the segregated South.[28]

Khan and other Indian Muslim seamen were living near the heart of Detroit's African American community on the east side of downtown Detroit at this moment of cultural and political ferment. No doubt, many of the men from the subcontinent kept to their own circles, living and socializing among Indian ex-seafarers and other immigrant Muslim autoworkers in their pocket of rooming houses on East Congress, Fort, and Lafayette Streets. As in New Orleans, however, a number of Indians married African American women and moved further into the residential center of Paradise Valley and Black Bottom, to the north and east of the immigrant boardinghouse district. British surveillance documents from the period show that Detroit's British Consul was keeping a close eye on this smaller group of more settled Indian ex-seamen. While the consul eventually expressed concern that "the lascars" were a radical element within a local Indian nationalist organization, the United India League of America, his first worry seems to have been that the ex-seamen had "married coloured women" and were associating with members of the "large influx of . . . Coloured people from the south," gaining the negative attention of local authorities and bringing disrepute to a group of Indian students then attending Michigan State University.[29]

It is unclear exactly where Khan himself took up residence in 1925—it appears to have been in or near the immigrant boardinghouse district— but he was quickly drawn to Black Bottom's cultural and entertainment district, and pulled into the local African American community's unfolding political activism.

In his memoir, Khan describes for the first time "hav[ing] the opportunity to get in close contact with . . . American Negroes" and to "appreciate [their] difficulties." This brought about a "revived political interest;" Khan now "made full use of [his] free time every week by attending . . . political, educational, or social meetings." He learned about the militant Marxist organization the African Blood Brotherhood, its newspaper, the *Crusader*, Garvey's United Negro Improvement Association and Black Star Line, and more generally, the frustrations of black ex-servicemen who returned to face unemployment and increased racial violence after the war. From his jail cell in India years later, Dada Khan wrote about this moment with passion, calling the United Negro Improvement Association the only "organization worth its name at the time" and expressing admiration for the self-sufficiency of the African American community in Detroit, which included both workers and "already, a middle-class educated section . . . such as lawyers, doctors, dentists, preachers, teachers, journalists, and some property and house-owners." As a whole, the community were "holding their own."[30]

Khan writes of two key figures who brought him into contact with "many political-minded . . . Negroes" in Detroit. The first was a roommate, whom Khan describes as a "South Indian who was brought up by American missionaries in [the] U.S.A." Although he does not specify the race of his roommate's adoptive parents, it is clear that as an adult, this South Indian was living in the black community and active within its church circles. The roommate began taking Khan to "Negro churches" in the neighborhoods where, in Khan's words, African Americans "led a segregated life as untouchables have to do in . . . India." Visits to services and meetings in these churches apparently became a part of Khan's routine for the months he lived in Detroit. The second person who introduced Khan to black political circles was Duse Mohammed Ali. Historian Richard Brent Turner has described Duse Mohammed as "a prominent member of London's Muslim community" in the 1910s who became Marcus Garvey's "mentor in Pan-Africanism." Duse Mohammed had published a journal, *The African Times and Orient Review*, from 1912 to 1920, in which he published "many articles on Islam in the British Empire, particularly in India," and developed a political vision that fused Pan-Africanism, anti-imperialism, and Pan-Islamic unity.[31] In the 1920s, he came to the United States and eventually settled in Detroit.

Dada Khan does not detail how he first came in contact with Duse Mohammed Ali. It may have been through some of the other Indian Muslims in Detroit who had begun attending the meetings and prayer services that Duse Mohammed was conducting under the auspices of a newly formed Islamic Society. Khan was impressed by the diversity of this group, in which Indians participated side by side with African, Arab, and African American Muslims. He was also drawn to Duse Mohammed's ideas of "mutual help . . . among the different oppressed peoples." The Sudanese Egyptian, writes Khan, had started "an organization at Detroit . . . to develop the worldwide commercial relations between all the colonial, semi-colonial, and oppressed people" and had "collected around him some middle-class Negro supporters of his plan apart from some Negro working people." What is interesting in Khan's account, however, is his suspicion both of Duse Mohammed's reliance on religion as the primary unifying force for oppressed peoples and of the elder figure's underlying motives. Identifying more with his black neighbors and coworkers than with his Muslim "co-religionist," Khan thought it wrong that Duse Mohammed Ali would take the hard-earned money of "Negro working people" in subscription fees to support his commercial schemes. Khan's relationship with Duse Mohammed, in other words, stands out not only, as Khan says, for the opportunity it provided for him to "[come] to know many more Negroes" in Detroit, but also as an indication of his own sharpening political vision, in which Khan increasingly came to see the importance of global solidarity based not on religion, but on the shared and overlapping oppression of the racialized, the colonized, and the "wage slave."

This vision, rooted in Khan's experiences as a maritime worker and an industrial worker, a colonial subject of British India and a racialized subject in the United States, came together in Detroit as Khan witnessed the grassroots African American movement in support of Ossian Sweet. Khan appears to have developed a strong connection to Detroit's working-class black community by the time of the Sweet trial, and was swept into the event, attending informational and support meetings in black churches and community spaces much as he had attended similar events in support of Indian independence in New York five years before. Khan was deeply moved by what he saw. "There [was] all sorts of [string]-pulling going on behind the scene to hinder [Sweet's] defence, and thus to deprive the accused of a fair trial. Negroes in the U.S.A., who were fully aware of the whites' treatment of their race rose to the occasion throughout the country. . . . Negro groups did not leave any stone unturned to rally the race in defence of the accused."[32] Describing one packed meeting that he attended "in the company of my South Indian friend" at Detroit's historic Second Baptist Church, Khan writes that "speaker after speaker poured out his heart to the audience in the most moving speeches." Then, "when the appeal was made for contributions for Dr. Sweet's defence fund," Khan continues, "everyone contributed whatever [they] could. By me were sitting some Negro working women of different ages. When the collection basket came, those who had no cash with them took off their earrings, finger rings, or whatever else [they had] to contribute towards the defence funds. . . . That day I saw how in face of a common danger, the Negro community stood united in defence of [a] man of their race."[33]

Haider Khan's description of the sustained organizing efforts of the African American community around Sweet's case makes clear that his experience of this time deepened his understanding of both the violent and the institutional sides of American racism; demonstrated to him what was possible when people came together around a common cause across various lines of difference (in this case class, age, and gender); consolidated his racial and political identification with African Americans; and ultimately stretched his own politics beyond the realm of anti-British anti-imperialism to an internationalism that was inspired by and rooted in his witness of African American popular protest. Ultimately, Khan's decision to pursue political training in the Soviet Union later in 1925 appears to have been as catalyzed by this experience of African American antiracist organizing as by his experiences as a worker or his meetings with the Soviet representatives who recruited him.

Dada Amir Haider Khan was clearly an extraordinary figure, both in terms of the incredible breadth of his travels, encounters, and experiences over the course of the seven years that followed his desertion from the SS *Khiva* in 1918 and in terms of the written record he left behind. This is precisely why Khan's account is so important—not because it represents, from beginning to end, the exact trajectory that other Indian Muslim followed in the 1910s and 1920s, but because it provides a picture of so many of the *different* pathways that Indian seamen took and so many of the places they lived and worked. After jumping ship in New York City in 1918, almost everywhere Khan went and in almost everything he did, there were other Indian ex-seamen who were there or who had been there before him. On the New York waterfront; in its boarding-houses and Indian-run restaurants and laundries; in the meetings of the FFI in New York City and the United India League of America in Detroit; in the American merchant marine; in munitions factories in New Jersey, railway workshops and steel foundries in New Jersey and upstate New York, and auto factories in Michigan; in Black Bottom rooming houses and Paradise Valley homes; in black churches and in the prayer meetings of Duse Mohammed Ali's Islamic Society in Detroit—in all these spaces through which Khan's trajectory passed, there were other Indian ex-seamen. His story thus gives us a sense of the possibilities that were open to Indian "seafaring men" as they moved through onshore networks in the United States—the pathways they followed and carved out; the spaces in which they lived, worked, and interacted; the encounters both within and outside Indian circles that were unique to their trajectories; and the transformations that were possible in the ways they saw themselves and the world.

CHAPTER 5

Bengali Harlem

There are West Indian, low class Mexican, low class Argentineans, low class Peruvians. They also come from East India. All of
them, however, when arrested, invariably [say they] are "Porto
Rican." In fact the incoming of these people is responsible for a
new racket. . . . We have come across groups lately in Harlem who
are selling fake Porto Rican birth certificates for $30 each.

—New York City Police Commissioner Mulrooney,
the *New York Age*, March 9, 1932

IF YOU HAD VISITED NEW YORK CITY in the spring of 1949, taken in a
Broadway show—say, *Death of a Salesman* or *South Pacific*—and then
happened to stroll along West Forty-Sixth Street looking to grab a meal
at one of the neighborhood's many and varied restaurants, you may well
have been tempted up a flight of stairs at number 144 to try the Indian
food at the Bengal Garden. The Bengal Garden was one of a handful of
Indian restaurants that had popped up in the theater district in recent
years. On entering this small, simple, rectangular space, you would have
likely been greeted and seen to your table by a Puerto Rican woman in
her midforties. This was Victoria Echevarria Ullah. She ran the front of
the restaurant and was stationed near the door. At a far corner table near
the back of the restaurant, you may have noticed a well-dressed and
distinguished-looking South Asian man, seated as if he were in his office,
speaking to one or more other men. He might have been speaking in Bengali or Urdu or English, or switching between the languages, depending
on his companions. This was Ibrahim Choudry, one of the owners of the

Bengal Garden, and a founder and officer of multiple community-based organizations, some East Pakistani, some Muslim American, and some interfaith. If you peeked into the back, you would have seen another South Asian man—solidly built, serious, and focused—doing everything from prepping to cooking to plating each dish, moving from one part of the kitchen to the next, sometimes swearing, and making the whole operation work. This was Habib Ullah, the restaurant's founder and other co-owner, and Victoria's husband. At the end of each night, after closing, all three headed uptown to go home. Habib and Victoria lived on the second floor of a five-story tenement building on a predominantly Puerto Rican block of East 102nd Street. Ibrahim Choudry had recently moved to a place on the other side of town, a ground-floor apartment on West Ninety-eighth Street, where his neighbors were Puerto Rican and Jewish.[1]

All three came to New York City between 1920 and 1935, and their lives intersected in Harlem. Choudry was likely the first to arrive in the city. He had been a student leader in East Bengal, had come to the attention of British colonial authorities, and had to flee India. He secured a job as a *serang* on an outgoing steamship, worked as a seafarer for a time, and deserted in New York City. Habib Ullah came to the city around the same time as Choudry. It is unclear how and why he left his village in the district of Noakhali at the age of fourteen, but at that young age he traveled to Calcutta and found a job on an outgoing ship. When his steamer reached the port of Boston, he either jumped ship or fell ill, and his ship continued without him. He could not read or write and barely spoke English, but somehow Habib made his way to New York City, where he lived with other Bengali ex-seamen on the Lower East Side and found work as a dishwasher and line cook. In the 1930s, Habib moved up the Lexington Avenue subway line to East Harlem, where more and more Bengalis were settling—and where he met Victoria. Victoria Echevarria had only recently come to the United States herself, from a neighborhood on the outskirts of San Juan, Puerto Rico. She was the eldest sister in a family of seven children, and when she was nineteen, her father died of a heart attack. Unable to find work in San Juan, Victoria set out on her own for New York City. She lived with some aunts and cousins who had settled in East Harlem, worked in factories, and started sending money back home.[2] The Bengal Garden was the result of these three individuals' pooling their expertise. Choudry put together the finances to start the restaurant; Victoria brought skills working with customers and handling the daily accounts; Habib brought his skills as a cook and his experience working in commercial kitchens throughout the city.

Their meeting and partnership grew out of the dynamic arena of migrations, encounters, and crossings that defined Harlem in the first half of the twentieth century. Harlem during this period is best known as the epicenter of the African American world. As thousands of African Americans joined the Great Migration in the opening decades of the twentieth century, New York City became a destination like no other, and Harlem became the neighborhood of all northern black neighborhoods. "To many oppressed within the limitations set up by the South," wrote Ray Stannard Baker in 1910, "it is indeed the promised land."[3] But Harlem was not just an end-point for southern migration; it was a destination for immigrants from other parts of the black diasporic world. By the time the first handful of Indian Muslim seamen moved uptown in the mid-1910s, the neighborhood around them was being transformed by thousands of immigrants from the English- and Spanish-speaking Caribbean: Jamaica, Barbados, the Bahamas, Puerto Rico, and Cuba. Choudry, Ullah, and other ex-seamen from the subcontinent were just a drop amid these larger streams of migrants, but they were one of several such smaller groups quietly settling into the uptown neighborhood, including Argentineans, Colombians, Mexicans, Panamanians, and Chinese.

As promising a place as it seemed, most Harlem residents in the 1910s–1930s struggled to get by. Since the turn of the century, more and more African Americans had moved uptown from other parts of the city in response to recurring waves of violence. By the interwar period, New York city was starkly divided and unequal; Harlem came to be, in the words of contemporary observers, a "city within a city," a "distinct nation," a "Negro community . . . with as definite lines of demarcation as if cut by a knife."[4] The neighborhood's housing and health conditions were poor, educational opportunities were limited, and the occupational structure of New York City was as segregated as its geography. Men of color were relegated to the city's lowest-paying jobs as unskilled laborers and service workers—porters, elevator operators, dishwashers. Women of color arriving from the South or the Caribbean found an even more limited range of occupations at significantly lower pay; close to three-quarters worked in personal and domestic service, while others labored in garment factories and other light manufacturing or operated boarding houses. Few of these jobs provided a living wage, so households had to pool resources to survive. The economic pressures on Harlem residents grew even more intense during the Depression. It was a context that could readily foster competition and conflict among the neighborhood's different groups.[5]

At the same time, as a space of what historian Earl Lewis has termed "overlapping diasporas," Harlem fostered new forms of identification and new formations of community. The neighborhood's varied inhabitants shared similar pasts and similar circumstances. They came to Harlem in the wake of antiblack violence in the South and the disruptions of British and U.S. rule in the Caribbean. Within one to two generations, most had moved from rural to urban settings, and all now faced forms of racial power in New York that were in some ways as oppressive as those they left behind. In Harlem, they maintained connections to previous lifeways and foodways and formed groups tied to shared origins: the Sons and Daughters of South Carolina, the West Indian Committee of America, the Club Borinquen.[6] But the neighborhood also brought people together across differences. It became a center for some of the era's strongest articulations of pan-African identity and anti-colonial internationalism, while intermarriage between African Americans and Caribbean immigrants brought members of different groups in contact with one another at the level of the personal, familial, and everyday.[7]

As they joined the flow into Harlem, South Asian Muslims became an important, if now forgotten, part of New York City and its uptown neighborhood. Many commuted downtown each day, crowded into subway trains with their African American, Puerto Rican, and West Indian neighbors, and worked beside them as doormen, elevator operators, dishwashers, line cooks and factory laborers. Others sold hot dogs from pushcarts along Harlem's main thoroughfares—Lexington Avenue, 110th Street, 116th Street. A handful saved enough money to open Indian restaurants in different parts of the neighborhood, and a select

few, like Choudry and Ullah, opened establishments in the heart of
midtown Manhattan. By the 1940s, members of this population, who
were predominantly from the maritime "sending" regions of East Bengal, established their own association, and spaces of daily gathering.
But they too shared much in their pasts and present with the other
groups around them. In Harlem they became part of a heterogeneous
Muslim community that included African Americans and immigrants
from Africa and the Middle East. And, as had happened in New Orleans,
Baltimore, and Detroit, a smaller number of these ex-seamen married
women from their adopted neighborhood, creating, together, a unique if
short-lived multiracial community.

Uptown Basti

When and how did a community of Bengali Muslim ex-seamen begin to
coalesce in Harlem? Dada Amir Haider Khan has provided a firsthand
account of the "colony" of Indian "seafaring men" who were living near
Manhattan's west-side waterfront, around 1920. The children of South
Asian men who jumped ship in New York in subsequent decades provide an equally vivid picture of the Bengali–Puerto Rican–African
American community that had formed by the 1940s and 1950s in Harlem and other parts of the city. What happened in the twenty intervening
years, between Khan's day and midcentury? Archival documents give us
some clues. The federal censuses of 1920 and 1930, draft registration records from the First World War, New York City directories, Manhattan
marriage certificates, and local news stories all bear traces of the working-
class Indian population that was settling into the city during the 1920s
and 1930s. Though scattered and disparate, these traces suggest a particular chain of entry into Manhattan: over time, Indian ex-seafarers moved
from New York's waterfronts—South Brooklyn, the Syrian district, and
Hell's Kitchen—first to the Tenderloin on Manhattan's West Side, then to
the Lower East Side, and then up the East Side elevated and subway lines
into Central and East Harlem.

During and immediately after the First World War, the archives show
that most of the city's working-class Indian population was living in the
Tenderloin, a few blocks from the West Side waterfront, in tenements

spread among the West Thirties and Forties. The characteristics of these men bear out Dada Khan's descriptions and closely mirror the characteristics of the Indian maritime and ex-maritime workforce. They were young, predominantly Muslim men, mostly nonliterate, working jobs in restaurants, hotels, and factories and on ships. The largest number were from Bengal, and the next largest groups appear to have been from Punjab and the Northwest Frontier, with a smaller number from Goa and Ceylon. Even as they were concentrated on the West Side, men from this demographic began to turn up in both the Lower East Side and Harlem during the war years. In 1918, for example, draft registrars recorded a twenty-five-year-old Indian Muslim man, Shooleiman Collu, living on Forsyth Street in the middle of the Lower East Side, working as an itinerant peddler.[8] Two years later, a federal census taker found Fayaz Zaman residing a few blocks away in a building of Jewish immigrants from Russia and Poland, working as a nickel plater in a local foundry. The Indian presence in Harlem at this time was larger, but less clearly tied to the maritime trade. There were several Caribbean migrants of Indian descent living in Central Harlem among other recent arrivals from British Guiana, Trinidad, and St. Vincent—Hugh and Rose Persaud, Lennox Maharage, Duncan Bourne, Byesing Roy—as well as men who had Anglicized their names—Edward Stevenson, Jack Amere, Joseph Harris. There was one Indian woman, Jane Williams, who was working as a maid for a Jewish family on West 120th Street, and there was Ranji Smile, a curry cook who had taken New York's high society by storm at the turn of the century and was now living in the West 130s. Yet, here again, scattered throughout the neighborhood, were men who fit the profile of escaped Indian seafarers: Nazir Ahmed, who was working as an elevator operator; Aladin Khan, a porter for a downtown candy company; Samuel Ali, a worker in a button factory; Mohammed Karim, a hotel cook.[9]

By the early 1930s, city and federal officials were recording a significantly larger population of working-class Indian men than previously, and their presence on the Lower East Side and in Harlem was becoming more concentrated and more distinct. About two dozen Indian Muslim men were living in the crowded tenements of the Lower East Side in a series of shared apartments on Clinton, Rivington, Norfolk,

Suffolk, Eldridge, and Orchard Streets. They were between nineteen and thirty-five years old and mostly worked in restaurants and hotels as doormen, porters, elevator operators, line cooks, busboys, dishwashers, countermen, and waiters. There were likely more of these men than what the documents show, as many would have thought it best to avoid census-takers and other officials. It is possible, in fact, that Indian men were drawn to the Lower East Side not just because of its low-rent tenements, but also because they could disappear into its dense population of immigrants from Eastern and Southern Europe. It is possible, in addition, that they were drawn to the neighborhood because of its kosher butchers, who, in the absence of a local Muslim community, provided the closest available approximation of halal meat. Uptown, however, the Indian population was even larger than it was on the Lower East Side. When federal census takers canvassed Harlem in April 1930, they recorded more than sixty-five Indian men residing at roughly forty-five different addresses throughout the neighborhood. Most of these men were clustered in two areas: East Harlem (in the eighteen city blocks between East Ninety-Eighth and 103rd Streets and Lexington and First Avenues), where their neighbors were primarily immigrants from Puerto Rico, Cuba, and the Dominican Republic, and lower Central Harlem (in the six city blocks bounded by West 112th and 118th Streets and Lenox and Fifth Avenues), where their neighbors were Puerto Rican, Cuban, African American and West Indian (Map 2).[10] It was here, New York's police commissioner claimed in 1932, that men from the subcontinent, barred from officially becoming part of the U.S. nation, sought to disappear into the communities around them, to pass, or even to gain new legal identities as Puerto Rican.[11]

By now, an increasing number of Indian Muslim ex-seamen were marrying within local communities of color. While roughly half the Indian population uptown in the 1930s were single men living as boarders or in small group households, one-third had married and were living with their Puerto Rican, African American, or West Indian spouses. The records of these unions are scattered among the thousands of New York City marriage certificates issued from the early 1920s through the late 1930s (Table 4). The majority of men listed in these records were in their twenties when they got married. They were either working in restaurants or doing other kinds of manual or semiskilled labor—ranging from silk

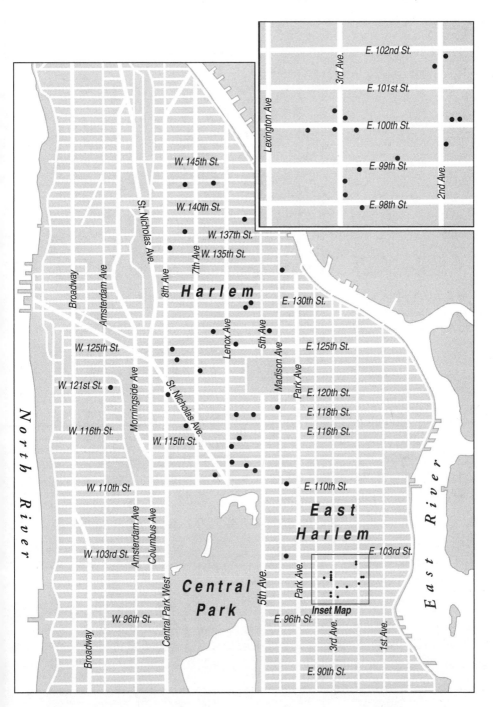

Map 2. Residences of Indians in Harlem, 1917–1937. Sources: USSS/DRC
WWI *Registration Cards* (various, 1917–1918); USDC/BC, *Population Schedules
for New York, NY* (various, 1920, 1930); CNY, *Certificates and Records of
Marriage* (various, 1920–1937); *New York Amsterdam News*, Marriage Notices and
Crime Reports (various, 1926–1937).

Table 4. Indian Mixed Marriages, Harlem and Lower East Side, 1922–1937

Date	Name	Age	Address	Color	Occupation	Birthplace
February 7, 1923	John Khan	22	1803 3rd Ave.	White	Laundry Worker	India
	Carmen Guzman	23	1985 2nd Ave.	White	—	Porto Rico
August 16, 1923	Mohammed Abcul	24	1803 3rd Ave.	White	Laundryman	India
	Sadie Simmonds	20	314 W. 133rd St.	Negro	—	Brooklyn, NY
January 3, 1925	Muslim Mia	24	341 1/2 W. 4th St.	Negro	Laborer	India
	Grace M. Dunbar	22	191 W. 134th St.	Negro	—	Elmira, NY
September 1, 1925	Rustum Alli	25	202 Broome St.	Colored	Mechanic	East India
	Beatrice Owens	21	202 Broome St.	Colored	—	Jacksonville, Florida
September 2, 1925	Abdul Hassan	28	70 Broome St.	White	Handyman	India
	Ethel LeVine	21	70 Broome St.	Colored	—	New York, NY
February 10, 1926	Solomon Khan	23	1808 3rd Ave.	White	Salesman	Calcutta, India
	Agnes Weeks	23	9 E. 130th St.	Colored	—	Barbados, BWI
July 10. 1926	Nawab Ali	24	222 E. 100th St.	Colored	Laundry Man	Calcutta, Br. East Indies
	Frances Santos	18	317 E. 100th St.	White	—	Porto Rico
June 2, 1927	Mokhd Ali	26	2971 W. 36th St.	White	Chauffer	Bangol, India
	Mable Leola Gibson	21	36 W. 128th St.	White	—	Baltimore, MD
April 1, 1929	Seconder Ali	30	69 W. 115th St.	White	Laborer	Bombay, India
	Maria Sedeno	27	54 E. 116th St.	White	—	San Juan, Puerto Rico

Date	Name	Age	Address	Race	Occupation	Birthplace
January 7, 1930	Wohad Ali	23	307 E. 100th St.	Colored	Laundry Work	India
	Maria Louisa Rivera	19	102 E. 103rd St.	Colored	—	Vega Baja, Puerto Rico
August 2, 1930	Caramath Ali	26	1978 2nd Ave.	White	Bell Boy	East India
	Carolina Green	27	230 E. 99th St.	White	—	Dominican Republic
August 2, 1930	Nawab Ali	29	222 E. 98th St.	Indian	Laundry Work	Calcutta, India
	Bernardina Colon	16	222 E. 98th St.	White	—	Juana Diaz, Puerto Rico
October 3, 1930	Kassim Ullah	27	329 Grand St.	Colored	Painter	East India
	Frances English	22	217 Grand St.	Colored	—	Carlisle, South Carolina
January 18, 1933	Habib Ali	23	90 Orchard St.	Colored	Waiter	Calcutta, India
	Dolores Velera	22	42 Rivington St.	Colored	—	Puerto Rico
December 14, 1934	Nabob Ali	28	57 E. 110th St.	White	Cook	Calcutta, India
	Maria Cleophe Jusino	22	57 E. 110th St.	White	—	Sabana Grande, P.R.
April 24, 1937	Kurban Ali	25	84 W. 115th St.	White	Silk Dyeing	India
	Esther Moulier	17	79 E. 109th St.	White	—	Santurce, Puerto Rico
June 26, 1937	Eleman Miah	27	39 W. 112th St.	East Indian	Cook's Helper	Calcutta, India
	Emma L. Douglass	22	183 W. 115th St.	Colored	—	Indianapolis, IN
August 23, 1937	Kala Miah	30	1769 3rd Ave.	Colored	Laborer	India
	Providencia Matas	26	46 E. 112th St.	Colored	—	San Juan, Puerto Rico

Proper names and place names are spelled as they appear on the original marriage documents.
Source: City of New York, *Certificates and Record of Marriage,* 1899–1937.

dyeing to automobile repair. Many listed "Calcutta" or "Bengal"—rather than simply "East India"—as their place of birth. The women they married were primarily in their late teens and early twenties and were either African American women from various parts of the United States—New York; Baltimore; Jacksonville, Florida; Carlisle, South Carolina—or women from Puerto Rico—San Juan, Vega Baja, Santurce—and in one case, the Dominican Republic. While the African American women in these records were consistently listed as "Colored" or "Negro" and the Puerto Rican women were in most instances classified as "White," the Indian grooms seemed to confound the city marriage clerks' understandings of race. When it came to "color," these men were classified in every possible way: white, colored, Negro, Indian, and East Indian.[12]

The mixed marriages did not go unnoticed in Harlem's local press. In the late 1920s, unions between Indian men and African American and Puerto Rican women began to appear in the pages of the neighborhood's most prominent black periodical, the *New York Amsterdam News*. Initially, these were simply entries among the newspaper's lists of the neighborhood's marriage certificate "issues"; in June 1927, for example, the issue of licenses to "Ali, Mokhd, 2971 West 36th street [and] Miss Mabel Leola Gibson, 36 West 128th Street" as well as to "Kriam, Abdul, 322 West 141st street and Miss Mildred Hayes, 242 West 146th street," were among a list of fifty-five "recent issues."[13] In 1932, a similar certificate issue warranted its own short paragraph. Under the headline "To Wed East Indian," the *Amsterdam News* wrote, "Nosir Meah, 27, who said that he was born in Bombay, India, has obtained a license to wed Miss Lillian Ponds, a domestic, 1926 Second avenue. Meah lives at 301 West 102d street."[14] By 1935, the *News* reported at greater length not merely on the issue of a marriage license, but also on the private reception following an Indian–African American wedding. Both the content and the tone of the article—familiar and matter-of-fact—suggest that such occurrences were gradually becoming a normal part of the social life of Harlem:

> The many friends of Mr. and Mrs. Syedali Miah, newlyweds, attended a wedding reception in their honor at their home, 260 West 125th Street, last Friday evening. The Miahs were married at the

Eighteenth Street Methodist Church . . . on April 5. The Rev. Charles F. Divine officiated. Mrs. Miah, formerly Miss Marguerite Richardson, is the daughter of Harper Richardson, 401 West 149th street. Her uncle, Charlie Anderson, with whom she made her home, is a well-known dancing teacher with studios at 2323 Seventh Avenue. Mr. Miah is a native of Bengal, India.[15]

The *Amsterdam News* did not merely report on the joyous moments of such marriages, however. Its pages suggest that these unions were complicated and that lives on both "sides" of each marriage could be precarious. On March 1, 1933, for example, the paper reported on the sentencing of "Kotio Miah . . . formerly of 267 West 137th street" to "two-and-a-half to five years" on charges of bigamy. "Miah's first wife, Belicia Jimenez," the *News* wrote, "a South American whom he married in 1927, claimed that he left her in 1932 to marry Carmen Jimenez, a Porto Rican, without obtaining a divorce. Miah's trial was unique in the annals of General Sessions in that the defendant was convicted, his attorney was fined $25 for contempt of court, and his six witnesses, all hailing from India, were arrested by immigration officials for unlawful entry into the country as fast as they left the witness stand."[16]

The appearance of Indian men in the *Amsterdam News*' crime reports provides another view of their entry into the everyday life of Harlem during the late 1920s and early 1930s. As in Kotio Miah's bigamy case, the Indians appeared in these reports both as accused perpetrators and as victims:

> March 10, 1926: Hubidad Ullah . . . said that he came uptown to have a good time with two other friends. . . . [T]hey were standing on the corner of 134th street and Lenox avenue when he saw [Fannie] Dials . . . whom he had known for about one week. . . . Hubidad said that she insisted upon them going to her apartment. . . . [He] said that he was invited into a separate room by the woman, who hugged and kissed him repeatedly. Having a slight craving for more whiskey, Hubidad . . . went into his pocket to get more money and . . . [discovered] his wallet [was missing].

April 9, 1930: Wyatt Griffin, 24, 103 West 121st street, was held without bail when charged by Abdul Mohammed, 2051 Seventh avenue,
with luring him into [a] hallway . . . where he is alleged to have attempted to rob [Mohammed] after threatening him with a blackjack.

April 23, 1930: Abdul Hack, 35, 225 East Ninety-ninth street, was
held without bail for a further hearing on a charge of illegally pos-
sessing drugs.

November 19, 1930: Abdul Kader, an East Indian, 124 West 127th
street, was taken to Bellevue Hospital for observation Thursday
evening by police after he had terrified tenants of the apartment in
which he lived. Kader brandished a revolver and shot at residents
until he was subdued by two policemen.[17]

While they present only glimpses of lives in moments of crisis, when
entanglements with sexual desire, petty crime, mental anguish, and violence erupted into public view, these early fragments of evidence suggest
an Indian population that was already part of the fabric of intimate relationships and daily struggles of Depression-era Harlem.

Hot Dogs and Curry

By the 1930s, Indian men were working in a wide variety of jobs across
the city; the ex-maritime population was integrating into the larger fabric of working-class life both in Harlem and in New York City as a whole.
The 1930 census shows that their occupations ran the gamut of service industry and semiskilled work: "counterman . . . chauffer . . . fireman . . .
porter . . . elevator operator . . . laundry worker . . . meat worker . . .
dress factory helper . . . mechanic . . . painter . . . packer . . . subway laborer."[18] For a smaller number of men, Harlem appears to have provided
a field in which to pursue different kinds of possibilities, beyond the
realm of service work and manual labor. S. Abedin, who listed his occupation as "shellac importer," shared an apartment on 119th Street in
Central Harlem with a mechanic, M. Yusef, and a restaurant laborer,
Ghulam Husein. Four self-employed "artists," Harry, Raymond, Abra-

ham, and Emanuel Rahman, lived on 111th Street and Lenox Avenue, and one "artist's model," Mougal Khan, lived on 129th Street between Fifth and Lenox Avenues.[19] For those who sought a way out of restaurant, hotel, and factory jobs, however, there appear to have been two much more common paths: either they found semi-independent work as food vendors on the streets or they opened restaurants and other small businesses of their own.

Helen Ullah, a Puerto Rican resident of East Harlem who married a Bengali ex-seaman—Saad "Victor" Ullah—in the mid-1940s, describes a string of Indian Muslim hot-dog vendors who were operating in East Harlem at that time, selling from pushcarts up and down Madison, Lexington, and Third Avenues. Much more than those who worked in factories all day or in the kitchens and basements of midtown restaurants and hotels, these men became a part of the everyday social landscape of Harlem, serving and interacting with the whole range of people who lived and worked in the neighborhood. They were also key to maintaining a fabric of community among the different Indian men and their families in the area; Indians would visit their friends' pushcarts on their way through the neighborhood each day, says Ullah, both to catch up on news and gossip— "to stop and say 'Hello, how are you?' and 'How are the kids?' and so forth"—and to eat the hot dogs themselves: "If it was pork, they wouldn't touch it, but they always knew it was safe to eat from other Indians' wagons." For Helen's youngest sister, Felita, the hot-dog vendors were a guarantee of safe passage through the neighborhood; as a child, she remembers navigating from one pushcart to the next, knowing that her brother-in-law Saad's friends would keep a watchful eye on her.[20] Those men who could save or raise enough capital, and who could navigate the legal terrain, went a step further to start up businesses and restaurants. The businesses were usually modest ventures. "They would set up . . . a little storefront," Ullah remembers, "and sell little knick-knacks . . . or they [would sell] . . . herbs and curry powders . . . spices." One Indian migrant became a neighborhood tailor. Another, who went by the name Paul, set up a small jewelry shop on East 103rd Street between Lexington and Third Avenues, which, beyond the actual business it did, became one of the favorite meeting places for the Bengalis who lived in the area, who would come to the shop to sit with Paul, drink tea, argue, and gossip.[21]

But restaurants were the most common venture that Indian ex-seamen pursued when they could gather the wherewithal, and by the 1940s and 1950s, several men had opened establishments locally in Harlem as well as in the Theater District in midtown Manhattan. The first Indian restaurant in New York City may have actually started in Harlem; for one year in 1913, the Ceylon India Restaurant—which would later be a center of Indian nationalist activity at its location on Eight Avenue and Forty-Ninth Street in midtown—was listed in the New York City Directory at an address on West 135th Street.[22] In 1933, the Harlem Restaurant Owners' Association had at least one Indian member,[23] and between the late 1940s and the late 1950s, advertisements for several Indian restaurants began to appear in the *Amsterdam News*. A 1946 advertisement—appearing just below an ad for "Club Sudan—formerly known as the internationally famous Cotton Club"—encouraged the *News'* readers to "Meet the 'Curry King' at India's Garden Inn," a restaurant on 121st Street and Manhattan Avenue that served "Delicious East Indian Dishes" alongside "American popular foods—steaks, chops, chicken."[24] In 1950, a small notice appeared amid advertisements for the Apollo Bar, Joe Wells's Restaurant and Music Bar, and Small's Paradise, announcing the opening of the Pakistan India Restaurant on Lenox Avenue between 119th and 120th Streets, Kajee and Miah, proprietors, specializing in "East Indian Curry and Rice and American Dishes."[25] When, in 1957, a South Asian immigrant named Eshad Ali took over proprietorship of the Indo-Pakistan Restaurant at 135th Street and Eighth Avenue, the *Amsterdam News* ran a feature article, describing it as a "gourmet's paradise," explaining the dishes Ali served, and noting that "[he] and his wife, Mamie, live in a modest apartment on 116th Street with their six children, whose ages range from four to thirteen." The next year, in 1958, Ali opened the Bombay India Restaurant on 125th Street and Amsterdam, an establishment that was in operation in the same location for thirty-five years.[26] Other Indian restaurants in Harlem have survived only in collective memory: one restaurant was operating out of a small basement in East Harlem in the mid-1940s; another, possibly named Ameer's, was on West 127th Street around Seventh or Eighth Avenue in the mid- to late 1960s; Syed Ali's restaurant was operating on East 109th Street, in the heart of Spanish Harlem, in the mid-1960s to early 1970s.[27]

These restaurants were important communal spaces for the ex-seamen from the subcontinent who had settled in Harlem. They could come to places like the Pakistan India Restaurant, Ameer's, Eshad Ali's, or Syed Ali's to eat familiar food, converse in Bengali or Punjabi, and discuss the events that were unfolding on the subcontinent in the turbulent years that followed Indian independence and the partition of India and East and West Pakistan. Over time, these establishments also became integrated into the daily life of African American and Puerto Rican Harlem. Miriam Christian, a housing activist who came to the neighborhood in the 1950s and initially worked as a columnist for the *Amsterdam News*, recalls that in the mid-1960s, she and her circle—which included other black journalists, artists, organizers, local politicians, and the restaurateur Joe Wells—used to have meetings, functions, and other "special occasions" catered by one of the neighborhood's Indian restaurants.[28] In an interview shortly before his death, the poet and East Harlem resident Sekou Sundiata described his own frequent visits to "Syed Ali's place" on East 109th Street in the late 1960s and early 1970s, where he remembered offering one of Ali's sons a sympathetic ear as he struggled with the prospect of taking on his father's business.[29] Miles Davis patronized Eshad Ali's Bombay India Restaurant on 125th Street, where according to percussionist James Mtume, he went partly to soak in the sounds of the music the proprietor played.[30] Since these were some of the first halal restaurants in Harlem, they also became spaces where South Asian and African American Muslims met and interacted. Ameer's on 127th Street, for example, became a regular spot for both groups; here, according to stories passed down to Alaudin Ullah, the youngest son of Habib Ullah, immigrant Muslims engaged in discussion and debate with members of Malcolm X's Organization of Afro-American Unity about their differing practices and interpretations of Islam.[31]

Those who opened Indian restaurants in midtown Manhattan were aiming for a different clientele. The first to venture into the heart of the city was the Ceylon India Inn. Its proprietor, K. Y. Kira, ran his Ceylon India Hindu Restaurant on Eighth Avenue on the edge of the Tenderloin from roughly 1914 to 1923 and then moved to the center of the theater district, on West 49th Street, just a few blocks uptown from Times Square. The move was precipitated by Kira's success in drawing increasingly large numbers of non-Indian customers, starting around the beginning of 1921, an event that created friction with the Indian seamen and students who had previously been able to sit at Kira's tables for hours at a stretch eating, drinking, and discussing the political situation in India.[32] Although Kira continued to use the Ceylon India Inn on West Forty-Ninth Street for the meetings and functions of expatriate nationalist groups, his move to the center of the Broadway district was clearly driven by business considerations; it was aimed at tapping into a growing desire for Indian food among the more adventurous members of New York's theatergoing crowd.[33]

Others soon followed Kira's lead. By the mid-1930s, the Ceylon India Inn was listed among Broadway theaters and restaurants as "New York's foremost—famous for delicious curries," but the Longchamps restaurant chain had now opened up a new venture across town on Madison Avenue on the East Side featuring a "magnificent new Indian restaurant" and an "Indian Terrace dining room."[34] Next, a small number of the more elite Indian immigrants and Indophiles in the city jumped into the fray: Sarat Lahiri, a musician, theater performer, and lecturer from Calcutta, opened the Bengal Tiger Restaurant on West 58th Street; Rustom Wadia, the son of a prosperous Parsi family in Bombay, opened the Rajah Restaurant on West 48th Street; and Trudie Teele, an American ex-missionary who had been stationed for fifteen years in Rangoon and Calcutta, hired a cook named Darmadasa and started the East India Curry Shop on East Sixtieth Street. The *New York Times* food critic Charlotte Hughes declared in 1939: "right now there is a mild scramble for the growing curry trade."[35]

It was in this context that a handful of Harlem's Bengali ex-seamen, some of whom had likely worked as cooks on board British steamships, took a chance on opening their own midtown "curry restaurants." One of the first—and perhaps the most important in terms of its role in the consolidation of the South Asian Muslim community in New York—was the Bengal Garden, the restaurant founded by Habib Ullah, operated by Habib and his wife, Victoria, and backed by Ibrahim Choudry. The Bengal Garden opened in 1948 one block south of the Ceylon India Inn, just above Times Square. Although it was a short-lived venture, the Bengal Garden appears to have owed its success to the front-of-house / back-of-house division of labor that Habib and Victoria Ullah worked out in the daily operation of the restaurant. The involvement of family members in these businesses would continue to be common; in Harlem, for example, Syed Ali's sons, who were of Bengali and African American descent, worked in the front of his restaurant, greeting and waiting on customers, and Mamie Ali ran the Bombay India Restaurant for many years after her husband Eshad's death.[36] This meant that these restaurants were racially and ethnically mixed not just in terms of their clientele, but also in terms of their operation and public face. In the case of the Bengal Garden, the first person that most customers saw when they entered the restaurant was not Bengali but Puerto Rican.

For Habib and Victoria, the Bengal Garden was the culmination of much longer trajectories. According to Victoria's sister Luz Maria Caballero, Victoria left San Juan at a time when the economic situation in Puerto Rico was bleak, in the mid- to late 1930s, but found the situation in New York almost as difficult, writing back to her family "that the wages were very low and the jobs were very bad in New York, too." Nevertheless, Victoria found factory work and began sending money back home. Around 1939, Victoria wrote to tell her family she had married Habib. Her sister recalls that she wrote that "she was happy to get married and Habib was a good man" and says that her family was not surprised that she had married a man from India: "there were a lot of Puerto Rican girls marrying Indians." In the next few years, over the course of the 1940s, Victoria had two children, Habib Jr. and Zubeida, helped her younger sister come to join her in New York, went to beautician school, and after the closing of the Bengal Garden opened her own beauty salon in the Bronx. "She was an ambitious person," says Caballero.[37] The Bronx salon became a new outlet for Victoria's skills with customers, business operations, and accounting.

It is unclear whether Habib Ullah first learned his kitchen skills as a worker on British steamers, but when his son, Habib Jr., was growing up in Harlem in the mid-1940s, his father had already been working as a line cook in the kitchens of New York restaurants and hotels for "many, many years." One of Habib Jr.'s early memories is of going to visit his father at the Silver Palm, on Sixth Avenue around Forty-Fourth Street. "It was a diner and the kitchen was downstairs in the basement," says Ullah Jr. "I went there as a kid and that was the first time I heard my father curse. When he was working he was saying 'Goddamn it, what the fuck, get that shit over here,' you know, he was screaming at people. I don't know if he was the head cook, but when he was working he was serious. That's where I first saw him working in a kitchen, but making American food."[38] After tiring of working for other people, and most likely at the urging of Victoria, Habib Sr. decided to try his hand at a restaurant of his own. Ullah started up the Bengal Garden with investments from Ibrahim Choudry and from another Bengali ex-seaman, whom Habib Jr. remembers only as "Mr. Ali," who had saved up $20,000 selling hot dogs from a pushcart on 110th Street.[39]

Despite the developing interest in Indian food among some New Yorkers, Habib and Victoria still had a difficult time making their restaurant work. The interest in curry noted by the *New York Times* in 1939 may well have waned by the time the Bengal Garden opened. There were also many more Indian restaurants in the Theater District by this time—some run by proprietors with greater resources and more promotional savvy—and Habib and Victoria had two investors to pay back. Habib Ullah Jr. believes that there were still too few Anglo-Americans ready to try Indian food in the late 1940s and early 1950s: "It was a struggle," he says, "because as good as the Bengal Garden was, back in those days most people didn't eat ethnic foods as much. 'You want to eat curry?' 'What's curry?' 'No, Indian food, it's too spicy. It's too hot.'"[40] In this sense, the presence of a large Caribbean population in Harlem may have made uptown a better location for Indian restaurants. West Indian establishments had been operating in the neighborhood for years by the 1940s, not only serving the local Caribbean community, but also, over time, familiarizing African Americans and others in Harlem with foods like roti and curry. One of the early Indian restaurants in Harlem was in fact opened by two Caribbean men of Indian descent—Seenandan and Persad.[41] Whatever the reason, Habib Ullah closed his midtown establishment after just one or two years and went back to being a line cook and dishwasher in other restaurants. A few years later Victoria passed away.[42]

However, the knowledge that Habib-Ullah learned and the skills that he gained from his experience of opening and running the Bengal Garden with Victoria now allowed Habib to play a crucial role within Harlem's Bengali community. In the 1950s and 1960s, Habib Ullah Sr. became the person from whom others in the community sought advice when they wanted to open restaurants of their own. This was the case for Syed Ali, when he opened his restaurant on 109th Street, for Masud Choudhury, when he opened a midtown restaurant in the 1950s, for Nawab Ali, a friend who opened the Kashmir Restaurant on West Forty-Fifth Street in 1960, and for many others:

> When a guy like Syed Ali or Nawab Ali wanted to start a restaurant, they would come for Pop and say, "I want to start a restaurant. What do I need to do?" And he knew. He knew where to go and what to do. So, he became a consultant to everybody. It started there. He'd say: "You don't need a lot of money up front." He says, "You get all the stuff on concession like your napkins, your silverware, your plates." He says, "You don't have to buy that stuff. You go in there and say 'I'm going to start a restaurant. I need so much of this and that.'" And they'll give it to you on concession because they know you'll pay them after a while and they want your business. So that's what he would [advise them on], and then he would help them set up the menu and certain things, tell them how to cook and whatever.[43]

Habib Ullah's experience with the Bengal Garden, in other words, expanded the base of knowledge among the city's Bengali migrants. Whether he was playing a consulting role out of generosity or to earn a little extra money later in his life when asthma forced him to scrape by on disability and Social Security, Ullah's advice enabled other ex-seamen to follow in his and Victoria's footsteps and ultimately operate more successful ventures than his own.

The Kashmir Restaurant, for example, which Nawab Ali operated with his son "Butch" working in the kitchen, ran successfully through the late 1950s and 1960s, until Ali decided to retire and return to his village in the newly created nation of Bangladesh in the early 1970s. The Kashmir benefited from its location a few doors down from what was, in the early 1960s, one of Manhattan's most popular music and dance venues, the Peppermint Lounge—home of go-go dancing and the

"Peppermint Twist"—which provided the Indian restaurant with a young, nighttime clientele. Even in its midtown location, however, the Kashmir remained, in part, a community space for other Bengalis. According to Habib Ullah Jr., Nawab Ali, like Ibrahim Choudry before him, saved a special table in the back corner of his restaurant where he served food to, and sat and talked with, Habib Sr. and others in his community whenever they dropped by. Ullah Jr. again emphasizes, however, that even a "successful" restaurant like the Kashmir did not make Nawab Ali a wealthy man, nor does he think this was ultimately the goal of those of his father's friends who took this route: "These guys weren't driving around in Cadillacs," Ullah Jr. says. "They were still living normal lives. I think starting their own business was their way of gaining some independence. They weren't looking to become rich."[44]

The Middleman

Like Dada Amir Haider Khan, Ibrahim Choudry went through a political transformation after coming to New York. The fact that he eventually Anglicized his name to Abraham in order to better suit his surroundings is emblematic of this transformation. His was not so much a politicization as a change in the focus and terrain of his organizing work. While Khan became a committed Indian nationalist during his years after jumping ship in the United States and then returned to the subcontinent to fulfill his political calling in the context of the independence movement there, Choudry left the independence movement early on and, after deserting *his* ship and settling in the United States, redirected his political energies to the task of building and consolidating a local South Asian Muslim community in New York City.

According to Choudry's brother Masud, young Ibrahim first became involved in politics in the early 1920s as a student in East Bengal. Like thousands of Indian Muslim men of his generation, he joined the Khilafat Movement, a Pan-Islamic, anti-imperialist agitation that arose after the British government refused to restore the Turkish Caliph to his throne after the conclusion of World War I. Although the Khilafat Movement was originally focused on the effort to force the British to follow through on this promise, it also became a conduit for the entry of many young Muslims into the Indian independence movement. This was particularly the case after Mohandas Gandhi sought to bring Khilafat and Indian National Congress leaders into common cause.[45] It is unclear where Ibrahim Choudry fit within these dynamics, and the specifics of his student political work in the early 1920s remain unknown. Like Sailendranath Ghose, however, Choudry ultimately became a wanted man and had to flee British colonial authorities via the merchant marine. Choudry, however, was not from the Calcutta elite—he came from a village in the district of Sylhet—so when he boarded a ship heading west, he did so not "disguised" as a seaman, but working as one. According to his brother, Ibrahim was working as a crew manager, or *serang*.[46]

In 1949, when Choudry applied for U.S. citizenship in the wake of the Indian naturalization bill that had passed Congress three years before, he submitted a Certificate of Arrival that stated he had arrived in the United States via the port of New York on the City Line ship the SS *City of Lahore*, on March 15, 1923.[47] There is no record, however, of the *City of Lahore* or any other City Line ship arriving in New York on March 15, 1923, nor did the *City of Lahore* arrive on March 15 of any other year in the 1920s. The ship did drop anchor in New York once in 1923, on August 27, but a note on its manifest declares that all its Indian crew were held on board and it left port without desertions. It is unclear, therefore, when exactly Choudry arrived in New York and how, many years later, he obtained from officials in the Immigration and Naturalization Office a signed Certificate of Arrival. By all accounts, Ibrahim Choudry did come to New York City in the early 1920s. It is unknown where he lived initially and what he did for work, but by the late 1930s, Choudry was already working among his countrymen uptown and on the Lower East Side, and in 1938, at the age of thirty-two, he married a young woman from Harlem, Catherine Aguilera. Catherine was seventeen years old and was also a recent immigrant to New York. She was born in Cuba to Puerto Rican parents who had moved to Guantánamo Bay after her father found work on the U.S. military base there. The family had then moved to East Harlem in 1936. Ibrahim and Catherine had two children, a daughter, Laily, in 1939, and a son, Noor, in 1942.[48]

It was around this time that Ibrahim Choudry embarked on his first large-scale community-building project. During the Second World War, the British government opened a series of clubs for British merchant sailors in Allied ports all over the world in an effort to keep up morale among the tens of thousands of seamen upon whom the war effort depended for the delivery of food, munitions, and supplies. Quarterly reports show that white British seamen regularly made use of these clubs, where they could engage in recreation of various kinds, but that the sizable population of Indian seamen working on British ships rarely set foot inside one of these clubs—not surprising given the racial dynamics of British maritime labor.[49] Two years after most of the British Merchant Navy Clubs—including one in New York City, on South Street— had already been established, Choudry appears to have been the main force behind convincing the British consul general in New York to open a separate club specifically for Indian seamen—the only one of its kind established for Indian workers throughout the entire global network of British Merchant Navy Clubs. Choudry became the first manager of the club, which occupied the two upper floors of a four-story building at 100 West Thirty-Eighth Street. The British Merchant Sailors' Club for Indian Seamen included a small prayer room, a recreation room, and a mess hall that seated eighty people, where visiting seamen could get fresh Indian meals, served three times a day by a staff cook, Secunder Meah. According to the club's records, its prayer room was equipped with "25 copies of Mohammedan Koran presented to Club by Viceroy of India's Special Purposes Fund." The recreation room had a "Film projector, Radio, Piano, Gramophone, Indian String Instruments, Chess, Checkers and Draughts . . . 6 tables, free note paper . . . [and] Indian papers and magazines."[50]

The records of the Indian Seamen's Club give us a sense of both the sheer number of Indian maritime workers going in and out of New York by the 1940s and the range of work that Ibrahim Choudry was doing among this population via the club. Within months of its opening, the British Merchant Navy Club for Indian Seamen in midtown Manhattan became the most visited of all the British Merchant Navy Clubs in the United States.[51] By the end of its first year, the club had had 66,221 visits by Indian seamen and had served 198,200 meals.[52] This enthusiastic reaction to the club was in part a sign of Choudry's foresight in recognizing a need and his skill in convincing British authorities to fill it, but it was also a result of his tireless work once the club opened. Choudry regularly went out to the docks all around the Manhattan and Brooklyn waterfronts to meet with incoming Indian crews and bring them in groups by city bus to the midtown club. He oversaw weekly prayer meetings, "special parties . . . on Mohammedan festivals . . . general recitations and songs, with drum accompaniment on Saturdays [with] local residents participating . . . [and f]ilm shows three nights a week," arranged "[e]xcursions . . . to the Bronx Zoo and Coney Island," procured complimentary tickets to the theater, and ran "bi-weekly English lessons." Choudry also took dictation in his office from nonliterate seamen who wanted to send letters back home and arranged visits for incoming sailors "to [the] homes of local Indian residents."[53] Beyond the specifics of Choudry's work, what is striking about the records of the British Merchant Navy Club for Indian Seamen is the acknowledgment that, by 1944, there was both a large Indian seafaring population and a smaller "resident" Indian population in New York City, of which men like Secunder Meah and the others listed as employees of the club— Sekunder Yassim, Salim Darwood, Wahed Ali—were all a part, and among whom Ibrahim Choudry was already clearly a leader.

During its short life span, the Bengal Garden also became an important space for the consolidation of New York's Bengali Muslim—or, after 1947, "East Pakistani"—community. This was in part because of Ibrahim Choudry's involvement in the restaurant and his use of the space for a range of different meetings and events. In the latter half of the 1940s, after his experience of running the Indian Seamen's Club on West Thirty-Eighth Street, Choudry became increasingly involved in building connections among the many ex-seamen who had settled in Harlem, elsewhere in New York, and across the river in New Jersey, as well as between this community and others in the city—particularly other Muslims. According to his son, Noor, Choudry was consumed by such work, which ranged from keeping a small spare room in his apartment for men who had just arrived in the city or had no place to stay, to helping ex-seamen with immigration problems, leading religious functions, and interfacing on his community's behalf with British, Indian, and Pakistani consular officials. Choudry even went from one New York–area hospital to the next, meeting with staff and asking them to call him whenever anyone was admitted to their care with the surnames Meah, Ullah, Uddin, or Ali. For many in the community, recalls Noor Choudry, his father "was the guy to call when there was a problem. That particular group," he continues, "was very, very tight, and if they called and they needed something, my dad was boom, gone. He would say: 'Son, there's a can of soup in the cupboard—I gotta go.' "[54]

Choudry was involved in a wide range of organizational and institution-building activities, in both Harlem and the larger city. He undertook most of this work under the aegis, or as a representative, of an organization he cofounded with Habib Ullah and others around 1947, the Pakistan League of America.[55] In 1944, when Choudry was running the Indian Seamen's Club on West Thirty-Eighth Street, he became involved with the India Association for American Citizenship, an organization that worked with Mubarek Ali Khan's Indian Benevolent Association to lobby Congress to grant citizenship rights to thousands of Indian workers and farmers who had settled in the United States in the 1910s and 1920s. In this effort, Choudry was allied against J. J. Singh and his India League of America, and when he wrote in his statement for the 1945 congressional hearings on Indian naturalization, "I am not speaking for the transient element—the student the business man, the lecturer . . . whose interests and ties in this country are temporary," it was likely as much a criticism of Singh and his more elite organization as it was a statement of Choudry's own position.[56] There also appears to be an air of defiance in Choudry's decision to start an organization, in distinction from J. J. Singh's India League of America, and call it the "Pakistan League of America." While the temptation may be to see the split between these two organizations in terms of nation and religion, especially at the moment that the sectarian violence of Partition was raging on the subcontinent, the most significant division between the groups they represented in the United States may in fact have been class. This is reflected in the *New York Times'* reporting on the first-anniversary independence celebrations of the two leagues in August 1948: the India League received the bulk of the *Times'* attention for their gala at the Waldorf Astoria Hotel, which featured a speech by J. J. Singh and "a short program of Indian ceremonial and temple dances in Oriental costumes," while the Pakistan League's parallel celebration at their clubhouse on the Lower East Side was given only brief mention. Ibrahim Choudry's complaint against "rich people from our nation who live in America" at a dinner for the East Bengali labor leader Aftab Ali a month earlier also appears to have been directed at J. J. Singh and the members of his league.[57]

This is not to say that the Pakistan League was formed merely in reaction to the more elite India League. The energy that Choudry had once put into the Indian Seamen's Club he now directed toward his work with the Pakistan League. By 1948, the league had a core membership of about 100–150 men—mostly, it appears, ex-seamen from East Bengali areas like Sylhet, Noakhali, and Chittagong who had become "East Pakistani" in absentia when the subcontinent was partitioned in 1947. The organization maintained an office on Eldridge and later Clinton Street, which, according to Habib Ullah Jr., doubled as its "clubhouse"— modeled, no doubt, on the Italian and Puerto Rican social clubs in the same neighborhood. The Bengal Garden restaurant became the primary location for the league's public events. This included a series of dinners between 1949 and 1951 honoring William Langer, the North Dakota senator who introduced the bill seeking citizenship rights for pre-1924 Indian migrants and then fought for its passage for seven years. These events, held on dates including Lincoln's and Washington's birthdays, featured speeches by Langer, Choudry, and other guests—Mubarek Ali Khan, Henry Tudor Mason, Hans Stefan Santesson—who had been involved with pushing the Langer bills in the 1939–1945 period. They were now part of an effort to get Senator Langer to introduce legislation opening up an immigration quota for the new state of Pakistan and granting naturalization rights to Pakistanis who had resided in the United States for four years or more. This effort was successful: Mubarek Ali Khan was the chief guest at a fourth dinner in 1951, at which he reported on Langer's introduction of the bill. In the mid-1940s, J. J. Singh had lobbied congressmen by wining and dining them in rooms he had taken in fancy Washington hotels. Now the Pakistan League was lobbying Langer by inviting him to the Bengal Garden, flattering him with Ibrahim Choudry's speeches and plying him with Habib Ullah's curry.[58]

It is significant that the activities of the Pakistan League of America— and of Ibrahim Choudry in particular—were reported as often in the pages of the *New York Amsterdam News* as in those of the *New York Times*. In addition to the fact that many of the Pakistan League's members were now longtime residents of Harlem—the *Amsterdam News'* home—Choudry cultivated relationships with the *News*, with Harlem's African American Muslim communities, and with a range of other communities and individuals throughout the neighborhood and the rest of the city. At one of the Bengal Garden's dinners honoring Senator Langer, "Mrs. Gerri Major of the *New York Amsterdam News*" was one of the invited guests, alongside the senator, as was the Italian American president of "local 325, Hotel and Restaurant Employees International Alliance," a local that, by this time, likely included a number of Bengali workers among its ranks.[59]

In August 1950, the Pakistan League cosponsored a banquet in Harlem that brought together a number of African American and immigrant Muslim associations—under the banner of the "Inter-Muslim Societies Committee"—to honor the arrival in New York of visiting Sufi Muslim missionary Maulana Mohammad Abdul Aleem Siddique, of Meerut, India. The dinner took place in the heart of the neighborhood, one block west of the Apollo Theater, at the offices of the International Muslim Society, an organization founded by two members of the Moorish Science movement, Dr. Abdul Wadud Beg and Dr. Rizkah Bey.[60] Choudry was one of the featured speakers at the banquet, whose attendees included immigrant Muslims from South Asia and the Caribbean, African American Muslims from Harlem, consular officials from Egypt, Iraq, and Yemen, and a prince of Kuwait.[61] One of the other sponsoring groups was the Muslim Brotherhood, USA, an organization cofounded by Talib Dawud, an African American Muslim with roots in the Ahmadiyya movement. Dawud was a well-known Harlem musician; he was a member of Dizzy Gillespie's band and husband of the vocalist Dakota Staton.[62]

In 1950–1951, Ibrahim Choudry's cousin took over the presidency of the Pakistan League.[63] While Choudry himself continued to play a central role in the organization, eventually coming back to the presidency later in the 1950s, he devoted increasing time to two causes that kept him in constant contact with a broader array of New York's Muslims as well as with leaders of other faiths. The first was his campaign to build a mosque in New York City, an effort that followed directly on Maulana

Siddique's call, during his 1950 visit, for "the Moslems of the United States to unite and pool their efforts to build a united organization and a mosque."[64] Choudry took to this challenge with great energy, building ties among different Muslim leaders throughout the city and initiating and coordinating a long-term fund-raising drive. Choudry even publicly called on Rita Hayworth, the Brooklyn-born Hollywood starlet, to pledge money for the construction of a New York mosque after her 1949 marriage to Prince Ali Aga Khan, then a representative of Pakistan in the United Nations General Assembly.[65]

When Choudry was reelected president of the Pakistan League in the mid-1950s, he joined a series of interfaith initiatives connected to New York's Presbyterian Labor Temple on the Lower East Side: in 1956–1957, he was a member of the Interfaith Committee for Peace in the Holy Land, which organized interracial, interfaith services in New York, petitioned the United Nations to strengthen their Middle East peace efforts, and sent delegations of Christian, Jewish, and Muslim leaders on philanthropic missions to the region; and in April 1960, Choudry was part of the Labor Temple's All Faith Task Force, which sent an open letter to Virginia governor J. Lindsay Almond condemning the jailing of two African American ministers who had challenged the whites-only policy of Petersburg Public Library. Choudry and the other members of the task force condemned the violation of "Negro citizens . . . rights of free speech, freedom of assembly, and freedom of religion, as well as equal protection under the law."[66] In 1958, Choudry drew upon his relationship with the Labor Temple and teamed up with two prominent African American Muslim leaders—Shaykh Daoud Ahmed Faisal, the founder and longtime leader of the Sunni group the Islamic Mission of America, and Ibrahim Guled of the International Muslim Society—to open the Muslim Children's Workshop, a center for the religious education of American-born Muslim youth, at the Temple's East Fourteenth Street address.[67]

Choudry's efforts at community building were emblematic of the transformation that New York's escaped South Asian seamen were undergoing as they became more rooted in Harlem and other parts of the city during the 1930s, 1940s, and 1950s. If they began their lives uptown as a small group of outsiders amid the much larger history-making migrations into Harlem, by midcentury they were deeply ingrained in the physical and social landscape of the neighborhood, in its cultural and institutional life, and in the cultural and institutional life of the city as a whole. They achieved this not by creating a closed enclave of their own but rather by living in an expanding set of concentric circles of identification and association. Like Harlem's migrants from Virginia, South Carolina, Barbados, Jamaica, Puerto Rico, and elsewhere, they formed their own ethnic organizations, within which they could speak a common language, draw on common pasts, share in their new challenges and experiences, maintain cultural and religious practices, and collectively pursue political goals, like the repeal of anti-Asian immigration and naturalization laws. But these organizations existed within a larger multiethnic context, and in their daily lives, these men were constantly stretching beyond the boundaries of "their own" ethnicity, language, and religion. The majority of New York's working-class South Asian Muslim population did not have the kind of public life that Ibrahim Choudry did; these men experienced the cross-racial and the interethnic at the level of the personal and the everyday—on their uptown streets, in their apartment buildings, and in their families.

CHAPTER 6

The Life and Times of a
Multiracial Community

He agreed to let me follow my religion while he followed his, He used to have the Koran, and he used to pray on his mat. I would go to church on Sunday, and he did his praying. We had different religions, but it worked out. And he said, yes, he would let me have my children be baptized in the Catholic religion and we'd bring them up as Catholics. But he would have his own religion, and I said, "Perfect."

—Helen Ullah

IN VIRTUALLY ANY major U.S. city today, you will find a commercial block, or several blocks, that are distinctly and visibly South Asian. At the heart of these "Little Indias," as they are often narrowly called, are usually a mix of businesses owned and run by immigrants from all over the subcontinent: India, Pakistan, Bangladesh, Nepal, Sri Lanka. There are South Asian restaurants and snack shops; jewelry stores specializing in gold wedding sets; clothing boutiques selling colorful saris, *salvaar kameez, loongis,* and *dupattas;* CD and DVD stores selling the latest Bollywood movies and Punjabi-, Bangla-, Tamil-, Telegu-, Urdu-, and Hindi-language music; electronics stores stocked with goods and appliances that switch between 110- and 220-volt electricity or between NTSC and PAL video standards; not to mention travel agencies and the offices of insurance agents and immigration lawyers. Visitors to such a neighborhood would have no doubt that they were in the midst of an immigrant community that had "arrived," that had become a clear and visible presence among all the other groups that made up that city.

The South Asian ex-seamen who settled in Harlem in the 1930s and 1940s were not legible in this way. While a handful managed to open small businesses—restaurants, variety stores, a jewelry store—these were not gathered together in a single location or on a single block. Rather, they were interspersed throughout uptown Manhattan, alongside Cuban botanicas, restaurants serving West Indian and "southern style" foods, Jewish-owned department stores, storefront churches, funeral parlors, sidewalk vendors and street preachers, small music clubs and massive jazz dance halls. The "community" these men constituted was also different from the communities that live near or congregate in today's "Little Indias" to eat and shop and socialize. To be sure, they had much that tied them together: most hailed from a few specific areas in East Bengal, almost all were Muslim, and they shared a set of experiences as former maritime laborers, as global migrants, and as industrial and service workers. They regularly congregated at the restaurants and businesses their countrymen had opened and at one another's apartments and homes. They looked out for one another; many prayed together; most gathered together at least once a year for the celebration of Eid. But the makeup of their communities was different from those of contemporary ethnic enclaves; in their day-to-day lives, the intimacies, friendships, and affiliations of these South Asian men extended beyond the borders of language, region, religion, and ethnicity to include the Puerto Rican, African American, and West Indian women that many had married; the extended families of these women: parents, brothers, sisters, cousins; the friends of their wives; their own friends and coworkers in factories, hotels, and restaurant kitchens; and their neighbors in the buildings and on the blocks that became their homes.

Of course, these men were all different. Some married and started families, while others continued to live in all-male shared apartments; some socialized primarily with other South Asian men, while others gradually cut their ties to the ex-seafaring population and instead developed diverse circles of intimates and acquaintances among the city's many migrant and immigrant communities. Most of the ex-seamen appear to have fallen between such extremes, moving each day between a multiplicity of friends, coworkers, and extended family and learning to shift between contexts and operate in multiple languages: Bengali, English, Spanish. The community that emerged from these men's migrations was thus not entirely "theirs"—that is, not entirely Indian or East Pakistani or Bengali in the way we might understand such terms today. It was these things but it was also something different, something more. This community was also comprised of, and belonged to, the dozens of women from the Caribbean and the South who made their lives with South Asian Muslim ex-seamen after their migrations intersected in New York. And the community was comprised of, and belonged to, the generation of children who were the result of these relationships, children who were, in contemporary terms, "mixed-race" and "bicultural," but who were, more than anything, *of* Harlem and, eventually, as the community spread outward, *of* the Bronx, Brooklyn, New Jersey, Long Island. As much as they were products of intermarriage and interracial relationships, these young men and women were products of New York City's working-class neighborhoods of color, of their tenements, streets, blocks, and schools. As they grew up in the 1940s, 1950s, and 1960s, they shared in and were formed by the pleasures, possibilities, and struggles of Puerto Rican and African American New York.

New Orleans' Bengali peddlers, their partners, and their children have left no clear firsthand record of the lives they made for themselves as residents of Tremé in the opening years of the twentieth century. South Asian seafarers settled in New York City later in the century, but the memories of their presence and daily lives are already faded and dispersed among scattered families and individuals. The pages that follow are drawn from the firsthand accounts of a small number of women and men, members of four interconnected families, who were part of the unique mixed community that existed in and expanded beyond Harlem from the 1930s to the 1960s: Helen Rodriguez Ullah; Laily Chowdry, Noor Chowdry; Habib Ullah Jr., Felita Ullah, Masud Choudhury, Luz Maria Caballero; and Alaudin Ullah. Their accounts are just a few—many remain to be told—and they are rooted primarily in the experience of Bengali intermarriage within Puerto Rican East Harlem. Their stories and memories are partial, fragmentary, and selective, as all stories and memories become with the passage of time. Yet, collectively, they give us insight into the complex lives and affiliations that came into being after a group of Muslim workers decided to leave behind British colonial India, escape from the exploitations of the maritime trade, evade the enforcers of the United States' anti-Asian immigration laws, and make New York City their home.

These personal accounts allow us to glimpse an alternate picture of South Asian American history, one in which migrants from the subcontinent built lives with and among people who had come to New York City—and to Harlem—from different parts of the country and the world and who shared class circumstances, living conditions, parallel experiences of racialization, and eventually neighborhoods and families, once they settled in the city. The stories of this hidden life of Harlem also make one thing certain: it is impossible to find the "South Asian America" of the pre-1965 era as if it were a neatly delineated ethnic neighborhood, with clear borders and clearly marked signs; this South Asian America was and continues to be embedded within other Americas, within Puerto Rican America, Afro-Caribbean America, and African America.

Relations

Each morning, Ursula Rodriguez boarded the Lexington Avenue elevated train at East 103rd Street, heading downtown with her second-eldest daughter, Jackie. Ursula and her husband had migrated to East Harlem from Puerto Rico in the early 1920s and moved to a tenement apartment on East 107th Street around 1931. It was now the late 1940s. Ursula and her daughter got off the train each day at Fourteenth Street, where Jackie proceeded to her school, Washington Irving High, and Ursula went to her job in a nearby factory. One morning, as Ursula and Jackie boarded a train filled with other Harlem commuters, a handsome young East Indian man whom Ursula thought looked a bit like the movie actor Sabu rose to his feet to offer her his seat. In the days that followed, this became part of the morning ritual. The young Indian, Saad Ullah, lived one subway stop uptown from the Rodriguezes and rode the same subway each morning to his job in a quilting factory downtown. He was not much older than Ursula's daughter Jackie and had taken notice of her, and now he made a point of getting a seat when he boarded the train at 110th Street, so he could offer it to Jackie's mother at the next stop. Eventually, his efforts to charm Ursula paid off; they struck up conversations during their rides downtown and Ursula invited Saad to visit the Rodriguez home.

But things didn't go exactly as Saad had planned. "When I saw him walk in," recalls Jackie's older sister Helen, "I thought, 'Well, okay!' He wanted to see my sister, though, not me. And he was very clear about it. He wanted to speak to Jackie, because she was the one he met on the subway every day. We all wound up going on a date, all three of us, Saad, Jackie, and myself. We saw a movie and he was very engaging. But my sister wasn't interested in him, so she told Saad, 'Go out with Helen.'" This is exactly what Saad Ullah now did, and after two more dates, on Christmas Eve, he proposed to Helen, "just like that!" "This was the third time I'd spoken to him," Helen now recalls. "My father said, 'This Indian doesn't fool around. He means business.'" The family liked him, though, as did Helen. "January the fifteenth of 1949 I married Saad Ullah," she now says, laughing, "and that's when I was introduced into the Indian community."[1]

In 1930, about half the Indian Muslim population in Harlem had consisted of single men living in short-term group households or letting out rooms from African American and Puerto Rican families. By the late 1940s, dozens of these men, like Saad Ullah, had married and settled within the neighborhood's other communities of color. Remembering this period, Helen Ullah describes Lexington Avenue between 102nd and 116th Streets as a kind of Indian corridor within East Harlem, where a scattering of young Bengali men, and eventually Bengali–Puerto Rican families, lived on or near the avenue. For her, the presence of these men was not out of the ordinary. East Harlem, she says, "was really a mixed community then. It was Puerto Rican, Jewish. There was even a synagogue right next to the school I attended, P.S. 72. And then close by there was an Italian neighborhood, running uptown from 106th Street. There were boundaries; we stayed on the other side of Park Avenue and Madison while the Italians stayed from Lexington Avenue down to First Avenue. And then toward 116th Street was the black community. And there were Chinese; there were quite a few

Chinese laundries."[2] The young men from Noakhali, Sylhet, and elsewhere in East Bengal were part of this larger social landscape. They
lived right in the center of East Harlem, and this proximity gave rise to
various opportunities for young Puerto Rican women and Bengali
men—who were referred to within the Puerto Rican community by the
Spanish "*Indios*"—to meet.[3]

In Helen Rodriguez's case, her future husband was especially persis-
tent in his efforts to get married and stay in the United States. Saad "Victor" Ullah had been working as a coal tender on a British steamship when
his ship docked in Baltimore in 1943.[4] He was just in his teens but had
already been in the maritime trade for some years, since early in the Second World War. He described his working conditions to Helen as "very
dark and very lonely . . . it seemed like all he did was shovel coal in the
bowels of the ship." On one voyage, Saad's ship was torpedoed and he
spent seven days in a lifeboat on the open sea before being rescued by
British forces. According to the story he later told Helen, however, Ullah
was an unwitting deserter: one day while his ship was still unloading in
Baltimore, one of Saad's shipmates asked him to come along with him to
do some sightseeing in the city. Although he had no money and didn't
know his way around Baltimore, he went along, relying on his shipmate
to guide him. When it started getting dark, Saad suggested they head
back to the ship, but his friend declared that he had no intention of going
back, that he was going to go to New York and Saad could either come
with him or go back to the ship himself. "Saad said, 'Well, that isn't fair,
because I don't know how to get back to the ship, and I don't have any
money.' So his friend says, 'Well, I guess you'll have to come with me.'
And that's what he did."[5]

The shipmate bought them tickets on a Greyhound bus to New York
and called ahead to make arrangements with other Indians who were already in the city. Saad's experience of arrival in New York City echoed in
some ways that of Dada Amir Haider Khan thirty years before, though it
also demonstrated the strength of the networks that had developed since
Khan's day: "Somebody met them at the Greyhound terminal and took
them to 114th Street in Harlem. Now, there was a lady; she was a black
lady. He stayed with her in one of her rooms, and there were other Indians [already] there. And in the morning, they took them to 103rd and

Lexington, and they met up with a man named Charlie. I don't know Charlie's Indian name, only the American name. And Saad stayed with Charlie there for a while, until they got him a job in a restaurant." Quickly tiring of the restaurant job, Saad Ullah found better work through two Jewish men he had met in the neighborhood who ran a quilt-making factory, and for the next several years, Ullah lived in Spanish Harlem and traveled to his job as a quilting-machine operator each day.[6]

After coming to Harlem, Saad Ullah developed a broad set of friends and acquaintances. Early on, he became friends with a young French Afro-Caribbean man, Marcel, who introduced him to his sister, "Frenchy," and her boyfriend, Abbas, another Bengali ex-sailor who had settled in Brooklyn. Helen describes Saad's new circle of friends as "very diverse . . . That group of young men were Puerto Rican, black, Chinese." It was among these friends that Saad changed his name: "when he went and met Marcel and Frenchy and the gang, the young men, they said they didn't like that name [Saad]. And they gave him the name Victor." It was also at this time, in the context of his daily routine in East Harlem, that Saad met, courted, and married Helen.

While Helen Ullah admits that Saad may have initially been in a hurry to get married to secure his immigration status in the United States, the two ended up as lifelong partners, married fifty-four years until his death in 2003. As the couple became closer, Saad cut his ties to his past on the subcontinent and was essentially adopted into Helen's Puerto Rican immigrant family. "My father says, Saad's a very good man, and an *Indio*. [laughing] My mother liked him, and so did my sisters and brother, and even though his speech was, you know, he had an accent, they accepted him for what he was. They said he was a hardworking man." On the other side, Helen now became part of two sets of friends and acquaintances with whom Saad spent time: on the one hand, the diverse group that gravitated around Abbas and Frenchy, who were married soon after Helen and Saad, and on the other, a community of Bengali–Puerto Rican families in East Harlem, who would get together on Sundays, shifting from one friend's house to the next from week to week.[7]

These Sunday events were primarily for the men, who would gather in the kitchen of whatever apartment they were in, cook an Indian meal, talk, and catch up with one another on what was usually their one day off from their restaurant or manufacturing jobs, while the women sat in a separate room. "They would put all the women in one room with the children," says Helen Ullah, "and the men went off to another room by themselves. And they did the cooking; the women didn't do any cooking." Most of these women, according to Ullah, were Puerto Rican and were older than she, having likely married their husbands in the 1920s and 1930s. It is unclear how long these Sunday gatherings had been going on in the neighborhood, but by the time Helen joined, the women had developed a network and sense of community among themselves, based on their shared experience of years of marriage to South Asian Muslim men. "They would tell me stories about how they and their husbands met, and they asked: 'Did I like being married?' If there was some argument with the husband, the women spoke to the other women—'Well, why did you fight?'—and try to counsel them. There was a camaraderie there with the older women, I think, and they would work it out, yes. They would work it out."[8]

Helen developed a bond with these women and stayed part of their group until she and Saad moved out of East Harlem, but she was uncomfortable with being placed in what she saw as a secondary social position and she made this clear to Saad from the start of their marriage. "I felt a separation there. The women didn't have too much of a say, and it looked like the men ruled the roost. But I told my husband, 'It's all right. I accept that—for *a while.*' I said, 'But you know, women should have their say.' And I think I got the point across." This was the first of many instances over the years, Helen says, in which Saad listened to her and changed to accommodate her opinions and concerns. Over time, the give-and-take of their relationship—its daily negotiations across Saad and Helen's differences—had a transformative effect on Saad Ullah. He and Helen ultimately moved out of Harlem to a racially mixed working-class area of Long Island and Saad became less interested in the city's Bengali community and closer to his extended, adopted Puerto Rican family and his smaller heterogeneous group of close friends.[9]

Saad's meeting with Helen's mother and sister was "chance"—it grew from the fact that the Rodriguezes and the young Bengali ex-seaman lived in the same neighborhood and shared the daily routine of traveling on the Lexington Avenue line to school and work each morning. Over time, however, the South Asian men who settled in Harlem and the women of color among whom they lived developed more deliberate ways of meeting one another to socialize, date, and marry. Masud Choudhury, a younger brother of Ibrahim Choudry who jumped ship in the 1940s, recalls that he and his South Asian friends made special trips to the Bronx to attend parties where they could meet Puerto Rican and African American women. Choudhury was also a close friend of Habib Ullah's, so when Victoria Ullah opened her beauty salon in the Bronx, Choudhury became a regular visitor, making the trip to flirt with Victoria's clients. Habib, Masud, and others also gained a reputation for their own parties held in East Harlem hotels, where they turned out in sharp suits, served homemade sandwiches, and played the latest Latin dance music.[10]

According to both Helen Ullah and Luz Maria Caballero, men from the subcontinent gradually gained a positive reputation among some members of Harlem's Puerto Rican community: the word was that they made good husbands. As a result, women who had already married Bengalis were asked to introduce sisters and friends to other *Indios*, or they simply made such introductions on their own initiative. Victoria Ullah, for example introduced Ibrahim Choudry to his first wife Catherine Aguilera, who was a friend of Victoria's. According to the Choudry's daughter Laily, Catherine was encouraged to marry Ibrahim despite a twenty-year age difference because he had a job at a time when Harlem was still recovering from the Depression. There were also more formalized channels for marriages. While middlemen had played a key role in other aspects of the Indian ex-maritime community's development—from John Ali to Ibrahim Choudry to a whole range of port-side and factory employment agents—one member of the New York circle, "Frenchy" Abbas, took on a different kind of middle-person role, setting up marriages between Indian ex-seamen and Puerto Rican, West Indian, and African American women.[11]

It is difficult to generalize about the marriages that arose from these varied contexts. In part this is because so few firsthand accounts now exist, and in part because the accounts that do exist contain gaps and silences. There were clearly different kinds of marriages. There were some that were brief, either because they were based on short-term desire or convenience or because they were characterized by conflicts and differences that were too great. Ibrahim Choudry's marriage to Catherine Aguilera did not last because it took a back seat to Choudry's community-based work. While Choudry's daughter was emphasizing the he was "a very fair man in all his dealings who loved people and lived in service to his fellow Bengalis," she says that he performed this work to the neglect of his wife and marriage. There were other mixed marriages, like those of the older, more conservative Puerto Rican women whom Helen Ullah met on Sundays, which were built upon on a family structure in which, in Helen's words, the men "ruled the roost." Some of these marriages may have lasted because the men and women largely inhabited their own separate social spheres with their own support systems. Other marriages of this kind may have hidden long-term conflicts and lasted only because the women were constrained by the social and economic consequences of leaving. These dynamics are not specific to interracial marriages but were likely inflected by the differences in language, beliefs, practices, and expectations specific to these particular relationships. There were other marriages, however, that were long lasting not because they adhered to a particular set of gender norms, but because they unsettled them: marriages like those of Habib and Victoria Ullah and Saad and Helen Ullah, in which the wives were independent women with their own working lives who were able to maintain a level of autonomy, and the husbands were flexible and open to change. These appear by all accounts to have developed into true companionate relationships.[12]

Congregation

Over time, these varied mixed marriages and the families to which they gave rise cohered into a unique New York area community. Although Harlem remained a center of gravity, by the 1950s and 1960s these families were increasingly spread out in different parts of the Bronx, Brooklyn, Long Island, and New Jersey. The Pakistan League of America held two major events each year that brought together its full membership of predominantly Bengali ex-seamen, their Puerto Rican, African American, and Afro-Caribbean wives, and all these couples' children. One of these events was the yearly celebration of Eid-al-fitr, the breaking of the fast at the end of the month of Ramadan. The league held a yearly Eid celebration from its inception in 1947, initially gathering at the Bengal Garden restaurant or at the league's clubhouse on the Lower East Side, and then, as these events got larger, in a series of banquet halls in the midtown hotels where its members were employed as kitchen workers and doormen.[13] By the 1950s and 1960s, the Pakistan League's Eid celebrations brought out hundreds of people. "In the early days, when I was younger," remembers Ibrahim' Choudry's son, Noor:

> we'd go to the Eids and there'd have to be three or four hundred people, maybe even more. The men would get there earlier and they'd do a lot of praying and it seemed like there were at least a hundred, hundred and fifty men only. After that it came time to have the big feast and the women would come. So then it was wall-to-wall people. I can remember one time they had twelve rows of tables, and these guys came marching out of the kitchen—had to be eight or nine of them with everything, putting it on the table family style— the rice, the bowls of chicken, everything. If you went home hungry it was your own fault. Eid was always a great celebration . . . it was a time when everybody was joyful.[14]

Sometime in the late 1940s or early 1950s, Ibrahim Choudry and other members of the Pakistan League also started the tradition of a yearly summer event, in which the organization would charter a boat to sail from a starting point on the New Jersey waterfront to the docks near the southern tip of Manhattan (where some of its members had likely deserted steamships years earlier) and then twenty-five miles up the East River and Long Island Sound to Rye Beach Playland, an amusement park near the New York–Connecticut border. "I remember standing on line in Battery Park," says Habib Ullah Jr., "and there were literally hundreds of people out there waiting to get on that boat—Bengali, Indian, Pakistani" men, their wives, and all their children. "And when the boat arrived, all the New Jersey families were already on board, so it really brought everyone together. There was a big picnic and there was a band on the boat and they would dance. This was how they renewed their bonds as a community."[15]

Both Habib Ullah Jr. and Noor Chowdry remember another type of family outing, one that points to the ties their fathers maintained to family and kin on the subcontinent as they simultaneously developed roots in and around New York City. On occasion, Ibrahim, Habib Sr., and other members of the uptown Bengali community would have an excursion to one of the waterfront areas to greet others from their home regions, who were still working in the maritime trade, as their ships lay in port. Habib Jr. remembers one of these trips vividly:

> We went to one of the ships once—I was a teenager at the time, and it had docked in New Jersey. Apparently the guys who were working on the ship were either friends or family members of some of the guys from the neighborhood, and a whole bunch of us went in three or four cars. The men were there and we visited them. It was a Sunday and the ship was closed, so everybody else was gone, but these Bengali guys stayed on the ship, and they did their own cooking for everyone who came to visit. We were all sitting around eating, and what I remember of that was that even their rice was hot. Forget the curry—their *rice* was hot. It almost killed me.[16]

These shipboard visits provided Habib Jr. and other members of the second generation with a brief glimpse of a world their fathers had once inhabited and which the children could know only partially and from the outside. For Habib Sr. and his generation, these trips to the docks were part of an ongoing relationship between the seamen who had deserted and settled in the New York area and others who remained in the trade, making their way through maritime circuits and moving back and forth to the subcontinent. The interplay between these two groups on the waterfronts of Manhattan, Brooklyn, and New Jersey dated back at least to the era of Amir Haider Khan; it was key to maintaining communication between men in New York and their families in Sylhet, Noakhali, and elsewhere.

After years in the United States, members of this community differed widely from one another in their engagement with the cultural and religious practices of Islam. Saad Ullah, for example, stopped going to the large, organized Eid celebrations after a while but maintained his own daily practice, unrolling a small prayer mat in the corner of his room each day to pray. He also agreed to have a Catholic wedding ceremony, three years after he and Helen were first married, when Helen expressed her desire to do so. Ibrahim Choudry was not only involved in Pakistani, Bengali, and Muslim American institutional and organizational work, but officiated at group religious observances, oversaw the preparation of bodies for burial, and was devout in his personal observance, praying five times a day. If he was on the streets of Manhattan when it was time for *namaaz*, his daughter Laily says, he would duck into a nearby phone booth to do his prayers. At the same time, like Saad Ullah, Choudry was generous and accepting of others' varied practices and actions, treating the members of his community who were less observant without a trace of judgment or condescension.[17] Habib Ullah Sr. was one of many among his friends who had relaxed his religious observances after coming to New York. It is possible that these men had developed a different relationship to Islamic practice before arriving in the United States, over the course of years of seafaring—or had not been strictly observant even before they went overseas. For these men, Islam consisted largely of the maintenance of dietary strictures, the observance of the yearly Ramadan fast, and the celebration of Eid at the end of fasting.[18]

Both Habib Ullah Jr. and Noor Chowdry note that many in their fathers' circles—the *"chachas"* (uncles), as the second generation referred to them—liked to gamble and smoke. These men would gamble even in the Pakistan League's clubhouse: "The ironic thing was," Habib Ullah Jr. says, "here are these guys sitting around the table playing poker, right? They're Muslims; you don't gamble, but they're playing poker, right? And then right on the wall above them—and I have this mental picture, I remember this—right above them on the wall, was a sign: 'No gambling allowed.' "[19] Noor Chowdry has similar memories about one of his *"chachas"* who, for a time, lived in his father's apartment's small spare room: "He worked evenings. And he'd come home real late at night. And all day, when he'd get up, you know, he'd just sit and play solitaire, over and over and over, for hours. And then I heard that he would go to the card clubs and play solitaire for money. For every card that you put up, you got so much money, and when you got up over a certain number, then the payout doubled. So you could win like a hundred dollars if you won the game or more. So that's what he loved to do."[20]

Because so many of the men in this group were not strictly observant, the norm within the mixed households appears to have been for husband and wife to maintain their separate faiths. This was the case, for example, with both Saad Ullah and Habib Ullah Sr., whose wives regularly attended Catholic churches in the neighborhood. Habib Ullah Jr. notes, however, that participation in each other's religious festivities was usually a one-way street: "the men never went to the churches on Easter, Christmas, whatever, but the wives would participate in their holidays, even if they didn't pray. They always were there for respect."[21] In a small number of cases, the wives of more religiously observant men did convert, or these men married African American women who were already practicing Muslims. Noor Chowdry remembers one such family that lived on West 112th Street in Central Harlem, that he used to visit with his father. On one visit, when Ibrahim Choudry brought a package of his favorite tea biscuits, Social Teas, it was not his Bengali friend, but the friend's African American wife who pointed out that the biscuits were made with lard, then took them and tossed them in the trash. "And then when we got home," Chowdry recalls, "we had Social Teas at home, so the first thing my father did, he reached in, took those, and threw them in the garbage! He was crushed. He loved those cookies."[22]

When it came to the second generation, their relationship to Islam largely depended on their fathers. Habib Ullah Sr., for example, de-emphasized both Islam and the Bengali language in bringing up his children because he wanted them to "fit in and become American." Significantly, "fitting in" was, in this case, not an assimilation into white American society, but an integration into the Ullahs' predominantly Puerto Rican section of East Harlem.[23] Ibrahim Choudry, however, tried to teach not only his son, Noor, but also Habib Ullah Jr. and other second generation youths the practices and the importance of daily observance. This happened later in Noor and Habib's childhood, in their early teens, at a time, perhaps, when Choudry was worried about the influences the two boys were growing up with in the United States. Up until then, Habib Jr. says, his knowledge about Islamic practice was minimal: "I would go to the prayers with my father and all that, but I didn't really know how to pray, because my father basically didn't know how to pray. [laughing] It was only later on when I was a teenager and my mother had passed away when Ibrahim Choudry started teaching me and Noor prayers." Choudry conducted these lessons in the home of his friend on West 112th Street: "he had a prayer room and we started going there once a week in the evening. And he was teaching us the different prayers, the beads, the rituals, how to wash before prayer. It was Choudry who taught us that." Noor took in what his father taught him but remembers with ambivalence some of the experiences that this observance brought with it—such as having to pray out in public on the side of the highway with his father and other community members during long road trips: "He'd ask me to do the call to prayer and I'd do it. But, you know, you see all these cars slowing down and staring at you and everybody's praying. And then you just had to get back on the bus and keep going."[24]

Generations

For the children of Bengali–Puerto Rican and Bengali–African American marriages, such experiences were part of daily life. This generation grew up shifting among a multiplicity of different cultural and religious practices, worldviews, languages, relations, and relationships within the context of their immediate and extended families, their schools, their neighborhoods, and the larger city of New York.

Noor Chowdry describes a childhood spent moving among a series of multiracial homes. In his first few years, he lived with his mother and maternal grandmother in East Harlem, speaking only Spanish until the age of six. Later he lived with his Bengali uncle, African American aunt, and his aunt's son, Hassan, in Belleville, New Jersey. Hassan was a jazz musician in his early twenties, and it was here, living with this part of the family, Noor says, that he himself fell in love with jazz. Noor spent hours listening to his cousin play saxophone. "I very seldom even saw Hassan. I heard him, and when the door was closed we were told, just leave, don't bother him. At night, he got out of there, doing his thing. I remember he played at clubs—jazz clubs in the city. And he just got me to the point where I said, 'I want to play the sax like him.'" Noor would also spend time with his father's friend Abdul, who had married and settled in another African American community in New Jersey and had a son Noor's age. Abdul ran a small business making perfumes and lotions, which he

sold door to door— an echo of the Bengali peddlers in New Orleans—
and Noor and Abdul's son often accompanied the father on his circuits
through working-class black neighborhoods, where, moving from one
home to the next, he would meet with his regular customers and make
his sales.[25]

Noor's descriptions of family events give us a sense of the larger multiracial community that had formed among and around groups of Bengali migrants by the 1950s. On holidays such as Thanksgiving and
Christmas, his father, Ibrahim, would pick up Noor and his sister, Laily,
in his car; then they would pick up Ibrahim's younger brother, Masud,
and his wife, Barbara, from West Harlem, then Ibrahim and Masud's
close friend Habib Ullah and his family from East Harlem. Then they
would all drive out to the house of Ibrahim and Masud's cousin Idris
Choudhury and his wife, Annie, in an African American section of the
suburb of Montclair, New Jersey. Among the South Asian men in this
group, two had married Puerto Rican women, two had married African
American women, and one had married a young working-class British
woman during a two-year stay in London in the 1940s. So when all the
women and men gathered in Montclair on the holidays, they brought
together a group of more than a dozen American-born cousins who were
Bengali and Puerto Rican, Bengali and African American, Bengali and
white, who grew up together as kin—hearing and speaking multiple languages, eating multiple kinds of home food, navigating multiple and
shifting racial, ethnic, and cultural identifications—all as part of a single
circle of extended family and friends.[26]

Habib Ullah Jr., who was part of this circle, remembers the group's
Montclair gatherings with fondness. From Habib Jr.'s perspective, it
becomes clear that the car rides out to Montclair foreshadowed a Bengali, Puerto Rican, and African American out-migration from Harlem
that was beginning to take shape even in the 1950s, but which would
accelerate in later years. The pathway from the Ullahs' tenement on
East 102nd Street to Masud Choudhury's apartment in a West Harlem
city housing project, to Ibrahim Choudry's residence in a West Side
apartment building, to Idris Choudhury's home in an African American suburban enclave outside the city was a path of modest class ascen-

sion even as it connected families and neighborhoods that were still predominantly of color. Idris Choudhury's wife, Annie, was part of an African American community in Montclair that had its roots in the Great Migration, when migrants from the postbellum South were drawn to the domestic and service jobs available among the New Jersey suburb's more prosperous white residents. By the 1940s and 1950s, when Idris and Annie were bringing up their children there, Montclair's black community was well established and varied, including both service sector workers and professionals. Driving out to Idris and Annie Choudhury's house for the day, remembers Habib Jr., "was a big thing for us. Because being city kids, that was for us like going to the country. And they had a big backyard, and so it was a lot of fun for us. It was different from what we knew."[27]

What Habib Jr. knew was East Harlem; it was here that his everyday life was rooted. Sometime in the late 1930s, Habib Sr. and Victoria had moved to a second-floor apartment in a five-story tenement building on East 102nd Street near the corner of Lexington Avenue. As Victoria helped other members of her family migrate from Puerto Rico over the next decade, they also settled nearby. After Victoria passed away in 1952, Habib Jr.'s sister went to live with her aunt Luz two blocks down East 102nd Street, in the housing projects between Park and Madison Avenues, while Habib continued to live with his father in their tenement apartment. Like most of the tenements in the neighborhood, the building that Habib Sr. and Jr. shared had no fans or air-conditioning, so it was sweltering in the summers; in the winter, the boiler would break down and leave them without heat and hot water. But what kept Habib Sr. there was the bond that neighbors had built with one another in the midst of their shared circumstances. "Each block," Habib Jr. remembers, "was like a neighborhood unto itself. You knew all your neighbors and your neighbors knew you—not only within the building, but on the block itself. You would know them by first name or nickname. So there was this sense of community." Throughout his childhood, Habib Jr. found a kind of belonging in which the simple fact of living on the block trumped other kinds of difference. "East 102nd Street," he remembers, "was about ninety-eight percent

Hispanic; there were a few blacks, and besides us, we had the Mahais and the Alis on the street. And it was fine—you were just accepted. 'You're Indian? All right, okay, come on, let's go.' Everybody hung out and just had a good time together and you weren't looked upon as anything strange. You were just one of the kids on the block."[28]

At the same time, Habib Jr. spent time with his Puerto Rican aunts, uncles, and cousins in other parts of the neighborhood, and he circulated in and out of the Bengali households that existed like pockets throughout East Harlem. Habib Jr. describes a constellation of South Asian men and mixed families living in nearby tenements among Puerto Ricans, Cubans, African Americans, and Italians. "We had several Indian families living right in our area, near East 102nd, 103rd Street. My father and I were there. Across the street was another family, the Mahais—they were Indian and black; down the block from us was Nawab Ali and his family. On East 103rd Street, there was Abdul Abbas and his family, and we had the Indian jeweler, Paul. Then there was another Indian—believe it or not, he changed his name to Brown—who had twin boys, and they lived on Ninety-Eighth Street between Park and Madison." A few blocks away, another Bengali had married an Italian woman and they had a daughter Habib's age named Sakina. In other parts of East Harlem there was Joe Mango, a close friend of Habib Sr. with whom he had lived on the Lower East Side when he first arrived in New York, and another ex-seaman who went by the name Charlie—the contact who had set up Saad Ullah with his first job on arrival from Baltimore. Habib Jr. remembers some South Asian men in the neighborhood only by a Bengali word for uncle: "We'd never call them by name; they were all just our *chachas*." Over time, some of these men moved farther out, like Nawab Ali, who moved with his wife and sons to the Bronx, and Abdul Abbas, who moved with his wife and daughters to Brooklyn. "In those days, that's how it was—there weren't defined neighborhoods of Indians. They were scattered all over the place." But Habib Sr. maintained contact with them all and took his son as he went calling on different friends through East and Central Harlem and into the outer boroughs.[29]

These individuals, households, and businesses, and his father's own home, formed a parallel universe to that of Habib Jr.'s Puerto Rican family and his immediate block. He and other "mutts like myself" developed a facility with moving in and out of all these different arenas. "You kind of lived a dual life," says Habib:

> Out on the street, if you had to be Puerto Rican, you were Puerto Rican; if you had to be black, you were black; if you had to be one of the kids from the block, you were one of the kids from the block. But when you got home, I know in my case my father always had the rice and curry going, and I would help him address his letters to his mother, back in what had become in those days East Pakistan. He couldn't write English or even Bengali, so Choudry or Joe Mango would come over and help him write the letters and I would address them for him, with my grandmother's name, Hazrat Hakem. So there was more of a cultural fix at home, an Indian atmosphere.

The duality of Habib Jr.'s daily experience was also reflected at an emotional register in the different ways he interacted with his "*chachas*" and his Puerto Rican family and friends. "With my Puerto Rican family, they embrace you, with my friends, you're slappin' five. Then, you go to the [Pakistan League's] clubhouse, where all the *chachas* are, it would be: 'Hello, boy, come here, tell me, how are you? How is school?' They were more reserved. So you learn, you adapt to that."[30]

Habib Ullah Jr. was able to move with relative ease among the multiple arenas—or dual sides—of his life in part because he was a boy and in part because he had a uniquely easy-going father. In the years that they lived together, Habib Sr. gave Habib Jr. great latitude in his day-to-day life, to the extent that he and his father during these years were more like roommates or brothers than father and son. He also emphasizes that the daughters of Bengali–Puerto Rican families had a different experience from his, that in general they stayed closer to their mothers and to the home and grew up essentially like other Puerto Rican girls and young women in East Harlem in the 1950s. Instead of moving through predominantly male Bengali spaces with their fathers as Habib did, they would have spent more time inside their apartments with their mothers and siblings or in different homes with the mothers' circles of family and friends or moving through a different set of public spaces: places of women's gathering like Victoria's Bronx salon, or the market, or church.

Habib Jr.'s wife, Felita, who grew up in a large Puerto Rican household a few blocks away from Habib elaborates:

> Girls were expected to come home from school and have dinner on the table and do chores. You were close to home or downstairs at the stoop, but not at the corners. In the evenings, you maybe visited your neighbor, but certainly by 8 o'clock, you were back. My mother said, "You can't be like white rice." You cannot be found in everybody's home. The weekend you spent cleaning, shopping. Saturdays, you would listen to the radio and they had live stuff on there and hit parade. You'd be singing all the latest songs. And definitely, you went to Mass every Sunday, all spiffed up. But church and activities like that, you did in groups, and visiting. So I don't know, we entertained ourselves, that's how it was.[31]

In retrospect, Habib Jr. now sees his father's inability to provide this kind of day-to-day structure as a limitation of Habib Sr.'s parenting abilities; he believes that a number of others in his father's group of exseamen, in different ways, lacked the skills and engagement that would have made them good parents. Some of Habib Jr.'s contemporaries had fathers who were absent or who moved in and out of their lives, while still others experienced ongoing conflicts over what their fathers would and would not allow them to do. Alaudin Ullah, Habib Jr.'s younger half brother, notes that many of his father's generation placed an unreasonable level of attention, pressure, and expectation on their eldest sons, while neglecting their younger sons and daughters. Alaudin questions Habib Sr.'s decision, for example, to give up his daughter to the care of her aunt Luz. Both Alaudin and Luz say this decision, based on Habib's inability or unwillingness to raise a girl on his own, took a heavy emotional toll on Zubeida. Laily Chowdry had a father who was much more involved in her life, but discovered that for all Ibrahim's openness, acceptance, and generosity toward the members of the multiracial community he helped forge, he did not want her to date black classmates at her high school. She now says that when she married the son of an Indian Muslim family from Trinidad whose parents were part of Ibrahim Choudry's circle in New York City, she did so mostly to please her father.[32]

The Bengalis were not the only fathers in Harlem—or in the United States—to subject their children to contradictions and double standards, nor was it uncommon in the 1950s, 1960s, and 1970s for daughters to experience the limitations or conservatism of their fathers more acutely than sons. Among the families that constituted this multiracial community, however, family gender dynamics played out in a particular way. When South Asian men either clashed with or were absent from their children, it was Puerto Rican, African American, and Afro-Caribbean women—the children's mothers, aunts, grandmothers, and other family members and friends—who raised them and provided them with stability, family, and community. These women took up the care of the Bengali men's children, especially their daughters, when the men were unwilling or unable to do so. This was just one of a number of factors that ultimately tied the second generation most closely to the communities around them; in their extended families, on their blocks, in their schools, and in the larger neighborhood, they became part of Puerto Rican and African American New York.

Dispersion

By the early 1970s, when the region once known as East Bengal, and then East Pakistan, became the independent nation of Bangladesh, the multiracial, multiethnic, and multireligious community that once came together in New York under the banner of the Pakistan League of America was already beginning to dissipate and disappear. The Muslim men from Sylhet, Noakhali, and elsewhere who had deserted British steamships in New York from the beginning of the First World War through the end of the second were dying off, their tombstones, marked with the star and crescent moon of Islam, accumulating in a section of a Staten Island cemetery purchased by the Pakistan League years before. The children of the second generation had largely assimilated—not into white American society and upper-middle-class suburbia but into working- and lower-middle-class Puerto Rican and African American communities. All but a few of those who once lived in Harlem had moved out—to Long Island, New Jersey, Florida, California. Habib Ullah Sr. was one of the few who stayed. For him, the area of Spanish Harlem where he settled in the late 1930s remained his home until he died in 1982. But Ullah was by no means stationary or static over these more than forty years. If Dada Amir Haider Khan moved through circuits that were global, even epic, in their scope, and was transformed by the experiences and the people he encountered, Habib Ullah traveled a set of more localized and routine circuits—through his adopted neighborhood and city. As such, Habib's life foregrounds everyday relationships and interactions as they would have played out for many of the South Asian Muslim men who settled in Harlem—in the intimate and localized spaces that normally remain inaccessible to history.

Habib was someone who enjoyed walking through his neighborhood engaging in what his son Alaudin describes as the "art of conversation." A typical daily circuit would have seen Habib chatting in English and a little Spanish with his Puerto Rican neighbors on his block, then walking up to Paul's, the Indian-owned jewelry shop on East 103rd, where he would sit and gossip for a while in Bengali and English, then up to Syed Ali's restaurant on 109th Street, where he would have lunch with more of his Bengali friends and hear news from the subcontinent. Then after lunch he might walk up to La Marqueta, Spanish Harlem's huge covered market, where he would go to a botanica run by an older Caribbean woman who supplied him with his spices, which she would mix into his trademark Indian masala. Next, Habib would take the train down to the Lower East Side to one particular Jewish fish seller to whom he had been going for years because he stocked a special kind of fish that Habib used in his curries. Then, finally, he would return to his apartment in East Harlem. This is a circuit that Habib Ullah made week after week, in one variation or another, over the course of the more than forty years that he lived in Spanish Harlem.[33] Such circulations bring to mind the philosopher Michel de Certeau's insights about the ways people transform the planned, imposed spaces of cities into actual lived places. De Certeau describes walking in the city as an act through which people forge unexpected paths, make the urban landscape their own, and thereby "organize a *here* in relation to an *abroad*, a 'familiarity' in relation to a 'foreignness.' "[34] Walking in Habib Sr.'s case, however, went beyond the act of claiming or refiguring a place; it was a means of forging new *human* relationships, often across racial, ethnic, linguistic, and gender differences, and maintaining those relationships through daily interaction and exchange over the course of a lifetime.

For the decades that Bengali and other Muslim men from the subcontinent were part of the social, cultural, and economic landscape of Harlem, these relationships were a condition of everyday life. Even those who created their own spaces and associated primarily with other men from the villages, districts, and regions they had left behind could not but be changed by the experience of navigating life, work, and leisure in the heterogeneous environment of their uptown neighborhood and the rest of New York City. Ironically, the passage of legislation expanding immigration and naturalization for people from South Asia heralded the end of both the Bengali community in Harlem and the cross-racial and interethnic dynamics that were such a central part of that community's formation and character. In part this was because the 1965 Immigration Act resulted not just in large numbers of new immigrants from the subcontinent, but also in a population of professionals and businesspeople who, in short order, by the early to mid-1970s, had formed distinct enclaves in the suburbs and outer boroughs of New York.[35]

There were other dynamics at work, as well. Again ironically, one of these was the formation of the independent nation of Bangladesh. In the mid-1940s, Mubarek Ali Khan and others arguing for the rights of Indian men who had migrated to the United States before 1924 often described this population as "stateless"—they had left their own country, which was under colonial rule, and started lives in the United States but had no right to citizenship in their new home.[36] This group's relationship to national identity only became more complicated in the years after Independence and Partition. While so many of the ex-seamen in New York identified with or became involved in the struggle for an independent India, over the course of less than thirty years they went from being subjects of colonial India to being Pakistanis to being Bangladeshis—all in absentia, as they remained in New York. As much as some, like Ibrahim Choudry, devoted themselves to the idea of the new nation of Pakistan that was taking shape thousands of miles away on the subcontinent in the 1950s and 1960s, the majority of the ex-seafaring population in New York by now lived out their daily lives at a more local register. Even their connections to one another were most strongly based upon region, language, and the shared experience of settlement in New York—and their lobbying efforts as the Pakistan League were focused on shoring up their ability to stay where they were.

The liberation war and formation of Bangladesh in 1970–1971 appears to have changed these dynamics, consolidating a sense of national identity at the same moment that the Bengali community in New York was growing due to post-1965 migration. The Pakistan League, which by some accounts had "grown dormant" by the late 1960s, was reactivated in this period and, after changing its name first to the East Pakistan League and then to the Bangladesh League, became the main vehicle for the efforts of Bengalis in the United States to publicize and build American support for the Bangladeshi nationalist struggle. The membership of the league now included many more professionals, businesspeople, and students, who had come to the United States since 1965.[37] While these members were devoted to the independence of Bangladesh, they appear to have had few ties beyond this shared cause to the earlier, working-class Bengali population that had settled in Harlem, let alone to the other communities of color with whom these earlier immigrants had built their lives.

Habib Ullah Jr. laments what was lost with this earlier generation. "There was a different atmosphere, a different attitude, a different way of life in those days," he says. "And I think it's sad. To a certain extent I understand keeping your culture, and I think my father's generation did to a great extent. But now South Asians keep their culture and put a wall around what is around them, and I think that's a disservice to the coming generations."[38] In a sense, though, Habib Jr.'s father epitomized not only the possibilities, but also the complexities and limits of the interracial relationships that Bengali Muslim ex-seamen built in 1930s-1960s Harlem. On the one hand, over the course of decades, Habib Sr. became deeply integrated into the life of East Harlem. He had left his village in Noakhali in his teens, so this neighborhood and the larger city around it truly became his home, where he both was rooted in a circle of other Bengali ex-seamen and also had a wide array of friends, acquaintances, and family members that stretched far beyond this South Asian circle, particularly among the Puerto Rican migrants, immigrants, and local residents who had also made East Harlem their home. He and Victoria built a partnership that reached across language, religion, ethnicity, and other lines of difference.

On the other hand, as his youngest son, Alaudin, points out, Habib Sr. was never able to move beyond the idea that he was incapable of raising his daughter, and he gave up responsibility for her after her mother died. And twenty years later, in his old age, Habib returned to Noakhali for the first time since leaving in the 1920s, and entered into an arranged marriage in order to bring a younger Bengali woman back to East 102nd Street to take care of him as his health began to fail.[39] This was another, much more localized and personal, consequence of the 1965 act, but one that puts into relief important larger questions about the longevity of the multiracial community that had once existed in Harlem. Was this a community that could have only existed in a particular place and time under a particular set of circumstances? Or does it point to dynamics and experiences of intermixture that continue to the present day in neighborhoods far beyond Harlem? Habib Ullah Sr. and his contemporaries may have sought to "get lost" after leaving their ships and entering the chaos and possibility of New York City eight decades ago, but the stories that their lives open up—along with the contradictions they reveal, the questions they raise, and the possibilities they suggest—should not be lost to history.

Conclusion

Lost Futures

A LAUDIN ULLAH STANDS ON the roof of a fifteen-story apartment block in East Harlem—one of the nine stark red brick towers and four low-rises that comprise the George Washington Carver Houses. Around him in every direction are the rooftops of other buildings, some supporting old wooden water towers, others flat, tarred, and patchy. From this height, there is little hint of the changes that are under way below. His father, Habib Ullah Sr., moved here to the projects in the 1970s from his longtime tenement apartment on 102nd Street, bringing Alaudin, his brother Karim, and their mother, Moheama. Habib's first wife, Victoria, had died many years earlier, and in the late 1960s, suffering from acute asthma and no longer able to work in restaurant kitchens, the elderly ex-seaman had returned for the first time in forty years to his village in Noakhali, in East Bengal, to remarry. Moheama was much younger but had already been married and divorced and now wanted to get out of the village. Habib offered to marry her and bring her back with him to the United States. Alaudin now recognizes that Habib was primarily looking for someone to care for him in his old age and insists his father should have known how difficult life would be here for his mother, who arrived in Harlem in 1967. By this time, the mixed Bengali—Puerto Rican—African American families that had once been a presence in

Central and East Harlem had largely left the neighborhood. When Karim and Alaudin were born, Habib decided to apply for one of the apartments in the Washington Carver projects. When one came through, on the top floor of one of the high-rises, Alaudin remembers that his father joked that he was moving his family to a penthouse apartment. He died less than ten years later, and Moheama, Karim, and Alaudin remained.[1] In 2010, they are the last family in Harlem with a direct connection to the community of South Asian ex-seamen that settled in the neighborhood in the 1920s–1940s.

It is a Sunday in early December. This is the day of the week on which, half a century ago, Habib and his friends would have gathered in the apartment of one of their fellow migrants from Bengal and spent hours cooking home food in the kitchen, while their wives chatted and children played in another room. Today the air is cool and crisp, and Alaudin looks south from the rooftop of his building, pointing out the tunnel where trains making their way into the city on the Harlem River line disappear underground after roaring past the projects. "That's Ninety-Sixth Street," he says. "That's where Spanish Harlem ends and the Upper East Side begins. When I was growing up, that was the Mason-Dixon Line. The white people stayed on their side, and we stayed on ours."[2] In recent years more and more of the wealthy New Yorkers who once stayed south of the Mason-Dixon Line have ventured uptown across the Ninety-Sixth Street border. Real estate developers have purchased one Harlem building after the next, inviting the migration of young professionals uptown as they rebrand Alaudin's part of the neighborhood "Upper Yorkville," the "Upper, Upper East Side," and "SpaHa."

Gentrification has been uneven, but it is just the latest in a series of changes that have gradually transformed the physical and social landscape of this part of the city. In the 1950s, Robert Moses had entire blocks of turn-of-the-century apartment buildings demolished in order to construct Washington Carver and the dozens of other housing projects that now tower above every part of Harlem.[3] In the ensuing decades, the neighborhood struggled with economic decline, aggressive policing, and social and political neglect. Many within the neighborhood's various different communities—the Bengalis included—migrated to other parts of the city or to working- and lower-middle-class suburbs in New Jersey,

Long Island, and elsewhere.[4] All of these processes have contributed to the loss of the neighborhood's many microhistories. The creeping gentrification of the present threatens to become a final sweep over the past, over the Harlem that was once home to Habib Ullah and Victoria Echevarria, Syedali Miah and Marguerite Richardson, Saad Ullah and Helen Rodriguez, Nawab Ali and Bernardina Colon, Ibrahim Choudry, Masud Choudhury, Joe Mango, Woheed Ali, and scores of other South Asian Muslims who escaped their ships to make new lives here.

The story is much the same in other cities. In New Orleans, the block that was once home to Moksad and Ella Blackman Ali and their four eldest children, in the city's Third Ward, is now part of a vast parking lot for the Superdome. The building at 1428 Saint Louis Street, which was home to the first recorded Bengali-Creole family in the city—Alef Ally, Minnie Lecompte, and their daughters Sadie and Viola—and that for decades afterward functioned as the Hooghly peddler network's main boardinghouse, was destroyed in the 1940s to make way for the Iberville Projects, now one of New Orleans' most impoverished and neglected public housing developments. A few blocks away, another parking lot stands in place of Sofur and America Ally's home on Orleans Avenue, once a site where peddlers newly arrived from West Bengal were introduced into the city and the Oriental goods trade. And Tremé's North Claiborne Avenue, once the thriving heart of New Orleans' black community and the site of shops run by Sofur Ally, Abdul Rahman, Abdul Fara, Towakkal Haldar, Abdul Jalil, Abdul Rohim Surker, and Abdul Hamid is now a wasteland of gravel lots, parked cars, and concrete columns running beneath Interstate 10, the raised highway built to direct traffic in and out of the city from its more affluent suburbs.[5] Hurricane Katrina took away lives and memories, split apart families, and destroyed photographs, documents, and other personal reminders of the past and has opened the door to a new era of gentrification. In Detroit, it is Interstate 375, the Chrysler Freeway, that cuts through the center of what used to be Black Bottom, and on the adjacent streets—Monroe, Lafayette, Fort, and Congress—desolate parking lots and massive concrete garages stand in place of the apartment buildings that were once rooming houses for Indian, Arab, and Afghan autoworkers. On Pennsylvania Avenue in West Baltimore, there is now a monument to commemorate the Royal Theater, but little else remains to suggest the rich cultural life that once flourished along the nearby blocks, let alone the Indian restaurant that operated in the center of this thriving midcentury African American neighborhood.

The South Asian peddlers and seamen who came to the United States between the 1880s and the 1950s left no obvious archives, no clear public record, and no single place to mark their presence. In their own day, many intended to "disappear"—at least to the authorities of a nation that would not legally admit them. The connections these men forged with other marginalized groups did not, for the most part, take the form of public political alliances, of movements or collective actions that might have left a mark on the historical record. Most of the men were nonliterate and left behind no letters, speeches, nor other written records of their thoughts and experiences. The everyday histories of working-class communities, of migrants and sojourners, of the racialized and the "illegal," are fleeting; perhaps more than anything, places give them solidity. These groups' pasts are kept alive in specific landscapes—buildings, parks, street corners, community centers, churches, mosques—by the people who lived them, remember them, and can narrate them. They are transmitted across generations through local stories, memories, and rumors. Decades of change in Tremé, in downtown Detroit, West Baltimore, and Harlem, have brought great losses to the communities that lived there, and amid these losses are stories of American immigration that diverge from the known, the expected, and the iconic.

A small number of men from South Asia were part of these histories. South Asian Muslim men once shared apartment buildings and city streets and, later, homes, families, and descendants with the residents of U.S. neighborhoods of color. They shared with those around them a similar set of conditions and social constraints; they shared some of the consequences of having dark skin in a society structured by race; they shared experiences of being excluded from power and full citizenship, of being relegated to manual labor and service sector jobs, of being uprooted, and, albeit in different ways, of being criminalized. They also shared daily lives and intimacies, conflicts and affinities, spaces of work and leisure, places and practices of worship. Now, posthumously, they share with their former neighbors the disappearance of the physical and social landscapes that supported their life pursuits and their complex families and communities. As surely as the lives of South Asian migrants became embedded within U.S. neighborhoods of color, the memory of their lives has vanished as these neighborhoods have been transformed and reconfigured by neglect, out-migration, gentrification, redevelopment, and urban renewal.

Some might say that this is not a significant loss. This was, after all, a small number of people. The number of Bengali silk peddlers working in the United States likely never amounted to more than a few hundred, and at most two or three dozen of these men stayed in New Orleans, Charleston, and other parts of the South after their network stopped operating. Likewise, the number of Indian seamen who successfully jumped ship likely only reached into the low thousands, spread over several decades, and perhaps fewer than fifteen hundred of these men spent extended periods of their lives or settled permanently in U.S. cities. In Harlem, the Lower East Side, New York City's outer boroughs, and New Jersey— the region where the largest number of South Asian ex-seafarers settled and intermarried—their community appears to have peaked in size during the 1940s and 1950s, at a time when events like the celebration of Eid drew about five hundred people each year, including the ex-seamen, their Puerto Rican, African American, and West Indian wives, and their mixed-race children.

But these numbers are deceptive. Between the 1880s and 1920s, in the years that vacationing and leisure travel first became part of the American popular experience, peddlers from Hooghly and Calcutta were a part of that experience; they became a regular, perhaps even expected, feature of working- and middle-class resorts from Atlantic City and Asbury Park through a chain of southern and Caribbean cities. At these sites, over the course of more than a generation, the peddlers would have interacted with hundreds of thousands of Americans. Likewise, between the early 1900s and the 1940s, groups of Indian seamen became a regular presence on the docks and around the waterfronts of major U.S. port cities, from Galveston to New York. If only a fraction ventured farther inland, moving on to restaurant and factory work, tens of thousands of Indian men passed in and out of port during these years, mingling with countless others at the water's edge: immigrants, arriving and departing travelers, maritime and waterfront workers, dockside merchants and businesspeople, restaurant and rooming-house keepers.[6] In the late nineteenth and early twentieth centuries, these peddlers and seamen at the resorts and waterfronts would have been the first East Indians that many Americans had ever seen face-to-face. The first "Hindoos" they encountered, the first people to represent "India" in their eyes, were neither Hindu "holy men" like Swami Vivekananda nor Sikh farm and mill workers like those on the West Coast, but Muslim men from areas of present-day West Bengal, Bangladesh, and Pakistan.

The importance of these men's stories, however, goes beyond such fleeting encounters. Their stories complicate a number of widely accepted notions about U.S. immigration in general and South Asian immigration in particular. Perhaps most significantly, they challenge expected patterns and trajectories of arrival, incorporation, and assimilation. Those peddlers and seamen who came to the United States between the 1880s and 1910s found a nation where "the Orient" was in vogue but Asian workers were the targets of exclusionary legislation and xenophobic violence. Those who arrived after 1917 were legally barred from entering the United States as immigrants—deemed undesirable and unassimilable on racial grounds, even as their goods and labor were in demand. All these factors shaped their relationship to the United States, their approach to working and operating within its borders, the spaces through which they could travel, and the places they ended up establishing roots. These varied constraints are also what make their stories so remarkable and illuminating. In order to access jobs and consumers in the United States, they forged pathways in and out of the orbits of two world powers. They made their way across 12,000 miles of ocean as deck passengers on colonial mail ships and steerage passengers in the cramped quarters of transatlantic steamers, or as members of the semicaptive colonial workforce in the engine rooms and kitchens of British merchant vessels; they made their way from port to port, across one border and then the next, as these ports and borders were policed and controlled with ever-greater vigilance to limit the global mobility of Asian migrants. Once they reached the United States, they were forced to navigate its racial dynamics and divisions and, ultimately, their own day-to-day existence as undocumented and illegal "aliens."

Their survival and "success" required the peddlers and seamen alike to be adaptable and strategic, to work collectively, to establish flows of information and means of mutual support. At times, they benefited from the competition between Britain and the United States. It was British shipping companies' fear of losing their edge over U.S. and other competitors, for example, that led them to push back against the restrictions of the 1894 Merchant Shipping Act and bring thousands of low-wage Indian maritime workers on voyages to ports in the U.S. Northeast, inadvertently setting the stage for those same seamen to jump ship and enter the onshore industrial and service economies of the United States. The peddlers, meanwhile, benefited from U.S. elites' emulation of their British imperial counterparts, at least in the fashion for "Oriental goods" and Orientalist narratives and fantasies. However, the peddlers and seamen also faced the combined power of both Britain and the United States, as the two nations collaborated in the development of global border and passport regimes and cooperated in the surveillance and policing of Indian populations within U.S. borders.[7]

In U.S. cities, the peddlers were too few in number and too transient to consolidate their communities in the form of ethnic enclaves. For the seamen, visible, identifiable enclaves simply may have not been in their interests. Instead of concentrated enclaves, both groups formed extensive networks of rooming houses, residences, point people, middle-people, and allies that stretched across multiple cities and states. Collectively, they used Americans' confusion over their "race" to their advantage, developing a fluid and contextual approach to their identity. They were "white" when they attempted to claim citizenship, "Hindoo" when selling exotic goods, "black" or "Porto Rican" when disappearing into U.S. cities or actively attempting to evade the immigration authorities. They were "*Indios*" on the streets of Spanish Harlem, and their Puerto Rican and African American wives were "East Indian" when they ran their Oriental gift shops or greeted customers in their restaurants. In the transnational movements, day-to-day negotiations, and strategic choices of these two groups of South Asian Muslims, we find the outlines of immigration stories far more complex than our national narrative can capture.

These stories also complicate specific assumptions about the time frame, geography, and dynamics of South Asian immigration and settlement in the United States. Almost twenty years ago, the ethnographer Karen Leonard published a groundbreaking study documenting the little-known history of early-twentieth-century Punjabi immigrants who partnered with Mexican and Mexican American women in the agricultural regions of California and the U.S. Southwest and lived out their lives in these areas through the midtwentieth century. In the years since the publication of Leonard's work, Punjabi-Mexican intermarriage has become a recognized part of the West Coast narrative of South Asian immigration in the pre-1965 period. Too often, however, the story of this mixed community has been treated as something singular and anomalous, rather than as an invitation to explore further the kinds of alliances and intimacies that early nonelite South Asian migrants pursued amid their era's anti-Asian legal regime, escalating anti-"Hindoo" violence, and hardened lines of racial segregation. It is increasingly clear that interracial relationships and multiracial communities were in fact not anomalous, but a central part of South Asian migrants' experiences in the first half of the twentieth century. This was the case not only for the Punjabi men who married in the West and Southwest and the Indian political exiles who found common cause with their African American, Caribbean, Irish, and Egyptian contemporaries in U.S. cities, but also, as Nayan Shah has recently shown, for Indian farm and mill workers who developed intimate bonds with other men on the West Coast of the United States and Canada.[8]

Nevertheless, two assumptions have persisted about the history of South Asians in the United States. The first is that little of significance occurred between the moment the U.S. shut its doors to South Asian immigration and naturalization in the 1917–1924 period and the moment the doors were "reopened" in 1965—or, to put it slightly differently, that the story of South Asians in America stopped in the early twentieth century and did not start in earnest again until thousands of professionals began to arrive in the late 1960s and 1970s. The evidence pieced together in the preceding chapters should give pause to this assumption; it suggests that, in fact, there has been an unbroken stream of migration from the subcontinent to the United States, much of it working-class and Muslim, that started well before the passage of the Asiatic Barred Zone Act and continued throughout the exclusion era.

In this sense, the histories of South Asian peddlers and seamen add to those uncovered by scholars of Chinese American history, documenting the many strategies migrants developed to carve out lives in the shadows a racist exclusionary immigration regime.[9] The stories of South Asian peddlers and seamen should also suggest, however, the many other "lost" histories yet to be uncovered—of South Asian women brought to the United States by wealthy families as nannies, cooks, nurses, and maids; of circus and exhibition workers, such as K. Y. Kira, who stayed after others moved on; of South Asians from Jamaica, Guyana, Trinidad, and elsewhere who participated in the Caribbean migration to U.S. cities in the early twentieth century; and of young people, like Amir Haider Khan's unnamed friend in Detroit, who were adopted by American missionary families in India and brought back to navigate the racial realities of a segregated United States.[10]

The second assumption that the peddlers' and seamen's stories call into question is that early South Asian immigrants' approach to race in the United States was characterized by the attempt to claim whiteness. This idea derives, in part, from the fact that historians of early Asian America have, rightly and understandably, focused much attention on South Asian immigrants' legal challenges to exclusion. As a result, Bhagat Singh Thind's Supreme Court case, in which he claimed that, as a "high caste Hindu," he was Aryan and thus Caucasian and thus a "white person" who should be eligible for citizenship in the United States, has come to occupy the center of the South Asian American narrative of the 1920s. A text authored by Rajani Kanta Das, an Indian student at Columbia University, around the same time the Thind case went up before the court, has also added to the notion that Indians "shunned Negroes" in the early twentieth century. In it, Das claimed that Indians did not associate with African Americans "partly due to [the Indians'] feeling of racial superiority and partly due to the fact that the negroes are socially ostracized by the Americans themselves."[11] It is unclear whose responses formed the basis for this study and its broad claims—whether Das interviewed the dozen or more ex-seamen who, by the 1920s, already lived in Harlem, just beyond the walls of Columbia University. By the time Thind's case was decided and Das's study was published, the grandchildren of Bengali peddlers were growing up as part of black New Orleans.

Some of these peddlers had made a similar attempt as that of Thind to gain citizenship based on a claim of being "white," but their lives, intimacies, and trajectories display a much more complex relationship to race, and to blackness, than either Thind or Das suggests. The same can be said of the many South Asian Muslim ex-seamen who settled in Detroit, Baltimore, and New York, whose memories have survived only because they have been kept alive within African American and Puerto Rican families.

Perhaps most significantly, the peddlers and seamen help us to see the neighborhoods of Tremé, Black Bottom, West Baltimore, and Harlem in an expanded light. At the very least, these should be understood as sites that are important to South Asian American history, alongside the more obvious locations where ethnic enclaves developed much later in the century. However, the South Asian stories lived out in neighborhoods of the black diaspora—on their streets and in their shotgun houses, tenements, and apartment buildings—also point to something crucial and often overlooked about these places themselves. These neighborhoods, so central to the cultural, political, and everyday life of African American, Creole, and Caribbean communities in the first half of the twentieth century, were also spaces of great multiplicity that fostered interactions, intermixtures, and a shared, if often contested, sense of belonging that was crafted in the give-and-take between different working-class migrants of color, none of whom were able to access fully the national promise of inclusion.[12] It is, of course, important not to idealize these spaces and their processes of collective place making. These were also sites marked by competition, division, and, at times, intergroup violence. But the stories of conflict have been told often and have overshadowed other experiences and dynamics—they are more dramatic and serve to confirm assumptions about the supposed incapacities of neighborhoods and communities of color. In fact, these neighborhoods and communities proved to be some of the only ones in the United States with the capacity to take in South Asian Muslim peddlers and seamen, to provide them with the possibility of establishing lives, livelihoods, homes, and home bases when their own regions were under colonial rule and when the official U.S. attitude toward South Asian migrants and sojourners ran from suspicion to exclusion.

In recent years, scholars have revealed the deep strain of internationalism that took root in black communities, newspapers, and religious, labor, and political organizations in the first half of the twentieth century. Throughout this period, African American, Caribbean, and Indian activists, artists, journalists, and intellectuals built ties with one another, engaged in dialogue, and were emboldened by a sense of common struggle against the injustices of racialized power both within the United States and across the colonized world. In the 1920s, Marcus Garvey's United Negro Improvement Association invited Indian expatriate nationalists such as Haridas Muzumdar to speak before thousands of its members at rallies in Detroit and New York City. Even earlier than Garvey, the Puerto Rican nationalist leader Pedro Albizu Campos had begun to speak of the parallels between British rule over India and U.S. rule over Puerto Rico, after meeting in Boston with the Indian poet Rabindranath Tagore. In the 1940s, W. E. B. DuBois and Paul Robeson staged a massive New York City rally in support of Indian independence under the banner of their organization, the Council on African Affairs, while a range of other African American leaders drew their own links to India: Howard Thurman, A. Philip Randolph, and Walter White all developed friendships and alliances with Indian nationalist leaders and advocated publicly for their cause. Throughout the 1920s, 1930s, and 1940s, internationalism was also part of the character of African American periodicals, where headlines about lynchings in the South and police brutality in northern cities shared space with reports about colonial violence in Africa and Asia, U.S. economic exploitation in Puerto Rico, and organized resistance, strikes, and independence movements in India, the Caribbean, Ethiopia, Nigeria. We are fortunate to have records of the interactions and alliances among major figures of this era, and of the ways that black newspapers articulated the connections between local and global struggles.[13] At the same time, we have known little of the ways this connectedness was lived out in people's everyday lives.

The pathways of South Asian peddlers and seamen illuminate this arena of everyday affiliation. It is a more intimate realm, beneath headlines and monumental events, one in which people came together across their differences not because they shared large-scale political struggles but because they shared small-scale everyday ones, not because they came in contact with one another in meeting halls and at rallies but because they met in their buildings, in their shops, on the corner, on the train. Even Dada Amir Haider Khan, who did attend political meetings in black churches, and who was transformed by what he saw there, entered into these spaces only after having witnessed, then experienced antiblack racism in his day-to-day work as a maritime laborer, and only after living on the peripheries of a black working-class neighborhood where he shared the ebb and flow of daily life with men and women who had come to Detroit from the Jim Crow South. Other seamen and peddlers kept largely to themselves, associating with those who came from their own region, spoke their language, and practiced their faith, before ultimately returning to the subcontinent. Still others took less explicitly political paths than Dada Khan but became more deeply connected than Khan to U.S. communities of color; they stayed in the United States for the rest of their lives, maintaining regular affiliations with one other, while simultaneously becoming part of African American and Puerto Rican families and neighborhoods. What these and other migrants of color found in black diasporic neighborhoods was what George Lipsitz, drawing on the African American religious scholar Theophus Smith, has called a "world-traversing and world-transcending citizenship," forged by peoples "cut off from ancestral homelands [and] denied full franchise and social membership in the United States." Denied national belonging themselves, South Asian Muslims found the means to make their lives in these places at the United States' racialized margins, bypassing the nation and instead forging connections that were transnational and local. Here, they depended not just on their own tenacity and kinship networks but also on the knowledge, labor, and partnership of other migrants and residents of color.

These dynamics point us to the important place of African American neighborhoods in U.S. immigration history. These were places that were shaped by southern migrants familiar with the worst aspects of racial power in the United States and by immigrants of color from other parts of the world who had experienced life under colonial rule. These neighborhoods were not just patchworks of separate enclaves through which different groups of immigrants passed on their way to the American dream. They were dense, heterogeneous spaces, that were home to multiple groups for whom the American dream was largely deferred or inaccessible, and the stories of South Asian migrants suggest that they fostered different possibilities, gave rise to different registers of community and affiliation, and allowed for different forms of immigrant assimilation and integration.

Alaudin Ullah has returned to his family's apartment, on the fifteenth floor of the Washington Carver Houses. He and his brother Karim sit on either side of their mother as she flips through old photo albums. She shifts in and out of Bengali and broken English, with the borinqueño Spanish appellation *papa* occasionally thrown in. She points out the different friends of her late husband Habib, along with their wives, children, and neighbors, and narrates fragments of stories and memories connected to each photograph. The people in these images are all gone now: individuals have passed away; families have moved from the neighborhood. A few men of Habib's generation moved back to East Bengal after it became the independent nation of Bangladesh. Alaudin and his family remain on their own somewhere between the vanished racially and ethnically mixed community in these fading photographs and the more homogeneous Bangladeshi community that has formed in the New York area since the 1980s.

In the opening years of the twenty-first century, Bangladeshis have become the fastest-growing Asian immigrant group in the United States. In New York City, recent Bangladeshi immigrants have settled in some of the same neighborhoods where deserting seamen lived almost a century ago—on the Lower East Side, and increasingly, again, in parts of Harlem— and many of the men in these areas work the same jobs that their counterparts did in the 1920s, 1930s, and 1940s as dishwashers, line cooks, and other restaurant laborers. They have had to navigate an era of anti-immigrant laws and public sentiment more severe in some ways than what the ex-seamen faced, because it has specifically targeted Muslims. But even among this community, there is little record and little memory of the men who came from their region in the first half of the twentieth century, let alone of the communities these men formed in Harlem, Detroit, and elsewhere, the connections they built with others and with one another, the paths they pursued under the radar of racist immigration laws, the women with whom so many partnered, and the children who were born of these relationships. In the meantime, the varied South Asian communities that exist across the United States continue to represent themselves publicly by trumpeting exactly the kinds of professionals and high-profile achievers that J. J. Singh and Mubarek Ali Khan presented to the U.S. Congress in 1945 as proof of South Asians' worthiness to join the U.S. nation. In this, the histories of working-class immigrants—of both the past and the present—are yet again obscured.

As the more affluent among the South Asian American community move into the mainstream of U.S. politics, business, and popular culture, Alaudin Ullah has in some ways taken on the mantle of his father's friend Ibrahim Choudry. Alaudin is not a community organizer, but an actor and playwright, and after years of interviewing anyone he could find who still remembered Harlem's Bengali community, he has transformed the history of his father's generation into theater. He now performs as Habib Sr. onstage, taking on the persona of his father and transporting his audiences to a moment in Harlem's past of which few are aware. Like Ibrahim Choudry once did in his letter to Congress, Alaudin reminds them of a population of workers who were forced to live with no legal status, who became part of the uptown neighborhood around them even as they remained largely invisible to the world outside, and whose stories have now disappeared. As was the case with Choudry, the mainstream press has periodically taken notice of Alaudin, and Alaudin has used each opportunity to speak up for the dishwashers and line cooks of his father's day, to correct the false impression that South Asians arrived on the United States' landscape only after the 1960s and came with scholarships to prestigious universities or with professional degrees in hand.

In all this, Alaudin Ullah has been guided by a photograph. This one is not in his mother's albums but is clear in his own memory. He saw the photograph as a child, in the early 1970s, he thinks in the apartment of Ibrahim Choudry. The photograph is of Choudry and Malcolm X standing together, amid a group of other African American and South Asian Muslims.[14] Alaudin has been trying for years to locate this image, which may now simply be the fading memory of a snapshot that no longer exists.

As he keeps searching, he is driven by more than just fact that the photograph might link one of his father's close friends to a larger-than-life figure of African American history. For Alaudin, this image stands for a past of which his father was a part—a past of everyday crossings and affiliations that, for this brief moment captured in a photograph, suggested the possibility of larger political solidarities. The image represents an idea that in the give-and-take of daily life, the experience of encountering, living among, and even conflicting with one another might lead different groups toward new understandings of community, shared struggle, and shared purpose. This is another reason the histories of South Asian peddlers and seamen are significant—not for the hidden pasts they reveal but for the possible futures that are connected to those pasts. These are the stakes of loss. It may be important to Alaudin Ullah that he find the lost photograph, but it is just as important for us to picture the future of community, solidarity, and inclusion that the image represents to him, and which was possible, however briefly, in the lives of men and women who are now gone.

Abbreviations

CNO/BH	City of New Orleans, Bureau of Health, *Certificates of Marriage*, Louisiana State Archives, Baton Rouge.
DCNY/PNY	District of the City of New York, Port of New York, *List of Passengers*, 1880–1896.[i]
CNY	City of New York, *Certificates and Record of Marriage*, 1899–1937, and *New York City Directory*, 1910–1933, New York City Municipal Archives, New York, NY.
UK/FOC	United Kingdom, *Foreign Office Correspondence*, 1900–1946, British National Archives, Kew Gardens, UK.
UK/IOR	United Kingdom, *India Office Records*, British National Library, London, UK.
UKBT/PL	United Kingdom, Board of Trade, *Passenger Lists, 1880–1920*.[ii]
USDC/BC	U.S. Department of Commerce, Bureau of the Census, *Population Schedules*, 1880–1930.[ii]
USDCL/BIN	U.S. Department of Commerce and Labor, Bureau of Immigration and Naturalization, *Petitions for Naturalization* and *Records of Naturalization*, 1908–1917.[ii]
USDCL/LMAP	U.S. Department of Commerce and Labor, *List or Manifest of Alien Passengers for the Immigration Officer at Port of Arrival*, 1907–1917.[i]
USDL/IS/LMAC	U.S. Department of Labor, *List or Manifest of Aliens Employed on the Vessel as Members of Crew*, 1917–1946.[i]
USDS/BC	U.S. Department of State, Bureau of Citizenship, *Passport Applications*, 1900–1924.[ii]

USDT/LMAP   U.S. Department of the Treasury, *List or Manifest of Alien Passengers for the Immigration Officer at Port of Arrival*, 1897–1906.[i]

USDC/SDNY   U.S. District Court of Southern District, New York, *Petitions for Naturalization*, 1910–1950, U.S. National Archives, Northeast Region, New York, NY.

USSS/DRC WWI   U.S. Selective Service System, *World War I Draft Registration Cards*.[ii]

[i] Accessed online via Ancestry Library Edition and EllisIsland.org.
[ii] Accessed online via Ancestry Library Edition.

Notes

INTRODUCTION: LOST IN MIGRATION

1. U.S. Congress, House Committee on Immigration and Naturalization (hereafter USC/HCIN), *To Grant a Quota to Eastern Hemisphere Indians and to Make Them Racially Eligible for Naturalization,* 79th Cong., 1st Sess., March 7–14, 1945.

2. Joan M. Jensen, *Passage from India: Asian Indian Immigrants in North America* (New Haven, CT: Yale University Press, 1988), 277; Montague A. Machell, *Muslim Valley Forge: An Introduction to Mubarek Ali Khan* (1949).

3. Harold A. Gould, *Sikhs, Swamis, Students, and Spies: The India Lobby in the United States, 1900–1946* (New Delhi: Sage Publications, 2006), 310–11; Jensen, *Passage from India,* 277.

4. Jensen, *Passage from India,* 42–56, 101–20; Mai Ngai, *Impossible Subjects: Illegal Aliens and the Making of Modern America* (Princeton, NJ: Princeton University Press, 2003), 40–41.

5. U.S. Congress, *Immigration Act of February 5, 1917,* 39 Stat. 874 (1917); U.S. Congress, *Immigration Act of May 26, 1924,* 43 Stat. 153 (1924); *United States v. Bhagat Singh Thind,* 261 U.S. 204 (1923); Jensen, *Passage from India,* 256–59, 265–67.

6. Machell, *Muslim Valley Forge,* 13, 24, 26; Gould, *Sikhs, Swamis, Students, and Spies,* 310–11; Jensen, *Passage from India,* 277; *New York Amsterdam News,* February 17, 1951, 18.

7. USC/HCIN, *To Grant a Quota;* see also U.S. Congress, Senate Committee on Immigration, *To Permit the Naturalization of Approximately Three Thousand Natives of India,* 78th Cong., 2nd Sess., 1944.

8. USC/HCIN, *To Grant a Quota.* See especially 70, 80–103, 142–51.

233

9. Ibid., 88.

10. Ibid., 76–77.

11. Vijay Prashad, *The Karma of Brown Folk* (Minneapolis: University of Minnesota Press, 2000), 4, 74–75.

12. L. P. Mathur, *Indian Revolutionary Movement in the United States of America* (Delhi: S. Chand, 1970); Sucheta Mazumdar, "Colonial Impact and Punjabi Emigration to the United States" and "Punjabi Agricultural Workers in California, 1905–1945," in *Labor Immigration under Capitalism: Asian Immigrant Workers in the United States before World War II*, ed. Lucie Cheng and Edna Bonacich, 316–36, 549–78 (Berkeley: University of California Press, 1984); Karen Isaksen Leonard, *Making Ethnic Choices: California's Punjabi Mexican Americans* (Philadelphia: Temple University Press, 1992); Prashad, *Karma of Brown Folk*; Gould, *Sikhs, Swamis, Students, and Spies*; Seema Sohi, "Echoes of Mutiny: Race, Empire, and Indian Revolutionaries on the Pacific Coast" (PhD diss., University of Washington, 2007); Maia Ramnath, Haj to Utopia: How the Ghadar Movement Charted Global Radicalism and Attempted to Overthrow the British Empire (Berkeley: University of California Press, 2011); Nayan Shah, *Stranger Intimacy: Contesting Race, Sexuality, and the Law in the North American West* (Berkeley: University of California Press, 2011).

13. On the larger history of South Asian labor on, and desertion from, British steamships, see Ravi Ahuja, "Mobility and Containment: The Voyages of South Asian Seamen, c. 1900–1960," *International Review of Social History* 51, no. S14 (2006): 111 41, Ahuja, "Networks of Subordination and Networks of the Subordinated: The Case of South Asian Maritime Labour under British Imperialism, c. 1890–1947," in *The Limits of British Colonial Control in South Asia: Spaces of Disorder in the Indian Ocean Region*, ed. Ashwini Tambe and Harald Fischer-Tiné (London: Routledge, 2009), 13–48; Gopalan Balachandran, "Conflicts in the International Labour Market: British and Indian Seamen, Employers, and the State, 1890–1939," *Indian Economic and Social History Review* 39, no. 1 (2002): 71–100; Balachandran, "South Asian Seafarers and Their Worlds: c. 1870–1930s," in *Seascapes: Maritime Histories, Littoral Cultures, and Transoceanic Exchanges*, ed. Jerry H. Bentley, Renate Bridenthal, and Kären Wigen (Honolulu: University of Hawaii Press, 2007), 186–204, Laura Tabili, *"We Ask for British Justice": Workers and Racial Difference in Late Imperial Britain* (Ithaca, NY: Cornell University Press, 1994); Rozina Visram, *Asians in Britain: 400 Years of History* (London: Pluto, 2002).

14. On gendered structures of early twentieth-century sojourning labor, see Sucheta Mazumdar, "What Happened to the Women?" in *Asian Pacific Islander American Women: A Historical Anthology*, ed. Shirley Hune and Gail Nomura (New York: New York University Press, 2003, 58–65; Donna Gabaccia, Italy's Many Diasporas (Seattle: University of Washington Press, 2000), 74–75, 83; Jennifer Guglielmo, Living the Revolution: Italian Women's Resistance and Radicalism in New York City, 1880–1945 (Chapel Hill: University of North Carolina Press, 2010), 13–16, 44–45, 67–72; Madeline Y. Hsu, Dreaming of Gold, Dreaming of Home: Transnationalism and Migration Between the United States and South China, 1882–1943 (Stanford:

Stanford University Press, 2000), 55–89; Erika Lee, At America's Gates: Chinese Immigration During the Exclusion Era, (Chapel Hill: University of North Carolina Press, 2005), 116–23.

15. Emma Lazarus, "The New Colossus," 1883; Mazumdar, "What Happened to the Women?" 59; Dirk Hoerder, *Cultures In Contact: World Migrations in the Second Millennium* (Durham: Duke University Press, 2002), 331–442.

16. Donna Gabaccia notes that different immigration scholars have identified different origins of the phrase "nation of immigrants." Its popular use as a description of the United States' national character—and a rhetorical marker of American Exceptionalism—dates to the mid-20th century; President Harry Truman deployed the phrase and the concept in debates over the McCarran-Walter Act in 1952, and the Anti-Defamation League published the book "*A Nation of Immigrants*," by then-Senator John F. Kennedy in 1959 (re-published posthumously by his brother Robert Kennedy in 1964). Donna R. Gabaccia, "Nations of Immigrants: Do Words Matter?" *The Pluralist*, Vol. 5, No. 3 (Fall 2010), 5–31; "Today's Immigration Policy Debates: Do We Need a Little History?" *Migration Information Source*, November 2006, http://www.migrationinformation.org/usfocus /display.cfm?ID=488, accessed 01/25/2012. Adam McKeown, argues that the United States' rhetoric of openness and its history of restriction, exclusion, and border controls are not in fact contradictory, but part of the "mutually constitutive processes of homogenization and differentiation" by which sovereign nation states formed themselves into a modern global system at the end of the nineteenth century. See Adam McKeown, *Melancholy Order: Asian Immigration and the Globalization of Borders* (New York: Columbia University Press, 2008), 5–7.

17. John Ali, Jr., Interview with the author, May, 2011; USDC/BC, U.S. Census, 1930, Population Schedules. Detroit City, MI: records for 566, 570, & 582 Lafayette Street E., 574 & 584 Fort Street E., and 569 Congress Street E.; The New York Age, March 9, 1932, cited in Irma Watkins-Owens, Blood Relations: Caribbean Immigrants and the Harlem Community, 1900–1930 (Bloomington: Indiana University Press, 1996), 200–01n31.

1. OUT OF THE EAST AND INTO THE SOUTH

1. USDT/LMAP, SS *St. Louis*, June 19, 1897; Vincent J. Cannato, *American Passage: The History of Ellis Island* (New York: HarperCollins, 2009), 50–51; John T. Cunningham, *Ellis Island: Immigration's Shining Center* (Charleston, SC: Tempus Publishing, 2003), 58–59, 62–63; "American Line's New Pier—To Be the Most Commodious on the North River," *New York Times*, February 26, 1893; "Fire on Ellis Island—It Broke Out Shortly after Midnight in the Furnace of the Main Building," *New York Times*, June 15, 1897; "Caring for Immigrants—New Arrangements in Consequence of Yesterday Morning's Fire on Ellis Island—Inspections on the Piers," *New York Times*, June 16, 1897; "Immigrants on the Piers—Ellis Island Clerks Hold the Examinations in Temporary Quarters Provided by Steamship

Lines," *New York Times*, June 17, 1897; "Fire on Ellis Island—Many Buildings Burned," *New York Tribune*, June 15, 1897; "The Ellis Island Blaze—Wonder Expressed That There Was No Loss of Life," *New York Tribune*, June 16, 1897; "The Weather," *New York Tribune*, June 19, 1897, 5; "Aftermath of the Big Fire—Ellis Island Is Now Simply a Desolate Ruin," *San Francisco Call*, June 16, 1897.

2. Lewis O'Malley and Monmohan Chakravarti, *Bengal District Gazetteers: Hooghly* (Calcutta: Bengal Secretariat Book Depot, 1912), 187; Siten Chakraborti and Radha Krishna Bari, *Handicrafts of West Bengal* (Calcutta: Institute of Art and Handicraft, 1991), 60; USDT/LMAP, SS *St. Louis*, June 19, 1897.

3. Cannato, *American Passage*, 50–51; Cunningham, *Ellis Island*, 58–59.

4. Cannato, *American Passage*, 87–90, 158; Cunningham, *Ellis Island*, 85, 121–22.

5. USDT/LMAP, SS *St. Louis*, June 19, 1897; Cunningham, *Ellis Island*, 62–63; "Settling the Immigrants—Arranging Accommodations at Barge Office," *New York Times*, June 18, 1897; "Five Thousand More Immigrants," *New York Times*, June 20, 1897; "Again at Ellis Island—New Immigrant Station to Be Opened Today," *New York Tribune*, December 17, 1900, as quoted in Cunningham, *Ellis Island*, 63; "Hindoo Peddlers Not Admitted," *New York Times*, June 27, 1897; UKBT/PL, SS *Paris*, July 8, 1897.

6. Adam McKeown, *Melancholy Order: Asian Immigration and the Globalization of Borders* (New York: Columbia University Press, 2008), 8, 114–16.

7. UKBT/PL, SS *Garth Castle*, July 31, 1897; O'Malley and Chakravarti, *Bengal District Gazetteers*, 187.

8. R. C. Dutt, *The Economic History of India* (London: K. Paul, Trench, Trübner, 1902); Sudipta Sen, *Empire of Free Trade: The East India Company and the Making of the Colonial Marketplace* (Philadelphia: University of Pennsylvania Press, 1998), 2–7, 120–43.

9. Claude Markovits, *The Global World of Indian Merchants, 1750–1947* (Cambridge: Cambridge University Press, 2000), 122–30.

10. In this, they resembled other groups of Indian and Chinese sojourning laborers of the era—a point that is explored in Chapter 2. Sucheta Mazumdar, "What Happened to the Women?" in *Asian Pacific Islander American Women: A Historical Anthology*, ed. Shirley Hune and Gail Nomura (New York: New York University Press, 2003), 58–74.

11. "A Teacher of the Vedanta," *The Critic: A Weekly Review of Literature and the Arts*, March 19, 1898, 200; "On Sin and Sinners—Swami Abhedananda of India Discusses the Subject at Mott Memorial Hall," *New York Times*, March 21, 1898, 10; "A Fascinating Hindoo—He Will Return to New York to Teach Philosophy—A Social Fad," *Kansas City Journal*, July 17, 1898, 14; Robert Love, *The Great Oom: The Improbable Birth of Yoga in America* (New York: Viking, 2010); "What Is Doing in Society," *New York Times*, October 29, 1898, 7; "What Is Doing in Society," *New York Times*, March 15, 1899, 7; "Bringing Temple Dances from the Orient to Broadway," *New York Times*, March 25, 1906, X2; Priya Srinivasan, "The Nautch Women Dancers of the 1880s. Corporeality, U.S. Orientalism, and Anti-Immigration Laws," *Women and Performance* 19, no. 1 (March 2009); Srinivasan, "The Bodies

beneath the Smoke or What's Behind the Cigarette Poster: Unearthing Kinesthetic Connections in American Dance History," *Discourses in Dance* 4, no. 1 (2007): 7–48; Carl T. Jackson, "The New Thought Movement and the Nineteenth Century Discovery of Oriental Philosophy," *Journal of Popular Culture* 9, no. 3 (1975): 523–48.

12. Robert Forbes and Terence R. Mitchell, *American Tobacco Cards* (Iola, WI: Antique Trader Books, 2000); Lynn Abbott and Doug Seroff, *Out of Sight: The Rise of African American Popular Music, 1889–1895* (Jackson: University Press of Mississippi, 2002), 154; "Sam T. Jack's Theater" (advertisement), *New York Times*, February 8, 1898, 12; "My Hindoo Man," words by Harry H. Williams, music by Egbert Vanalstyne (New York: Shapiro, Remick, 1905); "Down in Bom-Bombay," words by Ballard Macdonald, music by Harry Carroll (New York: Shapiro, Bernstein, 1915); "A New Coney Island Rises from the Ashes of the Old," *New York Times*, May 8, 1904, SM5; "Greater Luna Park," *New York Tribune*, May 8, 1904, A14; "Wild West at Garden—Two Bills, Pawnee and Buffalo, at Every Performance," *New York Tribune*, May 2, 1909, B2; "Wild West and Far East—Many Interesting Features Will Be Seen with Buffalo Bill and Pawnee Bill Exhibitions," *Jasper (MO) News*, September 12, 1909, 4; "Eight Hundred to Disband Here—Wild West Show to Close for Winter after Performance Tonight," *Times Dispatch* (Richmond, VA), November 6, 1909, 6; "Musical—Elephants a Feature with the Wild West Show," *Democratic Banner* (Mt. Vernon, OH), June 21, 1910, 2; "Buffalo Bill's Wild West and Congress of Rough Riders of the World—Pawnee Bill's Great Far East—An Oriental Spectacle" (advertisement), *Bisbee (AZ) Daily Review*, October 25, 1910, 3; Glen Shirley, *Pawnee Bill: A Biography of Major Gordon W. Lillie* (Lincoln: University of Nebraska Press, 1958), 164.

13. Edward Said, *Orientalism* (New York: Vintage, 1979), 31–42.

14. William R. Leach, *Land of Desire: Merchants, Power, and the Rise of a New American Culture* (New York: Vintage, 1994); Jennifer Scanlon, *Inarticulate Longings: The Ladies' Home Journal, Gender and the Promise of Consumer Culture* (New York: Routledge, 1995); *The Girl on the Magazine Cover: The Origins of Visual Stereotypes in American Mass Media* (Durham: University of North Carolina Press, 2000).

15. Kristin Hoganson, "Cosmopolitan Domesticity: Importing the American Dream, 1865–1920," *American Historical Review* (February 2002), par. 29, accessed August 25, 2008, http://www.historycooperative.org/journals/ahr/107.1/aho102000055.html.

16. Ibid., par. 5.

17. Ibid., pars. 5–9; Gina Marchetti, *Romance and the "Yellow Peril": Race, Sex, and Discursive Strategies in Hollywood Fiction* (Berkeley: University of California Press, 1993), 28–32.

18. Hoganson, "Cosmopolitan Domesticity," pars. 9–16.

19. Ibid., par. 7.

20. Alison Adburgham, *Liberty's: A Biography of a Shop* (London: George Allen and Unwin, 1975); Stephan Tschudi-Madsen, *The Art Nouveau Style* (Mineola, NY: Dover Publications, 2002), 188–206.

21. See, for example, "Cowperthwait's 'Reliable' Carpets—Special Sale" (advertisement), *New York Times*, December 7, 1898, 12; "W. & J. Sloane—Special Christmas Offering" (advertisement), *New York Times*, December 12, 1898, 4; "Ehrich Bros—Phenomenal Bargains" (advertisement), *New York Times*, December 4, 1898, 15.

22. "Cowperthwait's 'Reliable' Carpets—Special Sale"; "W. & J. Sloane—Special Christmas Offering"; "Ehrich Bros—Phenomenal Bargains"; "Vantine's Oriental Furnishings and Decorations" (advertisement), *New York Times*, February 13, 1898, 12; F. James Gibson, "Oriental Rugs," *New York Times Illustrated Magazine*, February 20, 1898, 12; *Vantine's: The Oriental Store*, retail catalog, (New York: A. A. Vantine, 1914).

23. Hoganson, "Cosmopolitan Domesticity," par. 22; the existence of Oriental gift shops on the boardwalks of New Jersey—Hamar's, Nabass & Kazaar, Shimamura & Co., Ching Hop Hing—is recorded in news reports on a series of turn-of-the-century fires in that area: "Spring Lake Fire—Northwest Wind Carries Flames from Building to Building," *New York Times*, September 20, 1900, 7; "Portion of Atlantic City Beach Swept by Fire Yesterday," *Chicago Tribune*, April 4, 1902, 3.

24. There is some disagreement in the record about the gendered division of labor in village- and workshop-based embroidery production in turn-of-the-century Hooghly. The *Bengal District Gazetteer*—the compendium of regional information compiled and used by British colonial administrators—stated in 1912 that "predominantly Mussalman [Muslim] ladies" did the work of embroidering *chikan* goods in silk and cotton. The article that appeared in the *Hindusthanee Student* in 1917 corroborates this, stating that the *chikan* embroidery "is generally carried on by the women folks [*sic*] in their homes," while a statement by the U.S. consul general in Calcutta, included in the 1908 report by the U.S. Department of Commerce and Labor, claimed that in Hooghly, "most of the embroidering on silk is done by men," while both women and men embroidered on cotton. Ships' records also list some of the men making their way to the United States to peddle *chikan* goods as "embroiderers," suggesting that at least to some degree both men and women were involved. O'Malley and Chakravarti, *Bengal District Gazetteers*, 187; N. C. Das, "Our Countrymen in the South," *Hindusthanee Student* 6, no. 1 (October 1917): 3; W. A. Graham Clark, Special Agent of the Department of Commerce and Labor, *Swiss Embroidery and Lace Industry* (Washington, DC: Government Printing Office, 1908), 42–43; U.S. Department of Commerce and Labor, *List or Manifest of Alien Passengers*, SS *Adriatic*, July 25, 1896; Royal Mail Steam Packet Company, *Passenger List*, SS *Oroya* (Colombo to London), January 12, 1908. A more recent account of Bengali *chikan* production states that women are the primary producers: Chakraborti and Bari, *Handicrafts of West Bengal*, 60.

25. Das, "Our Countrymen," 3. In stating, almost in shorthand, that the Hooghly peddlers had operated regionally, "until about a century ago before the decline set in," Das appears to have been referencing the work of R. C. Dutt, the nationalist economist who had just fifteen years earlier produced the first comprehensive analysis of the destructive impact of British rule on India's indigenous economy. Dutt's *Economic History of India* and its ideas about the evisceration of the Indian textile in-

dustry no doubt would have been well-known among the nationalist students who were the primary audience for *The Hindusthanee Student*. R. C. Dutt, *The Economic History of India* (London: K. Paul, Trench, Trübner, 1902).

26. There is disagreement over the exact extent to which the British were able to exert control over India's "inland trade"—the networks, markets, and mechanisms of exchange by which goods were bought and sold and moved from one location to another across Bengal and northern India during this period. Most recently, Sudipta Sen has argued that C. A. Bayly's emphasis on "the resilience of the indigenous commercial society" obscures the force and determination with which the East India Company sought control over the markets of the inland trade and underplays the disruptions caused by the Company's policing and regulation of sites of commerce, standardization of money, and imposition of concepts of capitalist political economy and "free trade." Sudipta Sen, *Empire of Free Trade: The East India Company and the Making of the Colonial Marketplace* (Philadelphia: University of Pennsylvania Press, 1998); C. A. Bayly, *Rulers, Townsmen, and Bazaars: North Indian Society in the Age of British Expansion, 1770–1870* (Cambridge: Cambridge University Press, 1983); Rajat Kanta Ray, "Asian Capital in the Age of European Domination: The Rise of the Bazaar, 1800–1914," *Modern Asian Studies* 29, no. 3 (1995): 449–554; Ray, "The Bazaar: Changing Structural Characteristics of the Indigenous Section of the Indian Economy before and after the Great Depression," *Indian Economic and Social History Review* 25 (1988): 263–318; see also Anand A. Yang, *Bazaar India: Markets, Society, and the Colonial State in Bihar* (Berkeley: University of California Press, 1998).

27. Das, "Our Countrymen," 5–6.

28. Markovits, *Global World of Indian Merchants*, 110–17, 119.

29. Charles E. Funnell, *By the Beautiful Sea* (New Brunswick, NJ: Rutgers University Press, 1983), 24.

30. Ibid., 32.

31. USDC/BC, *U.S. Census, 1900: Population Schedule* for Atlantic City, NJ, P1/W3/SD169/ED12/Sh16, P1/W3/SD6/ED10/Sh11, W1/SD169/ED4/Sh14–16; "Spring Lake Fire," *New York Times*, 7; "Portion of Atlantic City," *Chicago Tribune*, 3.

32. DCNY/PNY, *Lists of Passengers* for SS *Edam*, September 23, 1884; SS *California*, January 5, 1885; SS *Amerique*, April 2, 1885; SS *Waesland*, February 11, 1888.

33. For Waheed Bux, see USDCL/LMAP, SS *Albania* (San Cristobal, Panama, to New York), July 2, 1907; SS *Magdalena* (Colón, Panama, to New York), June 11, 1908; UKBT/PL, SS *Philadelphia* (New York to Southampton), October 3, 1908, SS *Mombassa* (London to Calcutta), October 10, 1908; USDCL/LMAP, SS *Majestic* (Southampton to New York), June 24, 1909; USDC/BC, *U.S. Census, 1910: Population Schedule* for Atlantic City, NJ, P3/W3/SD2/ED15/Sh15A; USDCL/LMAP, SS *Arabic* (Liverpool to Boston), June 27, 1912, listed as resident at one of the Hooghly network's key addresses in Calcutta, 13 Kerr Lane. For Mohammad Hossain, see DCNY/PNY, SS *Egyptian Monarch*, May 29, 1889; UKBT/PL, SS *Orinoco* (Colón, Panama, to Southampton), April 26, 1890; British India Steam Navigation Company, *Passenger List* for SS *Goorkha*, May 31, 1896; DCNY/PNY, SS *St. Paul*, June

6, 1896; UKBT/PL, SS *Campania* (New York to Liverpool), September 17, 1898; SS *Arabic* (Liverpool to Boston), June 27, 1912, named on the manifest as the father of another traveling merchant, Mohammad Khalik, and listed as resident at 13 Kerr Lane, Calcutta.

34. "Recent Events," *Brooklyn Eagle*, May 30, 1889, 4.

35. "Hindoos in America," *Chicago Daily Tribune*, July 19, 1891, 6.

36. Das, "Our Countrymen," 3.

37. DCNY/PNY, *Lists of Passengers* for SS *Armenia*, June 9, 1894; SS *Paris*, June 15, 1895; SS *St. Paul*, June 6, 1896; SS *St. Paul*, July 11, 1896.

38. Das, "Our Countrymen," 5–6.

39. Tom Murray, *Southern Railway* (St. Paul, MN: Voyageur Press, 2007), 39.

40. Eric Arnesen, *Waterfront Workers of New Orleans: Race, Class, and Politics, 1863–1923* (New York: Oxford University Press, 1991).

41. Kevin Fox Gotham, *Authentic New Orleans: Tourism, Culture, and Race in the Big Easy* (New York: New York University Press, 2007), 70–74; Alecia P. Long, *The Great Southern Babylon: Sex, Race, and Respectability in New Orleans* (Baton Rouge: Louisiana State University Press, 2004), 1.

42. Gotham, *Authentic New Orleans*, 70–72; Jasmine Mir, *Marketplace of Desire: Storyville and the Making of a Tourist City in New Orleans, 1890–1920* (PhD diss., New York University, 2005), 27.

43. "An Eighteenth Century Market in a Twentieth Century City—Progressive New Orleans Cherishes Its Old French Market," *Montgomery Advertiser*, December 27, 1903, 9.

44. Long, *The Great Southern Babylon*, 1–3, 165–69; Gotham, *Authentic New Orleans*, 35–44, 66, 70–77; Mir, *Marketplace of Desire*, 21–23, 27–28; Catherine Clinton, "Scepter and Masque: Debutante Rituals in Mardi Gras New Orleans" in *Manners and Southern History*, ed. Ted Ownby (Jackson: University Press of Mississippi, 2007), 81.

45. Henry Rightor, *Standard History of New Orleans, Louisiana* (Chicago: Lewis Publishing Company, 1900), 639–45; Reid Mitchell, *All on a Mardi Gras Day: Episodes in the History of New Orleans Carnival* (Cambridge, MA: Harvard University Press, 1995), 109; "Carnival at End—Krewe of Comus Give Their Parade in New Orleans," *Montgomery Advertiser*, February 2, 1903, 1; "Parade Knights of Momus Ushe[r] in the Mardi Gras," *Macon Weekly Telegraph*, February 23, 1906, 2; "New Orleans Greets Rex—Carnival Crowd Not So Large as in Previous Years," *Montgomery Advertiser*, March 3, 1908, 1; "Fire in New Orleans," *Macon Weekly Telegraph*, June 11, 1885, 1; Kristin L. Hoganson, *Consumers' Imperium: The Global Production of American Domesticity, 1865–1920* (Durham: University of North Carolina Press, 2007), 23, 288n52; Al Rose, *Storyville, New Orleans: Being an Authentic, Illustrated Account of the Notorious Red Light District* (Tuscaloosa: University of Alabama Press, 1974), 69, 77–80, 89, 146.

46. Virginia Meacham Gould, "'If I Can't Have My Rights, I Can Have My Pleasures, And If They Won't Give Me My Wages, I Can Take Them'. Gender and Slave Labor in Antebellum New Orleans" in *Discovering the Women in Slavery: Emancipating Perspectives on the American Past*, ed. Patricia Morton (Athens: University of Geor-

gia Press, 1996), 188–90; Juliet E. K. Walker, *The History of Black Business in America: Capitalism, Race, Entrepreneurship*, 2nd ed., vol. 1 (Chapel Hill: University of North Carolina Press, 2009), 90; Delia LaBarre, ed., *The New Orleans of Lafcadio Hearn: Illustrated Sketches from the Daily City Item* (Baton Rouge: Louisiana State University Press, 2007), 153.

47. Richard Campanella, "An Ethnic Geography of New Orleans," *Journal of American History* 94 (December 2007): 704–15.

48. "An Eighteenth Century Market," 9.

49. USDC/BC, *U.S. Census, 1900: Population Schedule* for New Orleans, LA, P3/W4/ SD1/ED36/Sh6–7; DCNY/PNY, *Passenger Lists* for SS *Egyptian Monarch*, May 29, 1889; SS *Paris*, June 15, 1895; SS *St. Paul*, June 6, 1896; SS *Adriatic*, July 15, 1896; British India Steam Navigation Company, *Passenger List* for SS *Goorkha*, May 31, 1896; UKBT/PL, SS *Campania*, September 17, 1898; Long, *Great Southern Babylon*, 116–17; "Not Very Dignified—Amusing Story of an Oriental Who Took a Bicycle Ride," *Biloxi Daily Herald*, May 5, 1900, 6.

50. "Not Very Dignified," 6.

51. The peddlers, the report continues, "may be seen at Atlantic City and other places squatted on the floor with their chikan work and some Indian jewelry, spread out in the most attractive manner." Clark, *Swiss Embroidery and Lace Industry*, 42–43.

52. USDCL/LMAP, SS *Adriatic*, January 25, 1908; SS *Celtic*, May 31, 1908; SS *New York*, October 4, 1908; SS *New York*, July 11, 1909; SS *Arabic*, July 20, 1909; *SS Celtic*, June 5, 1911; *SS Arabic*, July 11, 1911; SS *New York*, June 17, 1912; SS *Oceanic*, July 2, 1914; SS *St. Paul*, July 5, 1914. See also, for example, U.S. Selective Service System, Local Registration Board, New Orleans, LA, Registration Cards for Abdul Jobber Mondul, Abdul Jalil Mallick, Abdul Khollick Mondul, Abdul Sarkar, Abdul Waheed, Elias Mondul, and Fozlay Rohman (names reproduced here as they are transliterated in the draft registration records).

53. USDCL/LMAP, various, 1904–1917. The locations of these villages are as follows: Babnan, 22°54'31"N, 88°12'52"E; Sinhet, 22°53'50"N, 88°14'42"E; Alipur, 22°55'5"N, 88°10'30"E; Chandanpur, 22°52'44"N, 88°10'28"E; Mandra, 22°55'2"N, 88°7'8"E; Bandipur, 22°51'4"N, 88°9'21"E; Bora, 22°45'49"N, 88°15'41"E; Dadpur: 22°56'19"N, 88°11'47"E; Gopinathpur, 22°49'14"N, 88°03'00"E. Wikimapia.org, accessed December 16, 2010. In his 2002 *India Unbound*, Gurcharan Das describes meeting Golam Mondol, a young man from Babnan Village in Hooghly who had come to Calcutta to sell *chikan* work wholesale to a buyer at one of the city's large department stores. Describing his operation at the turn of the twenty-first century, Mondol stated, "The women do the embroidery and the men go out and sell the work. I concentrate on the south [of West Bengal] and my order book is bursting this year." Gurcharan Das, *India Unbound: The Social and Economic Revolution from Independence to the Global Information Age* (New York: Anchor Books, 2002).

54. This is the area surrounding the present-day Collin Street Mosque, due east of Park Street Station, and continues to be a Muslim-majority part of the city.

55. The relationships between newer and older members of the network, and between Hooghly villages and Collinga Bazar, are apparent in the home addresses that peddlers listed on ships' manifests on their way into New York. These groups of

co-travelers typically included one or two senior traders who listed home addresses in Collinga Bazar, Calcutta, and several other novice peddlers listing home addresses in Hooghly villages. See USDCL/LMAP, SS *Celtic*, May 31, 1908; SS *New York*, October 4, 1908; SS *Majestic*, June 24, 1909; SS *New York*, July 11, 1909; SS *Arabic*, July 20, 1909; SS *Adriatic*, June 24, 1910; SS *Celtic*, June 5, 1911; SS *Baltic*, November 20, 1911; SS *New York*, June 17, 1912; SS *Oceanic*, July 17, 1912; SS *Olympic*, July 2, 1913; SS *Oceanic*, July 2, 1914; SS *St. Paul*, July 5, 1914.

56. P. Thankappan Nair, *A History of Calcutta's Streets* (Calcutta: Firma KLM, 1987), 267.

57. Rudyard Kipling, "On the Banks of the Hugli," in *Wee Willie Winkie, City of Dreadful Night, and American Notes* (New York: H.M. Caldwell, 1899), 43–44.

58. Historian John Kuo Wei Tchen describes this milieu of port-city "intermingling" in his work on nineteenth-century Chinese settlement in New York City and has begun to expand upon the concept of hybrid "port cultures" in more recent work. John Kuo Wei Tchen, *New York Before Chinatown: Orientalism and the Shaping of American Culture, 1776–1882* (Baltimore: The Johns Hopkins University Press, 2001), xix–x; "Conceptualizing Port Cultures" (paper presented at the annual meeting of the Association For Asian American Studies, Austin, Texas, April 7–10, 2010).

59. British India Steam Navigation Company, *Passenger List* for SS *Goorkha*, May 31, 1896.

60. "Many of these ships carried only a few passengers, and some carried native passengers on deck. Fares, c1892, were £47 10s. to £52 10s. depending on accommodation." Ship's List Web site, accessed October 22, 2010, http://www.theshiplist.com/ships/lines/bisn.html; P&O Heritage Web site, accessed May 15, 2012, http://www.poheritage.com/our-history/company-guides/british-india-steam-navigation-company.

61. British India Steam Navigation Company, *Passenger List* for SS *Goorkha*, May 31, 1896. Contemporary accounts of Indian seamen who traveled this route are replete with stories of workers "going crazy" from the heat in the engine room, running above deck into the scorching sun, and ultimately jumping overboard in a desperate attempt to cool themselves. Dada Amir Haider Khan, *Chains to Lose: Life and Struggles of a Revolutionary* (New Delhi: Patriot Publishers, 1989), 90; "Crazed by Heat, Sailor Runs Amok," *New York Times*, August 15, 1926, E16.

62. DCNY/PNY, *List of Passengers* for SS *St. Paul*, June 6, 1896; "Shipping companies jammed as many as 2000 metal-frame berths into low-ceilinged compartments, which were usually divided into separate dormitories for single men, single women, and families. The air in these compartments was often rank with the heavy odor of seasickness. There was little privacy and immigrants found it difficult to keep themselves clean." Ellis Island National Monument Museum, Permanent Exhibit, photos and text on "Steerage," viewed October 9, 2010.

63. From about 1906 onward, they first traveled down the eastern Indian coast, most likely in local tramp ships, to Colombo, in order to pick up one of the steamers that the Orient Royal Mail Line ran between Australia and London via Ceylon. It is possible that larger groups of Hooghly's peddlers traveled together from Calcutta to Colombo, and then split up, with some taking the Orient Line westward through

the Suez and Mediterranean to London and the others taking the Orient's ships east and southward to Perth, Melbourne, and Sydney. Das, *Our Countrymen*, 3; O'Malley and Chakravarti, *Bengal District Gazetteers*, 187.

64. USDC/BC, *U.S. Census, 1910: Population Schedule* for New Orleans, LA, P2/W4/ SD1/ED59/Sh7A, P3/W4/SD1/ED60/Sh8A and Sh12A, P4/W4/SD1/ED62/Sh2B, P4/W5/SD1/ED74/Sh9A, P5/W5/SD1/ED77/Sh2B; DCNY/PNY, SS *Waesland*, February 11, 1888; USDT/LMAP, SS *St. Louis*, June 19, 1897.

65. "Railroad News," *Fort Worth Register*, June 6, 1897, 1; "East Indian Peddler Fined for No License," *Atlanta Constitution*, November 21, 1912, 4. While "Mohammed and Hamid Hassain" could have been the names of Syrian or Turkish peddlers, the absence in the archives of any other peddlers with these or similar names operating in this time and region besides the Mohammad Hossain, Shaikh Hossain, and Abdul Hamid who were active members of the Hooghly network strongly suggests that this is a reference to two of its members. USDC/BC, *U.S. Census, 1900, 1910: Population Schedules* for New Orleans, Louisiana and Dallas and Fort Worth, Texas; USDT/LMAP (various, 1895–1900).

66. USDC/BC, *U.S. Census, 1900, 1910: Population Schedules* for Asbury Park, Atlantic City, and Long Branch, New Jersey, and New Orleans, Louisiana (various); USSS/ DRC WWI, Local Registration Boards of New Orleans, LA; Charleston, SC; Memphis, TN; Chattanooga, TN; Galveston, TX; Dallas, TX; Birmingham, AL; Atlanta, GA; and Jacksonville, FL.

67. Clark, *Swiss Embroidery and Lace Industry*, 42–43.

68. All men between the ages of eighteen and thirty-five were required to register for the draft, regardless of nationality and immigration status. Immigrants who did not register were subject to deportation or conscription, so members of the Bengali network appear to have come out in significant numbers to register wherever they were working or residing.

69. "Tours to the Tropics—Hamburg American Line" (advertisement), *The Travel Magazine*, November 1907, 58; "A Calendar of Travel" and "The Royal Mail Steam Packet Co.—In Jamaica It's Summertime" (advertisement), *The Travel Magazine*, January 1908, 157–58, 161; "A Calendar of Travel," *The Travel Magazine*, February 1908, 230–32; S. L. Beckwith, "Havana: A City of Strange Peddlers," *Atlanta Constitution*, August 25, 1901, A9; May L. Baker, "School Teaching in Panama," *The Independent*, December 23, 1909, 1445–49.

70. United Kingdom, Board of Trade, *Passenger Lists for Ships Leaving UK 1890–1960*: SS *Tagus*, June 7, 1905; SS *Atrato*, December 19, 1906; SS *Orinoco*, May 8, 1907; SS *Orinoco*, July 8, 1907; SS *Trent*, January 22, 1908; SS *Atrato*, April 1, 1908; SS *Tagus*, February 17, 1909; SS *Magdalena*, May 26, 1909, accessed February 16–17, 2008, http://www.findmypast.com; Julie Greene, *The Canal Builders: Making America's Empire at the Panama Canal* (New York: Penguin, 2010), 21.

71. Greene, *The Canal Builders*, 51–52, 160–61; Winston James, *Holding Aloft the Banner of Ethiopia: Caribbean Radicalism in Early Twentieth Century America* (London: Verso, 1998), 26; Maia Ramnath, *Haj to Utopia: How the Ghadar Movement Charted Global Radicalism and Attempted to Overthrow the British Empire* (Berkeley: University of California Press, 2011), 150. Ships' records show that Punjabi men

were also traveling from Colón through Cuba and New Orleans on their way to the West Coast of the United States—a circuitous route that they had likely developed as a response to tightening immigration enforcement at West Coast ports. USDCL/ LMAP, SS *Ellis* (Belize to New Orleans), November 9, 1908; SS *Chalmette* (Havana to New Orleans), March 3, 1912; SS *Excelsior* (Havana to New Orleans), April 2, 1912; Nayan Shah, "Intimate Dependency, Race and Trans-Imperial Migration," in *The Sun Never Sets: South Asian Migrants in an Age of U.S. Power*, ed. Vivek Bald, Miabi Chatterji, Sujani Reddy, and Manu Vimalassery (New York: New York University Press, 2013).

72. Markovits, *Global World of Indian Merchants*, 110–56, passim.
73. USDCL/LMAP, Passenger Lists for: SS *Albania* (San Cristobal, Panama–New York), July 2, 1907; SS *Adriatic* (Southampton-New York), January 25, 1908; SS *Magdalena* (Colon, Panama–New York), June 11, 1908; SS Yoro (La Ceiba to New Orleans), Nov 16, 1919; SS Pastores (Cristobal to New York), Aug 15, 1920; UKBT/ PL, SS *Orontes* (Colombo-Tilbury), November 1906; SS *Atrato* (Southampton-Colon), December 19, 1906; SS *Orinoco* (Southampton-Colon), May 8, 1907; SS *Orinoco* (Colon-Southampton), July 8, 1907; SS *Oroya* (Colombo-London), December, 1907; SS *Trent* (Southampton-Trinidad-Colon), January 22, 1908; SS *Orotava* (Colombo-Plymouth), March 1908; SS *Atrato* (Southampton-Colon), April 1, 1908; SS *Tagus* (Southampton-Kingston-Colon), February 17, 1909; SS *Magdalena* (Southampton-Colon), May 26, 1909; USDS/BC, *Passport Applications* for: Fazleh Rehmond, American Legation, Panama, October 21, 1913.
74. Baker, "School Teaching In Panama."
75. S. L. Beckwith, "Havana: A City of Strange Peddlers," *Atlanta Constitution*, August 25, 1901, A9.
76. Erika Lee, At America's Gates: Chinese Immigration During the Exclusion Era, 1882–1943 (Chapel Hill: University of North Carolina Press, 2003), 39, 246; Mai Ngai, *Impossible Subjects: Illegal Aliens and the Making of Modern America* (Princeton, NJ: Princeton University Press, 2004), 18–19.
77. McKeown, *Melancholy Order*, 8, 114–16.
78. Ibid.
79. "Rug Peddlers Detained," *Baltimore Sun*, July 23, 1890, 1; "Hindoo Peddlers Not Admitted," *New York Times*, June 27, 1897, 23; see also "Seven Arab Peddlers," *New York Times*, October 15, 1888, 8; McKeown, *Melancholy Order*, 202–04; 249–55.
80. I draw here on Claude Markovits' definition of a trade network "as a structure through which goods, credit, capital, and men circulate regularly across a given space." Work still remains to determine the structure and workings of credit within the Hooghly peddler network. Markovits, *Global World of Indian Merchants*, 25.
81. USDC/BC, *U.S. Census, 1910: Population Schedule* for New Orleans, Louisiana: P2/ W4/SD1/ED59/Sh5; *U.S. Census, 1920: Population Schedules* for New Orleans, Louisiana: P5/W5/SD1/ED82/Sh5A; P5/W6/SD101/ED103/Sh1; P5/W5/SD1/ ED82/Sh4B; USDCL/BIN, U.S. Circuit Court for the Eastern District of South Carolina, *Petitions for Naturalization* for: Abdul Rohim Mondul (1900), Abdul Job-

ber Mondul (1901), Elahi Baksh Mondul (1905), Abdul Aziz (1908); Abdul Haq Mondul (1908); and Syed Abdul Ganny (1911).

82. UKBT/PL, SS *Campania*, September 17, 1898; USDT/LMAP, SS *Numidian*, September 14, 1902; USDC/BC, *U.S. Census, 1900: Population Schedule* for New Orleans, LA, P3/W4/SD1/ED36/Sh7, P9/W11/SD1/ED115/Sh18.

83. U.S. Congress, *An Act to Prohibit the Importation and Migration of Foreigners and Aliens under Contract or Agreement to Perform Labor in the United States, Its Territories, and the District of Columbia*, 48th Cong., 2nd Sess., February 26, 1885, Chap. 164, 23 Stat. 332 (1885).

84. The "Joynal Abdin" appearing on this manifest was a different person from Jainal Abdeen, one of the earliest members of the network to settle in New Orleans, who died in 1900. The later Joynal Abdin, however, became an important member of the network from 1904 forward, making trips through its U.S. and Caribbean circuits.

85. USDT/LMAP, SS *Teutonic*, June 2, 1904; USDCL/LMAP, SS *Oceanic*, July 17, 1912.

86. Das, *Our Countrymen*, 3.

87. USDS/BC, Passport Application for Fazleh Rehmond, American Legation, Panama, October 21, 1913, General Records of the Department of State, Record Group 59, National Archives, Washington, DC; USDC/BC, *U.S. Census, 1900: Population Schedule* for Neptune Township, NJ, SD168/ED138/Sh14.

88. USDS/BC, Passport Application for Abdul Gannie, Mays Landing, NJ, January 3, 1919; Passport Application for Noorul Huck, Houston, TX, July 2, 1918. The archives are full of similar sets of movements: Panch Courie Mondul is recorded traveling from Southampton, England, to Colón, Panama, in June 1905, from Liverpool to New York in May 1906, and from Liverpool to Bombay in July 1907. Abdul Barrick traveled from Naples, Italy, to New York in 1888, then lived at 10 Wesley Place, Asbury Park, NJ, in 1906, at 1428 St. Louis Street, New Orleans, LA, in 1908, and Charoh Village in the Hooghly District in 1909. Solomon Mondul traveled from Southampton to New York in 1896, lived at 1420 St. Louis Street in New Orleans in 1900, traveled from Liverpool to Atlantic City in 1906, lived in New Orleans in April 1910, traveled from Colón via Kingston, Jamaica, and New York to Asbury Park in August 1910, lived back in New Orleans in 1920, and finally, lived in Memphis, Tennessee, in 1930. USDC/BC, *U.S. Census, 1900: Population Schedules*; *U.S. Census, 1910: Population Schedules*; *U.S. Census, 1920: Population Schedules*; *U.S. Census, 1930: Population Schedules*; USDT/LMAP, USDCL/LMAP, UKBT/PL, various, 1888–1914.

89. "Burglars Made Rich Haul at the Shore," *Philadelphia Inquirer*, August 1, 1902, 3.

90. USDCL/LMAP, SS *Crib* (Belize to New Orleans), April 7, 1914; SS *Coppename* (Belize to New Orleans), October 19, 1914; SS *Coppename* (Belize to New Orleans), July 9, 1917; USDC/BC, *U.S. Census, 1910: Population Schedule*, New Orleans, LA, 1711 Conti Street; *U.S. Census, 1920: Population Schedule*, New Orleans, LA, 1825 St. Ann Street.

91. USDCL/LMAP, SS *Yoro* (La Ceiba to New Orleans), November 16, 1919. Interestingly, records show that by this time, at least one other set of peddlers—a group of Afghans headed by a merchant from Peshawar named Murad Mallik—was moving

through the infrastructure that the Bengali peddlers had built. In 1914, Mallik made two trips from Belize to New Orleans on his way to Atlantic City, where he had a residence and shop. In New Orleans, Mallik and three other Afghan traders stayed at 1711 Conti Street, one of the key households of the Hooghly network. It is possible, that Mallik was providing goods for members of the Hooghly network to peddle in Atlantic City and members of the Hooghly network were providing shelter for Mallik on his journeys between Central America and New Jersey. USDCL/ LMAP, SS *Crib* (Belize to New Orleans), April 7, 1914; SS *Coppename* (Belize to New Orleans), October 19, 1914; SS *Coppename* (Belize to New Orleans), July 9, 1917; USDC/BC, *U.S. Census, 1910: Population Schedule*, New Orleans, LA, 1711 Conti Street; *U.S. Census, 1920: Population Schedule*, New Orleans, LA, 1825 St. Ann Street.

92. The majority of these networks were confined to the Indian Ocean world and Southeast Asia, with the earliest being established in Muscat and Zanzibar and others following the expansion of the British Empire into East, Central, and Southern Africa, the Middle East, Ceylon, Burma, Malaya, and Mauritius. Most made their money either supplying Indian goods to Indian migrants and indentured laborers or operating general stores that catered to local populations in these various colonial sites. Claude Markovits, *Merchants, Traders, Entrepreneurs: Indian Business in the Colonial Era* (Houndmills, UK: Palgrave Macmillan, 2008), 221–24, 229–31, 237.

93. Ibid., 61.

94. See, for example: Dirk Hoerder and Nora Faires, "Preface," and Dirk Hoerder, "Introduction: Migration, People's Lives, Shifting and Permeable Borders," in *Migrants and Migration in North America: Cross-Border Lives, Labor Markets, and Politics*, ed. Dirk Hoerder and Nora Faires (Durham: Duke University Press, 2011), xii–xix, 21–23; Sucheta Mazumdar, "What Happened to the Women?" in *Asian Pacific Islander American Women: A Historical Anthology*, ed. Shirley Hune and Gail Nomura (New York: New York University Press, 2003, 58–65; Donna Gabaccia, Italy's Many Diasporas (Seattle: University of Washington Press, 2000), 74–75, 83; Jennifer Guglielmo, Living the Revolution: Italian Women's Resistance and Radicalism in New York City, 1880–1945 (Chapel Hill: University of North Carolina Press, 2010), 13–16, 44–45, 67–72; Madeline Y. Hsu, Dreaming of Gold, Dreaming of Home: Transnationalism and Migration Between the United States and South China, 1882–1943 (Stanford: Stanford University Press, 2000), 55–89.

2. BETWEEN "HINDOO" AND "NEGRO"

1. Mary Eliza Church Terrell, "Crossing the Color Line," *A Colored Woman in a White World* (Washington, DC: Ransdell, 1940), 376.

2. "How Dark Negroes 'Pass' Down South," *Jet Magazine*, September 8, 1955, 10–12. See also "Along Broadway at Night," *New York Times*, March 28, 1904, 9.

3. "Hindoos in America," *Chicago Daily Tribune*, July 19, 1891, 6; "Not Very Dignified—Amusing Story of an Oriental Who Took a Bicycle Ride," *Biloxi Daily Herald*, May 5, 1900, 6; S. L. Beckwith, "Havana: A City of Strange Peddlers," *Atlanta Constitution*, August 25, 1901, A9.

4. Alecia P. Long, *The Great Southern Babylon: Sex, Race, and Respectability in New Orleans* (Baton Rouge: Louisiana State University Press, 2004), 1; Jasmine Mir, *Marketplace of Desire: Storyville and the Making of a Tourist City in New Orleans, 1890–1920* (PhD diss., New York University, 2005).

5. Leon Litwack, *Trouble in Mind: Black Southerners in the Age of Jim Crow* (New York: Alfred A. Knopf, 1998), 238.

6. Ironically, the peddlers' fezes had led locals to describe them generally as "Turks." N. C. Das, "Our Countrymen in the South," *The Hindusthanee Student* 6, no. 1 (October 1917): 4.

7. Joseph Roach, *Cities of the Dead: Circum-Atlantic Performance* (New York: Columbia University Press, 1996), 245–59; Kevin Fox Gotham, *Authentic New Orleans: Tourism, Culture, and Race in the Big Easy* (New York: New York University Press, 2007), 42–44.

8. Roach, *Cities of the Dead*, 258–59; Henry Rightor, ed., *Standard History of New Orleans, Louisiana* (Chicago: Lewis, 1900), 640–45.

9. Rightor, *Standard History of New Orleans*, 640–45; Reid Mitchell, *All on a Mardi Gras Day: Episodes in the History of New Orleans Carnival* (Cambridge, MA: Harvard University Press, 1995), 109; Henri Schindler, *Mardi Gras Treasures: Float Designs of the Golden Age* (Gretna, LA: Pelican, 2001).

10. Robert Southey, "The Curse of Kehama," in *The Poetical Works of Robert Southey* (London: Longmans, Green, 1876), 548–627; Edwin Arnold, *The Light of Asia, or The Great Renunciation* (London: Trubner, 1879); Schindler, *Mardi Gras Treasures*, 34, 57; "Carnival at End—Krewe of Comus Give Their Parade in New Orleans," *Montgomery Advertiser*, February 2, 1903, 1. See also "Parade Knights of Momus Ushe[r] in the Mardi Gras," *Macon Weekly Telegraph*, February 23, 1906, 2.

11. "New Orleans Greets Rex—Carnival Crowd Not So Large as in Previous Years," *Montgomery Advertiser*, March 3, 1908, 1.

12. Joseph Logsdon and Caryn Cossé Bell, "The Americanization of Black New Orleans, 1850–1900," in *Creole New Orleans: Race and Americanization*, ed. Arnold R. Hirsch and Joseph Logsdon (Baton Rouge: Louisiana State University Press, 1992), 250–51, 257–61.

13. Arnold R. Hirsch and Joseph Logsdon, "Franco Africans and African Americans," in Hirsch and Logsdon, *Creole New Orleans*, 189–91; Logsdon and Bell, "Americanization of Black New Orleans"; State of Louisiana, *Separate Car Act*, 1890 La. Acts no. 111, 152; William Ivy Hair, *Carnival of Fury: Robert Charles and the New Orleans Race Riot of 1900* (Baton Rouge: University of Louisiana Press, 1986, 2008), 106–07.

14. Hirsch and Logsdon, Creole New Orleans, 189; Michael E. Crutcher, *Tremé: Race and Place in a New Orleans Neighborhood* (Athens: University of Georgia Press, 2010), 20–65; Richard Campanella, "An Ethnic Geography of New Orleans,"

Journal of American History 94 (December 2007): 704–15; Long, *Great Southern Babylon*, 130–31; Louis Armstrong, *Satchmo: My Life in New Orleans*, centennial ed. (Cambridge, MA: Da Capo Press, 1986), 7–8.

15. Hair, *Carnival of Fury*, 106–55; Litwack, *Trouble in Mind*, 280–83, 404–10.

16. "New York Has a Malay Colony," *New York Post*, November 22, 1900; "East Indian Peddler Fined for No License," *Atlanta Constitution*, November 21, 1912, 4.

17. USDC/BC, *U.S. Census, 1900, 1910: Population Schedules* for Asbury Park, Atlantic City, and Long Branch, NJ; New Orleans, LA; Charleston, SC; and Jacksonville, FL (various); USSS/DRC WWI, Local Registration Boards of New Orleans, LA; Charleston, SC; Memphis, TN; Chattanooga, TN; Galveston, TX; Dallas, TX; Birmingham, AL; Atlanta, GA; and Jacksonville, FL.

18. USDC/BC, *U.S. Census, 1910: Population Schedule* for New Orleans, Louisiana: P2/W4/SD1/ED59/Sh5; *U.S. Census, 1920: Population Schedules* for New Orleans, Louisiana: P5/W5/SD1/ED82/Sh5A; P5/W6/SD101/ED103/Sh1; P5/W5/SD1/ED82/Sh4B; USDCL/BIN, U.S. Circuit Court for the Eastern District of South Carolina, *Petitions for Naturalization* for: Abdul Rohim Mondul (1900), Abdul Jobber Mondul (1901), Elahi Baksh Mondul (1905), Abdul Aziz (1908); Abdul Haq Mondul (1908); and Syed Abdul Ganny (1911).

19. See for example: USDCL/BIN, U.S. Circuit Court for the Eastern District of South Carolina; *Records of Naturalization* for: Abdul Rohim Mondul (1902); Mohamed Kauser (1902); Abdul Jobber Mondul (1905); and Mohammed Ruhullah, (1905).

20. *United States v. Dolla*, 177 F. 101–05 (5th Cir. May–June 1910).

21. Ibid.

22. USDC/BC, *U.S. Census, 1900: Population Schedule* for Savannah, Georgia, SD1/ED65/Sh8; USDC/BC, *U.S. Census, 1910: Population Schedule* for Savannah, Georgia, W3/SD1/ED64/Sh20A.

23. CNO/BH, *Certificate of Marriage* for Abdul Hamid and Adele Fortineau; *U.S. Census, 1920: Population Schedules* for New Orleans, Louisiana: P5/W5/SD1/ED82/Sh4B; New Orleans, Louisiana, *City Directories for 1912–1919*.

24. Newspaper advertisements from the era show that Fara had recently opened an "East India Fancy Goods" shop along with two other members of the Hooghly network in the heart of the "Negro commercial district" along North Claiborne Avenue. "Mondul, Wahed, and Fara—Importers and Dealers in East India Fancy Goods" (advertisement), *New Orleans Herald*, April 22, 1920, 7; "East India Fancy Goods and Ladies Ready-to-Wear" (advertisement), *New Orleans Herald*, April 15, 1920, 12.

25. This is not to say the Syrians were "safe" from the racial violence of the era or unambiguously accepted as "white." See Sarah Gualtieri on the lynching of the Syrian grocer, Nola Romey, in Lake City, Florida in 1929. Sarah Gualtieri, *Between Arab and White: Race and Ethnicity in the Early Syrian Diaspora* (Berkeley: University of California Press, 2009), 120–34.

26. USDC/BC, *U.S. Census, 1900: Population Schedule* for Philadelphia, PA, W8/SD1/ED150/Sh3; Pittsburgh, PA, W8/SD18/ED129/Sh2; Cleveland, OH, W11/SD19/ED45/Sh10; St. Augustine, FL, P15/W4/SD2/ED143/Sh7; Houston, TX, P1/W2/

SD11/ED85/Sh11; Galveston, TX, W5/SD11/ED122/Sh8; Savannah, GA, Mailing District 4, SD1/ED65/Sh8; Charleston, SC (various); Atlantic City, NJ (various).

27. Michael Crutcher, "Historical Geographies of Race in a New Orleans Afro-Creole Landscape," in Richard H. Schein, ed., *Landscape and Race in the United States* (New York: Routledge, 2006) 30–31.

28. USDC/BC, *U.S. Census, 1900: Population Schedule* for New Orleans, LA, 3rd Precinct, Ward 4, Sup. Dist. 1, Enum. Dist. 36, Sheet Nos. 4, 6; Long, *Great Southern Babylon*, 104, 130–31, 138; Sanborn Fire Insurance Company, "New Orleans, Louisiana, 1895," in *Digital Sanborn Maps, 1867–1970* (Ann Arbor, MI: ProQuest).

29. Long, *Great Southern Babylon*, 138–39.

30. Ibid., 129.

31. Those apparently connected to the local entertainment and sex industry included an Irish barman at 1432 St. Louis Street, a German restaurateur at 322 Marais Street, an opera singer at 1418 Conti Street, a saloon keeper at 1428 Conti Street, and a large number of young women, living in groups of two and three, who appear to have been sex workers but listed their occupations euphemistically as "boarding-house keepers," "seamstresses," and "house girls." Nearby, for example, were Anna Howard and Amanda Flowers, two madams of the era, who both declared themselves to be "boardinghouse keepers," while their young female boarders included "seamstresses," "dressmakers," and a "house-servant." USDC/BC, *U.S. Census, 1900: Population Schedule* for New Orleans, LA, P3/W4/SD1/ED36/Sh5–12.

32. The rate at which properties were being turned over to the sex trade was staggering. According to one local historian, by 1910, "the (approximately) sixty addresses on Iberville Street [between Basin Street and North Claiborne Avenue] . . . had expanded to more than a hundred sixty, without additional structures being added." Al Rose, *Storyville, New Orleans* (Tuscaloosa: University of Alabama Press, 1974), 101; Sanborn Fire Insurance Company, "New Orleans, Louisiana, 1895" and "New Orleans, Louisiana, 1908," in *Digital Sanborn Maps, 1867–1970* (Ann Arbor, MI: ProQuest).

33. Long, *Great Southern Babylon*, 138–39; *U.S. Census, 1910: Population Schedules* for New Orleans, Louisiana, P4/W4/SD1/ED63/Sh3–4; P3/W4/SD1/ED60/Sh5-7.

34. USDC/BC, *U.S. Census, 1910: Population Schedule* for New Orleans, Louisiana: P2/W4/SD1/ED59/Sh5. Even with an older woman present, one wonders at the risks to which Alef Ally was subjecting his daughter. It is clear that Viola would have been in a precarious position as a teenage girl not only sharing a household with twenty men, but also living on the edge of Storyville, with its underage "sex circuses," as described by Roach, *Cities of the Dead*, 227-31.

35. On June 7, 1904, Joynal Abdin (a new arrival with the same name as Jainal Abdeen, who had died in New Orleans in 1900), was traveling from Liverpool to New York, and stated that he was on his way first to see his cousin Majan Ali at 15 Wellesley Place, Asbury Park, then to "Ali Monsoud" at 1428 St. Louis Street (this may have referred to either Monzur/Monsure Ali or Moksad Ali, both of whom were active in the city). On January 25, 1908, Majid Mondul, Baksh Rahman, and Abdul Aziz, traveling from Southampton to New York, were on their way to their "grandfather and friend" Fausley Mondul at 1428 St. Louis Street. On May 31, 1908, Tarzar Ali,

thirty, traveling from Liverpool to New York, with companions headed to Asbury Park and Atlantic City, was going to join his uncle Abdul Barrick at 1428 St. Louis Street. On September 12, 1908, Abdul Sircar, twenty-six, traveling from Southampton to New York, was on his way to his "brother Mocksyed Ally" (Moksad Ali) at 1428 St. Louis Street. On July 2, 1914, Eunoe Rahman, twenty-six, traveling from Southampton to New York with three companions on their way to Asbury Park, was going to join his uncle Kafeloddin Mondul (Kaliluddin) at 1428 St. Louis Street, though he was deported from Ellis Island. USDT/LMAP, SS *Teutonic*, June 2, 1904; USDCL/LMAP, SS *Adriatic*, January 25, 1908; SS *Celtic*, May 31, 1908; SS *St. Louis*, September 12, 1908; SS *Oceanic*, July 2, 1914. In 1917–1918, three Bengali peddlers who were of age for the military draft gave 1428 St. Louis Street as their home address when they registered: Abdul Gannie Mondul, twenty-four, Babur Ali, twenty-nine, and Dawood Rohman, twenty-two. USSS/DRC WWI, Local Registration Board, New Orleans, LA.

36. Sanborn Fire Insurance Company, "New Orleans, Louisiana, 1895," in *Digital Sanborn Maps, 1867–1970* (Ann Arbor, MI: ProQuest); Long, *Great Southern Babylon*, 131; Rose, *Storyville*, 72–96.

37. Long, *Great Southern Babylon*, 126.

38. Ibid., 1–4.

39. Crutcher, *Tremé*, 33–36; Samuel Charters, *A Trumpet Around the Corner: The Story of New Orleans Jazz* (Jackson: University Press of Mississippi, 2008), 51.

40. Long, *Great Southern Babylon*, 133.

41. Ibid., 129–30.

42. Rose, *Storyville*, 96; Mir, *Marketplace of Desire*, 4.

43. Abbott and Seroff point out that a contemporary theater owner in Chicago, Sam T. Jack, used the same poster, text, and promotional images, and presumably the same women, for his 1890 "Creole Burlesque Company," and his "Oriental Sensation Company," the latter of which purported to feature twenty Egyptian women. A later report noted that the "Oriental" company was 'made up of many New York City girls.'" The women who performed as "Oriental dancing girls" in Storyville included "Mademoiselle Rita Walker," a young woman whose madam took out a full-page advertisement in the District's illicit *Blue Book* to announce her as "one of the first women in America to dance in her bare feet." The District's Cairo Club built its main entertainments around "oriental dancers," though it is unclear what their origins were. Rose, *Storyville*, 69, 77–80, 89, 146. Lynn Abbott and Doug Seroff, *Out of Sight: The Rise of African American Popular Music, 1889–1895* (Jackson: University Press of Mississippi, 2002), 154.

44. "Claiborne Novelty Shop—Abdul Rohim Surker, Importer and Dealer in East India Fancy Needlework" (advertisement), *New Orleans Herald*, December 11, 1919; "East India Fancy Goods and Ladies Ready-to-Wear" (advertisement), *New Orleans Herald*, April 15, 1920, 12; "The East India Shop, S. M. Ally, Prop." (advertisement), *New Orleans Herald*, December 9, 1920, 12.

45. Rose, *Storyville*, 80.

46. E. J. Bellocq, *Storyville Portraits: Photographs from the New Orleans Red-light District, Circa 1912* (New York: Museum of Modern Art, 1970); Jay Moynahan, ed.,

The Blue Book of New Orleans (Spokane: Chickadee, 2006); Rose, *Storyville*, 79–80, 89.

47. While the wealthiest among the madams may have purchased their goods from luxury department stores like Maison Blanche, there were many other brothels in the area around St. Louis Street whose proprietors would have required less expensive Eastern fabrics, wall hangings, and rugs. Jessie Brown's establishment, next door to the Arlington, was subdivided into "as many as sixty-five" small rooms, each one of which was outfitted with a "good rug" to give customers a sense of class and luxury and set their rooms apart from common "cribs." Rose, *Storyville*, 79.

48. Das, "Our Countrymen," 4.

49. USDC/BC, *U.S. Census, 1910: Population Schedule* for New Orleans, LA (various).

50. Sanborn Fire Insurance Company, "New Orleans, Louisiana, 1908," in *Digital Sanborn Maps, 1867–1970* (Ann Arbor, MI: ProQuest); USDC/BC, *U.S. Census, 1910: Population Schedules* for 320 N. Roman Street, 323 N. Johnson Street, 1711 Conti Street, 413 N. Claiborne Avenue.

51. Das, "Our Countrymen," 4.

52. The records of such deaths are a grim testament to how deeply the lives of the Bengalis were entwined with the lives of their neighbors in black working-class New Orleans. Emilie Ally, Jainal Abdeen, Moksad Ali, Kahdidje Abdeen, and Frank Osborne were all killed by tuberculosis, Nofossur Abdeen Osborne by smallpox; Solomon Ally, Ballah Ally, Roheama Gertrude Ali, Koremia Ali, Mozar Ali, Mumbul Ali, Ismail Alley, Hilma Marta Hassan, Joynal Joseph Abdin, all children of mixed marriages, were dead before the age of fifteen. CNO/BH, Certificates of Death for Emilie Ali (1898), Jainal Abdeen (1900), Kathdeja Abdeen (1912), Moksad Ali (1918), Nofusur Osborne (1920), Frank Osborne (1924), Roheama Gertrude Ali (1899), Koremia Ali (1906), Ismail Alley (1907), Mozar Ali (1912), Mumbul Ali (1918), Solomon Ally (1918), Ballah Ally (1927), Joynal Joseph Abdin (1944), Hilma Marta Hassan (1945), Louisiana State Archives, Baton Rouge.

53. Although it is difficult to determine what kinds of hierarchies existed within the network, there are indications across the full range of sources cited in this and the previous chapter that their were men involved in the network who had different levels of education and literacy. While some of the earliest peddlers were described as speaking in "excellent English," Census enumerations record many of these men as not being able to read or write English. On official documents that required signatures, such as draft registration cards, a few of the men were able to sign their names in clean well-formed English or Bengali script, while a larger number appear to have signed with difficulty or were unable to sign in either language, marking documents with either an "x" or check mark.

54. Ibid., 4–5; Crutcher, *Tremé*, 52–53.

55. Das, "Our Countrymen," 4–5.

56. USDC/BC, *U.S. Census, 1900: Population Schedule* for New Orleans, LA, P3/W4/SD1/ED36/Sh6. Emily Lecompte, her mother, and her brother were racially categorized as "Black" in the 1880 census, with a clearly Creole, rather than Anglo-American, surname: USDC/BC, *U.S. Census, 1880: Population Schedule* for New

Orleans, LA, SD1/ED31/Pg49/Lines 19–22. She appears (as "Minnie") with Alef
Ally and their daughter, Sadie, on the passenger list of the SS *Adriatic*, traveling
from Liverpool to New York City in July 1896: DCNY/PNY, *List of Passengers* for
SS *Adriatic*, July 25, 1896, 2, lines 55–59. Birth records indicate that Alef Ally and
Emily Lecompte Ally were the parents of Mary Sadie (named "Aline" at birth) and
Viola: New Orleans Birth Records Index, 1790–1899: Certificate of Birth: Aline
Ally, 1892, vol. 6, November 25, 1892; Certificate of Birth: Viola Ally, 1897, vol. 115,
859, June 15, 1897.

57. Marriage certificates for these unions reveal interconnections on both the men's and
women's sides: Jainal Abdeen officiated and Yacoob Ali signed as a witness to
Moksad Ali's first marriage in 1892; Abdeen signed as a witness again to Moksad
Ali's second marriage in 1895; Moksad Ali in turn signed as a witness to Asa Alli's
marriage in 1897; Olga Santa Cruz married Abdul Rub ten years after her elder sister America had married Sofur Ally. CNO/BH, Certificates of Marriage for Moksad
Ally and Ada Wallace (1892), Jainal Abdeen and Florence Perez (1893), Moksad Ally
and Ella Elizabeth Blackman (1895), Shaik Aynnaddeen Mondol and Rita Albrier
(1896), Asa Alli and Aurelia Urbain (1897), Abdul Hamed and Adele Fortineau
(1900), Sofur Alli and America Santa Cruz (1900), Shaik M. Alley and Corinne Villar (1901), Bahador Ali Molar and Florence Gertrude Wilbert (1905), Joseph Abdin
and Viola Ida Lewis (1906), John A. Martin and Nofossu Abdeen (1909), Victor
Dupart and Sadie Ally (1909), Ensan Ally and Camille Basset (1910), Abdul Rub and
Olga Santa Cruz (1911), Maxest Ally and Ananise Sylvester (1911), Denis Schaff
and Viola Alley (1911), Hassin Abdul and Viola Wilson (1914), Frank Carey Osborn
and Nofossu Ella Abdeen (1914), Nazaf Alli and Juanita Marita Lambert (1916), Abdul Hamid and Emma Fortineau (1917), Hassan Abdul and Leonora Pavageau (1918),
Joseph Anthony Jensen and Hazel Adele Alley (1919), Louisiana State Archives,
Baton Rouge.

58. Their mothers and grandmothers worked in domestic service, and their fathers and
brothers were predominantly laborers on the docks, in factories, and in the various
construction trades. A number of the women lived in households headed by a single
parent, grandparent, or adoptive or stepparents after one or both of their biological
parents had died. The insecure futures that young women in these households faced
in a context in which pooling resources was crucial to survival may have made the
peddlers, as small businessmen with regular incomes, attractive as husbands or
partners. USDC/BC, *U.S. Census, 1880: Population Schedule* for New Orleans, LA,
Family of Ada Wallace, SD1/ED86/Pg32; USDC/BC, *U.S. Census, 1900: Population Schedules* for New Orleans, LA, Family of Adele Fortineau, P9/W5/SD1/ED51/
Sh15; Family of Corinne Villar, P9/W5/SD1/ED51/Sh19; Family of Florence Wilbert, P3/W4/SD1/ED36/Sh7; Family of Florence Perez, P6/W7/SD1/ED67/Sh21;
Family of Rita Albrier, P4/W7/SD1/ED65/Sh6; Family of Viola Ida Lewis, P6/W5/
SD1/ED48/Sh16; USDC/BC, *U.S. Census, 1910: Population Schedules* for New Or-
leans, LA, Family of Anaise Sylvester, P4/W5/SD1/ED74/Sh11A; Family of Juanita
Lambert, P6/W3/SD1/ED44/Sh2A; Family of Leonore Pavagneau, P8/W7/SD1/
ED117/Sh13A; Family of Viola Wilson, W11/SD1/ED186/Sh1B.

59. The one exception may be Minnie Lecompte, Alef Ally's partner, who appears to have traveled with Ally and their two daughters back to India for a visit in 1896. DCNY/PNY, *List of Passengers* for SS *Adriatic*, July 25, 1896: Page 2, Lines 55–59.

60. Sucheta Mazumdar, "What Happened to the Women?" in *Asian Pacific Islander American Women: A Historical Anthology*, ed. Shirley Hune and Gail Nomura (New York: New York University Press, 2003, 58–65.

61. Jennifer Guglielmo, *Living the Revolution: Italian Women's Resistance and Radicalism in New York City, 1880–1945* (Chapel Hill: University of North Carolina Press, 2010), 13-16, 44–45, 67-72; Donna Gabaccia, *Italy's Many Diasporas* (Seattle: University of Washington Press, 2000), 74–75, 83. See also: Madeline Y. Hsu, Dreaming of Gold, Dreaming of Home: Transnationalism and Migration Between the United States and South China, 1882–1943 (Stanford: Stanford University Press, 2000), 55–89; Erika Lee, At America's Gates: Chinese Immigration During the Exclusion Era, (Chapel Hill: University of North Carolina Press, 2005), 116–23.

62. Das, "Our Countrymen," 4.

63. The question of how and where these men and women met is a bit more complex. An analysis of the women's addresses suggests proximity was a factor, but not in ways that might be expected. Only one member of the Hooghly network married a woman from the immediate area around Storyville, where most of the peddlers lived between the 1890s and 1910s. Bahadoor Ali, one of the seven Bengali men living at 1420 St. Louis Street in 1900, married Florence Wilbert, a young African American woman who lived with her widowed mother, a dressmaker, in the same building. In another instance, proximity appears to have figured in a different way. Two women from the same block of Carondelet Avenue on the uptown side of Canal Street, Ida Lewis and Anaise Sylvester, married two Bengali peddlers, Joseph Abdin and Maxest Ally, five years apart. CNO/BH, Certificates of Marriage for Moksad Ally and Ada Wallace (1892), Moksad Ally and Ella Elizabeth Blackman (1895), Aynnaddeen Mondol and Rita Albrier (1896), Ensan Ally and Camille Basset (1910); Certificates of Death for Moksad Ali (October 13, 1918) and Sofur Ally (May 2, 1936), Louisiana State Archives, Baton Rouge; USDC/BC, *U.S. Census, 1900: Population Schedule* for New Orleans, LA, P3/W4/SD1/ED36/Sh6; *U.S. Census, 1910: Population Schedule* for Beat 5, Hancock County, MS, SD6/ED29/Sh10A; *U.S. Census, 1920: Population Schedule* for New Orleans, LA, P4/W5/SD1/ED80/Sh20A; *U.S. Census, 1930: Population Schedules* for New Orleans, LA, P6/W5/B177/SD11/ED36-76/Sh7B, P6/W5/B183/SD11/ED36-76/Sh16A.

64. Campanella, "An Ethnic Geography of New Orleans."

65. Crutcher, *Tremé*, 52–53.

66. Ibid., 53–55.

67. Das, "Our Countrymen," 4; "Mondul, Wahed, and Fara—East India Fancy Goods and Ladies Ready-to-Wear" (advertisement), *New Orleans Herald*, April 15, 1920; "Fozlay Rohman, Importer and Dealer in Oriental and Domestic Fancy Goods" (advertisement), *New Orleans Herald*, December 23, 1920, 12; "Special Bargains for Xmas Credit or Cash—It Will Pay You to See Me—Claiborne Novelty Shop—Abdul

Rohim Surker—Importer and Dealer" (advertisement), *New Orleans Herald*, December 11, 1919, 12.

68. Crutcher, 57; Tony Scherman, *Backbeat: Earl Palmer's Story* (Washington: Smithsonian Institution Press, 1999), 9.

69. CNO/BH, Certificates of Birth for Aline [Mary Sadie] Ally (November 25, 1892), Nofossur Abdeen (June 13, 1893), Monzure Ally (July 7, 1895), Kadaza [Kadhidje] Abdeen (December 26, 1896), Cayamus [Karamouth] Ally (July 7, 1897), Viola Ally (June 15, 1897), Ishamel Abdeen (October 16, 1898), Rohema [Roheamon] Ali (April 18, 1900), Abraham Ally (September 2, 1901), Abdul Gane Hamid (February 1, 1902), Isaac Ally (June 10, 1904), Louisiana State Archives, Baton Rouge. USDC/BC, *U.S. Census, 1900: Population Schedules* for New Orleans, LA, P3/W4/SD1/ED36/Sh6, P16/W3/SD1/ED33/Sh8; *U.S. Census, 1910: Population Schedules* for New Orleans, LA, P4/W5/SD1/ED74/Sh9A, P5/W5/SD1/ED77/Sh2B; *U.S. Census, 1910: Population Schedule* for Beat 5, Hancock County, MS, SD6/ED29/Sh10A.

70. The changing racial classifications of this family over the course of three censuses are notable in their demonstration of the contingency, subjectivity, and instability of the U.S. Census's racial classifications: in 1910 Sofur Ali was recorded as "Hindu" and America and their children as "Mulatto;" in 1920 the entire Ali family was categorized as "White;" and in 1930, America was recorded as "Black" while Sofur and the children were categorized as "Hindu." CNO/BH, Certificate of Marriage for Sofur Ally and America Santa Cruz (1900); USDC/BC, *U.S. Census, 1900: Population Schedule* for New Orleans, LA, P3/W4/SD1/ED36/Sh7; *U.S. Census, 1910: Population Schedule* for New Orleans, LA, P5/W5/SD1/ED77/Sh2B, *U.S. Census, 1920 Population Schedule* for New Orleans, LA, P5/W5/SD1/ED82/Sh5A; *U.S. Census, 1930: Population Schedule* for New Orleans, LA, P6/W5/B177/SD11/ED36-76/Sh7B.

71. USDCL/LMAP, SS *Celtic*, October 18, 1908; USDS/BC, Passport Application for Roston Ally, New Orleans, LA, November 7, 1918. Brandon Ally (descendant of Sofur and America Ally), e-mail correspondence with the author, July 20, 2008, and November 24, 2010.

72. CNO/BH, Certificates of Marriage for Moksad Ally and Ada Wallace (1892), Jainal Abdeen and Florence Perez (1893), Moksad Ally and Ella Elizabeth Blackman (1895), John A. Martin and Nofossu Abdeen (1909), Frank Cary Osborn and Nofossu Abdie (1914); Certificates of Death for Jainal Abdeen, January 21, 1900, and Kathadje Abdeen, November 5, 1912, Louisiana State Archives, Baton Rouge; USDC/BC, *U.S. Census, 1900: Population Schedule* for New Orleans, LA, 400 S. Pierce Street. (Names are reproduced here as they are transliterated in the original documents.)

73. Eric Arnesen, *Waterfront Workers of New Orleans: Race, Class, and Politics, 1863–1923* (New York: Oxford University Press, 1991), 34–73, *passim*.

74. CNO/BH, Certificates of Death for Nafoosa Osborne, April 7, 1920, and Frank Osborne, November 1, 1924, Louisiana State Archives, Baton Rouge; USDC/BC, *U.S. Census, 1920: Population Schedule* for New Orleans, LA, 225 S. Johnson Street; *U.S. Census, 1930: Population Schedule* for New Orleans, LA, 1629 N. Johnson Street, 1725 Iberville Street.

75. CNO/BH, Certificate of Marriage for Moksad Ally and Ellen Elizabeth Blackman (1895); Certificate of Birth for Monzure Ally, July 7, 1895; USDC/BC, *U.S. Census, 1880: Population Schedule* for New Orleans, LA, SD1/ED80/Pg52; *U.S. Census, 1900: Population Schedule* for New Orleans, LA, P9/W11/SD1/ED115/Sh18.

76. USDC/BC, *U.S. Census, 1920: Population Schedules* for Chicago, IL, 5631 Lafayette Avenue; Los Angeles, CA, 777 Gladys Avenue.

77. CNO/BH, Certificate of Death for Moksad Ali, October 13, 1918; *U.S. Census, 1910: Population Schedule* for Beat 5, Hancock County, MS, SD6/ED29/Sh10A; *U.S. Census, 1920: Population Schedule* for Bronx, NY, WAD5/SD2/ED271Sh7A.

78. City of New York, Board of Health, Certificate and Record of Marriage for Bahadour M. Ali and Margaret B. L. Carree, Certificate No. 26075, August 20, 1923; Roston Ali and Pearl Pierce, Certificate No. 33040, October 29, 1924, New York City Municipal Archives, New York, NY; USDC/BC, *U.S. Census, 1930: Population Schedule* for New York, NY, WAD21/BL/SD24/ED31–1019/Sh6B.

79. "Dancer's Parents of Varied Races—Father of Bahadoor Ali Turkish Subject, Mother New Orleans Creole," *Baltimore Afro-American*, March 27, 1926, 6.

80. Bardu Ali, "Bardu Ali Remembers," in Redd Foxx and Norma Miller, *The Redd Foxx Encyclopedia of Black Humor* (Pasadena, CA: Ward Ritchie Press, 1977), 121–29; George Lipsitz, *Midnight at the Barrelhouse: The Johnny Otis Story* (Minneapolis: University of Minnesota Press, 2010); Vladimir Bogdanov, Chris Woodstra, and Stephen Thomas Erlewine, *All Music Guide to the Blues*, 3rd ed. (San Francisco: Backbeat Books, 2003), 432; Eugene Chadbourne, "Bardu Ali," entry for *All Music Guide*, online edition, accessed May 15, 2009, http://www.allmusic.com/artist/bardu-ali-p535639/biography.

81. U.S. Supreme Court, *United States v. Thind*, 261 U.S. 204 (1923); Joan M. Jensen, *Passage from India: Asian Indian Immigrants in North America* (New Haven, CT: Yale University Press, 1988), 42–58; Mai Ngai, *Impossible Subjects: Illegal Aliens and the Making of Modern America* (Princeton, NJ: Princeton University Press, 2004), 38–50.

82. USDS/BC, Passport Application for Roston Ally, New Orleans, LA, November 7, 1918; USDC/BC, *U.S. Census, 1910: Population Schedule* for Long Branch, NJ, SD3/ED79/Sh8A; DCNY/PNY, *List of Passengers* for SS *Paris*, June 15, 1895; USDCL/LMAP, SS *Oceanic*, June 29, 1905.

83. USDCL/LMAP, SS *Cedric*, September 16, 1923.

84. USDS/BC, Passport Applications for Abdul Rub Mollah, Washington, DC, February 4, 1919, and August 1, 1922; USDC/BC, *U.S. Census, 1880: Population Schedule* for St. Louis, MO, SD1/ED74/Pg20; *U.S. Census, 1900: Population Schedule* for St. Louis, MO, W23/SD11/ED342/Sh1; *U.S. Census, 1910: Population Schedule* for St. Louis, MO, W26/SD10/ED418/Sh3A, W17/SD10/ED266/Sh13B; *U.S. Census, 1910: Population Schedule* for New Orleans, LA, P3/W4/SD1/ED60/Sh8A; *U.S. Census, 1930: Population Schedule* for French Lick, IN, SD13/ED59–1/Sh14B.

85. USDS/BC, Passport Applications for Abdul Rub Mollah, Washington, DC, February 4, 1919, and August 1, 1922; USDCL/LMAP, SS *City of York*, June 14, 1921; SS *Cherbourg*, February 17, 1925; SS *Columbus*, January 18, 1936; USDC/BC, *U.S.*

Census, 1930: Population Schedule for French Lick, IN, SD13/ED59-1/Sh14B; Parke Flick, "Maple Street History," letter to the editor, *Springs Valley Herald*, 1999, accessed December 12, 2008, http://www.ingenweb.org/inorange/fls_maple _street.htm.

86. James H. Madison, *A Lynching in the Heartland: Race and Memory in America* (New York: Palgrave McMillan, 2003); USDC/BC, *U.S. Census, 1920: Population Schedule* for French Lick, IN, SD3/ED137/Sh17A.

3. FROM SHIPS' HOLDS TO FACTORY FLOORS

1. The Western or Gregorian calendar date on which this celebration occurred in Brooklyn corresponds on the Islamic calendar to within a day of 23 Dul q'idah, one of two dates on which different Shi'a groups mark the eighth Imam's death. According to scholar Raza Mir, the observance for many such dates would have followed in form the observance of Eid-al-fitr, involving a similar sacrifice and feast. Raza Mir, Interview by the author, conducted via email, May 2012.

2. "Lascar" was a British colonial term for Indian seamen derived from the Persian "lashkar," referring to sailors or military encampment laborers. As Ahuja points out, South Asian maritime workers used a variety of terms to refer to themselves: "khalasis," "jehazis/jehajis," "ag-wallahs," "pani-wallahs," among others. Ravi Ahuja, "Networks of Subordination—Networks of the Subordinated: The Ordered Spaces of South Asian Maritime Labour in an Age of Imperialism (c. 1890–1917)," in Ashwini Tambe and Harald Fischer-Tiné, eds., *The Limits of British Colonial Control in South Asia: Spaces of Disorder in the Indian Ocean Region* (London & New York: Routledge, 2008), 14.

3. "Lascar Sailors Here Honor the Malah—Native Feast of the Far East Observed on Ships with Oriental Crews," *New York Times*, December 30, 1907, 3.

4. "Crews of Lascars—The Knight Companion and Algoa Both Manned by these East Indiamen," *Dallas Morning News*, October 4, 1896, 19.

5. Ahuja, "Networks of Subordination," 13–16, 23–24; G. Balachandran, "South Asian Seafarers and Their Worlds: c. 1870–1930s," in *Seascapes: Maritime Histories, Littoral Cultures, and Transoceanic Exchanges*, ed. J. Bentley, R. Bridenthal, and K. Wigen (Honolulu: University of Hawai'i Press, 2007), 187–191; Dinkar Desai, *Maritime Labour in India* (Bombay: Servants of India Society, 1939), 33–34; Laura Tabili, *"We Ask for British Justice": Workers and Racial Difference in Late Imperial Britain* (Ithaca, NY: Cornell University Press, 1994), 41–48.

6. According to figures cited by historian Gopalan Balachandran, the number of Indian seamen on British ships rose from 24,000 to 52,000 between 1891 and 1914. The latter figure amounted to 17.5 percent of the British maritime labor force. This would rise to about a quarter of British maritime workers in the interwar period. G. Balachandran, "South Asian Seafarers," (2007), 188; G. Balachandran, "South Asian Seafarers and Their Worlds: c. 1870–1930s" (paper presented at Seascapes, Littoral Cultures, and Trans-Oceanic Exchanges, Library of Congress, Washing-

ton, DC, February 12–15, 2003), par. 8, accessed July 9, 2006, http://www.history cooperative.org/proceedings/seascapes/balachandran.html.

7. Balachandran, "South Asian Seafarers" (2007), 188; Balachandran, "South Asian Seafarers" (2003), par. 9. On engine-room labor, see Laura Tabili, *"We Ask for British Justice,"* 49.

8. Because they sought to remain hidden and most were sojourners, it is difficult to establish with certainty exactly how many Indian seamen jumped ship in U.S. ports from the 1910s to the 1940s. Census records suggest that at any particular moment in the 1920s–1930s, between ten and fifty ex-seamen were working and residing in each of about a dozen U.S. industrial towns, including Chester and Bethlehem, Pennsylvania; Youngstown, Ohio; Buffalo and Lackawanna, New York; and Detroit and Dearborn, Michigan, and between fifty and a hundred men were working in the service sector in New York City. A conservative estimate would, in other words, place three or four hundred Indian maritime deserters in the United States at any one time during this period. This number would have fluctuated widely due to various conditions in the industry and, eventually, due to the Second World War. In the early 1920s, government officials and some newspapers claimed that there were between 1000 and 3000 Indian seamen in the country illegally, though this was likely an exaggeration meant to stoke anti-immigrant sentiment. But given that so many of these seamen appear to have moved through one or more onshore locations in the United States within a matter of months or years, and then cycled back out of the country, it is safe to assume that in the three decades between 1914 and 1944, the total number of desertions reached into the low thousands.

9. UK/FOC FO371/9614 (A2858).

10. Peter Linebaugh and Marcus Rediker, *The Many-Headed Hydra: Sailors, Slaves, Commoners, and the Hidden History of the Revolutionary Atlantic* (Boston: Beacon Press, 2000), 150–51; Herman Melville, *Moby Dick: or, The Whale* (London: Humphrey Milford, 1922); Amitav Ghosh, *Sea of Poppies* (New York: Farrar, Straus and Giroux, 2008).

11. Linebaugh and Rediker, *Many-Headed Hydra,* 150.

12. Rozina Visram, *Asians in Britain: 400 Years of History* (London: Pluto Press, 2002), 54.

13. Tabili, *"We Ask for British Justice,"* 49. See also R. H. Thornton, *British Shipping* (Cambridge: Cambridge University Press, 1959), 70, 83 ,87, 250; Joe Stack, "Shooting Ashes on the Old George Washington," *The Hawsepipe* 8 (February–March 1989), cited in Tabili, *"We Ask for British Justice,"* 210–11nn18, 19, 20.

14. Dada Amir Haider Khan, *Chains to Lose: Life and Struggles of a Revolutionary* (New Delhi: Patriot Publishers, 1989), 90.

15. Visram, *Asians in Britain,* 54; Tabili, *"We Ask for British Justice,"* 48; Balachandran, "South Asian Seafarers" (2007), 188–89.

16. Tabili, *"We Ask for British Justice,"* 43–44.

17. Ibid., 43–44, 50.

18. Desai, *Maritime Labour in India,* 20; Ahuja, "Networks of Subordination," 22–25; Balachandran, "South Asian Seafarers" (2007), 188.

19. Ahuja, "Networks of Subordination," 22–23; Tabili, *"We Ask for British Justice,"* 52.
20. Ahuja, "Networks of Subordination," 21–25; Tabili, 44–46.
21. Dirk Hoerder, *Cultures in Contact: World Migrations in the Second Millennium* (Durham: Duke University Press, 2002), 373–75, 380–83.
22. Hoerder, *Cultures in Contact*, 377–83, Sucheta Mazumdar, "Colonial Impact and Punjabi Emigration to the United States," in Lucie Cheng and Edna Bonacich. Labor Immigration under Capitalism: Asian Immigrant Workers in the U.S. Before WWII (Berkeley: University of California Press, 1984), 318–19.
23. Ahuja, "Networks of Subordination," 24; Hoerder, *Cultures in Contact*, 373–75. The most thorough examination of the imposition of British taxation and land tenure policies in India is Ranajit Guha's classic study of the Permanent Settlement, *A Rule of Property for Bengal*. While Ahuja points out that the region of Sylhet, one of the most important "sending" regions for men entering the British maritime trade, was one of the few areas of Bengal not subject to the Permanent Settlement, other aspects of the British regime—for example, the introduction of private property, fixed yearly taxes, and tax-farming—appear to have had a damaging effect on smallholders in the region. Ranajit Guha, *A Rule of Property for Bengal: An Essay on the Idea of Permanent Settlement* (New Delhi: Orient Longman, 1982).
24. In describing these dynamics in colonial Punjab, Mazumdar writes that smallholding peasants were often kept unaware of the clause in their mortgage agreements that allowed for moneylenders to take possession of their land upon default. "[M]ost of the moneylenders," she writes, "were also land-hungry agricultural entrepreneurs." Over time, however, the stakes of mortgaging land must have become clear. The Kashmiri former seaman, Amir Haider Khan, for example, intimates that the most common reason for rural men to migrate to the port cities and enter the maritime labor force was to "pay back the userer's loan" in order to "save a few acres of land from being expropriated by moneylenders or the state." Mazumdar (1984), 321–24; Haider Khan, 70.
25. Ahuja, "Networks of Subordination," 24–31.
26. Ibid., 17–18.
27. Tabili, *"We Ask for British Justice,"* 42–46; Ahuja, "Networks of Subordination," 14–17; Balachandran, "South Asian Seafarers" (2007), 188; Visram, *Asians in Britain*, 55, 225; Khan, *Chains to Lose*, 66; Conrad Dixon, "Lascars: The Forgotten Seamen," in *Working Men Who Got Wet*, ed. Rosemary Ommer and Gerald Panting, 265–77 (Newfoundland: Maritime History Group, Memorial University of Newfoundland, 1980), 272.
28. Although unemployment appears to have been chronic among Indian maritime workers throughout the first half of the twentieth century, figures are available only for the latter part of this period. In 1939, Dinkar Desai, general secretary of the Seamen's Union of Bombay, estimated that out of a total number of 235,000 Indian seamen (140,000 in Calcutta, 70,000 in Bombay, 25,000 in Karachi), only one of four men were employed at any one time. A later report by James L. Mowatt, an official of the International Labour Office in Geneva, presented similar findings "250,000 to 300,000 [seamen] for 65,000 jobs available annually." Desai, *Maritime*

Labour in India, 39–44; James L. Mowatt, *Seafarer's Conditions in India and Pakistan* (Geneva: International Labour Office, 1949), 8.

29. On the formation of Indian maritime trade unions in the interwar period, see Balachandran, "South Asian Seafarers" (2007), 191–94.

30. When a British shipping company sought to hire an Indian crew in Calcutta or Bombay, the company's representative would first approach a local *ghat serang*, who would bring a group of potential *serangs* to the office of the port's shipping master. Here, one of the master's clerks would advise the shipping company's representative, helping him to select a *serang* (or a series of *serangs* for different ship's departments) from the mustered group. The chosen *serang* was then given a set period of time to assemble a full crew of workers according to the needs of the ship. The *serang* would return to the shipping office with his chosen men, and after the shipping company's representative had inspected and accepted each of the crew, the group was signed on together under a binding contract for a period ranging from six months to two years. Desai, *Maritime Labour in India*, 31; Mowatt, *Seafarer's Conditions*, 16–22.

31. Desai, *Maritime Labour in India*, 32–35; Mowatt, *Seafarer's Conditions*, 16–26 passim.

32. Khan, *Chains to Lose*, 70. In his 1939 study of the Indian maritime industry, Dinkar Desai described a Calcutta *serang* who was given 22 rupees per person per month to distribute as wages to the fifteen members of his deck crew. According to Desai, the serang took anywhere from 1 to 10 rupees off the top of each person's salary, for "a total monthly [cut] of Rs. 88 out of a . . . pay bill of Rs. 330." Ahuja emphasizes that this was a system in which shipping companies were complicit—debt and dependency turned the Indian seaman "into the 'docile' and 'reliable' workman that [British] shipmasters and companies celebrated"—while Balachandran notes that when Indian seamen began to organize unions in the 1920s and 1930s, the reform of "corrupt recruitment practices" became one of the first targets of their agitations. Desai, *Maritime Labour in India*, 33–34; Ahuja, "Networks of Subordination," 30; Balachandran, "South Asian Seafarers" (2007), 193.

33. Khan, *Chains to Lose*, 90.

34. "Crazed by Heat, Sailor Runs Amok," *New York Times*, August 15, 1926, E16.

35. What was then described as "madness" and "suicide" might now just as easily be understood as moments of breakdown in the system upon which these ships depended for their smooth functioning; they were moments in which ships' officers pushed the system to its limits, and seamen resisted in whatever limited way they could. Ravi Ahuja, "Mobility and Containment: The Voyages of South Asian Seamen, c.1900–1960," supplement, *International Review of Social History* 51 (2006): 111–41. See also: Tabili, *"We Ask for British Justice,"* 45; Visram, *Asians in Britain*, 56.

36. Visram, *Asians in Britain*, 56; Tabili, *"We Ask for British Justice,"* 45–49.

37. Visram, *Asians in Britain*, 55–56; in fact, adds Tabili, Indian firemen's "high mortality and frequent disappearances, deaths from beri-beri, 'heat apoplexy', heart failure, 'dementia', and suicide, suggest that many men, particularly firemen, may literally have been worked to death." Tabili, *"We Ask for British Justice,"* 45.

38. Visram, *Asians in Britain*, 55.

39. Indian seamen who contemplated escape also faced the more informal social control of their Indian middlemen—both the *serangs* who were charged with watching and controlling Indian crews during each voyage and the *ghat serangs* in Indian home ports, who could harass Indian seamen's families if these men did not return from a voyage to pay off their debts. Ahuja, "Mobility and Containment," 116–17; 120–21; 132–35; United Kingdom, Board of Trade, British Merchant Shipping Act, Part 2, Sec. 169–83 (1894). For a first-person account of the disparities in the provisions for Indian and English and European sailors, see: Khan, *Chains to Lose*, 77–78.

40. Visram, *Asians in Britain*, 225–53; Tabili, *"We Ask for British Justice,"* esp. 81–112, 161–77; G. Balachandran, "South Asian Seafarers" (2003).

41. Khan, *Chains to Lose*, 76.

42. United Kingdom, India Office Records, Copy of Secret Letter, dated September 16, 1929, from the Commissioner of Police, Bombay, to the Deputy Director, Intelligence Bureau, Simla, P&J(S) 1769/1929.

43. Haji Shirajul Islam and Nawab Ali, interviewed in Caroline Adams, ed., *Across Seven Seas and Thirteen Rivers: Life Stories of Pioneer Sylheti Settlers in Britain* (London: Eastside Books, 1994), 95–96, 77. Haider Khan describes being approached when his ship docked in Vladivostok in 1915 by "an officer in a Czarist militia uniform who . . . asked in signs whether we had any American shoes to sell." Khan, *Chains to Lose*, 103.

44. Khan, *Chains to Lose*, 89.

45. Ibid., 101.

46. "Murder on the High Seas: Capt. Lyall Cut to Death by a Lascar Cook," *New York Times*, December 8, 1890, 9.

47. "Can't Keep Faith in Jail: Hindus Held for Murder, Ask to Be Allowed to Prepare Their Food," *New York Times*, July 19, 1913, 3.

48. "40 Rioting Lascars Fell Ship Officers," *New York Times*, November 9, 1930, 28.

49. Visram, *Asians in Britain*, 56–57.

50. Balachandran, "South Asian Seafarers" (2007), 191, 194–98; Tabili, *"We Ask for British Justice,"* esp.: 81–112, 161–77; Visram, *Asians in Britain*, 225–53.

51. Tabili, *"We Ask for British Justice,"* 137–38.

52. Balachandran, "South Asian Seafarers" (2007), 191.

53. Visram, *Asians in Britain*, 66, 68; Tabili, *"We Ask for British Justice,"* 140–45; Balachandran, "South Asian Seafarers" (2007), 197.

54. Visram has uncovered references as far back as the nineteenth century to British women who were married to or cohabited with Indian and other "coloured" sailors. Tabili writes that the women who entered into these relationships were largely from maritime families themselves—the daughters of sailors, dockworkers, and others connected to the trade. Because they were more likely to be literate in English and were more skillful in navigating state and city bureaucracies, these women came to play a number of crucial roles in the assimilation of Indian men into local economies and communities. See: Adams, *Across Seven Seas*, 73, 98, 184, 199–200; Tabili, *"We Ask for British Justice,"* 145; Visram, *Asians in Britain*, 68.

55. Visram, *Asians in Britain*, 196–97. Tabili points out that it was up to individual shipping companies to find and prosecute deserters, and while agents of these companies did canvass dockside areas in pursuit of deserting crew members, their willingness to expend resources on such efforts was limited, and police in localities farther removed from the site of desertion were not particularly concerned with how Indian men had entered the country. Tabili, *"We Ask for British Justice,"* 151.

56. Tabili, *"We Ask for British Justice,"* 140.

57. Ibid., 136–37.

58. Ibid., 121.

59. Ibid., 140–42.

60. Khan, *Chains to Lose*, 122–23; Visram, *Asians in Britain*, 208–09, 257; Adams, *Across Seven Seas*, 146–8.

61. Shah Abdul Majid Qureshi, in Adams, *Across Seven Seas*, 146, 148.

62. Tabili, *"We Ask for British Justice,"* xx; Ahuja, "Mobility and Containment," xx; UK/IOR: Government of Bombay, Marine Department Order No. 519 (March 15, 1920) and No. 1899 (November 20, 1920), IOR/P/10793, A 73–76, 243–48, 341–44.

63. "Why Lascars Were Left in the South—English Law, It Is Said, Did Not Permit Bringing Them North," *New York Tribune*, November 23, 1901, 16; U.S. Congress, House Committee on Merchant Marine and Fisheries, *Lascar Seamen Investigation*, 76th Cong., 1st Sess. (June 16, 1939), 2.

64. Roger Daniels, *The Politics of Prejudice: The Anti-Japanese Movement in California, and the Struggle for Japanese Exclusion* (Berkeley: University of California Press, 1962), 28; Hyman Weintraub, *Andrew Furuseth, Emancipator of the Seamen* (New York: Arno Press, 1979), 112; Asiatic Exclusion League, *Proceedings of the Asiatic Exclusion League, 1907–1913* (New York: Arno Press, 1977).

65. See Furuseth's testimony, for example, in U.S. Congress, House Committee on Immigration and Naturalization, *Alien Seamen and Stowaways: Hearings before the Committee on Immigration and Naturalization*, 62nd Cong., 1st Sess. (1912); U.S. Congress, House Committee on Immigration and Naturalization, *Deportation of Alien Seamen: Hearings before the Committee on Immigration and Naturalization*, 69th Cong., 1st Sess. (1926); U.S. Congress, House Committee on Immigration and Naturalization, *Deportation of Deserting Alien Seamen: Hearings before the Committee on Immigration and Naturalization*, 69th Cong., 2nd Sess. (1927).

66. "[N]o alien excluded from admission into the United States . . . and employed on board any vessel arriving in the United States," the law stated, "shall be permitted to land in the United States." U.S. Congress, *An Act to Regulate the Immigration of Aliens to, and the Residence of Aliens in, the United States*, H.R. 10384, Pub. L. 301, 39 Stat. 874, 64th Cong. (February 5, 1917).

67. Ibid.

68. Ahuja, "Mobility and Containment," 120–21, 132–35.

69. During this period, representatives of the shipping companies Ellerman and Bucknall, Graham and Company, the Hall Line, and the City Line lobbied the British government to lift the winter ban on Indian seamen entirely, but failed to sway the Board of Trade, who formally reaffirmed the ban in July 1920. In correspondence

dated February 6, 1920, the Hall Line revealed that they were still gaining dispensations to use Indian deck crews on North Atlantic voyages at the time of their writing. UK/IOR: IOR/P/10793, A 73–76, 243–48, 341–44.

70. The Ellerman Line appears most prominently in these records; they were running Indian-manned steamships back and forth between New York and various British ports throughout the late 1910s and early 1920s. The fact that Ellerman tended to employ Bengali seamen in greater numbers than others from the subcontinent may account for the higher percentage of Bengalis—as opposed to men from Punjab and the Northwest Frontier—among the ex-maritime populations in U.S. cities and factory towns. USDL/IS/LMAC, SS *Carmania*, January 1, 1919; SS *Kasama*, January 2, 1919; SS *Lowther Castle*, January 4, 1919; SS *Karimata*, January 6, 1919; SS *Kandahar*, January 10, 1919; SS *Clan Macintyre*, January 13, 1919; SS *Malancha*, January 17, 1919; SS *Clan Cunningham*, January 19, 1919.

71. USDL/IS/LMAC, SS *Carmania*, January 1, 1919; SS *Kasama*, January 2, 1919; SS *Lowther Castle*, January 4, 1919; SS *Karimata*, January 6, 1919; SS *Kandahar*, January 10, 1919; SS *Clan Macintyre*, January 13, 1919; SS *Malancha*, January 17, 1919; SS *Clan Cunningham*, January 19, 1919.

72. Based on an analysis of ships' records via search tools developed for the Ellis Island Arrivals Database by Dr. Stephen Morse, Gary Sandler, and Michael Tobias. The highest numbers were in 1918 (at the height, it appears, of the period in which the "lascar-line" provision was relaxed due to wartime shipping needs) and the lowest numbers were in the early 1920s, when the lascar line was reinstated and there was a worldwide slump in shipping. USDL/IS/LMAC, various, 1917–1924, accessed online via EllisIsland.org; Enhanced Ellis Island Database, accessed April 2–4, 2007, http://stevemorse.org/ellis2/ellisgold.html.

73. Robin Dearmon Jenkins, "African Americans," and Drew Philip Havély, "Mobilization (U.S.)," in James D. Ciment and Thaddeus Russell, *The Home Front Encyclopedia: United States, Britain, and Canada in World Wars I and II* (Santa Barbara: ABC-CLIO, 2006) 214, 389–91.

74. "Strikers Migrate to Take Rail Jobs," *New York Times*, July 12, 1922, 2; Khan, *Chains to Lose*, 126–28, 307, 314–15.

75. He was luckier than many of these men; after five months, he was fired from the job and sent back to Manhattan after he talked back to a superior. Khan, *Chains to Lose*, 126–28, 130–32.

76. "Rail Shop Strike at Deadlock Here," *New York Times*, July 9, 1922, 2; "Strikers Migrate," 1–2; Khan, *Chains to Lose*, 307.

77. In the only official statement by federal authorities, the *Times* reported that the "Assistant Immigration Commissioner said that there had been 'no attempt to round up Hindus at Jersey City or anywhere else' by his agents." "Strikers Migrate," 2.

78. "New York Has a Malay Colony," *Duluth News Tribune*, reprinted from *New York Post*, November 23, 1900.

79. USDC/BC, *U.S. Census, 1920 and 1930: Population Schedules*, See *infra* note 84; Khan, *Chains to Lose*, 121–26, 306–10; UK/FOC: FO371/5675 (A3331, A4156); FO371/9614 (A2858); FO371/11169 (A2383); Habib Ullah Jr., interview by the au-

thor, New York, NY, October 2004; Helen Ullah, interview by the author, Fort Lauderdale, FL, 2008; John Ali Jr., interviews by the author, May and July 2011. These networks and onshore worlds communities mirror those which had formed in Britain in the same period, particularly in the roles played by boardinghouses, other ex-seamen and their wives. See: Tabili, *"We Ask for British Justice,"* 135-50.

80. USDC/BC, *U.S. Census, 1920: Population Schedules*, Hillsboro Township, New Jersey, SD204/ED129/Sh23A/23B/57B; Bethlehem City, Pennsylvania, SD7/ED82/Sh3B/9B; Chester City, Pennsylvania, W3/P2/SD2/ED123/Sh2A, 9B; Youngstown, Ohio, W2/PD/SD265/ED157/Sh6A; W2/PH/SD265/ED161/Sh7B, 8A; Detroit City, Michigan, W3/SD145/ED90/Sh4A, 4B, 10B; W11/SD145/ED327/Sh6A, 7B; ED705/Sh3A; ED791/Sh7B; USDC/BC, *U.S. Census, 1930: Population Schedules*, Lackawanna, New York, W1/SD7/ED15-420/Sh3A, 8B, 9A, 9B; Dearborn City, Michigan, P13/SD18/ED82-896/Sh42B; Detroit City, Michigan, W1/SD21/ED8/Sh8A; W3/SD21/ED64/Sh2A, 4A, 4B, 5A, 10B; W5/SD21/ED113/Sh7A, 8A; John Ali Jr., interviews.

81. City of Lackawanna, New York, USA, *History of the City of Lackawanna*, accessed May 3, 2012, http://www.ci.lackawanna.ny.us/ history.html.

82. USDC/BC, *U.S. Census, 1920: Population Schedules*, Lackawanna, NY, W1/SD21/ED306/Sh43B, 53A, 62B.

83. USSS/DRC WWI, Local Registration Board, Erie County, NY, various; see especially the record for Hasmatula Serang.

84. USDC/BC, *U.S. Census, 1930: Population Schedules*, Lackawanna, NY, W1/SD7/ED15-420/Sh3A, 8B, 9A, 9B; Dearborn City, MI, P13/SD18/ED82-896/Sh42B; Detroit City, Michigan, W1/SD21/ED8/Sh8A; W3/SD21/ED64/Sh2A, 4A, 4B, 5A, 10B; W5/SD21/ED113/Sh7A, 8A.

85. 1920 and 1930 census records show a constellation of Indian shared houses and boarding houses on East Monroe, Lafayette, Fort and Congress Streets, between Brush and Hastings Streets. Amir Haider Khan describes arriving in Detroit in 1925 to find many of the ex-seamen he had known in New York City five years before, and details the role of one "educated Indian" employed by Ford who acted as a kind of agent, placing ex-seamen in assembly-line work. USDC/BC, *U.S. Census, 1920: Population Schedules*, Detroit City, Michigan, W3/SD145/ED90/Sh4A, 4B, 10B; W11/SD145/ED327/Sh6A, 7B; ED705/Sh3A; ED791/Sh7B; USDC/BC, *U.S. Census, 1930: Population Schedules*, Detroit City, Michigan, W1/SD21/ED8/Sh8A; W3/SD21/ED64/Sh2A, 4A, 4B, 5A, 10B; W5/SD21/ED113/Sh7A, 8A; Khan, *Chains to Lose*, 390-92. See also British intelligence reports on the clandestine network connecting the New York City waterfront with Lackawanna, Youngstown, and Detroit: FO371/9614 (A2858).

86. USDC/BC, *U.S. Census, 1920 and 1930: Population Schedules*, Detroit City, Michigan, (see *supra* note 90); Jeremy Williams, *Detroit: The Black Bottom Community* (Charleston: Arcadia, 2009), 17, 31-3, 36; Ernest H. Borden, *Detroit's Paradise Valley* (Charleston: Arcadia, 2003), 12-14.

87. Khan, *Chains to Lose*, 391.

88. USDC/BC, *U.S. Census, 1930: Population Schedules*, Detroit City, Michigan, (see *supra* note 90).

89. Ali, interviews.

90. Ali, interviews; Helen Ullah, interview; Qureshi, in Adams, *Across Seven Seas, 146, 148.*

91. Tabili, *"We Ask for British Justice,"* 46; Visram, *Asians in Britain,* 56.

92. Helen Ullah, interview; Khan, *Chains to Lose,* 133, 306–10; Habib Ullah Jr., interview by the author, Fort Lauderdale, Florida, 2008. See also: Tabili, *"We Ask for British Justice,"* 135–50.

93. Helen Ullah, interview; Noor Chowdry, interview by the author, Los Angeles, CA, January 2006; Habib Ullah Jr., interview, 2004; Khan, *Chains to Lose,* 121–26, 306–10; UK/FOC: FO371/5675 (A3331, A4156); FO371/9614 (A2858); FO371/11169 (A2383).

94. Khan, *Chains to Lose,* 122–24.

95. Ibid., 122–32, 166. Dada Khan writes ironically that he was guided through the process of "renouncing my position as a British subject" by a British seaman. The loophole he used was a recurring theme of International Seamen's Union president Andrew Furuseth in testimony before Congress in the 1910s and 1920s. Furuseth's insistence that the loophole be closed was part of the labor leader's long-running crusade to keep Chinese and Indian seamen out of the United States. See his testimony in U.S. Congress, House Committee on Immigration and Naturalization, *Alien Seamen and Stowaways: Hearings before the Committee on Immigration and Nationalization,* 62nd Cong., 1st Sess. (1912); U.S. Congress, House Committee on Immigration and Naturalization, *Deportation of Alien Seamen: Hearings before the Committee on Immigration and Nationalization,* 69th Cong., 1st Sess. (1926); U.S. Congress, House Committee on Immigration and Naturalization, *Deportation of Deserting Alien Seamen: Hearings before the Committee on Immigration and Nationalization,* 69th Cong., 2nd Sess. (1927).

96. Khan, *Chains to Lose,* 123.

97. Ibid., 122–23, 141; Cheryl Lynn Greenberg, *"Or Does It Explode?" Black Harlem in the Great Depression* (New York: Oxford University Press, 1991), 22.

98. Gilbert Osofsky, *Harlem, the Making of a Ghetto: Negro New York, 1890–1930* (New York: Harper and Row, 1966), 12–13, 46–50; Cheryl D. Hicks, *Talk with You Like a Woman: African American Women, Justice, and Reform in New York, 1890–1935* (Chapel Hill: University of North Carolina Press, 2010), 59, 68–79, 88; USDC/BC, *Census of the United States, 1920: Population Schedules* for New York, NY, SD 1., ED 295 and 777, records for West 36th, 37th and 38th Streets (various addresses).

99. USDC/BC, *Census of the United States, 1920: Population Schedules* for New York, NY, records for 672 Eighth Avenue, 236 West 61st Street, 254 West 41st Street, 266 West 38th Street, 324 West 43rd Street, 330 West 59th Street, 439 West 36th Street; *Census of the United States, 1930: Population Schedules* for New York, NY, records for 253, 778 and 780 Eighth Avenue, 393 West 29th Street, 533 West 29th Street; USSS/DRC WWI, Local Registration Board, New York, NY, Registration Cards for Abdul Mohammed, Ali Allihassan, Amir Haider Atta Mohammed, Abdul Aziz, Abraham Pira, A. Hussaine, S. M. D. Pereira, Stanley Lionel, Jacob Joseph; Khan, *Chains to Lose,* 215–16, 278–86.

100. Khan, *Chains to Lose*, 166–67.

101. Ibid., 306–10.

102. USDC/BC, *Census of the United States, 1920: Population Schedules* for Detroit City, Michigan, W3/SD145/ED90/Sh4A, 4B, 10B; W11/SD145/ED327/Sh6A, 7B; ED705/Sh3A; ED791/Sh7B; USDC/BC, *Census of the United States, 1930: Population Schedules* for Detroit City, Michigan, W1/SD21/ED8/Sh8A; W3/SD21/ED64/Sh2A, 4A, 4B, 5A, 10B; W5/SD21/ED113/Sh7A, 8A.

103. Ahuja, "Networks of Subordination," 27–28; Adams, *Across Seven Seas*, 72–73, 98, 117, 150–51; Khan, *Chains to Lose*, 133, 154–55, 306–10.

104. USDC/BC, *Census of the United States, 1930: Population Schedules* for Detroit City, Michigan, W3/SD21/ED64/Sh2A, 4A, 4B, 5A, 10B.

105. USDC/BC, *Census of the United States: 1920: Population Schedules* for Chester, PA, records for 27, 33, and 38 Graham Street; USDC/BC, *Census of the United States: 1930: Population Schedules* for Chester, PA, record for 524 Front Street; Ali, interviews.

106. Ali, interviews.

107. Ibid.

108. Letter from Agnes Smedley, Friends of Freedom for India to Santokh Singh, Ghadr Party, San Francisco, Sep 30, 1920, Kartar Dhillon Papers, in possession of Professor Vijay Prashad, Trinity College, Hartford, Connecticut.

109. Ali, interviews.

110. Ibid.

111. "Hold Six Indian Seamen Here for Alleged Mutiny," *Afro-American*, August 1, 1925, 9.

112. See, for example: Sudarshan Kapur, *Raising Up a Prophet: The African-American Encounter with Gandhi* (Boston: Beacon Press, 1992); Gerald Horne, *The End of Empires: African Americans and India* (Philadelphia: Temple University Press, 2009); Nico Slate, *Colored Cosmopolitanism: The Shared Struggle for Freedom in the United States and India* (Cambridge: Harvard University Press, 2012).

4. THE TRAVELS AND TRANSFORMATIONS OF AMIR HAIDER KHAN

1. Among those who know of his life and work, Amir Haider Khan is often referred to, with both respect and affection, using the honorific "Dada." I use the honorific here periodically in this same sense, but out of consistencey with the rest of the book, I will, through most of the chapter, refer to Dada Khan using his surname, Khan. I use Dada Khan's full name, without "Dada," in the title of the chapter, because the chapter title is meant to refer to the historic Amir Haider Khan—that is, the young man, before he returned to India to join the independence struggle.

2. Dada Amir Haider Khan, *Chains to Lose: Life and Struggles of a Revolutionary*, ed. Hasan Gardezi (New Delhi: Patriot Publishers, 1989), 130–32.

3. Ibid., 314–15.

4. Ibid., 128.

5. Ibid., 131, 141, 144, 157, 169, 218, 258.

6. Maia Ramnath, *Haj to Utopia: How the Ghadar Movement Charted Global Radicalism and Attempted to Overthrow the British Empire* (Berkeley: University of California

Press, 2011), 95–115; Joan M. Jensen, *Passage from India: Asian Indian Immigrants in North America* (New Haven, CT: Yale University Press, 1988), 19–20, 168, 241–42. (New Haven, CT: Yale University Press, 1988), 19–20, 168, 241–42; Michael Silvestri, *Ireland and India: Nationalism, Empire and Memory* (London: Palgrave Macmillan, 2009), 13–45; Harold A. Gould, *Sikhs, Swamis, Students, and Spies: The India Lobby in the United States, 1900–1946* (New Delhi: Sage Publications, 2006), 231–260; UK/FOC: FO371/5675 (A3331, A4156); FO371/9614 (A2858); FO371/11169 (A2383).

7. L. P. Mathur, *Indian Revolutionary Movement in the United States of America* (Delhi: S. Chand, 1970); Jensen, *Passage from India*; Harold A. Gould, *Sikhs, Swamis, Students, and Spies: The India Lobby in the United States, 1900–1946* (New Delhi: Sage Publications, 2006); Seema Sohi, "Echoes of Mutiny: Race, Empire, and Indian Revolutionaries on the Pacific Coast" (PhD diss., University of Washington, 2007) Ramnath, *Haj to Utopia*. British concerns about Ghose's relationship to the Indian seafaring population originally centered on suspicions that the FFI was recruiting seamen in New York to smuggle guns and pamphlets back to India. In 1919–1920, British authorities were watching an Egyptian boardinghouse keeper and maritime employment agent named Mohammed Abdou, whom they suspected of working in concert with the FFI in New York City to place their "agents" on outgoing ships. Abdou was accused of aiding groups of seamen to desert British ships in port so he could place other seamen on board these ships in his role as an employment agent. For a brief period in 1922 authorities at the India Office in London suspected that Ghose himself was intending to take things a step further by opening his own shipping employment agency in New York as a front for the smuggling of these materials. It is unclear whether this was simply a rumor that put British authorities in a panic or something Ghose was indeed contemplating. It does seem that there were quite a few Indian seamen transporting small arms back to the subcontinent in the 1920s and that the authorities were having a difficult time policing this trade. The correspondence running between the India Office, the Foreign Office, the Colonial Government in India, and various British Consuls in North America and Europe about the smuggling of small arms by seamen was quite extensive. It includes records, for example, of the arrests of Indian seamen caught bringing arms into India that they allegedly purchased in European ports such as Marseilles and Antwerp. Some of these seamen who were transporting a pistol or two at a time may have been doing so merely as a way of supplementing their pitiful wages through this and other types of black marketeering. For others, it was clearly a form of engagement in the independence struggle. UK/FOC: FO371/5675 (A3331, A4156); FO371/9614 (A2858); FO371/11169 (A2383); Mr. Ferrard (India Office) to R. Sperling, Esquire (Foreign Office), FO371/7300 (A7068); UK/IOL, Copy of Secret Letter, dated September 16, 1929, from the Commissioner of Police, Bombay, to the Deputy Director, Intelligence Bureau, Simla, P&J(S) 1769/1929.

8. Khan, *Chains to Lose*, 94-7.

9. Ibid., 151–52.

10. Ibid.

11. Ibid., 207.

12. Because Khan wrote this first volume of his memoir while being held in a British colonial jail, it is likely that he purposely withheld the name of this "Ghadr Sikh" in in order to protect him.

13. Khan, *Chains to Lose*, 210.

14. Ibid., 211.

15. Ibid., 211–14. It should be noted that, while Dada Khan was sensitive enough to re-mark upon the gendered division of labor with regard to the considerable work of or-ganizing the FFI's conference, his failure to comment critically on the use of the orga-nization's female volunteers as sexualized and exoticized lures for fund-raising—or for that matter, to recognize the gendered nature of his new sense of revolutionary camaraderie as he strode down the city streets "in the company of representatives of the Gadar Party"—perhaps shows the limits of his critique of gendered power relations at the time he wrote this part of his memoir in the 1940s.

16. Khan, *Chains to Lose*, 216.

17. The copies of *Ghadar di Gunj* that the "Ghadr Sikh" gave Khan, he writes, "con-tained very simple revolutionary poems, direct appeals for action, in Punjabi Urdu which could be understood even by illiterate persons. I used to recite them to my-self whenever I was alone. They helped instill in me a burning patriotism, a will to action, no matter how risky." Khan, *Chains to Lose*, 216.

18. Ibid., 217–18.

19. Ibid., 148.

20. Ibid., 140.

21. Ibid., 140–41.

22. Ibid., 140.

23. Ibid., 313–14.

24. "I wanted to get away from the waterfront and everything associated with it," he writes. Ibid., 314.

25. Ibid., 322–23.

26. Ibid., 327–29.

27. Michael A. Gomez, *Black Crescent: The Experience and Legacy of African Muslims in the Americas* (Cambridge: Cambridge University Press, 2005), 259–60. See also: Richard Brent Turner, *Islam in the African American Experience* (Bloomington: University of Indiana Press, 2003), 83–90. While Duse Mohamed Ali is often cred-ited with having founded the Universal Islamic Society in 1926, both Dada Khan's account and records of incorporation suggest that the organization dates to the fall of 1925. Khan, *Chains to Lose*, 422–24. Duse Mohammed Ali's own account, that he was invited to Detroit by "some Indian Muslims . . . in New York" to help them in "establishing a prayer room with a regular system of weekly prayers," suggests that members of the ex-maritime community may have had a hand in the beginnings of Duse Mohamed's Detroit activities. Khambiz GhaneaBassiri, *A History of Islam in America* (Cambridge: Cambridge Universiy Press, 2010), 206.

28. For a detailed account of the Ossian Sweet case, see Kevin Boyle, *Arc of Justice: A Saga of Race, Civil Rights, and Murder in the Jazz Age* (New York: Henry Holt, 2004).

29. UK/FOC: Dispatch from British Consul, Detroit, MI to the Rt. Hon. Austen Chamberlain, M.P., His Majesty's Principal Secretary for Foreign Affairs, Foreign Office, London, England, Dec 2, 1925, FO 371/10639 (A6330). See also: UK/FOC, Dispatch from British Consulate, Detroit, MI to the British Embassy, Washington, D.C., September 25, 1929, FO 371/13534 (A6872).
30. Khan, *Chains to Lose*, 415–16.
31. Turner, *Islam in the African American Experience*, 83.
32. Khan, *Chains to Lose*, 417.
33. Ibid., 420–21.

5. BENGALI HARLEM

1. Habib Ullah Jr., interviews by the author, New York, 2004, 2005, and Fort Lauderdale, FL, 2008; Noor Chowdry, interview by the author, Los Angeles, CA, 2006.
2. Habib Ullah Jr., interviews; Noor Chowdry, interview; Masud Choudhury, interviews by the author, New York, 2004, 2006, 2008; Luz Maria (Echevarria) Caballero, interview by the author, Miami, FL, January 2008.
3. Gilbert Osofsky, *Harlem, the Making of a Ghetto: Negro New York, 1890–1930* (New York: Harper and Row, 1966), 34.
4. Osofsky, *Harlem*, 71, 77–80, 87–93; Cheryl Lynn Greenberg, *"Or Does It Explode?" Black Harlem in the Great Depression* (New York: Oxford University Press, 1991), 13–15.
5. Greenberg, *"Or Does It Explode?"* 18–26, 69–74. See also: Cheryl D. Hicks, *Talk With You Like a Woman: African American Women, Justice, and Reform in New York, 1890–1935* (Charlotte: University of North Carolina Press, 2010), 23–52.
6. Osofsky, *Harlem*, 32, 135; Jesse Hoffnung-Garskof, "The World of Arturo Alfonso Schomburg," in Miriam Jiménez Roman and Juan Flores, eds., *The Afro-Latin@ Reader: History and Culture in the United States* (Durham: Duke University Press, 2010), 79–81.
7. Hoffnung-Garskof, "The World of Arturo Alfonso Schomburg," 70–72, 79–81; Winston James, *Holding Aloft the Banner of Ethiopia: Caribbean Radicalism in Early Twentieth Century America* (London: Verso, 1998), 122–84.
8. USSS/DRC WWI, Local Registration Board, New York, NY, Certificate of Registration for Shooleiman Collu.
9. USDC/BC, *U.S. Census, 1920: Population Schedules* for New York, NY (various).
10. Other Indian men were scattered across the rest of Central Harlem, stretching all the way up to West 141st Street and St. Nicholas Avenue. USDC/BC, *U.S. Census, 1930: Population Schedule* for New York, NY (various addresses).
11. Irma Watkins-Owens. *Blood Relations: Caribbean Immigrants and the Harlem Community, 1900–1930* (Bloomington: Indiana University Press, 1996), 201n31.
12. New York City Department of Health, *Certificates of Marriage*, 1922–1937, New York City Municipal Archives, New York, NY.
13. "Issue Recently," *New York Amsterdam News*, June 15, 1927, 17.

14. "To Wed East Indian," *New York Amsterdam News*, February 24, 1932, 9.

15. "Newlyweds Feted," *New York Amsterdam News*, April 27, 1935, 7.

16. "Bigamist Sentenced to Term in Prison," *New York Amsterdam News*, March 1, 1933, 14.

17. "Out for Good Time; Loses $140," *New York Amsterdam News*, March 10, 1926, 1; "City News Briefs—Harlem Court," *New York Amsterdam News*, April 9, 1930, 8; "City News Briefs—Harlem Court," *New York Amsterdam News*, April 23, 1930, 5; "Runs Amok with Gun," *New York Amsterdam News*, November 19, 1930, 2.

18. USDC/BC, *U.S. Census, 1930: Population Schedule* for New York, NY (various addresses).

19. USDC/BC, *U.S. Census, 1930: Population Schedule* for New York, NY, Block A, Sup. Dist. 24, Enum. Dist. 31-909, Sheet No. 10B; Ward 17AD; Block D, Sup. Dist. 23, Enum. Dist. 31-786, Sheet No. 31A; Block D, Sup. Dist. 24, Enum. Dist. 31-922, Sheet No. 6B.

20. Helen Ullah, interview by the author, Miami, FL, January 2008; Felita Ullah, interview by the author, Fort Lauderdale, FL, January 2008.

21. Helen Ullah, interview; Habib Ullah Jr., interview, 2005.

22. New York City, *City Directory, 1915–16*, Municipal Archives, New York, NY.

23. "Restaurants Adopt Scale," *New York Amsterdam News*, September 6, 1933, 3.

24. "Meet the 'Curry King' at India's Garden Inn" (advertisement), *New York Amsterdam News*, January 12, 1946, 18.

25. "Now Open—Pakistan India Restaurant" (advertisement), *New York Amsterdam News*, March 4, 1950, 18.

26. Sara Slack, "In the Midst of Harlem: East Indian Dishes Feature of New Shop," *New York Amsterdam News*, March 16, 1957, 18; "Bombay India Restaurant" (advertisement), *New York Amsterdam News*, May 3, 1958, 15.

27. Masud Choudhury, interview, 2004; Alaudin Ullah, interview by the author, New York, December 2006; Habib Ullah Jr., interview, 2005.

28. Miriam Christian, interview by the author, New York, 1996.

29. Sekou Sundiata, interview by the author, Brooklyn, New York, May 2007.

30. Paul Tingen's biography, *Miles Beyond,* describes a series of meetings between Davis and Mtume in 1972 at a restaurant that was almost certainly the Eshad Ali's: "Miles and I would often go to this restaurant at 125th Street in Harlem," Mtume says, "and discuss some of the influences he was hearing. It was an Indian restaurant, and obviously they were playing Indian music, and it was at that point that he was telling me about the idea of using the electric sitar and tablas." Paul Tingen, *Miles Beyond: The Electric Explorations of Miles Davis, 1967–1991* (New York: Watson-Guptill, 2001), 130.

31. Alaudin Ullah, interview, 2006.

32. Dada Amir Haider Khan, *Chains to Lose: Life and Struggles of a Revolutionary* (New Delhi: Patriot Publishers, 1989), 215.

33. It is unclear exactly when the Ceylon moved, but it was sometime between mid-1923, when records show that K. Y. Kira's wife, Elizabeth, took out a twenty-one-year lease on the West Forty-Ninth Street address, and mid-1925, when articles in the

New York Times indicate that another restaurant, the Garden of India, had occupied the Ceylon's former location on Eighth Avenue. Interestingly, the *Times* articles described a meeting of expatriate radicals at the Garden of India, in which Mahatma Gandhi "was condemned as a coward, and an armed revolution was advocated." This was in contrast with the meetings held at the Ceylon India Inn at its new location, which were very much in support of Gandhi's leadership and strategies back on the subcontinent. *New York Times*, "Commercial Space Leased—Two West Side Midtown Buildings in Long Term Leases," *New York Times*, July 12, 1923, 29; "Indians Here Want Revolution," *New York Times*, June 29, 1925, 2; "Buddhist Upbraids Western Christians," *New York Times*, December 21, 1925, 24; "Hail Policies of Gandhi," *New York Times*, December 5, 1930, 19.

34. "Opens Today—The Outstanding Restaurant Creation of the Century" (advertisement for Longchamps Restaurants), *New York Times*, October 4, 1935, 2; "Where Everybody Goes to See Everybody Else" (advertisement for Longchamps Restaurants), *New York Times*, October 17, 1936, 3; "Ceylon India Inn" (advertisement), *New York Times*, May 25, 1938, 26.

35. "Sarat Lahiri—Hindu Musician was Actor and Proprietor of Restaurant" (obituary), *New York Times*, May 6, 1941, 21; "The Rajah Restaurant—Delicious Curries, Bombay Cooking" (advertisement), *New York Times*, June 12, 1927, X9; "To Mark Gandhi Birthday," *New York Times*, October 10, 1939, 28; "News of Food," *New York Times*, February 7, 1949, 23; "News of Food," *New York Times*, September 1, 1953, 20; Clementine Paddleford, "The Real Thing! These Curry Recipes Come Straight from India. Try Them . . . ," *Los Angeles Times*, October 15, 1944, E20; Charlotte Hughes, "For Gourmets and Others: Curry Comes to the Table," *New York Times*, March 12, 1939, 53; USDCL/LMAP: SS *Rotterdam*, January 26, 1923.

36. Sekou Sundiata, interview, 2007.

37. Luz Maria Caballero, interview by the author, Miami, FL, January 2008; In earlier editions, Zubeida's name was listed as Humaira.

38. Habib Ullah Jr., interview, 2008.

39. Ibid., 2004, 2005, 2008; Noor Chowdry, interview, 2006.

40. Habib Ullah Jr., interview, 2008.

41. In a 1946 advertisement in the *Amsterdam News*, the proprietors of India's Garden Inn at Manhattan Avenue and West 121st Street listed themselves as "Seenandan and Persad." Neither are names that would have been common among Muslim seamen from Bengal or Punjab, and the latter, "Persad" is a spelling that is used predominantly in the Caribbean. Ship records indeed do show that at least one Persad family had migrated to Central Harlem from British Guiana by way of Trinidad in the 1920s and was living there, at 2323 Seventh Avenue at the corner of West 136th Street. One member of this family, Andrew Persad, later associated with Ibrahim Choudry and some of the city's other Bengalis and may have been the proprietor of India's Garden Inn. "Meet the 'Curry King' at India's Garden Inn" (advertisement), *New York Amsterdam News*, January 12, 1946, 18; USDCL/LMAP, SS *Vandyck*, March 7, 1924, SS *Voltaire*, June 28, 1924; "Memorial Meet Honors Late Y. Meherally," *New York Amsterdam News*, August 19, 1950, 14.

42. Habib Ullah Jr., interviews, 2005, 2008.

43. Ibid., 2008.

44. Ibid.

45. On the Khilafat Movement, see Gail Minault, *The Khilafat Movement: Religious Symbolism and Political Mobilization in India* (New York: Columbia University Press, 1982); M. Qureshi, *Pan-Islam in British Indian Politics: A Study of the Khilafat Movement, 1918–1924* (Boston: Brill Publications, 1999).

46. Masud Choudhury, interview, 2004.

47. USDC/SDNY, *Petition of Naturalization* for Abraham Choudry formerly Ibrahim Choudry also known as Ibrahim Chawdry, Petition No. 582344, November 1, 1949.

48. Ibid; Laily Chowdry, interview by the author, by phone, May, 2012.

49. UK/FOC, FO 371/42909-42911.

50. The report also included details of the food served in the dining hall. Breakfast consisted of a simple menu of cereal, fruit, eggs, toast, rice, and tea or coffee, while the midday dinner included "Curried fish, beef, or chicken" and an evening supper "Curry and salad, cake, tea or coffee." UK/FOC, *Quarterly Report on Operations, Statement of Accounts, and Estimated Expenditures and Receipts, British Merchant Navy Club for Indian Seamen, New York,* June 1, 1944, FO 371/42909/W9435.

51. UK/FOC, FO 371/42909-42911.

52. "Events of Interest in Shipping World—Club Aids Indian Seamen," *New York Times*, May 28, 1944, 34.

53. UK/FOC, *Quarterly Report.*

54. Noor Chowdry, interview, 2005.

55. Ibid. Choudry was also the organization's first president.

56. U.S. Congress, House Committee on Immigration and Naturalization (hereafter USC/HCIN), *To Grant a Quota to Eastern Hemisphere Indians and to Make Them Racially Eligible for Naturalization: Hearings before the Committee on Immigration and Naturalization on H.R. 173, H.R. 1584, H.R. 1624, H.R. 1746, H.R. 2256, H.R. 2609,* 79th Cong., 1st Sess., March 7–14, 1945, 76–77, 144–46. In the latter pages of the transcript of the hearings, Choudry is listed as secretary of the India Association for American Citizenship on various letters of support that the association submitted for inclusion in the official record of the hearings.

57. "Pakistan Leader Speaker—Urges Countrymen Not to Desert Their Ships Here," *New York Times*, July 7, 1948, 5; "Freedom of India Celebrated Here—Pakistan League Dinner Also Observes End of First Year Since British Release," *New York Times*, August 16, 1948, 8.

58. Habib Ullah Jr., interviews, 2004, 2005, 2008; "Freedom of India Celebrated Here"; "Events Today," *New York Times*, February 20, 1949, 64; Gerri Major, "Town Topics—Tribute to Lincoln," *New York Amsterdam News*, February 10, 1951, 10; "Pakistan Group to Honor Sen. Langer," *New York Amsterdam News*, February 19, 1949, 32; "Sen. Langer Is Honored by Pakistanis," *New York Amsterdam News*, March 3, 1951, 18; "League Hears Dr. Ali Khan," *New York Amsterdam News*, June 23, 1951, 22. The lobbying of Senator Langer and others in Congress by members of New York's Bengali/Pakistani community appears to have given rise to a separate group connected to the Pakistan League, which took on the name "The Non-Partisan League." On J. J. Singh's style of lobbying, see Harold A. Gould, *Sikhs,*

Swamis, Students, and Spies: The India Lobby in the United States, 1900–1946 (New Delhi: Sage Publications, 2006), 308–09, 316–20.

59. "Sen. Langer Is Honored By Pakistanis."

60. Samir Abed-Rabbo, "The Neglected Focus," *Journal of the Institute of Muslim Minority Affairs* 5, No. 1 (1984): 64–66.

61. "Moslem Leader, Honored at Dinner, Urges Unity," *New York Amsterdam News*, August 19, 1950, 13.

62. Later in the 1950s, according to Clegg, Dawud became "the most belligerent critic of the legitimacy of the Nation of Islam as an Islamic movement." Claude Andrew Clegg, *An Original Man: The Life and Times of Elijah Muhammad* (New York: St. Martin's Griffin, 1998), 132. See also: Yvonne Yazbeck Haddad and Jane I. Smith, *Muslim Minorities in the West: Visible and Invisible* (Lanham, MD: Altamira Press, 2002), 79. Ibrahim Choudry was also described as the "Secretary of the Muslim Brotherhood of the United States" in an item in the *Amsterdam News* the next year, though it is not clear whether this was actually the case. "Town Topics," *New York Amsterdam News*, June 9, 1951, 18.

63. "M. Chowdhury Heads Local Pakistan League," *New York Amsterdam News*, December 2, 1950, 20.

64. "Moslem Leader, Honored at Dinner, Urges Unity," *New York Amsterdam News*, August 19, 1950, 13; "Muslim Leader at Town Hall, September 10," *New York Amsterdam News*, September 2, 1950, 13.

65. Gerri Major, "Town Topics," *New York Amsterdam News*, June 9, 1951, 18; "Moslems Observe Day of Sacrifice," *New York Times*, September 1, 1952, 28; Habib Ullah Jr., interviews, 2004, 2008; Alaudin Ullah, interviews, 2005, 2006, 2008. It took more than twenty years, but Choudry and the others he had enlisted within the Muslim community eventually succeeded in establishing the Madina Mosque on First Avenue and East Eleventh Street in Manhattan, in the neighborhood now known as the East Village. It is still one of the most active mosques in the city, although it is now threatened by the gentrification of the neighborhood.

66. "A Call to Prayer for Peace in the Holy Land" (paid advertisement), *New York Times*, April 20, 1956, 14; "Group Hits Jailing of Virginia Ministers," *New York Amsterdam News*, April 23, 1960, 5.

67. "Muslims Open New Center for Children," *New York Amsterdam News*, March 1, 1958, 10. On Shaykh Daoud Ahmed Faisal, see: Turner, *Islam and the African American Experience*, 120. Choudry's connection to Faisal may have gone beyond the organizational in the sense that Faisal's wife and cofounder of the Islamic Mission, Mother Khadijah Faisal, according to Turner, was of mixed South Asian and Afro-Caribbean ancestry. When Khadijah Faisal died at the age of ninety-three in 1992, her obituary in the *New York Times* noted that she was born in Barbados. "She and her husband," the *Times* wrote, "worked to bring immigrant Muslims and new American converts to the faith together in one mosque. The success of their effort was evident at her funeral there yesterday, where Muslims from Pakistan and Morocco prayed shoulder to shoulder with American black converts." "Sayedah Khadijah Faisal Is Dead—Co-Founder of Mosque Was 93," *New York Times*, September 10, 1992.

6. THE LIFE AND TIMES OF A MULTIRACIAL COMMUNITY

1. Helen Ullah, interview by the author, Fort Lauderdale, FL, 2008.
2. Ibid.
3. USDC/BC, *United States Census, 1930: Population Schedules* for New York, NY (various addresses); Helen Ullah, interview; Luz Maria Caballero, interview by the author, Miami, FL, January 2008; Felita Ullah, interview by the author, Fort Lauderdale, FL, January 2008.
4. Although he shared the common surname Ullah with Habib and a number of other Bengali ex-seamen in New York City, Saad was not related to Habib or any of these others. He had no relations in the United States when he left his ship in Baltimore.
5. Helen Ullah, interview.
6. Ibid.
7. Ibid.
8. Ibid.
9. Ibid.
10. Masud Choudhury, interviews by the author, New York, NY, April 2005, July 2008; Alaudin Ullah, interviews by the author, New York, NY, April 2005, August 2006; Habib Ullah Jr., interview by the author, New York, NY, October 2004, April 2005; Habib Ullah Jr., interview by the author, Fort Lauderdale, FL, January 2008.
11. Helen Ullah, interview; Luz Maria Caballero, interview; Laily Chowdry, interview by the author, by phone, May, 2012.
12. Noor Chowdry, interview by the author, Los Angeles, CA, January 2006; Helen Ullah, interview; Habib Ullah Jr., interviews, 2004, 2005; Alaudin Ullah, interview by the author, New York, NY, October 2004; Alaudin Ullah, interviews, 2005, 2006.
13. Habib Ullah Jr., interviews, 2004, 2005, 2008; Noor Chowdry, interview. See also "Moslems in New York Gather for Prayer," *New York Times*, June 25, 1952, 4.
14. Noor Chowdry, interview, 2006.
15. Habib Ullah Jr., interview, 2005, interview by the author, by phone, May 2012; Helen Ullah, interview.
16. Habib Ullah Jr., interview, 2008.
17. Helen Ullah, interview; Laily Chowdry, interview.
18. Habib Ullah Jr., interview, 2005.
19. Ibid.
20. Noor Chowdry, interview, 2006.
21. Helen Ullah, interview; Habib Ullah Jr., interview, 2008.
22. Noor Chowdry, interview, 2006.
23. Habib Ullah Jr., interview, 2005.
24. Habib Ullah Jr., interview, 2008; Noor Chowdry, interview, 2006.
25. Noor Chowdry, interview, 2006.
26. Ibid.; Habib Ullah Jr., interview, 2004.
27. Patricia Hampson Eget, "Challenging Containment: African Americans and Racial Politics in Montclair, NJ, 1920–1940," *New Jersey History* 126, no. 1 (2011): 1–17; Habib Ullah Jr., interview, 2004.
28. Habib Ullah Jr., interviews, 2004, 2005.

29. Habib Ullah Jr., interview, 2004.

30. Ibid.

31. Felita Ullah, interview by the author, by phone, May 2012.

32. Habib Ullah Jr., interviews, 2004, 2008; Habib Ullah Jr., interview by the author, by phone, May 2012; Alaudin Ullah, interviews, 2005, 2006, 2008; Noor Chowdry, interview, 2006; Laily Chowdry, interview.

33. Habib Ullah Jr., interview, 2005; Alaudin Ullah, interviews, 2005, 2006.

34. Michel De Certeau, *The Practice of Everyday Life* (Berkeley: University of California Press, 1984), 130.

35. Maxine P. Fisher, *The Indians of New York City: A Study of Immigrants from India* (New Delhi: Heritage, 1980); Arthur W. Helweg and Usha M. Helweg, *An Immigrant Success Story: East Indians in America* (Philadelphia: University of Pennsylvania Press, 1990). For some of the city's earlier Bengali restaurant owners, these developments brought opportunities for expansion. Syed Ali, for example, moved his restaurant from 109th Street in Spanish Harlem to the stretch of Indian restaurants and shops that was beginning to form on Lexington Avenue around Twenty-Eighth Street in the late 1970s and early 1980s. Yet here, with new competition and a less devoted clientele, his business eventually failed.

36. See, for example: USC/HCIN, *To Grant a Quota to Eastern Hemisphere Indians and to Make Them Racially Eligible for Naturalization: Hearings before the Committee on Immigration and Naturalization on H.R. 173, H.R. 1584, H.R. 1624, H.R. 1746, H.R. 2256, H.R. 2609*, 79th Cong., 1st Sess., March 7–14, 1945, 142–43.

37. A. M. A. Muhith, *American Response to Bangladesh Liberation War* (Dhaka, Bangladesh: University Press, 1996), 7–8.

38. Habib Ullah Jr., interview, 2005.

39. Habib Ullah Jr., interview, 2008; Alaudin Ullah, interviews, 2006, 2008.

CONCLUSION: LOST FUTURES

1. Alaudin Ullah, interviews by the author, 2004–2008.

2. Alaudin Ullah, interview by the author, December 2010.

3. Robert Caro, *The Power Broker: Robert Moses and the Fall of New York* (New York: Vintage, 1975).

4. Habib Ullah Jr., interview by the author, Fort Lauderdale, FL, January 2008; Noor Choudhury, interview by the author, Los Angeles, CA, January 2005.

5. Michael E. Crutcher, *Tremé: Race and Place in a New Orleans Neighborhood* (Athens: University of Georgia Press, 2010), 20–65; George Lipsitz, *How Racism Takes Place* (Philadelphia: Temple University Press, 2011), 224.

6. On port cultures and the New York waterfront, see: John Kuo Wei Tchen, New York Before Chinatown: Orientalism and the Shaping of American Culture (Baltimore: Johns Hopkins University Press, 2001).

7. Adam McKeown, *Melancholy Order: Asian Immigration and the Globalization of Borders* (New York: Columbia University Press, 2008).

8. Karen Isaksen Leonard, *Making Ethnic Choices: California's Punjabi Mexican Americans* (Philadelphia: Temple University Press, 1992); Nayan Shah, *Stranger Intimacy: Contesting Race, Sexuality, and the Law in the North American West* (Berkeley: University of California Press, 2011).

9. Madeline Y. Hsu, *Dreaming of Gold, Dreaming of Home: Transnationalism and Migration between the United States and South China, 1882–1943* (Stanford, CA: Stanford University Press, 2000), 55–89; Mai Ngai, *Impossible Subjects: Illegal Aliens and the Making of Modern America* (Princeton, NJ: Princeton University Press, 2003); Erika Lee, *At America's Gates: Chinese Immigration during the Exclusion Era* (Chapel Hill: University of North Carolina Press, 2005), 147–220.

10. See census records for Nora Boyce, governess; Eveline Bagle, nurse; Alice Byan, domestic; Gobin Roy, porter; H.D. Persaud, elevator operator; USDC/BC, U.S. Census, 1910: *Population Schedules* for New York, New York: SD1/ED1160/Sh1B; SD1/ED1142/Sh3B; *Population Schedule* for Philadelphia, Pennsylvania: W22/SD1/ED400/Sh2A; USDC/BC, U.S. Census, 1930: *Population Schedules* for New York, New York: SD23/ED31-784/Sh6A; SD24/ED31-886/Sh18A; Dada Amir Haider Khan, *Chains to Lose: Life and Struggles of a Revolutionary* (New Delhi: Patriot Publishers, 1989), 420.

11. Rajani Kanta Das, *Hindustani Workers on the Pacific Coast* (Berlin: Walter de Gruyter, 1923), 109.

12. Scholars have addressed such dynamics of intermixture using a variety of generative concepts: "overlapping diasporas," "polyculturalism," "conviviality," "the intimacies of four continents." Earl Lewis, "To Turn as on a Pivot: Writing African Americans into a History of Overlapping Diasporas," *American Historical Review* 100 (June 1995): 765–87; Brent Hayes Edwards, "The Uses of Diaspora," *Social Text* 19, no. 1 (2001): 45–73; Robin D. G. Kelley, "People in Me," *ColorLines* 1, no. 3 (Winter 1999): 5–7; Vijay Prashad, "From Multiculture to Polyculture in South Asian American Studies," *Diaspora* 8, no. 2 (1999): 185–95; Paul Gilroy, *Postcolonial Melancholia* (New York: Columbia University Press, 2004); Lisa Lowe, "The Intimacies of Four Continents," in *Haunted by Empire: Geographies of Intimacy in North American History*, ed. Ann Laura Stoler, 191–212 (Durham, NC: Duke University Press, 2006).

13. Sudarshan Kapur, *Raising Up a Prophet: The African-American Encounter with Gandhi* (Boston: Beacon Press, 1992); Colin A. Palmer, "Pedro Albizu Campos," *Encyclopedia of African-American Culture and History, Volume 1* (Detroit: Macmillan Reference, 2005), 67; Penny Von Eschen, *Race against Empire: Black Americans and Anticolonialism, 1937–1957* (Ithaca, NY: Cornell University Press, 1997); Richard Brent Turner, *Islam in the African American Experience* (Bloomington: University of Indiana Press, 2003); Vijay Prashad, *Everybody Was Kung-Fu Fighting: Afro-Asian Connections and the Myth of Cultural Purity* (Boston: Beacon Press, 2001); Gerald Horne, *The End of Empires: African Americans and India* (Philadelphia: Temple University Press, 2009); Nico Slate, *Colored Cosmopolitanism: The Shared Struggle for Freedom in the United States and India* (Cambridge: Harvard University Press, 2012).

14. Alaudin Ullah, interview by the author, New York, NY, May 2005.

Acknowledgments

THIS PROJECT WOULD not have been possible without Alaudin Ullah, who, more than fifteen years ago, approached me with the desire to make a film about his father. It was Alaudin's father's extraordinary story that prompted me to begin searching the archives for traces of a population of early-twentieth-century South Asian immigrants who appeared to have been completely passed over by recorded history. As my research progressed over the course of the last several years, it was enriched by countless conversations with Alaudin and by his coordination of and participation in interviews with members of his extended family and other surviving members of what I have called here the "Bengali Harlem" community. I am deeply grateful for the openness and trust of those who agreed to these interviews: Noor Chowdry, Habib Ullah Jr., Masud Choudhury, Moheama Ullah, Karim Ullah, Laily Chowdry, Hamid Choudhury, Barbara Choudhury, Helen Ullah, Luz Maria Caballero, Rafael Caballero Jr., and Alaudin Ullah himself. Alaudin and I continue to work on a documentary film that will be a companion to this book, entitled *In Search of Bengali Harlem*. I am also grateful for the assistance of Shamsul Islam, Medha Jaishankar, and Naeem Mohaiemen in shooting a number of the videotaped interviews and for their insights about the history that was unfolding as we recorded each one. I would like to thank

Brittany Jones, the great-granddaughter of Mustafa "John" Ali, a Sylheti seaman who jumped ship in Baltimore in the 1920s, for contacting me as I was completing the book, and John Ali Jr., her grandfather, who graciously fielded my questions over the course of two phone interviews. These interviews added considerably to the histories of South Asian maritime networks and industrial labor explored in Chapter 3 and deepened my understanding of the presence of Indian ex-seamen in West Baltimore and Chester, Pennsylvania.

I have been incredibly fortunate in the number of people who have engaged critically with my research and writing over the last decade, and in the enthusiasm, encouragement, and guidance they have shown the work. This includes first my dissertation adviser, Andrew Ross, whose sharp critical insight, detailed comments, and continuing advice have been invaluable, and my dissertation committee members, Gayatri Gopinath, Adam Green, and Faye Ginsburg, who pushed my thinking in new directions and encouraged me to write with greater confidence. Vijay Prashad's engagement with this project has extended through every phase, from its inception to its final revisions; his example and advice, his critical readings of multiple drafts, and his friendship have fueled this book's creation. I am grateful to George Lipsitz and to one anonymous reviewer for their close and careful reading of the book in its manuscript form and for their generative and encouraging feedback. I cannot thank Junaid Rana enough for introducing me to the writings of Dada Amir Haider Khan, which proved to be a turning point for this project, and for reading and commenting on the manuscript in its near-final form. Robin D. G. Kelley encouraged me early on to pursue census-based genealogical research, a turn that transformed virtually every aspect of the project. Jigna Desai and Khyati Joshi engaged with my writing on New Orleans as editors of an anthology on Asian Americans in the U.S. South; their careful readings, suggestions, and insights deepened and strengthened the work here. In the final stretch, Miriam Jimenez generously read and commented on the chapters on Harlem, as did Noor and Laily Chowdry, Habib Ullah Jr., and Alaudin Ullah. Larry Powell did a close reading of one of the chapters on New Orleans, and Jennifer Guglielmo advised me on the larger framing of the book while providing an inspirational example of engaged popular historical writing in her own work. I am grateful to all of them for their time, care, and guidance.

At NYU, I was lucky to have a brilliant cohort of friends working on different aspects of the South Asian diaspora, combining the insights of comparative ethnic studies, global political economy, ethnography, and critical historiography; Miabi Chatterji, Sujani Reddy, and Manu Vimalassery were my immediate intellectual family over the years this project was developing, and I owe much to our conversations and collaborations, which expanded the vision for this book. I was also fortunate for the teaching, mentorship, advice, and direction of a number of brilliant scholars in NYU's Program in American Studies and Department of Social and Cultural Analysis—Lisa Duggan, Jack Tchen, Nikhil Singh, Juan Flores, Walter Johnson, Arlene Davila, Thuy Tu, and Minh-ha T. Pham. Madala Hilaire and I started at the American Studies Program the same year, and she always had my back, shepherding me through the bureaucracy in the midst of a thousand other demands on her time. At MIT, I have found unwavering support from my senior colleagues, Jim Paradis, Tom Levenson, Ken Manning, Helen Elaine Lee, Junot Diaz, William Uricchio, Ian Condry, Emma Teng, Jing Wang, Abha Sur, Chris Capozzola, and Nick Montfort. Thank you to Magdalena Reib, Nick Altenbernd, Maya Jhangiani, and Shinika Spencer for their help and guidance in the day-to-day work at MIT. Beth Coleman was my link between the worlds of New York City and Cambridge, music and scholarship, and buoyed me with friendship, advice, and radio.

At conferences, workshops, and invited talks, and in private conversations and consultations, numerous others have engaged with the research and writing that has taken shape in this book; these friends, colleagues, and mentors have pushed me and the work forward over many years, drafts, versions, and revisions. They include Hishaam Aidi, Rich Blint, Jacqueline Nassy Brown, Alicia Camacho, Hazel Carby, Aniruddha Das, Tamina Davar Shilpa Dave, Sohail Daulatzai, Michael Denning, Pawan Dhingra, Brent Hayes Edwards, Kale Fajardo, Jeremy Glick, Juan Flores, Peter James Hudson, Inderpal Grewal, Zareena Grewal, John Hutnyk, Vanessa Agard Jones, Anna Arabindan-Kesson, Aisha Khan, Amitava Kumar, Scott Kurashige, Hugh Kesson, Sunaina Marr Maira, Purnima Mankekar, Biju Mathew, Raza Mir, Manijeh Moradian,

Alondra Nelson, Fiona Ngo, Mimi Nguyen, Gary Okihiro, Dawn Peterson, Gautam Premnath, Uzma Rizvi, Amrik Saha, Nayan Shah, Sandhya Shukla, Lok Siu, Seema Sohi, Gayatri Chakravorty Spivak, Rajini Srikanth, Anantha Sudhaker, and Laura Tabili. I am also greatly indebted to Sucheta Mazumdar, Karen Isaksen Leonard, Joan Jensen, Paul Gilroy, Earl Lewis, Richard Brent Turner, Sudarshan Kapur, Hasan N. Gardezi, G. Balachandran, Ravi Ahuja, and Rozina Visram, whose combined scholarship provided a foundation for this book.

Joyce Seltzer recognized the importance of the histories that I have endeavored to record here, championed my work at Harvard University Press, and saw me through the stressful and demanding process of writing my first book; I am sincerely grateful to her for her faith and commitment and to her assistants, Brian Distelberg and Jeanette Estruth, and the book's production editor, Edward Wade, for patiently working with me and advising me in the various stages of the book's preparation. Phil Schwartzberg was equally patient with me in the preparation of the book's maps; his work has enriched the book and helped bring the geographies of South Asian settlement to life. My thanks to a number of archivists who helped locate images and documents for the photographic section of the book: John Gartrell at the Afro-American Newspapers Archives and Research Center in Baltimore, Jackie Rose at the *Philadelphia Inquirer*, and Trevor Plante, Robert Ellis, and Amy Reytar at the National Archives in Washington, D.C.

Portions of Chapters 2, 5, and 6 are reproduced with permission from an earlier essay of mine, "Overlapping Diasporas, Multiracial Lives," in *Black Routes to Islam*, edited by Manning Marable and Hishaam D. Aidi (New York: Palgrave Macmillan, 2009) and the book's epigraph is reproduced with permission from Édouard Glissant's *Poetics of Relation*, translated by Betsy Wing (Ann Arbor: University of Michigan Press, 1997). I am grateful to both publishers for permission to reproduce this material, and to Gita Rajan and Vinay Lal for providing an early platform for my research in "'Lost' in the City: Spaces and Stories of South Asian New York, 1917–1965," *South Asian Popular Culture 5.1* (2007).

My parents John G. Bald and Suresht Renjen Bald taught me by example about love, justice, and connection across lines of supposed difference and of the possibilities for creative, intellectual, and political engagement in the world. And there are not enough words to thank my partner, Kym Ragusa, who read and listened to innumerable drafts of this book and contributed her critical acuity, prodigious skills as a writer and editor, and sensitivity to the human lives represented in, and passed over by, the archives. This project has been enriched beyond measure by the personal and intellectual journey that we have been on together for the past twenty years.

Index

Tables are indicated by t following the page number. Maps are indicated by m following the page number.